Date Due

THE HISTORY OF
THE ENGLISH NOVEL

THE HISTORY OF
THE ENGLISH NOVEL

By Ernest A. Baker, D. Lit., M.A.

THE HISTORY
OF THE
ENGLISH NOVEL

By Ernest A. Baker, D. Lit., M.A.

Albert *1869 - 1941*

Volume VIII

From the Brontës to Meredith:
Romanticism in the English Novel

New York

BARNES & NOBLE, INC.

First published 1937
Reprinted 1950 by special arrangement with
H. F. & G. WITHERBY, LTD.
326 High Holborn, London, W. C. 1

Printed in the United States of America

PREFACE

As usual, and in fact inevitable in a work on this plan, there is some overlap at both ends of the present volume. But this brings out all the more clearly that the group of novelists under review were the ones affected by the arrival in fiction of the romantic influence which had revivified poetry in a previous generation. What is called "the Romantic Revival" showed itself in the work of Charlotte and Emily Brontë, and culminated in Meredith, affecting the novelists in between to a lesser but appreciable extent. It was not the spurious Radcliffian romanticism which even that great classic, Sir Walter Scott, often dabbled in, but that of Wordsworth, Keats, and Shelley. It was to have its backwash in the period described by some as "the Romantic Nineties." This view of the literary history of the time is illustrated and, it is hoped, substantiated in the following pages.

My thanks are due again to a large number of librarians for supplies of books, especially those named in the preceding volume. It is sad that I cannot again thank personally the son of Meredith, the late Mr W. M. Meredith, for having generously allowed me to quote what was necessary from his father's works. He gave me this permission on behalf of the Trustees, and to his fellow-trustees therefore I here express my indebtedness and my gratitude. Once again, I am under a deep obligation to Dr Edith C. Batho, of University College, London, for her watchful care in revising the proofs.

E. A. B.

5

CONTENTS

FROM
THE BRONTËS TO MEREDITH
ROMANTICISM IN THE ENGLISH NOVEL

CHAPTER I

THE BRONTËS—CHARLOTTE

In all the work of all the novelists from Jane Austen and Maria *No sign* Edgeworth to Dickens and Thackeray scarcely a hint has *as yet* emerged, beyond Peacock's gibes in *Melincourt* and *Nightmare in fiction of the* *Abbey*, that any one of them was much affected by the mental *Romantic* and spiritual disturbance which now appears the great literary *revival* event at the beginning of the century, the event which purified and renewed the very nature of poetry.[1] The perturbation did not, in fact, spread at once to this secondary and more prosaic department of imaginative activity. The novel went quietly on as if nothing extraordinary was happening. Certainly, the art of fiction did not stand still. Jane Austen, if she had lived, would have read Thackeray with an enjoyment in which her perception of a different attitude of mind, another angle of vision, new revelations and new truths, was no slight ingredient, and Scott would for other reasons have rejoiced in Dickens. These newcomers were their own offspring, or at least came of the same ancestry as themselves; they were their natural and direct successors. All alike were the heirs of Fielding and Smollett, Richardson and Sterne, and one after the other they had improved their inheritance. Manners and customs apart, which are always changing, there was little to mark them off as belonging to another age. The novelists had undergone no revolution of mind or soul; they were still faithful to the eighteenth century, still engrossed by the outward spectacle, fascinated by life's multitudinous variety, exhilarated by its humours or not unendurably touched by its pathos, but as yet unawake to the call of the deeper imagination, unaccustomed to look within, unable, as Carlyle said of Scott, to go beneath

[1] See also Volume VI. 14–15; and, as to Scott, chap. ix., especially 221–224.

the skin and get to the heart. The novel had not yet faced the urgent but less tangible realities; it had found all it wanted in the more obvious half of life, in the commerce of workaday existence or the tragi-comedies of clashing affections, thwarted ambitions, and evildoers brought to account. Only the poets hitherto had ventured into the region of semi-conscious feeling, the penumbra that borders and casts its shadows upon the visible scene, the twilight in which the heart is a touchstone, the soul a powerful talisman. All this remained a closed book to the novelist, a marginal tract into which the mere prose-writer did not stray, hardly even such roamers as Lamb and Hazlitt or such an adventurer as De Quincey. It would have been to grasp and scrutinize man's spiritual being, as well as his outward lineaments; and no fiction had as yet presented a living soul. And that sense of "something far more deeply interfused" which awed and exalted the romantic heart was still outside the apprehension of the novelist. What had allied Wordsworth, Coleridge, and Blake,[1] Shelley and Keats, as partners in one and the same movement, though they differed from each other profoundly, was this resurrection of the spirit. Here, at any rate, they were at one; this was above all the Romantic inspiration.[2]

Now a tendency to break accepted canons — When such deeper perceptions came at length into fiction, they were bound to put some strain on the working formula which has served so far as a rough specification of the novel, "the interpretation of human life by means of fictitious narrative in prose."[3] Prose itself was showing signs of breaking loose from established restraints. De Quincey, not to mention the effervescent and obstreperous Christopher North, is a capital instance. Carlyle wrote prose which is poetry rather than oratory, except that it was meant to be more than overheard. Dickens, especially when he was responding in his own way to Carlyle's fierce humanitarian war-cries, with little

---

[1] Blake was not known to Wordsworth till 1812, or to Coleridge till 1818.

[2] See L. Cazamian: "L'Intuition panthéiste chez les romantiques anglais" (*Études de psychologie littéraire*, 1913), on the vanity of that exalted sense, experienced by Wordsworth and Coleridge, of being in tune with the infinite, and of seeing into the life of things, man through Nature coming into touch with the universal spirit.

[3] Volume I. 15.

inkling, however, of Carlyle's larger purport, waxed lyrical in *Bleak House* and elsewhere, as well as in his Christmas rhapsodies. Charlotte Brontë grew tumid and rhetorical in her impassioned moments, though her sister Emily's prose, while it continually did the work of poetry, always obeyed the very letter of the law. Meredith, however, was soon to evolve a style betwixt and between, claiming rights of its own; whilst lesser novelists, notably Charles Kingsley, rushed into facile lyricism when excitement turned their heads. Hardy and Conrad were among the few who stepped along the sublime altitudes with a gait that did not offend against decorum. But there was a predisposition among novelists to ignore or repudiate the old understanding that a work in prose must be a sedate intellectual treatment of what is either fact or some abstraction or close equivalent of fact. The novel was outgrowing its old limitations, and to express itself adequately had to refashion even the medium in which it worked.

There is a curious overlap in the history of fiction at this era. Such novelists as Jane Austen and Maria Edgeworth, Thackeray and Trollope, loyal to the old tradition, stood above the turmoil, serene, critical, amused; at the utmost, they were sensitive and compassionate spectators. Those, on the other hand, who felt the new impulse were not content to look out on life; they were in it. Their books were their means of working out their own salvation and that of the world at large. They would not if they could have cut themselves loose and held aloof from the common problem, how to live. A gospel they must find, for themselves and for others. Everything was at stake. Life was a course of abstruse and anxious study; they must go deeper into themselves, and so learn to see more deeply into others, thus clarifying at least some part of the infinite complexity. They discovered aims and missions. Fiction in such hands became the novel militant. Dickens was caught by the new earnestness; he became one of the fighters. Disraeli joined once or twice in the fray. It was not merely that the novelist waxed sentimental or impassioned over incidents and situations that wrung his heart; such situations were only the nodes and crises of a perpetual conflict in which

The belated advent of Romanticism in the novel

he and the rest of the human family were vitally involved. Fiction to such writers was a very serious affair, in which they are seen eagerly and anxiously striving to find their bearings, to discover a way of life, to save their own souls in saving humanity.[1] In this they were of the same company as the poets, Wordsworth, Keats, Shelley, Tennyson, Browning, Matthew Arnold. Many, indeed, wrote poetry themselves, the Brontë sisters, Kingsley, Meredith, George Eliot, William Morris, Hardy, Stevenson, D. H. Lawrence, not to mention some still living; and whatever its quality it was an overflow of the same imaginative force, and a totally different thing from the playful minor verse of Peacock and Thackeray. It was, in short, a poetical or at least an imaginative revival in fiction of which the Brontës were the pioneers, a re-establishment of that vital correlation with poetry which Fielding had repudiated, even when he defined the novel as "A comic epic in prose." The novelist was refusing to be strictly circumscribed any longer by prose limits, and reasserting the rights of creative energy, as was forecast in the discussion with which this work opened.[2] In Wordsworth and his fellows, the English genius had liberated itself from the inhibitions of natural instinct, spontaneity, enthusiasm, free imagination, which had dominated so long. It rejected the worn-out phrases and formulæ which had passed for thought but repressed originality. It was tired of repetition. It was not afraid of becoming metaphysical. For the soul was at last awake to its own existence and its relations to a complex and perhaps inscrutable universe. And now the novelists were to follow on the same track; a literature of manners was to give place to a literature of the spirit.

The term "Romanticism" ambiguous   It is that equivocal term "Romanticism" which has been the stumbling-block and confused history, making us apt to overlook the curious indifference of novelists in that same age to the change of depth and scope which regenerated poetry,

[1] The absence in English literature during the Romantic period of such works as *Adolphe, René, Corinne*, has been remarked. In poetry there were examples enough of the practice of writing and living the same work of art. The Brontë novels were, surely, the same thing in fiction.
[2] See Volume I. 13–21.

a disregard for what in the historical retrospect seems the outstanding event in literature. The general label has been affixed to poets and novelists without enough heed to its ambiguousness. Badges and ensigns have been sought and found, "Strangeness and beauty," "the renascence of wonder," and so on, to characterize a very miscellaneous crowd, phrases which usually omit the distinctive essence, through the fallacy which confounded different schools.[1] The romanticism of Wordsworth and Coleridge was a radically different thing from the romanticism of Scott and his followers, or that of Byron, which left its impress on Hope, Trelawny, Lytton, and others, and especially on Disraeli, who travestied his master in *Ixion*, competed with him, perhaps unwittingly, in *Contarini Fleming*, and drew his portrait in *Venetia*. Scott's romanticism came from other sources than that of Wordsworth and his group, and if theirs is the true Romanticism then his should evidently bear a different label.[2] Scott was a poet of limited range, but one of the greatest creators of character, whose vision was spellbound by the heroism and splendour of bygone ages—one to whom the past was as vivid and as concrete as the present, human nature being ever the same. Hence it was the easiest thing in the world for him to substitute something like the genuine article for the sham Gothic of Mrs Radcliffe and her tribe. He wrote novels which were a speaking likeness of periods dead and gone, and sometimes dabbled in the stagy supernatural of Horace Walpole, Beckford, and "Monk" Lewis, thus being inevitably associated with the whole company as another romantic; for these were so termed, not unreasonably, since they did write romances or romantic novels. But he was as untouched by the Romanticism of the great poets as were the rococo novels of Mrs Radcliffe herself, who, though

[1] Of the merely tendentious use of the word "Romanticism," as standing for everything to which a critic is opposed, the works of Professor Babbitt are the most erudite example. So too L. Reybaud calls Romanticism "le triomphe absolu de l'individualisme" (*Le Romantisme*, 1926), individualism being regarded as the most formidable of anti-social influences.

[2] The older romanticism, or pseudo-romanticism, was considered in Volume V. in the chapters on the Novel of Sentiment, the Novel of Sensibility, and the Gothic Novel. See also Volume VI. 14-15, on Jane Austen's and Maria Edgeworth's immunity, and as to Scott, chaps. vi.-ix.

she was to outlive Keats and Shelley, published the last of them the year before the *Lyrical Ballads*. Scott's disciples, however, went on with their romantic novels right through the nineteenth century, often lighting upon the strangeness and beauty that dazzled them in peoples and events of their own time, as well as of the past. Literary historians must answer for it when there is any confusion between these votaries of the romance that is as old as the hills and a newer and sublimer thing. Historians have a weakness for evolving formulas merging together all the impulses and ideas and efforts at originality in all the writers of a given age, and then of tracing the sources in the writers who happened to have preceded. So, among the antecedents of Romanticism, not only the fiction of terror and suspense, but even the novels of sensibility, are counted by some of them as germs and springs and sources. And then these critics point to the growing sense of human brotherhood in Scott, Miss Edgeworth, Galt, Dickens, and Thackeray, as another indubitable trait of Romanticism, linking those novelists with the poets. It is true that a warm feeling for all sorts and conditions of men becomes more and more prevalent as the cold intellectualism of the Augustan age fades into the past. But why mix this up with what was of a wider and very different order, the great revival in poetry, even though one of the first-fruits of this revival was a return to nature, including the nature of the humblest of mankind? The novel had returned to nature half a century before, and was never again to desert nature, except in the affectations and morbidities of the sentimentalists and the artificial frightfulness of the amateurs of terror. That affectionate trust in humanity which characterized the novel in the Romantic era had characterized it ever since the beginnings of modern fiction in Defoe and Fielding. It was as apparent in Goldsmith's *Vicar of Wakefield* as in his poems of the homely virtues. It was as prominent a trait in Cowper, Burns, and Crabbe, as in Wordsworth, with his reverence for the plain Cumberland dalesman, that humble seer of eternal realities. Lamb's essays are rich with it. This was his humanism. The Wordsworthian sense of the divinity of man deepened and glorified that sense of brotherhood, and in novelists who were Wordsworth's disciples was to have no small share in bringing fiction into line with the new poetry.

It was not till half a century after the *Lyrical Ballads*, not till Wordsworth and Coleridge were silent or had lost their inspiration,[1] and Keats, Shelley, and Byron were in their graves, soon followed by the yet unrecognized Blake, when poetry had fallen into the trough again after the great tidal wave of imaginative activity, that fiction was to have its Romantic revival, with results not less epoch-making in its own sphere. The poetic awakening had fallen flat so far as the public were concerned. The new age had seen Romantic poets but not Romantic readers, understanding and assenting readers, that is. It had not been a revival in the sense that the general consciousness had received, accepted, and responded to the new vision and the new doctrines. In the retrospect to-day it looks a colossal event; but, though Wordsworth succeeded Southey as Poet Laureate in 1843 and his works went into a fair number of editions, Shelley and Keats, who might have been expected to be at least as popular, had no public worth mentioning,[2] and Blake was unknown to the world at large. The poets who now had to satisfy the cravings of the reader of verse were such as Clare, Bloomfield, and Bernard Barton, Moore, Rogers, and Campbell, Milman, Kirke White, Letitia Landon, Mrs Hemans, Eliza Cook, Hartley Coleridge, and "Festus" Bailey. Beddoes, the only

The Romantic revival in fiction

---

[1] It seemed as if the ageing Wordsworth had himself forsaken his youthful ideals. Browning's "Lost Leader" was an unfair attack; Wordsworth was not a time-server or turncoat. But he had outlived and was afraid of his own Wordsworthianism. He was so affected by what his editor calls a "change of audience," and had lost so much of the old spirit of defiance, that in rewriting large parts of *The Prelude*, that incomparable study of the growth of the poetic personality, he often changed its pantheistic mysticism into the pious sentiments of a strict Anglican churchman. It reminds one of Coleridge's tampering with philosophic concepts and trans-mogrifying his metaphysical theorem into a geometrical allegory of the Trinity (*Table-Talk*, 51). In Professor de Selincourt's edition of *The Prelude*, the poem as written in the years 1798–1805 is printed side by side with the amended version of 1850. But if Romanticism was largely dead in Wordsworth it was not dead in all those who read him, and was about to have a second spell of life in the novel.

[2] Sir Henry Jones relates how difficult Browning's mother found it to secure copies of "Mr Shelley's atheistical poems," and how Browning got to know about Keats from his acquaintance with Shelley (*Camb. Lit. Hist.*, xiii. 53).

VOL. VIII.—B

one with a touch of greatness, was an obscure recluse, most of whose work did not appear till after his death. These it was who had to fill the gap before the arrival of Tennyson and Browning, to be followed by Clough and Arnold, and then the Rossettis, Coventry Patmore, William Morris, and Barnes, the Dorsetshire poet. And now Tennyson and Browning were in the leading seats of the orchestra, Carlyle had begun to shake the world, and Ruskin was taking up his parable, when the event happened which was to have like effects in fiction to those which had transfigured poetry. In fact, the awakening came at the time of what literary historians style the second Romantic revival,[1] the moment when poetry and much else were near the brink, or right over it, of another change, which this time carried readers with it, and so made the results of the earlier Romantic movement deep and lasting. And the share of the novel in this further awakening has scarce had justice done it. Poetry can go on, and must go on if there are poets, even in the absence of readers; the novel cannot. But now a handful of novels by two unknown girls, who were poets themselves and imbued with the poetic philosophy of Wordsworth and his fellows, carried the new Romanticism, the gospel of the imagination, into quarters which did not study poetry. Novels which were read by all could not fall flat.[2]

England was entering upon the era of scientific and commercial activity, with which poetry was too often to come to terms, at no small cost to its integrity. But in the Brontë sisters and Mrs Gaskell, George Eliot and George Meredith,

---

[1] T. S. Omond calls it the "Neo-Romantic Revival," and regards the two Brownings and Tennyson as the protagonists, and succeeding in a regenerative effort in which Keats had failed. Incidentally, he says of Emily Brontë, "She cannot be called a poet" (*Periods of European Literature*, xi., *The Romantic Triumph*, 57-58 and 121).

[2] It is time to protest against the view which ignores the part of the Brontës in the spiritual reaction evident in fiction as well as in poetry, and even classifies them with those who reject Romantic idealism. To take one instance, Madeleine L. Cazamian (*Le Roman et les idées en Angleterre*, 1923) rightly points out "Pendant la séconde moitié du siècle, le problème de la vie spirituelle s'impose, non comme prétexte à moraliser, mais comme le sujet inévitable le plus fréquent, le plus brûlant, le plus actuel" (10). But she brackets Charlotte Brontë and Mrs Gaskell with Dickens and Thackeray as representing "la réaction contre l'idéalisme romantique . . . dans le roman" (56).

the novel maintained its independence, as poetry had done *Closeness*
forty years before. It liberated itself from the inhibitions *of the*
which thwarted instinct and repressed imagination; it looked *analogy*
and thought for itself, and became a faithful and penetrating *with the*
critic of life, prophesying even of man's future. In the hands *former event*
of such writers, a change came over fiction corresponding to
the earlier change in poetry, a change of attention from outer
to inner, a concentration of vision, a sudden illumination.
The novel, also, began to trust to the inner light. Intellect
and reason had been the faculties it relied upon hitherto;
now imagination and instinct claimed their share in the interpretative and creative work. Fiction regains a place beside
or only a little below poetry, dares to speak for the soul, to
sound the deeps of personality, to face the enigmas of evil and
death. It had to go through this revolution; it was its only
hope of salvation; it had like poetry to escape from prison. The
novel had not yet emerged from the eighteenth into the full
light of the nineteenth century, into the light of Romanticism.
It had not yet divined that vision of an ampler world which
had flashed upon the poets. The novelist was now called
upon to perform his share, a great and invaluable share if he
took himself seriously, in the work of enlightenment; he must
go deeper into himself and others, and so learn to interpret
life creatively, evolving such an ideal of personality as would
satisfy the soul and enable men to find their true selves in an
otherwise unintelligible universe.

Some such thing was to happen to the novel as might con- *What if*
ceivably have happened, had it been sufficiently developed in *the novel*
the full tide of the Elizabethan potency of imagination to stand *had*
the weight of all that was then put upon drama. Drama is *attained*
the least confined in scope of all forms of fiction. In the *ripeness*
greater Shakespearian plays, the whole universe of things, *Shake-*
seen and unseen, is brought before the mind. There is no *speare's*
interdict on the revelation of the heart; the passions speak *time!*
without constraint; speculation is at its most imaginative
pitch. This was the prerogative of creative literature before
the blighting classical code fell upon poetry and drama. But
Elizabethan prose fiction was not yet ripe for creative work;

it was only a nondescript offshoot of literature, in the shape of such elementary stuff as the cony-catching tracts, the picaresque chap-books, and some erotic romances which were conceived as poems in prose. Uncertain of its aims and standing, it continued to exist as it were on sufferance, and had to wait for its coming of age till after the ascendancy of comedy at the end of the seventeenth century. Fielding came after Congreve and Vanbrugh, and after Addison, Steele, and Pope, all of whom were absorbed by the mere superficies of life. Prose was the medium, and prose the spirit, of fiction when it achieved independence. But what if Marlowe, or Webster, or even Shakespeare, had written novels, and not merely as a passing diversion, but as efficient vehicles for matters as great as those which went into their plays! In this Victorian day there was no drama worth talking about; and Charlotte Brontë, George Eliot, Meredith, and then Hardy and Conrad, were about to make the novel as ample in compass and as critical and creative as the stage-play had been when it retained its formal and spiritual union with poetry. Henceforth it enjoys the powers and privileges of a sister art, a blood-relation to both poetry and drama. A century before it had turned its back on poetry; but now the unnatural divorce was to be repudiated. The one indemnification for all it had sacrificed then was that it had learned in the great prose age of Defoe, Fielding, and Richardson to come into the most intimate contact with the prose of life. It had learned realism. This was worth the temporary loss of the higher privileges, especially as Cowper, Crabbe, and Wordsworth had shown, if the Elizabethan playwrights had not already done so, that realism is one of the ways in which the loftiest creative imagination may find its goal.[1] Yet the separation had lasted so long and was

---

[1] It is difficult to subscribe to Professor Abercrombie's dictum, "There is an element directly opposed to romanticism: it is realism. The true antithesis, then, is between romanticism and realism" (*Romanticism*, 33). He says, "Romanticism is a withdrawal from outer experience in order to concentrate on inner experience" (*Ibid.*, 51). But Wordsworth, for instance, often concentrates upon outer experience, which he interprets in the light of inner experience; and his realistic portrayal of Cumbrian dalesmen, though the spiritual outlook may be different, is not more different intrinsically from the realism of Flaubert, or D. H. Lawrence, or James Joyce, than from that of Cowper or Crabbe. And, among the novelists now under scrutiny, Charlotte and Anne Brontë were, surely, realists, in that their novels were

so complete, through the assumption that fiction must be
based upon and limited by a purely intellectual and therefore

faithful transcripts of what they had experienced. Charlotte gave this an imaginative
interpretation. It might be risky to aver that Emily's *Wuthering Heights* was composed of fundamentally similar elements, combined in different proportions. We
know even now too little about her outer experience, and her inner experience and
her outlook upon the world were those of a mystic. But even that transcendently
imaginative work is firmly based on a realistic substructure, the faithful portraiture
of rough and homely rustic life and character. For the great Romantics were
realists in so far as they saw clearly, and they were realists in the technical sense
when they portrayed what they saw with all possible faithfulness, penetrating
further, however, and revealing more than the general run of novelists. Shelley
and Keats themselves were far better realists than those novelists who, as Henry
James put it in his preface to *The American*, "palm off" on us "the disconnected and
uncontrolled experience—uncontrolled by our general sense of 'the way things
happen.'" These are the romantics who cast but a negligent and astigmatic eye
at realities, and depict their nightmare visions and wanton fancies in such shapes
and colours as show what little regard they have for any sort of veracity. Theirs is
not a serious treatment of either outer or inner experience. The antithesis to be
sought is one between moral and emotional interests, preferences, and ideals, rather
than the one predicated by Professor Abercrombie. It is a matter of personal
attitudes and mental habits—of honesty, earnestness, and the imagination which is
deeper and fuller insight, compared with the morbid or affected sentimentality,
the cultivated sensibility of such as the Mackenzie school, or the insincerity and
artificiality of the Gothic novelists. There will be plentiful instances in later pages
of thoroughgoing realism profoundly absorbed in the inner experience. The
antithesis, in short, should be between the votaries of a meretricious romance and
the poets and novelists who instinctively sought truth to both inner and outer
experience. The trouble is that the great poets of this era were called Romantics,
or Romanticists; the term Classical would have been nearer the mark for Wordsworth and Coleridge, Keats and Shelley. For the so-called Romantic movement
was a revival and a recovery, a return to the main current of healthy, vigorous,
developing life, which had been forsaken ever since the Elizabethan age—and, of
course, a repudiation of the falsehoods recently "palmed off" in poetry and fiction.
In the novel, perhaps, this is more clearly manifest than in poetry, for here there
was no comprehensive break with the past; development went on continuously
from Fielding onwards. Scott was a mixture of classical and romantic; his genius
classical:

"L'inspiration est romantique, l'art est classique" (Georges Lafourcade),
his easy-going concessions to prevailing tastes the other thing. Byron, who ran
eighteenth century, was always going off into stagy heroics; but even he was
sincere at bottom. Romantic poetry seems to open up the infinite; the poet is a
seer. So is it with all great art—Homer, Shakespeare, Michelangelo, Turner, Dante,
Praxiteles, Goethe, Rodin. Consider the realism in each of them; estimate the
part respectively of inner and outer experience. The Romantic revolt and all the
rest of it was not a new departure—at any rate, in English literature—but a re-
assertion of true principles of art. ". . . Art is not the cancelling of the actual
and imperfect, and the putting in its place of a vague and fanciful perfection that
is only an illusory abstraction after all; it is the transfiguring of the actual by the
ideal that is actually immanent in it. The actual hides in itself an ideal that is its
true reality and destination, and this hidden ideal it is the function of art to reveal.
The artist is a seer, whose eye pierces to the secret of which the natural fact is the
sign and prophecy. He is a magician, whose hand releases the spirit imprisoned in
matter, and transforms the brute token into the breathing and speaking body. And
as the ideal in the whole of Nature moves in an infinite process towards an Absolute

prosaic interpretation of the facts of existence, that it was not to be annulled without protest. It is very significant, however, that after this there was only one novelist of eminence who maintained the eighteenth-century attitude, Anthony Trollope.

Carlyle's part in this revival

The influence on the novel of one great man who would have disdained to write such a thing himself, Thomas Carlyle, must not be overlooked or under-estimated at this turning-point in the history of fiction. Carlyle was at the moment a much more imposing and stimulating figure than either Tennyson or Browning, whose chief work was yet in the future. He wrote prose, a prose of his own make; but it was the imagination of a poet that he brought to bear on history, biography, and the philosophy of life. His books approximate in spirit and in style to epic or drama; they are fiery imaginative enunciations of his view of the world. He had recently been teaching that biography is the very essence of all books worthy of the name, biography which traces the development of souls. The effect of his doctrine on such a mind as Browning's, intent on this very problem of the inmost life, is patent, and also upon George Eliot's and Meredith's. But it is not less evident in the case of Charlotte Brontë, whose novels are all biographies, and all concerned with this development of soul, of an independent personality, as envisaged by Carlyle. She, too, would have subscribed to his faith in intuition—the intuitions of "the wise and noble-minded." [1] For, in the novel, more intimately and not less poignantly, the soul was reawakening, and contemplating itself amid its trials and tribulations, its deep secret life, its doubts and questionings, and celestial or infernal ecstasies. It was the individual soul, rather than the social being, the arithmetical unit, or the part of an organic complex, as heretofore, which had become the central theme, man finding himself and evolving through

Perfection, we may say that art is in strict truth the apotheosis of Nature. Art is thus at once the exaltation of the natural towards its destined supernatural perfection, and the investiture of the Absolute Beauty with the reality of natural existence" ("The Art-Principle in Poetry," in G. H. Howison's *Limits of Evolution* (1901)).

[1] Perhaps she was not aware of how much she owed Carlyle. She told an interviewer that she "reverenced the dignity of his life, though she disliked his writings" (J. Storrs-Smith, of the *Free Lance* (March, 1868), cited by Delafield, 203).

personal rather than social relations.[1]   The eighteenth century
had been the heyday of social intercourse; this was the form
in which civilization then expressed itself.   Society was the
urbane ordering of personal attitudes; the individual tended
to be submerged; personality was not yet a problem.

Social life is the sphere of comedy.   Any excess of indivi- *The*
dualism is a kink in the prevailing order; too much idiosyncrasy *belated*
is only a source of amusement.   But now the individual *change*
becomes the centre of philosophic interest; and intimacy, *from the*
18th to
personal relations, are seen to be, not only the root of human *the 19th*
community, but also a principal factor in the spiritual develop- *century*
ment of the human being.   This, perhaps, is the noblest end *point of*
visible to contemplation; the ideal companionship of kindred *view*
souls is at any rate the consummation which the new fiction
aims at, instead of the merely sensual or sentimental union
which had been the traditional goal of romance.   The novel
was caught at last in the spiritual current which had swept
poetry onward, the vision which illuminates and resolves
the baffling complexities, discords, and conflicts, and redeems the
disasters of mundane existence, the vision that perceives the
infinite in the finite.   And it had reached this point of vision,
not by seeking any transcendental revelation, but by opening
its eyes to the world within.   The novel of the Brontës and
George Eliot is not content merely to feed curiosity and
provide entertainment; it is a summons to the inherent
seriousness, the tragic stakes, of the life we are all faced with.
It seeks to resolve the mysteries and contradictions by seeing
clearly all that is in question, and all that may be achievable
by man.

The struggle for self-realization is a more serious matter *Emerg-*
than the friction of odd idiosyncrasies; it inevitably involves *ence of*
tragic issues.   The conflict is that of the individual with a *the tragic*
issues
world of inimical forces.   Whether they end disastrously or *of life*
with happiness for those chiefly concerned, Charlotte Brontë's
novels invariably have this character of tragic conflict; and

[1] See Professor John Macmurray's admirable account of the changes in the conception of personality from Descartes and Hume to thinkers of the present day, in
" The Unity of Modern Problems " (*Journal of Philosophical Studies*, iv. 14).

George Eliot, in *Adam Bede*, *The Mill on the Floss*, *Romola*, and *Middlemarch*, sets forth still more deliberately and resolutely the fatal course of the strife between the individual and the hard facts which eventually break him, if he falls short in the wisdom and strength to realize his higher self. Meredith, in *The Ordeal of Richard Feverel*, *Beauchamp's Career*, and other novels, works out corresponding themes; and Hardy and Conrad were to follow by different paths. There had been tragic novels ever since *Clarissa* and *Amelia*, or such as had passed for tragic. But the mere heaping up of pathos does not suffice to make tragedy. Most of them were but exaggerated appeals to the sensibilities, gross stimulants of the pleasure there is in tears and the contemplation of grief and suffering. These were not the stern yet compassionate studies of the agonizing ordeals met with in the most commonplace existence, not views of the soul at odds with its environment. Mrs Inchbald's *Simple Story* and *Nature and Art* [1] were among the few that had anything of the real stuff of tragedy; but both were polemical in intent, and thus open to the suspicion of being deliberately overcharged. Mrs Sheridan's *Sidney Bidulph* [2] was a studied effort to heap up a banquet of pathos; like Frances Brooke's *Charlotte Mandeville* [3] or Mackenzie's *Julia de Roubigné*,[4] it drove violently at the springs of horror and commiseration, in the manner taught by Baculard d'Arnaud and Prévost.[5] On the other hand, the gruesome narratives long drawn out by Amelia Opie, Mary Wollstonecraft, and Mary Hays, were vehement and provocative appeals against what they regarded as the injustices of the world as at present constituted, and the same disqualification lies against Godwin's *Caleb Williams*. Even Scott's *Bride of Lammermoor*, and *St Ronan's Well* even before he altered the ending, had too much of the gloom and terror prepense of Gothic romance to be accepted as austere tragedy. And a similar frontal attack on the feelings tends to disable the claims of Lockhart's and Hogg's novels of insensate passion, crime, and remorse.

[1] See Volume V. 250–252.
[2] *Ibid.*, 141–144.   [3] *Ibid.*, 144–145.   [4] *Ibid.*, 108–111.
[5] Chap. vi., "The Novel of Sensibility."

Lytton's *Eugene Aram* and *Falkland* were commonplace melodramas woven about the time-honoured motives of crime and nemesis. As to the Irish novelists, whose temperament inclined them to tragedy, the Banims and Griffin ruined their best work with melodrama and gratuitous horror; and there was too much of the same weakness in Carleton, several of whose novels were otherwise sound examples of the primitive tragedy of heroic endurance beaten to the ground by calamity.[1] Of that finer tragedy of the human being waging a losing battle for the unattainable, or out of its nobler self creating the fury which will destroy it, tragedy of the type of *Hamlet* or *Lear*, there is hardly a glimpse before the Brontës, George Eliot, and Meredith.

Nothing was further from the minds of Charlotte Brontë (1816–1855) and her sisters when they began writing novels than the idea that they were heading a revolt or voicing a protest, though they had courage enough for anything. Charlotte, in fact, when she wrote *Jane Eyre*, the first of hers to secure publication, confessedly made an effort to write like other people, or at any rate to produce something more to the taste of her publishers and the ordinary reader, since her earlier attempt, *The Professor*, had not been acceptable. But all three—Anne Brontë must be included, for her two novels, though of small account in themselves, were similar in origin and in their simple candour—followed the inner light. They looked in their hearts and wrote, and they wrote of the things with which they were most familiar. They were more intelligent and more interested in intellectual matters, and much more widely read, than most inhabitants of a country parsonage; they had digested a good many novels, and knew what the public was used to. But one thing was certain: they would tell what they believed to be the truth. They were very serious young persons, and not likely to make any concessions even to what was then regarded as proper reticence. Then they were poets all three, steeped in the Wordsworthian feeling for Nature as our living mother, speaking to her children in the fields and streams, and shadowing forth messages for the

The Brontë departure

---

[1] See Volume VII., chap. i., "The Irish Novelists."

spirit in her visible graces and sublimities. All this was household knowledge, it was the breath of life, to the Brontë children. Poetry, which had hitherto had little attention paid it in fiction, except in the more flowery romances, was now to take its place in the life-history of a sensitive and imaginative woman or of a man who was no mere worldling. Their own lives were serious and troubled enough; and, as their fiction was to be made out of it, there was not likely to be much of the comedy arising from the contrasts and collisions of incongruous characters, which was the staple of most current works of fiction when they were anything more than stories of intrigue or adventure or sentimental love-tales. Passion found its voice again, and spoke unashamedly of many things which had been cloaked or dissembled under a mask of propriety, distantly alluded to in euphemisms and ambiguities, or ignored as if they did not exist. Charlotte Brontë's outburst at Jane Austen's disregard of the passions is famous: "The passions are perfectly unknown to her; she rejects even a speaking acquaintance with that stormy sisterhood." [1] Charlotte might have said with Emerson, "Passion adds eyes, is a magnifying glass," for it made her see with more intensity, even if it over-coloured much that she saw. To be so earnest in the contemplation of her own and other people's existence was to be keenly alive to the tragic issues, to all that had been left out in the novels of manners or of paltry intrigue which she had read.[2] For the drawing-room background which was the fashion, she would substitute a background of infinity. More particularly, and it was this which brought her into the wars with reviewers and made her a byword with straitlaced readers, she frankly uncovered the inviolate world of women's instincts and natural yearnings for sympathy and sexual realization, and the tragedy of the woman misunderstood was given a publicity that scandalized convention. Then she broached the insistent theme of personality: what are we to make of ourselves? where is our goal and compass? The question was handled

[1] Letter to W. S. Williams, 12th April 1850.
[2] The twenty "clever, wicked, sophistical, and immoral French books," that she read in 1840 did not include Balzac, whom she did not read till later on (Sinclair, 115, n.).

with the courage and earnestness befitting the most solemn of all problems. But it was still for women that she was most concerned, for women's right to the same self-responsibility as men's: "What was I created for, I wonder? Where is my place in the world?" muses Caroline Helstone, in *Shirley*. A way must be found to make life square with ideals. To evolve a rich and free personality was an end in itself, none more worthy, none more reasonable, in our ignorance of the constitution of the universe, and faith in some ultimate reality which we apprehend through our liberty of action. The value of personality is absolute and intrinsic; it is our firmest intuition, our only certainty. This was a basic conviction which she shared with the mystical Emily, however different may have been their attitudes to orthodox religion.

The Brontë sisters were not abstract thinkers, and did not *Its his-* come with any theory or philosophy of fiction to originate a *torical* movement; they made something like a revolution without de- *im-* signing it, through their instinctive repudiation of so much that *portance* was generally accepted. If Charlotte and Emily Brontë were the Wordsworth [1] and Blake, it was not till Meredith that the Coleridge appeared of this phase of the Romantic revolt. He was the one to expound theories, in his scattered aphorisms and in his great essay on *Comedy*, the latter dealing with aspects of creative literature which were almost entirely outside their purview. They were not humorists, and comedy has little place in their fiction, except as one of the minor relaxations of literary routine. Charlotte often made an effort to be facetious as a concession to readers' expectations, but it seems to have gone against the grain. George Eliot was to reinstate humour, still keeping it subordinate, and not, like Trollope, the disciple of Smollett and Dickens and Thackeray, perceiving it everywhere, and, where found, making the most of it. With her, as with the Brontës, character, not characters, was the primary interest. In Meredith's novels, it was not the comedy of humours, but the more subtle comedy of excess and

---

[1] Charlotte must have been conscious of her affinity to Wordsworth; she sent *The Prelude*, that great spiritual autobiography, as a present to Mrs Gaskell, on its publication in 1850 (Gaskell, xxi.).

extravagance, want of sanity and proportion, that predominated, and this is to tragedy only as the other side of the shield. In his exalted vision of a consummated personality, and in the ardent young figures, "noble strength on fire," who aim at it, he is of the Brontë creed. The Brontës were not great masters of the art of fiction; but they were full of a rapturous sense of life, and they had pre-eminently the power of infusing it. They were a force not to be measured by four immature novels, even including *Wuthering Heights*, and their historical importance far outweighs their positive achievement, great as that was.

Brontë-ana

This is a history of the novel, not of the novelists, and it would be superfluous to go far into the maze of contradictions, uncertainties, and obstinate enigmas to which the largest amount of biographical writing ever devoted to three young women is by no means an infallible guide. All required here is the minimum of personal detail necessary to the understanding of their work and its genesis. Fortunately, the essential facts are known to everyone interested, and a general familiarity with these may safely be taken for granted. More indeed is known about the Brontës than about any similar family of writers, although some points are still obscure, and the character of Emily will always remain largely inscrutable.[1]

[1] Though the literature is so large, and Mrs Gaskell's *Life of Charlotte Brontë*, in spite of reticences and deliberate suppressions, is still the most live biography, there is no single one of all these biographical studies which can be accepted in its entirety. Thus, one of the most penetrating and illuminating was written before the publication of the Heger letters in 1913; but in the edition which followed that disclosure the writer refused to modify her general thesis. That disclosure may or may not have been unfair to Charlotte Brontë's memory; but, at any rate, we should like to have the views such an analyst of character would have formed with the full data before her. The Brontë sisters have, of course, been "psychoanalysed"; a whole book has been put together to demonstrate, with suitable elaboration, what is obvious to anyone, that Charlotte suffered from "repressed personality." A number of curious works by champions of Charlotte, Emily, or Branwell Brontë prove to the satisfaction of the writers that their favourite was sole author of the works of the others. Among the least trustworthy are some of the contributions from contemporaries, who prided themselves on having known the family or members of it personally, and volunteered statements which chronology or other facts show to be untrue. Others, like Mrs Oliphant, have been actuated by prejudice amounting almost to spite, and their testimony and comment had better be rejected altogether: Miss Delafield, in the best summary of the Brontë literature, ignores Mrs Oliphant. Even Charlotte Brontë was very careless in some of her statements, and her inaccuracies have been exposed, *e.g.* by Mr Benson

From their childhood till long after the age when such *Juvenile* amusements usually pall, the three sisters and their brother *writings* were always imagining and writing scenes and stories, with *of the* but the vaguest idea that some day they might appear before *and* the world as authors. Emily's and Anne's ecstatic absorption *sisters* in the "Gondal Chronicles" is now a well-known story; Charlotte and Branwell also had their secret papers dealing with the Angrians and other imaginary peoples. Some of this highly romantic stuff has now been published, and it can be seen how far the Gondal epic was a sort of mental background to Emily's poems, and indirectly even to *Wuthering Heights*.[1] Their father was an author in a small way, publishing stories of a mild didactic order and some minor poetry; and it must not be forgotten that his children had Celtic blood from both sides, he being Irish and their mother from Cornwall. Charlotte's voluminous early works, though not so voluminous as Mrs Gaskell thought,[2] and her precocious efforts "to analyse character," [3] were an apprenticeship to the craft of fiction the value of which she acknowledged in the preface to her first book, *The Professor*, the one that was declined by every firm and had to wait for publication till after her death.[4] Indefatigable romancers as they were, it was not till after Charlotte's final return from Brussels, at the beginning of 1844, and the subsequent failure of their project for running a school or having a few pupils at home, that they took up more seriously their early dream of public authorship. Charlotte's accidental discovery of the secretive Emily's poems was the event which

---

(*Charlotte Brontë*, xii.), who also points out absurd misunderstandings on Mrs Gaskell's part (*Ibid.*, 31). Excellent spadework was done by C. K. Shorter, which has been utilized by writers possessed of real insight; and the researches of the Brontë Society have been almost too fruitful. The quarrels of the commentators and re-interpreters are, unfortunately, quite as irritating as they are amusing.

[1] See Shorter's *Charlotte Brontë and her Circle* (1896) and *The Brontës: Life and Letters* (1908), Mrs Gaskell, v., and Mrs E. H. Chadwick's *In the Footsteps of the Brontës* (1914).

[2] Gaskell, v., corrected by Benson, 31.

[3] Ellen Nussey says she began the practice when she was five years old (letter quoted by Delafield, 35).

[4] "A first attempt it certainly was not, as the pen which wrote it had been previously worn a good deal in a practice of some years." "In many a crude effort, destroyed almost as soon as composed," she tells how she had got over any taste for the ornamented and redundant, and had come to prefer the plain and homely.

presently led to this scheme for publishing, and the first-fruits were contained in the little volume of *Poems, by Currer, Ellis, and Acton Bell* (1846), which was a dead failure, though its publication had cost them nearly £50.[1] But all three sisters were now busy writing stories, and as soon as finished these were offered to one publisher after another, Anne's *Agnes Grey* appearing with Emily's *Wuthering Heights* late in 1847, but Charlotte's novel, *The Professor*, meeting with a general refusal. Though it was the last to be published (1857), and might never have seen the light at all but for the celebrity won by her three later novels, there is good reason for considering her first work first.

"The Professor": autobiography, like the rest

Charlotte Brontë's four novels are all autobiographical; free transcripts, that is, of what she herself went through or witnessed at very close range—autobiography of the introspective and self-revealing kind. Outside their home life at Haworth, the joys as well as the sorrows of which preoccupied them above everything else, the three sisters had extremely little experience; they were ignorant of the ways of the world, and their shy disposition and intense reserve kept them peculiarly innocent. But Charlotte had recently gone through a trial of her feelings and fortitude which had left such an indelible impression, and now proved such a key to the feminine heart, that she was to use it again and again. She was to tell the story four times, with circumstantial changes which half disguise the facts. It was the assurance that she had told the truth, "that she had described reality," which Mrs Gaskell repeatedly notes as the one thing that satisfied Charlotte Brontë[2]; the one reality she thoroughly knew was herself and her small world. And she was no mere spectator. She was always striving to get down to the ultimate truth, to reach what might be called the sensations of the soul, for these were the only sensations that interested her. She had fallen in love with M. Heger; not in any vulgar sense, such as it irritates her friends even to hint at; but she had recognized in him the

---

[1] Two copies were sold, before the rest of the stock was sold for paper-linings for boxes (Benson, 194).

[2] *E.g.* in the passage quoted by Delafield, 152–154.

type of man which was the natural complement to the woman she felt herself to be, strong precisely where she was weak, nervous, diffident, and morbidly self-conscious. In him she worshipped her ideal of masculine strength, intellect, authority. To say she was in love is not to suppose that in any circumstances she would have enacted the "practical modern French novel" which Crimsworth apprehended if he stayed under the roof of Mlle Reuter after her union with the unsuspecting Pelet.[1] In the case of Charlotte Brontë there could never have been any actual "conflict between passion and duty."[2] But this was the most disturbing event of her whole life, the life which she lived over and over again in her novels. When she had learned to write fiction better, she gave a fuller and more moving account of this great episode in *Villette*, whereas *The Professor* is a very quiet, matter-of-fact, unheightened version. It is indeed an inversion of the actuality, since the actors are put into opposite rôles—or opposite sexes. Crimsworth, the professor, who tells the story and has the feelings and the outlook of a Charlotte Brontë, is here in pursuit of the young girl, who, though in love with him and the first to acknowledge it,[3] has too modest a sense of her own worth, and is too conscious of what she thinks her duty, to yield until duty coincides with love. Frances has the character which Charlotte prized in woman, with the calm determination and power of resistance which Lucy Snowe, in the later novel, found the hardest thing in the world to maintain. Crimsworth, on the other hand, is in the position of Lucy in the *pensionnat*, watched jealously by Mlle Reuter, who likes him better than Pelet, her intended, and strains every nerve to estrange him from Frances Henri.[4] This spying, crafty, insincere Zoraïde Reuter is recognizably

[1] Chap. xx.

[2] As observed in *The Times* leader commenting upon the four letters to M. Heger printed in that issue, 29th July 1913.

[3] She writes in the farewell letter returning the twenty francs, "I am afflicted— I am heart-broken to be quite separated from you; soon I shall have no friend on earth. But it is useless troubling you with my distresses. What claim have I on your sympathy? None; I will then say no more.—Farewell, Monsieur " (chap. xix.).

[4] Notice that Crimsworth is short-sighted, like Charlotte Brontë, and also like Paul Emanuel. Another small touch is the "Monsieur" with which Frances always addresses Crimsworth, even after they are married; it is like Jane Eyre's "Sir" to Mr Rochester, even when they are lovers.

a sketch from the same original as Mme Beck, in *Villette*; and even in Pelet, the slighter portrayal of a thoroughly French Belgian, there is a dash of Paul Emanuel's humours, though he is a totally different man at bottom. The topography is the same, and many small touches were repeated when the story was entirely recast in *Villette*. The dull, good-looking pupils, Eulalie, Hortense, and Caroline, impenetrable to Crimsworth's teaching, reappear in the Mlles Blanche, Virginie, and Angélique, who are the bane of Lucy Snowe's life at Mme Beck's. Then the three teachers, Mlles Zéphyrine, Pélagie, and Susette, whose "ordinariness" Crimsworth finds intolerable and hardly expressible in plain English, are evidently the Mlles Blanche, Sophie, and Marie Haussé depicted with no little resentment in one of Charlotte's letters to Emily.[1] The "perfidious, mercenary, and dry-hearted" Zéphyrine may be identified at once with Mlle Blanche, "the regular spy of Mme Heger," and no doubt appears once more in Mlle Zélie St Pierre, in *Villette*, "a Parisienne, externally refined, at heart corrupt, without a creed, without a principle, without an affection." In both books, there is the same dislike of the Flemings, whose "deformity of person and imbecility of intellect" are laid to the account of climate, and moral short-comings to the effects of Romish priestcraft. Sylvie, the least exceptionable pupil, "was even sincere, as far as her religion would permit her to be so"; but "her whole soul was warped to a conventual bias," and she gave "her independence of thought and action into the hands of some despotic confessor." But these are minor points compared with the identity of the principal actors and of the affection, which persons and circumstances conspire to thwart, eventually uniting them. *Jane Eyre* is the same story in a different shape, and in the love of the despised governess for the master who is a married man comes nearest to the Heger affair. In Caroline Helstone's passionate and for a long while hopeless adoration of Robert Moore, in *Shirley*, the tale is still further transformed. Frances Henri is the regular Brontëan heroine, with the distinction that she has the strength to submit, and accept her

---

[1] Quoted by Benson, 115.

lot without tempestuous plaints, repinings, and rebellions; and so she is happier in the end than she had dared to expect. Charlotte Brontë yearned to be like that; but, alas! she had the pangs, but not the reward. She did not get her Crimsworth. In *Jane Eyre* and *Shirley*, she brought about a satisfactory termination for her lovesick heroine by force, arbitrarily solving the problem that in her own case had been insoluble.[1] The special beauty of *Villette* is in the very different ending: sundered in the flesh, the lovers achieve their union in the spirit.

In the preface, Charlotte excommunicated everything romantic and meretricious. She subscribed to no school, to no influence; and can be seen feeling her way, as it were by the method of trial and error, to a kind of fiction that would convey reality as she saw it. She was not yet sure what should be put in and what left out. The result is a pedestrian story, only too carefully observant of the finger-posts of her own personal experience. Put side by side with the storms and excitements of her later novels, it is decidedly tame. The leading figures are satisfactory, all but Crimsworth, whose invincible integrity and "sardonic disdain"[2] do not fascinate the reader as they do Mlle Zoraïde. All Charlotte's male characters are, of course, a woman's men, or women in shape of man; Crimsworth, unfortunately, is that and nothing more. But Frances Henri is at least as admirable in her quiet way as her sister-heroines; and Mlle Reuter and Pelet, though not elaborate portraits, are concrete enough for the little drama in which they perform. But there is a perfunctory, unfinished look about the supernumeraries; it is too evident that they have only a casual connexion with the story; they are simply background, mere filling. And, as they have nothing particular to do, they can justify their presence and display what character they have only by discursive talk. Already, the

A laboured and unequal story

[1] Probably Janet Spens is right in the theory that in *Shirley*, as in *Villette*, the love-affair should have had a tragic termination. Charlotte probably meant Caroline to die—of love-sickness? Shirley would then have married Robert Moore. But Charlotte lost Anne just then (chap. "Valley of the Shadow of Death") and had not the heart for tragedy (English Association: *Essays and Studies*, xiv.).

[2] "'Que le dédain lui sied bien!' I once overheard her say to her mother: 'il est beau comme Apollon quand il sourit de son air hautain.'"

difference stares one in the face between those characters in Charlotte's novels who are drawn with perfect understanding, created, or re-created, out of her impassioned consciousness, and those who are merely observed. These latter are only half alive. She has watched and reflected, and tries conscientiously to get to the bottom of them. The others she knows through and through, without trying; they are of her own begetting. It is clear that Yorke Hunsden, the plain-speaker who makes a hobby of the candour which hurts, was a man that interested her; but his portrait had to be finished later on, in the Hiram Yorke of *Shirley*. Few of the other minor characters were worth completing. Charlotte Brontë never had the command of light-hearted, sprightly dialogue, ready for use at any moment; here it is sadly to seek; and the mere exchange of serious or half-serious sentiments between such persons as Crimsworth and his brother or the crotchety Hunsden is as dull as some of the disquisitions which give a foretaste of George Eliot.[1] The reader accustomed to humour is disappointed; the painstaking and often censorious and caustic analysis of traits and motives seems an arid substitute. But how much worse would it have been had Charlotte feigned the gift of humour which she had not, like so many who followed her!

"*Jane Eyre*"
The Professor had gone the round of the publishers, and came back at last from Smith, Elder, & Co., with two pages of criticism, instead of the usual terse formula, and with the intimation that a three-volume novel would be favourably considered. Charlotte had one nearly ready; her own sagacity had told her that the public wanted something different from *The Professor*, and she had anticipated the demand for "a more vivid interest." *Jane Eyre*, begun in the summer of 1846, appeared in October 1847, under the pseudonym of "Currer Bell." Perhaps her imagination had been liberated by her sister's *Wuthering Heights*; Emily had had no misgivings in letting her genius have full rein. But it is easy to see how a diffident young woman who had first ventured only upon a sober tale evolved out of her own most sacred experience

---

[1] *E.g.* chapter-opening xix., on the study of real life.

would speedily acquire the boldness and freedom needed to win a public. In fact, she explains it in the preface to her posthumous novel, *The Professor*: "Until an author has tried to dispose of a manuscript of this kind, he can never know what stores of romance and sensibility lie hidden in breasts he would not have suspected of casketing such treasures." It was not merely her own breast that was so susceptible. She observes, not without irony, "Men in business are usually thought to prefer the real; on trial the idea will be found fallacious: a passionate preference for the wild, wonderful, and thrilling—the strange, startling, and harrowing—agitates divers souls that show a calm and sober surface." This time, the romanticism which she had repressed was to have full fling, and even to be enhanced with a romanticism of older date which had thrilled and harrowed tastes not yet awake to the higher call. She must have read Le Fanu's tale of the bigamist whose blind wife terrorizes her innocent supplanter, and, probably without remembering the source, reproduced the cardinal features.[1] But, if to this extent her plot was borrowed, she established her own dramatic idea, and worked it out to the conclusion that satisfied her own logic. She forgot all about Le Fanu, and she forgot much else; for *Jane Eyre* was written at white-hot speed, and many reminiscences which haunted her imagination, from Mrs Radcliffe and other romancers, went unconsciously into her pen-pictures of gloomy old mansions, grim interiors, and scenes that shook as well as pierced the heart. The semi-supernatural phenomena of mysterious voices, ghostly laughter, and omens and premonitions, might be identified as the time-worn furniture of Gothic romance; but they were realities in a life lived on such a plane of emotional exaltation as Jane Eyre's, or Charlotte Brontë's.[2]

[1] See the ample synopsis of this story in the *Camb. Lit. Hist.*, xiii. 414–416. There is less to be said for the contention of Janet Spens (*Essays and Studies*, xiv.) that *Jane Eyre* was based on Richardson's *Pamela*; the plot features in which the two stories coincide are simply the stock-in-trade of much fiction at this date.

[2] Everybody then, if not now, believed Jane Eyre to be Charlotte herself; "but she always denied it calmly, cheerfully, and with the obvious sincerity that characterized all she said" (Harriet Martineau, quoted by Delafield, 248). But if she had denied that Jane and Frances, Caroline and Lucy were projections of herself, and the ordeals they go through only different versions of her own, she would have to be disbelieved, though her honesty would not be in the slightest degree impugned.

Little Helen Burns, when she ought to be attending to Miss Scatcherd's reproofs, loses the sound of the querulous voice, and falls into a sort of dream that she is far away in Northumberland, and that the noises around her are the bubbling of the little brook at home. Jane, and Charlotte, believe that sympathies exist "whose workings baffle mortal comprehension," between distant and perhaps estranged relatives; "signs, for aught we know, may be but the sympathies of Nature with man." Hence the dream when she was six years old, followed by the summons home to her sister's deathbed, a recollection which gives dreadful significance to the image of a wailing babe haunting her mind at Mr Rochester's, and, sure enough, heralding the news that her cousin John has committed suicide and Aunt Reed is dying. Charlotte saw nothing miraculous in such perceptions; they are supposed to be characteristic of high-strung organizations. She may perchance have read *Moll Flanders*, or heard of the voice calling Moll's runaway husband that reached him miles away in Delamere Forest [1]; it was the sort of incident that she would fully believe in. A different kind of incident, because it is not subjective, is the sudden storm and the crash of thunder which ends the idyllic scene in the orchard, where Rochester asks Jane to be his wife and she accepts him. The great horse-chestnut under which they had been sitting was rent in twain.[2] This may be described as sham-supernatural or as an extreme example of the "pathetic fallacy"; Hardy has a similar presage of tragedy in *A Pair of Blue Eyes*, where the church-tower falls down just as Elfride, who has never told Knight the secret which will be fatal to their happiness, says to him, "He shall be my strong tower and refuge."

A new sort of realism

Clumsiness and glaring improbabilities in the plot, blunders and absurdities in the picturing of a society to which Charlotte Brontë was a complete stranger, were as nothing beside the fierce sincerity with which she depicted life as it had imprinted itself on her quivering sensibilities, from childhood to woman-

---

[1] See Volume III. 197, and cp. *Jane Eyre*, xxxv. She told Mrs Gaskell that "It is a true thing; it really happened" (Shorter: *Charlotte Brontë*, 165).

[2] Chap. xxiii.

hood. The reality was in herself; and the narrowness of her
actual experience was far more than made good by its intensity.
It would not be correct to say that Charlotte and Emily had
to make bricks without straw: they had ample resources in
themselves which the right kind of experience released and
made creative. The absurdities and improbabilities escape
challenge in the fervency and conviction of the story-telling;
the snags vanish in the rush of the current. For the frankness
and honesty are transparent. This was how the world
appeared, this was what had happened, to them. It was the
simple truth they were telling, both Charlotte and Emily,
unlike as it might be to commonplace experience, and, happily,
they put it in the form of autobiography; with the pose
of omniscience and impersonality commonly assumed by a
novelist it would continually have looked absurd. It has
often been said of *Jane Eyre*, as well as of *Wuthering Heights*,
that it is not a mere novel. The latter had better be described
outright as a sort of poem. As to *Jane Eyre*, it is a rendering,
not of life as it is observed, but of life as it is felt, as it is known
in its elements. / It has been called "idealized realism" [1]; at
any rate, it is impassioned realism, and may be termed idealistic
in that Charlotte Brontë was projecting her moral dilemma
on the imaginative screen, essaying her own solution by the
touchstone of realities. / It was a sort of pragmatism before
such a theory had been formulated. The plot and the bizarre
situations and incidents in which she set forth her inner history
might be sheer melodrama, but they were true subjectively:
her honest and scrupulous mind would not let her go beyond
what she knew by deepest experience. First there was the
urgent problem of her wounded heart, her yearning for peace
and content; and then her hunger for liberty, for self-
realization, in which she voiced the feelings of all her sex. And,
last but not least, there was the acute sense of the struggle for
life, always present in her aching heart, as the virtual head of
the family of children at Haworth, with the dread of what
Branwell might do next haunting her like an incubus. These
were the motives that subconsciously shaped her stories. Auto-

[1] Bonnell, 207.

biography was the inevitable form, and she adopts the regular autobiographical plan, beginning with childhood and girlhood, and going on to the great episode which unsettled her modest scheme of life and generated the drama of her novels.[1]

Struggles of a repressed person- ality

Charlotte suffered all her life from frustration.   Emily was the only one of the sisters whose personality could not be repressed.   Charlotte rebelled, but timidly, dreading the consequences, ineffectually.   Her puritanism, her father's rule, the cramped circumstances at Haworth, and the submissiveness inculcated upon her sex, restrained her, in life.   But she felt that her submission had been exacted, the everlasting suppression rankled, and she avenged herself in her books.   The greatness of soul which she put into Jane Eyre belonged to herself, as did the other characteristics of the little governess, plain, but a "savage, beautiful creature" in her conquering charm, diffident, but when her mind was made up "never was anything at once so frail and so indomitable"; but they belonged to herself only as what she wanted to be.   In her contacts with the world, the actual Charlotte remained timid, self-conscious, shy, and by no means the conqueror depicted in her heroine.   Little Jane's outburst at Aunt Reed's is the kind of rebellion she would like to have ventured:

"I am glad you are no relation of mine: I will never call you aunt again as long as I live.   I will never come to see you when I am grown up; and if anyone asks me how I liked you, and how you treated me, I will say the very thought of you makes me sick, and that you treated me with miserable cruelty."

"How dare you affirm that, Jane Eyre?"

"How dare I, Mrs Reed?   How dare I?   Because it is the *truth*.   You think I have no feelings, and that I can do without one bit of love or kindness; but I cannot live so: and you have no pity.   I shall remember how you thrust me back— roughly and violently thrust me back—into the red room, and locked me up there, to my dying day; though I was in

---

[1] She had read and admired George Sand, though she was not quite satisfied even by *Consuelo*.   Dimnet quotes her approval of George Sand's mingling of poetry and feeling with her portraiture of life, and remarks on the combination in both novelists of inner truth and external improbability (see especially pp. 52–53).   Mary Robinson (Mme Duclaux) rightly called Charlotte Brontë "un poète lyrique" (48).

THE BRONTËS—CHARLOTTE

agony; though I cried out, while suffocating with distress, 'Have mercy! Have mercy, aunt Reed!'"[1]

This, and the exaggerated reminiscences of the horrors of Lowood school, with the portrait of Mr Brocklehurst, the "black-marble" despot, are her long-deferred vengeance, and it is satisfactory to know that some of it did not miss the mark.[2] Liberty was what she craved above all:

I tired of the routine of eight years in one afternoon. I desired liberty; for liberty I gasped; for liberty I uttered a prayer; it seemed scattered on the wind then faintly blowing. I abandoned it and framed a humbler supplication; for change, stimulus; that petition, too, seemed swept off into vague space: "Then," I cried, half desperate, "grant me at least a new servitude!"[3]

When the half-starved and shivering little girl looks over the "high and spike-guarded" wall at Lowood, and sees the fells and the beck, now through wild rain and whirling sleet and now under the blue skies and serenity of May, she has her first faint glimpse of Mother Nature, though not yet will she know the harmony and calm which there is in that communion for Nature's children.

All this I enjoyed often and fully, free, unwatched, and almost alone: for this unwonted liberty and pleasure there was a cause to which it now becomes my task to advert.

The cause was the disorganization in the school due to the outbreak of fever, when "forty-five out of the eighty girls lay ill at one time." Jane's beloved friend, little Helen Burns, was dying, and Jane's eyes are opened now to things beyond. It is an incident related with extreme pathos, but with something very different from the didactic unction of those who would draw a salutary moral from a child's death. Helen stands for Charlotte's eldest sister, Maria, who was taken home

[1] Chap. iv.
[2] Dickens's Dotheboys Hall, in *Nicholas Nickleby*, dates from 1839. The Rev. W. Carus Wilson may have been libelled in Mr Brocklehurst. But it does not matter. Charlotte Brontë's ogre is true; it is one of the ugly figures that loom up out of many, or most, memories of childhood.
[3] Chap. x.

to die of consumption. Charlotte, Emily, and Elizabeth were removed a little later, and Elizabeth died too. Charlotte had loved to talk to the thoughtful and intelligent Maria, and this touching conversation with the dying Helen may have been the echo of a real one. A new train of thought had entered Jane's mind with the sickness of her little friend:

"This world is pleasant—it would be dreary to be called from it, and to have to go who knows where?"

And then my mind made its first earnest effort to comprehend what had been infused into it concerning heaven and hell; and for the first time it recoiled, baffled; and for the first time glancing behind, on each side, and before it, it saw all round an unfathomed gulf; it felt the one point where it stood—the present; all the rest was formless cloud and vacant depth: and it shuddered at the thought of tottering, and plunging amid that chaos.

Then she is summoned to Helen's bedside:

"Where are you going to, Helen? Can you see? Do you know?"
"I believe; I have faith; I am going to God."
"Where is God? What is God?" [1]

She has awakened to the ultimate problem. The keynote of death is struck which was to sound from beginning to end of the Brontë novels, as it sounded in the Haworth household. Hitherto, fiction had shunned such thoughts, or the sceptical and sardonic spirit of the eighteenth century had ruled: "One world at a time, please!" as the free-thinking *grande dame* had politely retorted to the offer of ghostly consolation on her death-bed. It is the revival of imagination in the novel, the entry of romance, not mere Waverley romance, but that of Wordsworth, Keats, Shelley, and Blake. Here it may sound childish, and even stilted; but it is all the truer and more earnest for its childishness.

Nature poetry The Wordsworthian attitude to nature is the other side to this haunting sense of the mystery of life. It would be risky to assert that the Brontë sisters would not have had their in-

[1] Chap. ix.

tense passion for the moors environing their gloomy parsonage had they not read the romantic poets. At all events, they did read them, and there are passages enough in their books which sound like an echo of Wordsworth himself. Several occur in *The Professor*, injured a little by over-writing but sincere in their inspiration, such as the vignette of the storm-washed city and the mighty rainbow, or the scene in the Protestant cemetery, where the remains of Martha Taylor, Charlotte's friend, actually lay. It is in this quiet spot that Crimsworth finds Frances, whom he has long been seeking in vain. *Jane Eyre* and the two subsequent novels are full of this nature poetry, marred at times by the "pathetic fallacy," but for the most part imbued with a disinterested worship, if that sense of close kindred, of intimacy, and of an affection which is almost a complete remedy for mortal ills, may be termed disinterested.

I touched the heath: it was dry, and yet warm with the heat of the summer-day. I looked at the sky; it was pure: a kindly star twinkled just above the chasm ridge. The dew fell, but with propitious softness; no breeze whispered. Nature seemed to me benign and good; I thought she loved me, outcast as I was; and I, who from man could anticipate only mistrust, rejection, insult, clung to her with filial fondness. To-night, at least, I would be her guest—as I was her child: my mother would lodge me without money and without price.[1]

Then there is the eloquent passage inspired by the moors above Hathersage, in the Peak of Derbyshire, the village which she calls Morton, where she finds St John Rivers and his sisters. Diana Rivers seems to be her first venture at an image of her own sister Emily. These are still the moors of the Pennine, the same as the moors of Haworth.

I saw the fascination of the locality. I felt the consecration of its loneliness: my eye feasted on the outline of swell and sweep—on the wild colouring communicated to ridge and dell, by moss, by heath-bell, by flower-sprinkled turf, by brilliant bracken, and mellow granite crag.[2] These details

---

[1] Chap. xxviii.
[2] Of course, it was not granite; young parsonage ladies did not yet "do" elementary geology.

were just to me what they were to them—so many pure and sweet sources of pleasure.[1]

Nature haunts her dreams, sleeping or waking, when Jane is in love, and still uncertain of the character and intentions of Rochester: the wind has "a sullen, moaning sound," and there is "a mournful under-sound, whether in the house or abroad I could not at first tell, but it recurred, doubtful yet doleful, at every lull: at last I made out it must be some dog howling at a distance." This is the old romanticism, the cult of symphonious atmosphere; and even in the exquisite little snatch of Wordsworthian music preluding Jane's first sight of Mr Rochester the same art, or artfulness, is latent:

On the hill-top above me sat the rising moon; pale yet as a cloud, but brightening momently: she looked over Hay, which, half lost in trees, sent up a blue smoke from its few chimneys; it was yet a mile distant, but in the absolute hush I could hear plainly its thin murmurs of life. My ear too felt the flow of currents; in what dales and depths I could not tell: but there were many hills beyond Hay, and doubtless many becks threading their passes. That evening calm betrayed alike the tinkle of the nearest streams, the sough of the most remote.[2]

Mr Rochester   Rochester was probably not drawn from any particular original, but conjured up by Charlotte Brontë as a concrete embodiment of her masculine ideal. He is not a likeness of M. Heger, but offspring of the dream inspired by Heger.[3] He is a creation, and a fine creation, too, in spite of obviously Byronic traits. A gentleman who behaves so eccentrically and even outrageously, and yet commands the reader's sympathies and is always fully alive, must have something in him both as an objective character and as the result of literary parturition. Rochester has moral courage enough for anything, moral or immoral; he dares bigamy with supreme nonchalance, has presence of mind in the most alarming situations; he also has wit, eloquence, and a sardonic humour

---

[1] Chap. xxx.   [2] Chap. xii.
[3] The relation of Crimsworth, Rochester, Paul Emanuel, and other characters to M. Heger is well discussed by Mackay, 63–65.

which is his nearest resemblance to Paul Emanuel, or M. Heger. And with all this he is a magnificent lover. It was one of Charlotte's triumphs over actuality that Rochester gives Jane the satisfaction which in one of her poems of passionate love faced by indifference she allots to a man:

> There was a sort of quiet bliss
> To be so deeply loved,
> To gaze on trembling eagerness
> And sit myself unmoved.[1]

But it was not Charlotte Brontë's part so much to depict *The* remarkable characters, as to show live characters acting remark- *other* ably. Here was the strength of her dramatic genius, here *charac-* were its limitations. There are finer characters in fiction than *ters* Jane Eyre, there is none with a more dynamic personality. It is what Jane thinks, and feels, and does, that gives her this life and force; nothing else counts, not even the smallness and plainness on which Charlotte laid so much stress, as if she were avenging herself on fate for her own physical shortcomings. Jane delineates herself, dramatically. So do the others. Their attitude to life, their temperament, the kind of soul they have, are revealed in their actions, rather than in mannerisms and tricks of social demeanour or of speech, such idiosyncrasies as might be catalogued. It was not Charlotte Brontë's habit to introduce her characters with a formal inventory of peculiarities. Hers was a more natural way, at least a way that looks more like nature and less artificial. Things are usually in full swing when the first chapter opens; the reader hears things said and sees things done; and, if this is not enough to make the speakers and actors clear and substantial to the eye of imagination, then a few particulars are let fall which tell the reader what he wants to know. But it is the drama that defines the characters: no play-bill is necessary to the play. In Charlotte

---

[1] *Gilbert*, i.—"The Garden." Most of Charlotte Brontë's poems written at this period are concerned with the bitterness of separation, especially from one who is lukewarm or disdainful of the other's passionate affection; *e.g.* "Stanzas":

> My love is almost anguish now,
> It beats so strong and true;
> 'Twere rapture, could I deem that thou
> Such anguish ever knew.

Brontë's novels there is much more description of stage and scenery than of persons, and this because the environment is a shaping factor in their lives. Those who stand out most are those who have aroused most feeling. Jane Eyre, or Charlotte Brontë, cherishes a warm affection or a fierce hostility towards such as Mrs Reed, or Mr Brocklehurst and Miss Temple, the ogre and the angel of Lowood school, or the frivolous society at Thornfield Hall, or St John Rivers and his sisters. Even those who play but an insignificant part may enjoy a sharp definition owing to such acute dislike as she visits on the heads of the nasty mistress at Lowood, Miss Scatcherd, and the repulsive children of Mrs Reed. Strong feeling provokes her to exaggerate unconsciously those traits which have annoyed her or otherwise affected her vision; hence the worldly people at the big house become the caricatures of humanity which they actually seemed to the hostile eyes of the governess, just as Mr Brocklehurst and Mrs Reed are the embodiments of malignancy which they were in the eyes of the downtrodden child.[1] Jane Eyre says, "I could never rest in communication with strong, discreet, and refined minds, whether male or female, till I had passed the outworks of conventional reserve, and crossed the threshold of confidence, and won a place by their heart's very hearthstone."[2] It was impossible for her to be intimate with those who excited this instinctive antipathy, or really to understand them: they were a sealed book. She was bound to treat them unfairly. In spite of Charlotte's enthusiasm for French literature, M. Heger never succeeded in eradicating the over-emphasis and exaggeration in her style, her story-telling, or her presentment of character. But what does it matter? It does not matter here, for in one, and that the most important sense, there is only one character and one subject in *Jane Eyre*, Jane herself; the rest, whether men and women or stocks and stones, are only the things that impinged on her consciousness and determined her attitude and her actions.[3]

[1] Cp. Bonnell (207) on this tendency to "magnify" her portraits of those whom she disliked. [2] Chap. xxxii.

[3] A good instance of a character that she neither loved nor hated, one that left her cold, is St John Rivers. He is one of those observed characters who are so

Shirley (1849) is a very different novel from *Jane Eyre*. "Shir-
Charlotte Brontë was dismayed and bewildered by the invec- ley"
tives hurled by the reviewers at her unblushing frankness, the
alleged coarseness and unwomanliness, of her treatment of what
she thought the most vital problems. So she fell back on
something more like normal fiction, without reverting to the
sober literalism of *The Professor*. In *Shirley*, she wrote a
novel in the somewhat desultory style of reminiscences, dealing
with the people around her or in the houses where she had
lived as a governess, her personal friends or obnoxious acquaintances, those people above all who had impressed themselves
on her imagination. The book is full of portraits, and most
of them were recognized; in fact, it was this more than anything else that led to the identification of "Currer Bell" and
the lifting of the veil of anonymity. It is a general delineation
of provincial life within a radius stretching considerably
beyond the village of Haworth, and she looks back over a tract
of recent history beginning a few years before she was born.
For this part of the West Riding had been the battle-ground
of operatives and mill-owners during the industrial troubles
incident to the Orders in Council of 1807–1812. Her dear old
friend and schoolmistress, Miss Wooler, had told her tales of
the Luddites, and she sent for a file of the *Leeds Mercury* of
that period to make sure of the details. The attack on William
Cartwright's mill in 1812 suggested the attack on Moore's
mill in the Hollow, described in one of the most graphic and

utterly inferior to those whom she drew from the heart outwards. His original
was the Rev. Henry Nussey, brother of her friend Ellen, who had once proposed
to Charlotte and been rejected; their natures were incompatible. He became
vicar of Hathersage, and Charlotte stayed there with Ellen, when she became
familiar with the Derbyshire moorlands. Jane Eyre tries hard to like St John, but
cannot love him, and declines his urgent appeal to go with him as his wife to
India. She can be seen making great efforts to do him justice. She goes so far as
to persuade herself that he feels the spell of the moorland as she feels it. "He
seemed in communion with the genius of the haunt; with his eyes he bade farewell
to something" (chap. xxxiv.). But it is impossible to accept such a contradiction
of his superiority to everything earthly. Mary Taylor said, "It's a bit of your
absurd charity to believe in such a man" (Sinclair, 83). Charlotte herself admitted
that the character of Dr John, in *Villette*, was a failure because "it lacked the germ
of the real"; and, as Miss Sinclair observes, "whenever Charlotte Brontë 'took' a
character, as she took the unfortunate curates and Mr St John Rivers, the result
was failure" (*Ibid.*, 142). As to the surface accuracy of the portrait of Nussey, see
Wroot, 59–65.

poetical chapters, "A Summer Night." [1]   Thus the dramatis
personæ are composed almost entirely of characters whom she
had closely studied, but externally rather than by that power
of being inside them which vitalizes even such bizarre figures
as Mr Rochester and Paul Emanuel, or the two old maids of
Briarfield, whose hearts given to good works, though they
themselves were inured to privation, pain, and ingratitude,
were a sufficing bond of sympathy and understanding.   "You
must not think, reader," says she, "that in sketching Miss
Ainley's character, I depict a figure of imagination—no—we
seek the originals of such portraits in real life only." [2]   But,
for the most part, she kept so close to what she had witnessed
that imagination was hampered.   All sorts of local events and
incidents that have little bearing on the story are conscientiously retailed, as if she felt herself under an obligation to
complete a panorama of rural life in Yorkshire, once having
entered upon the theme.   Nowhere else is Charlotte Brontë
so much a mere spectator.   Often she is reduced to the part
of analyst and commentator, on some incidental personage, as
in this little essay on Hiram Yorke, a character in which she
gives what was left over in the sketch of Yorke Hunsden, in
The Professor, the whole making a study of Mr Joshua Taylor,
father of her bosom friend Mary Taylor:

As Mr Yorke did not possess poetic imagination himself, he
considered it a most superfluous quality in others.   Painters
and musicians he could tolerate, and even encourage, because
he could relish the results of their art; he could see the charm
of a fine picture, and feel the pleasure of good music; but a
quiet poet—whatever force struggled, whatever fire glowed,
in his breast—if he could not have played the man in the
counting-house, or the tradesman in the Piece Hall, might
have lived despised, and died scorned, under the eyes of
Hiram Yorke. [3]

True, this is the single one of her novels that is not autobiographical in form; yet it is autobiographical in matter.   For,
though her heroine Caroline Helstone is to a great extent a

---

[1] See Wroot (87–92) on her sources for the history.
[2] Chap. x., "Old Maids."   [3] Chap. iii.

portrait of her friend Ellen Nussey,[1] the story of her heart is Charlotte's story, and the ups and downs of her fond passion for Robert Moore are the drama of *Jane Eyre* or *The Professor* in a new shape. It is, in short, the old story, but not intensified into violent drama, or melodrama, love unrequited overshadowing the whole monotonous existence óf the girl in the unsympathetic parsonage, and all the more poignantly from her conviction that the chief obstacle to her happiness is the beauty of her dearest friend, Shirley Keeldar. For there is a second heroine, and she so important that she gives the novel its title; and there are two heroes, the story before it comes to a conclusion oscillating round two different poles. How is the confused drama given any sort of unity?

The plot, as it stands, but surely not as Charlotte foresaw *The plot* it, however tentatively she began, runs as follows: Caroline loves Robert Moore, who does not respond, and who after a while is attracted by Shirley. Everything points to a tragic end to Caroline's innocent hopes. Then, suddenly, expectations are reversed. Robert Moore does propose to Shirley, but only on a momentary impulse of a mercenary kind, to save himself from bankruptcy by marrying a rich wife. Shirley, with her piercing insight,[2] easily sees through the falsehood, and rejects him contumeliously. Then Louis Moore, that bluestocking in breeches, more of a nonentity even than Crimsworth, in *The Professor*,[3] appears from nowhere, and carries off the divine Shirley; and Robert, when the repeal of the Orders in Council leaves him again on the highway to prosperity, offers his hand to Caroline, and is thankfully accepted. To put it baldly, the plot comes undone, instead

[1] Charlotte denied this; but the question, often discussed, is well summarized by Wroot (97–102). Shirley tells Caroline, "You resemble none of the rest, Lina: there are some prettier faces than yours here; you are not a model beauty like Harriet Sykes, for instance; beside her, your person appears almost insignificant, but you look agreeable—you look reflective—you look what I call interesting." Which fits Charlotte Brontë like a glove.

[2] Shirley's preternatural acuteness is shown in her having guessed that Mrs Pryor was Caroline's mother, long before they proceeded to enlighten her (chap. xxvi.).

[3] Swinburne did not think much of either hero, but he was withering about Louis. "Robert Moore is rather dubious than damnable as a study from the male; but for his brother the most fervent of special pleaders can hardly find much to say on that score" (*Charlotte Brontë*, 54).

of being resolved according to reason or probability. Mrs Gaskell does not say that Charlotte changed her mind half-way through the story, and abandoned the tragic ending foreshadowed; but she describes at great length the pitiable state of mind in which Charlotte found herself at the critical point, and so indicates that there were sufficient motives. Branwell had died, and after him Emily, since she began the novel; and now—a still more grievous blow to Charlotte, who was wrapt up in her—Anne, too, died.

The pen, laid down when there were three sisters living and loving, was taken up when one alone remained. Well might she call the first chapter that she wrote after this, "The Valley of the Shadow of Death."

But, even before that, in the chapter called "An Evening Out" which immediately precedes it, there are signs that she had reached a point of suspense and perplexity. This is nothing but an aimless recital of sentimental tribulations, with a break, and what looks suspiciously like a postscript, in which the second hero, or pseudo-hero, Louis Moore, is suddenly introduced—another of her pedagogues and the worst of the lot! [1]

Caroline and Shirley, and their ideas   Charlotte Brontë is not content to let the story speak for itself: Caroline and Shirley must be women with ideas, which they discuss with each other as well as illustrate in their lives. The main theme of the story, woman in love and so at the

[1] Rebecca West was naturally upset by the over-flavoured sentimental menu of "An Evening Out," which she singles out as "an extreme example" of Charlotte's practice of working upon people's feelings (*The Great Victorians*, "Charlotte Brontë," 56–57). It is an account of an evening spent by Caroline at the Yorkes', when, as Mrs Gummidge would have put it, everything goes "contrary," and her love-sick heart is tortured by everyone's cruel indifference; and it ends, but for the long "postscript," with one of Charlotte's most eloquent manipulations of the pathetic fallacy. "This is an autumn evening, wet and wild. There is only one cloud in the sky; but it curtains it from pole to pole. The wind cannot rest; it hurries sobbing over hills of sullen outline, colourless with twilight and mist. Rain has beat all day on that church tower: it rises dark from the stony enclosure of its graveyard; the nettles, the long grass, and the tombs all drip with wet. This evening reminds me forcibly of another evening some years ago: a howling, rainy autumn evening too—when certain who had that day performed a pilgrimage to a grave new-made in a heretic cemetery," etc. This allusion to the burial of Jessie Yorke (drawn from Martha Taylor, who was buried outside Brussels) is a gloomy touch which seems to argue that here, rather than in the subsequent chapter, starts the debacle of Charlotte Brontë's plot, as originally outlined.

mercy of the other sex,[1] reopened all the social questions
which had been excogitated by Jane Eyre or implied in her
personal battle with circumstance. Whilst she listened at
Thornfield Hall for Grace Poole's blood-curdling laugh, Jane
used to ruminate by fits and starts on the plight of the millions
condemned to inaction and "in silent revolt against their lot."
"Women feel just as men feel; they need exercise for their
faculties, and a field for their efforts, just as their brothers
do."[2] Her long duel with Rochester was fought for her sex
as much as for herself—Charlotte Brontë implies as much in
her outbursts of indignation against the existing state of things.
Caroline Helstone, as an innocent girl shyly in love with her
handsome, domineering cousin, and tortured by alternate
hopes and despairs, is an appealing and exquisitely natural
figure. When she resigns herself to be set aside for Shirley,
without ceasing to love them both; when she feels that she
indeed gave Robert up, gave him up to Shirley, the first
moment she saw her, "rich, youthful, and lovely," and will not
grudge them their happiness, though it is at the cost of hers—
then, poor little Caroline is the most beautiful of Charlotte's
heroines. But she, too, has to be pressed into the service.
Caroline has to give her mind to the cause of all her sisters in
adversity, and to exchange preachments with Shirley on man
and woman, love and marriage, in the style of an amateur
sociologist.[3] There is something wrong with the world,
especially the world of women. Like Jane Eyre, she has to lift
up her voice for liberty, and for some equality between the
sexes. She even broaches the momentous question of the value
and purpose of life itself: "What was I created for, I wonder?"

---

[1] It is, of course, absurd to talk as if Charlotte Brontë were the first novelist to
deal with love from the woman's point of view. *Pamela* and *Clarissa* must not be
forgotten, nor Jane Austen's *Persuasion*. The intervals between Richardson and
Austen, and Austen and Brontë, are not incommensurable.

[2] *Jane Eyre*, chap. xii.

[3] Caroline was evidently rounding on Charlotte's critics in some of her tirades.
"Obtrusiveness is a crime; forwardness is a crime; and both disgust: but love!—
no purest angel need blush to love! And when I see either man or woman couple
shame with love, I know their minds are coarse, their associations debased. Many
who think themselves refined ladies and gentlemen, and on whose lips the word
'vulgarity' is for ever hovering, cannot mention 'love' without betraying their
own innate and imbecile degradation: it is a low feeling in their estimation connected
with low ideas for them" (chap. xvii.).

But the quiet and gentle Caroline, whose only strength was in her power of self-renunciation, hardly seems the right champion for such daring views; the strong-minded and imaginative Shirley would have been a better exponent. Shirley is, indeed, a living solution of the problem of a free and lofty personality. But her deliverances on the relations between the sexes are only a weak echo of Jane Eyre's, though her uncle, Mr Sympson, calls them "Preposterous stuff!—indecorous! —unwomanly!" and stammering with horror ejaculates, "Unladylike language! Great God!—to what will she come?" Yet all she has said is that "Before I marry, I am resolved to esteem—to admire—to *love*." And she adds later the betraying clause, her husband must be her master: "I will accept no hand which cannot hold me in check." She withers Robert Moore, after his insincere declaration; but it is a pity that she winds up with sheer rodomontade:

"Lucifer—Star of the Morning!" she went on, "thou art fallen. You—once high in my esteem—are hurled down; you —once intimate in my friendship—are cast out. Go!"

Shirley, as Mrs Gaskell said, was meant to be a portrait of Emily Brontë as she would have been "in health and prosperity." She is a beautiful and poetic creation; but she is not Emily. Charlotte, as all the evidence shows, was never intimate with Emily, and to comprehend and reveal that elusive soul was beyond her. There are, undoubtedly, characteristics taken from the life. She had often watched and wondered at her sister's odd ways:

Shirley takes life easily: is not that fact written in her eye? In her good-humoured moments, is it not as full of lazy softness as in her brief fits of anger it is fulgent with quick-flashing fire? Her nature is in her eye: so long as she is calm, indolence, indulgence, humour, and tenderness possess that large grey sphere: incense her,—a red ray pierces the dew,— it quickens instantly to flame.[1]

Even this is evidently written with effort; but the hymns to Nature which she puts in Shirley's mouth, and the descant

[1] Chap. xxii.

on the woman-titan who far transcended Milton's Eve, are not worth two sentences of *Wuthering Heights*. Charlotte's famous epitaph to that book, the comparison with the colossal statue hewn out of the granite block, is grandiose and almost sublime; but it shows that to her Emily and her book were unintelligible.[1]

This is the richest of Charlotte Brontë's novels in characters drawn directly from life.[2] Many she had known so long and familiarly that they were, so to speak, cradled anew in her imagination, and have some of the vitality of her most creative work. And, if she blended together traits from different individuals, the results were so much the better. For instance, the old Cossack, Mr Helstone, is believed to have been drawn partly from a striking original, the Rev. Hammond Roberson, and partly from Charlotte's father [3]; whilst it is averred that such features as his masterfulness and abrupt, caustic manner were recollections of M. Heger.[4] Robert Moore, who is not nearly so lifelike, may have had an unidentified original, but is, obviously, in the main an idealization of strength and virility: Charlotte could never moderate her respect for masculine efficiency. That homely but remarkable person, Hortense Moore, was a fuller picture of the Mlle Hausse of the Brussels *pensionnat* who had been slurred in her correspondence with Branwell. The Rev. Cyril Hall was a former vicar of Birstall, a character in his way; the Yorkes were her friends, the Taylors; the curates, whom she savagely scourged rather than satirized, all recognized themselves, and Charlotte was disgusted when she learned that they enjoyed the fun. She was the most personal of novelists. Probably, her instinctive veracity led her to exaggerate for the sake of emphasis, which would account for the imputation of coarseness in her portraiture. It is the coarseness of a hard etching. Such keen,

The other characters

[1] Let us, however, not be ungrateful for what we have got. Swinburne pointed out that it is the only study of Emily from the life by a real intimate (*Charlotte Brontë*, 81–86). At any rate it conjures up a livelier vision than Branwell's clumsy portrait in the National Portrait Gallery.

[2] Wroot devotes some fifty pages to these identifications.

[3] Wroot, 105–108.

[4] "He is just the Belgian professor with the imagination and the tender heart omitted from his composition" (Mackay, 64).

systematic observation made for sharp distinctions, exaggeration of oddities, and a certain vigour which was a substitute for the inner life which came from instinctive understanding. There is neither one thing nor the other in her caricatures of Mr Sympson and the Misses Sympson or the Misses Nunnely, who pronounce Shirley and her like "unsexed," and look at her "as quiet poultry might look on an egret, an ibis, or any other strange fowl.

What made her sing so? *They* never sang so. Was it proper to sing with such expression, with such originality— so unlike a school-girl? Decidedly not: it was strange, it was unusual. What was *strange* must be *wrong*; what was *unusual* must be *improper*. Shirley was judged." [1]

Charlotte Brontë saw through the dull conventionalism and everlasting pose of the genteel. Even the amiable Mrs Pryor comes in for shrewd analysis of her narrow-mindedness. It is she, with her caste prejudices, who is hurt by what she thinks the arrogance of a "man of the people." This was worthy William Farren, who, as Caroline was well aware, had "very fine feelings "; but "he knew when he was misjudged, and was apt to turn unmanageable with such as failed to give him his due." It is, indeed, in her drawing of such as Joe Scott, William Farren, and Moses Barraclough the Methody that Charlotte Brontë proves the soundness of her study of characters that she had known. She contemplated the labour troubles from the employer's point of view; she was a stanch Tory. Yet she shows both sides fairly, and so gives a truer and more poignant account than Disraeli had done in *Sybil* (1845) or Dickens was about to do in *Hard Times* (1854). Listen to Farren pleading with the obdurate Moore, and note the skilful infusion of broad Yorkshire in the dialogue:

"I've not much faith i' Moses Barraclough," said he, "and I would speak a word to you myseln, Mr Moore. It's out o' no ill-will that I am here, for my part; it's just to mak' an effort to get things straightened, for they're sorely a crooked. Ye see we're ill off—varry ill off: wer families is poor and pined.

[1] Chap. xxxi.

We're thrown out o' work wi' these frames: we can get nought
to do: we can earn nought. What is to be done? Mun we
say, wisht! and lig us down and dee? Nay: I've no grand
words at my tongue's end, Mr Moore, but I feel that it would
be a low principle for a reasonable man to starve to death like
a dumb creatur':—I willn't do't. I'm not for shedding blood:
I'd neither kill a man nor hurt a man; and I'm not for pulling
down mills and breaking machines: for, as ye say, that way o'
going on 'll niver stop invention; but I'll talk—I'll mak' as
big a din as ever I can. Invention may be all right, but I
know it isn't right for poor folks to starve. Them that governs
mun find a way to help us: they mun mak' fresh orderations.
Ye'll say that's hard to do:—so mich louder mun we shout out
then, for so much slacker will t' Parliament-men be to set on
to a tough job." [1]

Charlotte Brontë's object was not local colour, but fidelity
to what she knew.

The final rehandling of the crucial passage in her life, "*Vil-*
which she had touched over-diffidently in *The Professor* and *lette*"
used unconsciously as material in *Jane Eyre* and *Shirley*, is
her last novel, *Villette*, which she sat down to write after
reluctantly deciding not to take advantage of her popularity
by forcing *The Professor* upon her readers. In that first essay,
she had taken the easy line of autobiography, without realizing
the difficulties and the stumbling-blocks. Crimsworth had
been merely the reporter, the sensitive plate on which the
sensations were impressed; and her efforts to individualize
him, by giving him the abrupt, sarcastic, imperious manner
of the born preceptor, had left him the mere shadow of a
man. Paul Emanuel, now that she had the courage to tell
all the truth, comes to life without effort on her part, for he
was her heart's image of the man who had roused her to the
very soul. She reverts here to straight autobiography, for
the indirect method in *Shirley* had landed her in serious difficulties; but not literal autobiography. It is the drama as it
had reshaped itself in her mind after years of reflection; the
essential facts, as she lived them over again, falling into due

[1] Chap. viii.

relief with the accents in the right places. She had now
acquired a better sense of values, as is most clearly proved by
her decision to give the drama a tragic ending. As Mrs
Gaskell records, her father was "anxious that her new tale
should end well; he disliked novels that left a melancholy
impression." "But the idea of M. Paul Emanuel's death at
sea was stamped on her imagination, till it assumed the distinct
force of reality; and she could no more alter her fictitious
ending than if they had been facts which she was relating." [1]
Her artistic conscience was becoming infallible. As already
noted, *Shirley* would have had a tragic conclusion, but for the
melancholy circumstances that made it unbearable for her to
dwell any longer on grief and suffering. The utmost concession she would allow to her father's appeal was to wrap her
meaning in a cryptic sentence, which those who cannot endure
the truth may choose to misunderstand, to "leave sunny
imaginations hope"—"let them picture union and a happy
succeeding life." She herself asked for no such thing. She
was content. She had brought about the harmony which is
afforded to mortals. The ideal end had been attained, the
discords were resolved, the lovers are united in the spirit
though separated in the world of space and time.

Autobio-
graphy in
essence
Devotees of Charlotte Brontë still exist who are up in
arms at any suggestion that *Villette* is based upon the fact of
a passionate affection for M. Heger. To what has already been
said here on this point it need only be added that her imagination would never have been content with a mere reconstruction;
the realism she sought was a concrete interpretation of such
an intense spiritual conflict as she had passed through, bringing
out its ideal significance. She wanted to give more than the
mere facts and yet evade the facts, to state in the most moving
way all that it meant for her without reproducing the actual
circumstances; and she almost succeeded. But her strength
was not in invention. Tell-tale details crept in; it sounds
like the record of actual events; and at Brussels more was read
into them than the facts warranted. [2] Mrs Gaskell, in her

[1] Gaskell, xxv.
[2] Mr Benson does not believe that she tried to avoid any identifications. "Whether
or no she actually muttered *je me vengerai* to that lady [Mme Heger] when she left

biography two years after Charlotte's death, probably to avoid
unpleasantness for those still living, suppressed those parts of
the letters to M. Heger which revealed the overwhelming nature
of Charlotte's sentiments.   Charlotte Brontë herself, as usual,
was too modest; it doubtless never entered her head that
posterity would be so interested in her life that every scrap of
evidence throwing light on such a vital episode would be raked
up and scrutinized, and that the letters to her idolized preceptor revealing all her secrets would be pieced together and
published for all the world to read.   Those letters,[1] however,
merely confirmed what critical insight as well as eyes eager for
scandal had now already perceived.[2]   The disguises which she
had bestowed upon the Hegers and the teachers and pupils
in the Brussels *pensionnat* were too transparent.   The life
of Lucy Snowe was another of Charlotte Brontë's idealized
autobiographies.

Pondering over the actual, she would fain have evoked *Pro-*
another reality, not the facts but the inmost truth.   But *foundly*
actuality had its revenge.   Banal incidents come in that would *sub-*
never have been thought of had they not occurred; others, *jective*
which no doubt had the ideal truth that Charlotte Brontë
required, are exaggerated and given a forced picturesqueness
producing an air of fantasy.   Such, for instance, is Lucy's
nocturnal escapade after Madame Beck gives her the drugged
potion.   She wanders out at random, and finds herself in the
park—

in a land of enchantment, a garden most glorious, a plain
sprinkled with coloured meteors, a forest with sparks of ruby
and golden fire gemming the foliage; a region, not of trees
and shadow, but of strangest architectural wealth—of altar and
of temple, of pyramid, obelisk, and sphinx; incredible to
say, the wonders and the symbols of Egypt teemed throughout
the park of Villette.

Brussels for the last time, she had kept these things in her heart . . . and now
releasing them she took her revenge" (281).

[1] See *The Times*, 29th July 1913.

[2] Sir T. Wemyss Reid guessed or was otherwise aware of the secret which Mrs
Gaskell had suppressed, unless she saw only parts of the letters (*Charlotte Brontë:
a Monograph*, 1877), and Angus M. Mackay took the same view (in *The Brontës:
Fact and Fiction*, 1897).

It is like a dream, the dream of a girl sick and desperate with amorous longing; and, as in a dream, she meets the most unexpected persons without being in the least surprised. "In five minutes the secret was mine," the secret of the great fête; and soon Lucy sees and overhears things which are the key to other secrets. All this is a very romantic excursion from the dull realism of the Rue Fossette; if it were not an actual incident, picked out from her memories and fancifully embroidered, it would be the most far-fetched expedient a novelist could invent for clearing up Lucy's perplexities. As usual with the still fumbling realist, the unlikeliest things are those which really took place; and, if an incident looks probable, it is probably an invention. Pure fiction shuns the exaggerated, which is the pitfall of that which is founded on fact. But, as in *Jane Eyre*, the apparent artlessness—and it was no doubt a genuine artlessness—with which she takes up one after another the common events of a young girl's life, the seeming inconsistencies, which are not inconsistencies after all, such as the tenderness for Dr John Bretton which comes to naught and is followed soon by the real business, the strange love-affair with Paul Emanuel, conspire to impose the illusion of reality. Such tokens of Lucy's veracity are all the stronger for being involuntary and accidental; who could doubt that she is telling the truth? So, the rambling introductory chapters follow the haphazard line of real autobiography, and are the best possible preamble to what follows, giving as they do the clues to the girl's odd character, especially that blind honesty, the fanatical, bigoted candour, and aggressive frankness, which got both the character and the author into hot water. Like *Jane Eyre*, it reads, not like a novel, but as the most ingenuous of self-revelations, like the confession poured into the ear of Father Silas. Life as it struck upon her retina, in sharpest contours, in minutest precision, is the sum and substance of *Villette*, along with Lucy's reactions, of which a perception of the comic was not one, though she and her creator were exasperated by the absurd. A daguerreotype of any original in all the enormity of his humour is her best substitute for the comic. But, in spite of all the clumsiness and the superfluities, the story, all that matters, is told with a strong, firm accent, well under control.[1]

Observation in *Villette* is better balanced with her more pro- *The* found portraiture than in *Shirley*; Lucy herself, Paul Emanuel, *charac-* and Mme Beck are of this supreme order. The charming little *ters* witch, Paulina, who reappears in the more commonplace shape of the Countess de Bassompierre; Dr John, with whom, like Lucy, Charlotte is half in love; his mother, Mrs Bretton, and the aged Miss Marchmont, who in one of the earliest chapters strikes the favourite keynote of death, and the frivolous Count de Hamal and Ginevra Fanshawe, stand out from among the crowd of incidental characters, as people to be loved or hated, in contrast with the mob for whom "hatred would be too warm a feeling," as Charlotte described the daily population at the Rue d'Isabelle in one of her letters home.[2] Dr John is the ordinary virtuous and sensitive young man, seen by a woman's approving eyes, like Crimsworth or St John Rivers. He was drawn with great care from a most worthy original, her publisher, Mr George Smith, as a conscious tribute of admiration; and George Smith recognized himself, or at any rate discovered that he "stood for Dr John."[3] Lucy's fondness for Dr John is an affair of the head, not the heart; she loves his sunny temperament, admires his sterling character; he has the qualities which she esteems, but not that compulsive affinity which would have defied reason. All this is expounded in the curious dialogue between Reason and her aching heart, when this was the solitary hope she had to cling to.

This hag, this Reason, would not let me look up, or smile, or hope: she could not rest unless I were altogether crushed, cowed, broken in, and broken down.

For Lucy was altogether too strange and solitary a being for the steady and humdrum Dr John; her quest for a sortable

---

[1] "A work is great, when it has ceased to matter that it is bad" (C. E. M. Joad, *Return to Philosophy*, p. 235). It applies to the work of Emily as well as of Charlotte Brontë.

[2] Letter to Branwell, quoted by Shorter (*Charlotte Brontë*, 68).

[3] It was the George Smith that founded the *Dictionary of National Biography*.

mate must needs be long and difficult. Charlotte Brontë, as her habit was with the characters that gripped her, said she did not like Lucy Snowe [1]; the reason being that, deliberately or by some indefinable coercion, she put her own faults and shortcomings into Lucy, the faults and weaknesses which she could never eradicate. Lucy Snowe is the truest of all portraits of Charlotte Brontë.[2] No one could depict better than Charlotte herself her shyness and want of self-possession, her acute consciousness of this, her painful sensitiveness to duty, and, with all that, the indomitable will, when her blood was up, which gave her the self-possession and presence of mind, and a conquering strength equal or superior to Jane Eyre's. Twice Madame Beck, whose self-possession is absolute, knowingly takes advantage of Lucy's curious weakness to prevent her seeing Paul Emanuel. Lucy knows all the time what Madame is doing and what she is missing. The first time, she is in her room, but can hear Paul's voice inquiring for her and the lying excuse of Mlle St Pierre; yet she makes no move till it is too late.

As that street door closed, a sudden amazement at my own perverse proceeding struck like a blow upon me. I felt from the first it was me he wanted—me he was seeking—and had not I wanted him too? What, then, had carried me away! What had rapt me beyond his reach? He had something to tell; he was going to tell me that something: my ear strained its nerve to hear it, and I had made the confidence impossible. Yearning to listen and console, while I thought audience and solace beyond hope's reach—no sooner did opportunity suddenly and fully arrive, than I evaded it as I would have evaded the levelled shaft of mortality.[3]

The other time was when Paul pays the school his farewell visit before starting for the West Indies. He went the round;—

he came to the last pupil; he turned. But Madame was before me; she had stepped out suddenly; she seemed to magnify

---

[1] See Sinclair, 153–154, citing Gaskell, xxv.

[2] Swinburne (81–83) has a fine passage on this identity of character, "with the consolation and support of her genius withdrawn"; he congratulates Wemyss Reid on detecting the likeness.   [3] Chap. xxxiii.

her proportions and amplify her drapery; she eclipsed me; I was hid. She knew my weakness and deficiency; she could calculate the degree of moral paralysis—the total default of self-assertion—with which, in a crisis, I could be struck. She hastened to her kinsman, she broke upon him volubly, she mastered his attention, she hurried him to the door—the glass door opening on the garden. I think he looked round; could I have but caught his eye, courage, I think, would have rushed in to aid feeling, and there would have been a charge, perhaps a rescue; but already the room was all confusion, the semicircle broken into groups, my figure was lost among thirty more conspicuous. Madame had her will; yes, she got him away, and he had not seen me; he thought me absent.[1]

It is like a score of incidents recorded of Charlotte Brontë, even after she had become a famous woman; she would nervously shrink into herself, not merely from the applause which always embarrassed her, but from an introduction that she knew would give her intense pleasure. The aptitude for misery was constitutional with Charlotte as with Lucy. The pangs that drove her, though a Protestant, to the confessional at St Gudule, are an historical fact, like many other incidents transferred to Lucy's account; Mrs Gaskell thought fit to omit this one. Lucy's incurable lack of hope, and, "deeper than melancholy," the heart-break which she nursed and cherished, with her love of solitariness, were all Charlotte's. Her delight in storms and in everything that testified to the might and majesty of nature was the simple obverse of all this. When the whole seminary, during the thunderstorm, were crowding round the night-lamp in the dormitory, praying aloud, she was out on the ledge outside her casement, revelling in it. She could not go in.

Too resistless was the delight of staying with the wild hour, black and full of thunder, pealing out such an ode as language never delivered to man—too terribly glorious, the spectacle of clouds split and pierced by white and blinding bolts.

After the confession, she found herself entangled in a maze of small streets, when a storm which had abated came down

1 Chap. xxxviii.

again with renewed violence.   Lucy was near exhaustion, but she bent her head to meet it.

My heart did not fail me at all in this conflict; I only wished that I had wings and could ascend the gale, spread and repose my pinions on its strength, career in its course, sweep where it swept.

It was then that her physical forces gave way, and she was picked up unconscious, and coming round discovered that she was with friends, the Brettons, whom she had lost sight of for years—one of various coincidences with which the story is clumsily articulated.   This joy in the strength and turbulence of nature was not unconnected with her worship of masculine strength, her readiness to yield even to arrogance.   It was not only Paul Emanuel's insight and quick understanding of the slighted girl that conquered her, but, still more, her instinctive admiration for strong, masterful, peremptory characters: the power to command was the godlike in men. He was her vision of M. Heger; yet much of him came out of her own soul.   He was her ideal counterpart: with all his childishness and impulsiveness, he had the qualities that she most prized, spontaneity, transparency of heart, indomitable courage, and, in spite of the "shameless disregard of magnanimity," in which "he resembled the great Emperor," a generosity really sublime.   His "crochets and eccentricities" were the laughter of the school; but "How often," murmured I to myself, "has this man, this M. Emanuel, seemed to me to lack magnanimity in trifles, yet how great he is in great things!"   He begins by bullying her, his recognized characteristic, in which he is exactly like Rochester; but in both cases the very best of the woman is brought out by the contact; in both, the great-souled, solitary being finds herself when she finds—her master?—nay, her destined mate in a world overcrowded with the vile, the petty, and the inane.   That seems to be what Charlotte Brontë was driving at.   Both M. Emanuel and Mr Rochester sin, as characters in a novel, if they do sin, not by inconsistency, but rather by too much consistency, truth and logic pushed to the bounds of extravagance—the almost inevitable result of idealizing what excites fervid admiration. If anywhere, it is in the antics of this man of learning and of profound wisdom that Charlotte Brontë senses the comic.[1] Whether she attains it is a question. M. Emanuel often attains the height of absurdity, of sublime absurdity; he is not far from it in the famous scene where he deliberately tries to exasperate Lucy's feelings of patriotism, and succeeds. In the pretty incident of the birthday present which he thought she had forgotten, and his heroism when she smashes his spectacles, the comical is tenderly combined with something more affecting. Perhaps here some symptoms of a sense of humour may be detected in Charlotte Brontë by the expert in such matters. Assuredly, she does not show it in her sarcastic characterizations of people of whom she had a low opinion; in this, of Miss Fanshawe, for instance:

"And what would *you* give to be *me*?" she inquired.
"Not a bad sixpence—strange as it may sound," I replied.
"You are but a poor creature."
"You don't think so in your heart."
"No; for in my heart you have not the outline of a place: I only occasionally turn you over in my brain."

Compare with this chaff the still heavier-handed comment on a magnificent Continental "fine woman":

With one of these beauties I once had the honour and rapture to be perfectly acquainted: the inert force of the deep, settled love she bore herself, was wonderful; it could only be surpassed by her proud impotency to care for any other living thing. Of blood, her cool veins conducted no flow; placid lymph filled and almost obstructed her arteries.[2]

It gave her immense satisfaction to turn the tables on anyone, the curates in *Shirley* for example, and she could hit off conceit and self-complacency with the malicious irony appropriate, as

[1] She did not think him wise. "He was a man, not wise in his generation, yet could he claim a filial sympathy with 'the dayspring on high'" (chap. xxix.). But what she means here is innocent of worldly wisdom.
[2] Cp. the very Corellian account of Rachel's acting, and the similar description of the "meaty" Cleopatra (chap. xix.).

in her general characterization of English country ladies in the same novel:

Whether young or old, pretty or plain, dull or sprightly, they all (or almost all) have a certain expression stamped on their features, which seems to say, "I know—I do not boast of it —but I *know* that I am the standard of what is proper; let everyone therefore whom I approach, or who approaches me, keep a sharp look-out, for wherein they differ from me—be the same in dress, manner, opinion, principle, or practice— therein they are wrong." [1]

It is an effective gibe, like the one at the Christian ladies at sales of work, who levy exorbitant prices on the "heathenish gentlemen":

The proceeds of such compulsory sales are applied to the conversion of the Jews, the seeking up of the ten missing tribes, or to the regeneration of the interesting coloured population of the globe.

But a humorist would have made a good deal more of Barraclough, the "preaching tailor," who heads the attack on Robert Moore's machines, and is undeniably a character. Charlotte only vents on his head her rooted dislike of Non-conformists: "Do you want a subscription to a new Ranter's chapel, Mr Barraclough?" and represents him taking to heart Moore's irony:

"You seem a fine fellow," said Moore, quite coolly and drily; "you don't care for showing me that you are a double-dyed hypocrite, that your trade is fraud: you expect indeed to make me laugh at the cleverness with which you play your coarsely farcical part, while at the same time you think you are deceiving the men behind you." [2]

The comic, in short, made no great appeal to Charlotte Brontë: life to her was too real, too earnest; and she was certainly not one to subscribe to "the vile English tradition that humour is a literate quality," [3] though in much of her prose she complied only too willingly with what was then the

[1] Chap. vii.   [2] Chap. viii.   [3] George Moore, *Avowals*, 74.

golden rule, that a facetious lightness is the perfection of style—without, however, achieving lightness. The comic side of the Brussels adventure is inevitably more apparent to that critical onlooker, the reader, than to either Crimsworth or Lucy Snowe, or to Charlotte Brontë, for whom those two were too much herself to be viewed so disinterestedly. Some detachment is indispensable for any glimpse of the underlying comedy of things, and detachment was more than she could arrive at in her view of a world in which she had endured and agonized. Charlotte Brontë detested Fielding; she could never see through the ironical nonchalance to his tender humanity. It is a wonder that she could put up with Thackeray's besetting levity, as well as his humour and satire. As to the repugnance which she felt towards Jane Austen, it has been well pointed out that she herself was too often a fit subject for that lady's raillery.[1] Her failings in other respects were not unconnected with her lack of that alert eye for the grotesque which not only gives the positive delight of laughter, but also ensures sanity and proportion. Yet perhaps Charlotte Brontë had still more genius, certainly more intensity of genius, than either her predecessor, Jane Austen, or George Eliot, her successor. She died in her fortieth year, after a life giving few opportunities of fruitful experience: she had barely finished her apprenticeship, and only begun to have the confidence and sureness of judgment and execution which more genial circumstances and a more leisurely training gave the other two to start with.

[1] *E.g.* Benson (63–64), on her letter refusing Henry Nussey; cp., however, the fun and badinage among the girls at Haworth (72–73).

CHAPTER II

THE BRONTËS—EMILY AND ANNE

EMILY BRONTË (1818–1848) is still more of a wonder. It is not merely that she died at thirty and yet left a book which stands apart from all other works of fiction, and a number of poems realizing a strength of feeling and beauty seldom attained by more accomplished poets of either sex, not to mention the voluminous romancing, dreaming, and poetizing with which she amused herself and her brother and sisters without any idea that it would be exhumed some day for others to read. But Emily was in herself one of the rarest characters in either fiction or reality, and what she wrote is as interesting as a key to such a personality as in its purely literary appeal. Incidentally, her novel, if novel it can be called without some strong qualifying adjective, takes precedence among works of prose fiction as the one most exceeded in bulk by the volume of writings about it, not all written in vain. And she herself has hardly fallen short of this as a subject for critical and psychological study, controversy, and sheer heroine-worship. She never courted such fame. Her poems were written for her private satisfaction, to disburden and console her own mind. They were her secret meditations, prayers, prophetic dreams; and she was bitterly hurt when Charlotte read them—it seemed as if it had given her soul away. Charlotte's shyness and solitariness were but weaknesses of the flesh compared with the secrecy and remoteness of Emily, whom she ironically described as "not naturally gregarious." Emily shunned acquaintances beyond the narrow circle of her home and a few friends, and even with these she maintained her reserve. There was no common measure between Charlotte's diffidence and Emily's self-reliance. Emily was strong, she was happy, in her deep inner life.

> Why I have persevered to shun
> The common paths that others run,
> And on a strange road journeyed on,
> Heedless, alike of wealth and power—
> Of glory's wreath and pleasure's flower.

So she hugs her loneliness, in one of her minor poems; and, in another, more revealing, she salutes her truest friend, Imagination:

> Oh, my true friend!   I am not lone,
> Whilst thou canst speak with such a tone!
>
> So hopeless is the world without;
>   The world within I doubly prize;
> Thy world, where guile, and hate, and doubt,
>   And cold suspicion never rise;
> Where thou, and I, and Liberty,
> Have undisputed sovereignty.

Liberty was her great craving; to be herself, to live her own life, to cherish what to her was no mere dream but the final reality. Like Wordsworth, she had her moments of intense vision, when she seemed to see into the life of things. Cheerfully busied in her household tasks, cooking, baking bread, sewing, and brooding over the world within which was her sufficing refuge from the dark world around her, or wandering on her beloved moors where she was at home with the infinite, she was happy, happier far than Charlotte. She, too, has her dialogue with Reason:

> Stern Reason is to judgment come,
> Arrayed in all her powers of gloom.

But she turns to an advocate with brighter eyes, and tells "why I have chosen thee," Imagination—

> A comrade, for by day and night
> Thou art my intimate delight.

Charlotte did not understand her sister; the pair were the obverse of each other; the Shirley whom she painted so lovingly is but a half-portrait. Emily, who was self-reliant to a fault, could make a confidant of the childlike Anne, and,

An enigma to the average mind apparently, the talented ne'er-do-well Branwell Brontë may even have had some obscure part in her strange masterpiece, *Wuthering Heights*. But for those who could not enter into her inner world there was something mysterious, intractable, and even savage about Emily; they could as soon have made friends with Catherine Earnshaw or the terrifying Heathcliff. Many of the riddles lurking in her poems will probably never be solved. Who, for instance, was so passionately lamented in "Yes, thou art gone," and in "Remembrance"? Who was it lay—"Cold in the Earth—and the deep snow piled above thee," "through fifteen wild Decembers"? Was it only a personification of the many human lives cut off in early youth? Could it be no personal loss that had stricken her, but sorrow for all the golden dreams that had perished, with a stern resolve to face the residue of life, without despair but "without the aid of joy"? In the case of Emily Brontë there cannot be two answers to such a question. She was only twenty-eight when the poems were published,[1] and there is no record of any love-affair of hers, either "fifteen wild Decembers" before or at any other date. That she was once in love with the flirting curate, the Rev. Mr Weightman, with the pretty face and the engaging manners, is pure guesswork: there is not an atom of evidence that he or any other identifiable person was the object of her lament.[2] As Maeterlinck finely put it, nothing ever happened to Emily Brontë, and yet everything happened.[3] "It was as if everything happened to her more personally and more profoundly than to others, for everything

---

[1] According to Shorter and C. W. Hatfield (*Complete Poems of Emily Brontë*, 7) "Remembrance" was written by March, 1845.

[2] The supposed love-affair with Weightman is the subject of a book by a novelist, but not a novel, *Haworth Parsonage* (1927), by Isabel Clarke. It is also believed in by E. and G. Romieu, authors of *The Brontë Sisters* (1931); see pp. 91–96. But the *reductio ad absurdum* of the conjectural literature about Emily's supposed love-affair is the recent book by an American lady, *The Life and Eager Death of Emily Brontë* (1936), based on a misreading of "Love's Farewell"—Charlotte's pencilled gloss—as the name of a lover, Louis Parensell (see *Times*, 29th August 1936).

[3] "Aucun evènement ne s'arrêta jamais au seuil de sa demeure; mais il n'est pas un évènement auquel elle avait droit qui n'ait eu lieu dans son cœur avec une force, une beauté, une précision et une ampleur incomparables. Il ne lui arrive rien, semble-t-il, mais tout ne lui arrive-t-il pas plus personnellement et plus réellement qu'à la plupart des êtres, puisque tout ce qui se produit autour d'elle, tout ce qu'elle entend, se transforme chez elle en pensées, en sentiments, en amour indulgent, en admiration, en adoration pour la vie?"—*La Sagesse et la destinée*, cii.

that she perceived or heard of was transformed into thoughts and feelings, into compassionate love, into admiration, into adoration of life." The Weightman fable is only a specimen of the conjectures put forward, often with strange confidence and acrimony, to clear up some obscurity, by those who cannot rest without a reasonable explanation of everything said or done by one so little swayed by ordinary reason as Emily Brontë. Emily has suffered from the cranks and monomaniacs as much as Charlotte from the philistines. Better to admit that she was not as other women are, and by patiently weighing what she said in verse or prose try to fathom her meaning. If her ideas are often remote, nothing could be more lucid than her language. Careful analysis and comparison of her famous story and her poetry, especially by those whose interests have given them a sympathetic understanding of the visionary flights in both, are likely to be the most effective method of interpreting Emily Brontë. For it is obvious that she was a mystic; not deeply versed in mystical lore, but a mystic by natural disposition. She was one of those to whose rapt gaze the world about them seems to melt away and give place to the deeper realities of the world beyond. To her, as to the author of *Adonais*, the life we see is but a screen, blinding the eyes to that which is dimly discerned by a chosen few. "The thing that irks me most," says Catherine Earnshaw, "is this shattered prison. . . . I'm wearying to escape into that glorious world, and to be always there: not seeing it dimly through tears, and yearning for it through the walls of an aching heart; but really with it, and in it."

That outburst of Catherine's has its counterpart in many *The* passages of Emily's verse, notably, in the inspired account of *mystic* the mystic vision in "The Prisoner." First, the hush of peace. *vision*

> Then dawns the Invisible; the Unseen its truth reveals,
> My outward sense is gone, my inward essence feels:
> Its wings are almost free—its home, its harbour found,
> Measuring the gulf, it stoops, and dares the final bound.
>
> Oh! dreadful is the check—intense the agony—
> When the ear begins to hear, and the eye begins to see;
> When the pulse begins to throb, the brain to think again;
> The soul to feel the flesh, and the flesh to feel the chain.

But she would lose no throe of this "rapturous pain," "that divinest anguish"; she longs for the vision to return. In the poems, and in *Wuthering Heights*, there is evidence enough scattered about to convince the adept in occult learning that Emily had had the mystical experience; her eyes had been unsealed.[1] The narrow life in the Haworth parsonage, the dull household routine, was the platform from which she soared in spirit into other realms. She was happy amid the drudgery, for she was thus free of both worlds. The one opened out from the other: it was but the opposite side of reality. She loved Earth too intensely to endure any separation. That is the whole burden of the lines ending,

> We would not leave our nature home
> For *any* world beyond the tomb.
> No, mother, on thy kindly breast
> Let us be laid in lasting rest,
> Or waken but to share with thee
> A mutual immortality.[2]

She pined away whenever she was long absent from Haworth; Charlotte's love of home and the moorlands was nothing to the passion of Emily's, which was a religion. She loved Earth, but it was that one spot of Earth which was her spiritual home. It was amid those cherished objects, the moors and becks, and the rough and primitive, half-savage dwellers in the solitudes, that she had her intimations of another state. Through them she was to paraphrase her vision. She found

---

[1] "That experience, that ἔνωσις, or immediate union with the divine, which Porphyry tells us that his master attained four times in six years and he himself once, that blinding experience had been Emily's" (J. C. Smith, "Emily Brontë, a reconsideration," in *Essays and Studies of the English Association*, v., 1914, pp. 146–147). Still more authoritative is Mr Charles Morgan (*The Great Victorians*—"Emily Brontë," 67) on "the complete mystical experience that Emily appears to have enjoyed at some time in her early youth; her abiding desire, which made all other desires relatively unimportant to her, for repetition of it; or a partial re-experience —one of many, as I interpret her—from which in an agony of spiritual disappointment, she had been dragged back." J. C. Smith pertinently calls attention also to the "genii-life," the visions and the trances experienced by Shirley.

[2] She also wrote in *The Genius of Earth* :

> Few hearts to mortals given
> On earth so wildly pine;
> Yet few would ask a heaven
> More like this earth than thine.

the transition perfectly natural from the plain, fearless, un-sentimental realism, with which she drew their harsh visages, to the transcendent spiritual ecstasies which she believed she shared with such as Catherine and Heathcliff. Catherine expresses Emily's passion for the Haworth moors when she tells Nelly how miserable she felt when she dreamt that she was in heaven:

"Heaven did not seem to be my home; and I broke my heart with weeping to come back to earth; and the angels were so angry that they flung me out into the middle of the heath on the top of Wuthering Heights; where I woke sobbing for joy."

Born of such perceptions, *Wuthering Heights* has the character and tone of some primeval myth or rude saga, an emanation of the moorlands, embodying the deepest and the loftiest in-stincts of human nature in a handful of primitive folk and two or three more sophisticated people from the world outside. Such fiction resembles Charlotte's as little as any, except that the significant characters in both differ from the common run in novels, in being living souls, perhaps the first since Shakespeare's. But Emily's are conceived on a towering scale. Catherine Earnshaw and Heathcliff are of the same stature as the Brunhilds and Sigurds and Gudruns of ancient epic, and they speak in the same large accents. There was indeed a myth-making faculty in Emily, recognizable in the fragments of story that jut out, as it were, from poems which are otherwise pure lyrics, and clearly manifest in the childish inventions and romantic transmutations of the Gondal chronicle. History, current events at home and abroad, the tales they had read, and all that stirred the imaginative hearts of Emily and Anne, went into this secret ledger. The Gondal epic was a sort of diary, in which the events that moved them most intensely were recorded in a poetic symbolism of their own. Catherine and Heathcliff had their prototypes in the Gondal legend, in "cursed Zamorna" and the woman of whom he was robbed.[1]

---

[1] Mrs Humphry Ward's suggestion that Emily had read Hoffmann's weird story, *The Entail*, simply illustrates the straits to which the searcher for origins is reduced in the case of the Brontës. Undoubtedly, the grim atmosphere is similar in both

Crude and ultra-romantic as these were, often reminiscent of Byron and the Gothic novelists, Emily had projected into them her own passionate soul, as she presently did into Heathcliff and Catherine. "Emily," said the wondering Mrs Gaskell, "must have been a remnant of the Titans—great-granddaughter of the giants who used to inhabit the earth." [1] It was a true word, though uttered by one who saw even less into the depths of that strange character than Charlotte had done, when she tried to portray her in Shirley.

"Wuthering Heights"
No work of literature was ever more inseparably identified with a definite spot on the earth's surface than Wuthering Heights (1847); and yet it is a drama of elemental conflict and suffering that might have been played out on any stage. It is the story of a passion unfettered by the limitations of the world and the flesh; time and place, though so definitely particularized,[2] are almost irrelevant; it is of any region and any age of mankind's perennial agony. At the end, the lover left on earth seeks union with the beloved even in the grave. And he attains it; for Emily has not merely grasped the modern idea of the supreme value of the individual soul, which realizes itself in its personal life and in mutual understanding, complete harmony, virtual identity with its destined mate; she sees the personality and the consummated union as eternal facts, which mortality itself cannot annul.[3]

> There is no room for Death,
> Nor atom that his might could render void.

Charlotte was much more orthodox in her heterodox ways of contriving the marriage of true minds; Emily, innocent

tales—the sense of a spirit-world close at hand—except that the ghastliness is very German and very corporeal, especially when the manifestations occur. As to the entail motive, there is no real correspondence; and old Francis is not more like old Joseph than many another crusty old servant would be, plagiarized from the Gothic romancers.

[1] Chap. xxvii.

[2] E.g. in Mrs Dean's conscientious effort to fix the date of Hindley's assault on the jealous Heathcliff, as the summer of 1778—i.e. nearly twenty-three years before (chap. vii.).

[3] "Belief in the personal and positive immortality of the individual and indivisible spirit was not apparently, in her case, swallowed up or nullified or made nebulous by any doctrine or dream of simple reabsorption into some indefinite infinity of eternal life" (Swinburne, 266).

libertine that she was, defied convention. Catherine, at the very moment when she is deciding to marry Linton, as a matter of worldly wisdom and natural expectation, declares to Nelly her unalterable sense that she and Heathcliff are fundamentally and irrevocably one.[1]

"It would degrade me to marry Heathcliff now; so he shall never know how I loved him: and that, not because he's handsome, Nelly, but because he's more myself than I am. Whatever our souls are made of, his and mine are the same; and Linton's is as different as a moonbeam from lightning, or frost from fire."

And then she relates how she wept in her dream, to find herself in heaven, away from Wuthering Heights, away from Heathcliff.[2] She knows she is doing wrong; she knows it in her heart of hearts:

"*Here!* and *here!*" replied Catherine, striking one hand on her forehead, and the other on her breast: "in whatever place the soul lives. In my soul and in my heart, I'm convinced I'm wrong."

Never will she forsake Heathcliff: "I shouldn't be Mrs Linton were such a price demanded!" With her good-natured husband's aid, she will save him from Hindley and help him to rise. Worldly connexions and worldly prejudices are of no concern to them; theirs is a bond that nothing in this existence or the one beyond can break. "Nelly, I *am* Heathcliff! If all else perished, and *he* remained, *I* should still continue to be; and if all else remained, and he were annihilated, the universe would turn to a mighty stranger: I should not seem a part of it."

The probabilities of average human nature do not apply to

---

[1] Love, not sex, is the bond of indissoluble union. The rash and innocent marriage of Catherine and Edgar Linton, when she avowedly loves Heathcliff as if he were part of her very being, is proof enough of Emily's innocence.

[2] Cp. *Aucassin et Nicolete:* "En Paradis qu-ai je à faire? je n'i quier entrer, mais que j'aie Nicolete, ma très douce amie, que j'aim tant " ("What have I to do in Paradise? I don't want to go there, but to have Nicolette, my sweetest love, whom I love so") (*Nouvelles françaises du 13e siècle,* ed. L. Moland and C. d'Héricault, 1856, 242–243).

Realism
the basis
such a story. It has reached the dimensions of that tragedy in which the confines of mundane existence are broken down. And yet the strange thing is that a story which soars to the extreme heights of poetry is nevertheless based on the firmest and plainest realism: not alone the setting, which is as solid as the moorland rocks.[1] Catherine and Heathcliff, though

[1] As to the extent of this realism, a flood of light has been recently shed on the question where Emily Brontë found the germs of her characters, or the moulds into which she poured her conceptions of masculine strength and untamable will, by those who have studied the Methodist magazines read at Haworth parsonage, and the records of the violent revivalist movements going on in those parts in her time and earlier (see particularly *Methodist Good Companions* (1935), by Mrs G. Elsie Harrison: *e.g.* chap. v., "Reactions in Haworth Parsonage"). As might well be supposed, Emily was not intimate with the country people of the West Riding, even those round about her. Charlotte said: "I am bound to avow that she had scarcely more practical knowledge of the peasantry among whom she lived, than a nun has of the country-people that pass her convent gates" (Gaskell, xvi.). But Mrs Brontë was a Methodist from Cornwall, like the aunt who took her place; and the atmosphere at the parsonage "was steeped in Methodism." The young folk read what Charlotte called "mad Methodist magazines, full of miracles and apparitions and preternatural warnings, ominous dreams, and frenzied fanaticisms." (As Mrs Harrison remarks, George Eliot also read these thrillers, and perhaps it was there that she found the story of Hetty and her murdered baby, in *Adam Bede*. She too had a Methodist aunt, whom she idealized in Dinah Morris.) Jabes Branderham, in Mr Lockwood's dream of the sermon "divided into four hundred and ninety parts" and of his protest which excites a riot in the chapel, had his original in the Rev. Jabez Bunting (1779–1858), the clergyman who turned Wesleyan and became a mighty force among the Methodists. He was the central figure in an uproarious incident at the opening of a chapel at Woodhouse Grove, where the Brontës' uncle John Fennel was headmaster of a school, the school, in fact, where Patrick Brontë met his future wife and that Aunt Bramwell came from. The "rappings and counter-rappings" which Lockwood eventually traces to the tapping of the fir-cones on the window were a reminiscence of the row in the chapel, and by no means the only details literally reproduced from incidents now authenticated. A previous incumbent of the Haworth living (1742–1763) had been William Grimshaw, Methodist preacher and friend of Wesley. His denunciations in broad Yorkshire are echoed by old Joseph, who seemed to Lockwood "the wearisomest self-righteous Pharisee that ever ransacked a Bible to rake the promises to himself and fling the curses to his neighbours." The Brontë girls knew all about the good-hearted but rugged and boisterous Grimshaw, head of the Haworth Round. Sowden's Farm, on the brow of the hill, is the old parsonage to which Wesley came, and may safely be identified with Wuthering Heights, Ponden Hall, across the moor, being similarly recognizable as Thrushcross Grange (Harrison, 118–119). Other corroborations abound. The Earnshaw legend is the Grimshaw legend, and the general brutality in *Wuthering Heights* is that of the Haworth Round. It all shows how solid Emily had laid her realistic foundations. It shows also that her sense of humour was not defective, like Charlotte's. Only compare her Joseph with Charlotte's timid kitcat of Barraclough, the obnoxious Methody. She gets comic relief out of this profane representative of the apostolic Grimshaw, without any such change of tone as would have turned tragedy into farce and have jarred upon the feelings. It is the man's unconscious nature.

"'Thank Hivin for all! All warks togither for gooid to them as is chozzen, and piked out fro' the rubbidge! Yah knaw whet t' Scripture ses.' And he began

they represent and express such daring conceptions, are not merely drawn realistically, they are realists themselves. Perfectly clear-sighted in their outlook on the rest of the world, they see each other exactly as they are. Catherine tells the lovelorn Isabella, fascinated by Heathcliff's rugged strength and superiority to other men, what he really is: "an unreclaimed creature, without refinement, without cultivation; an arid wilderness of furze and whinstone."

"Pray don't imagine that he conceals depths of benevolence and affection beneath a stern exterior! He's not a rough diamond—a pearl-containing oyster of a rustic: he's a fierce, pitiless, wolfish man. I never say to him, 'Let this or that enemy alone, because it would be ungenerous or cruel to harm them'; I say, 'Let them alone, because I should hate them to be wronged': and he'd crush you like a sparrow's egg, Isabella, if he found you a troublesome charge. I know he couldn't love a Linton; and yet he'd be quite capable of marrying your fortune and expectations! avarice is growing with him a besetting sin. There's my picture; and I'm his friend."

And, after the last wild interview, after the tempest of despair and the caresses that bite like curses, when Nelly Dean tells Heathcliff that Catherine's life has closed in a gentle dream, and prays that she may "wake as kindly in the other world," this is his answer:

quoting several texts, referring us to chapters and verses where we might find them."
    The blending of gloom and grotesquerie, of sardonic humour with terror, is inimitable. Had Emily wanted to be a novelist, she would have been one of the greatest, if she had lived. Humour she kept in proper restraint; she was a poet, writing tragedy the most austere. There is nothing incredible in the argument that the religious passion of such as Grimshaw for the Divine Lover was translated by her "into the language of human love," or that Grimshaw's ecstasies, during which "the communicants were sometimes held in Haworth church for hours together," suggested the wild transports of Heathcliff. The passion of *Wuthering Heights* is sexless: Heathcliff cries, "My soul's bliss kills my body." Emily was revolted by the Methodist view of evil and the doctrine of eternal punishment; she was a rebel, an individualist; her religion was an affair between herself and God. "It was Emily Brontë's violent reaction to the Methodist doctrine of sin that made her best poetry" (Harrison, 133). That is true with some grains of allowance. And, certainly, Heathcliff, with "no sort of fear of hell and Satan or of an outraged God," is a withering retort to the plaintive, pusillanimous Methodist who, as Grimshaw put it, hoped "to go creeping into heaven at last" (*Ibid.*, 135).

"May she wake in torment!" he cried, with frightful vehemence, stamping his foot, and groaning in a sudden paroxysm of ungovernable passion. "Why, she's a liar to the end! Where is she? Not *there*—not in heaven—not perished—where? Oh! you said you cared nothing for my sufferings! And I pray one prayer—I repeat it till my tongue stiffens—Catherine Earnshaw, may you not rest as long as I am living! You said I killed you—haunt me, then! The murdered *do* haunt their murderers, I believe. I know that ghosts *have* wandered on earth. Be with me always—take any form—drive me mad! only do not leave me in this abyss, where I cannot find you! Oh, God! it is unutterable! I *cannot* live without my life! I *cannot* live without my soul!"

It is the negation of polite romance ; all this is death to sentimentalism. The matter - of - factness mingled with Heathcliff's heaven-defying transports appears memorably in his instructions to the sexton: his coffin to be placed close to Catherine's, and a plank removed from each so that their dust will mingle. Heathcliff is thoroughly credible; he is consistent in act and speech and emotion, from the appalling incident when he curses himself for having put out a hand and saved the life of his enemy's son,[1] to the demoniac imprecation when he tells the dying Cathy that the kisses and tears she has wrung out, "they'll blight you—they'll damn you."

[1] That incident (chap. ix.) inevitably calls up the scene in *Hamlet* which Dr Johnson found "so atrocious and horrible," where Hamlet will not slay his uncle while at prayer, and waits for a moment when he can catch him in some act

That has no relish of salvation in't.

Heathcliff is like Hamlet in combining realistic vision, matter-of-factness, with the imagination that looks beyond. Coleridge said that in Hamlet Shakespeare "intended to portray a person, in whose view the external world, and all its incidents and objects, were comparatively dim, and of no interest in themselves, and which began to interest only, when they were reflected in the mirror of his mind. Hamlet," he continues, "beheld external things in the same way that a man of vivid imagination, who shuts his eyes, sees what has previously made an impression on his organs" (*Lectures on Shakspere*, ed. T. Ashe, 1893, 159—with Ashe's punctuation). Much of this applies to Emily Brontë's Heathcliff. On the other hand, Heathcliff might be taken as an example of Blake's anarchic individualism. Blake would have admitted him to his heaven. "Men are admitted into Heaven not because they have curbed & govern'd their Passions or have No Passions, but because they have cultivated their Understandings. The Treasures of Heaven are not Negations of Passion, but Realities of Intellect, from which all the Passions Emanate Uncurbed in their Eternal Glory. The Fool shall not enter into Heaven let him be ever so Holy." "This world of Imagination is Infinite & Eternal, whereas the world of Generation,

All the others who figure in the story, including the pair *The sub-* through whom, by an awkward expedient, it gets itself told, *sidiary* are entirely subordinate, mere accessories to the terrific duel *charac-* between the protagonists; but they sustain their parts and *ters* help to establish the realistic solidity. Isabella, the commonplace, giddy young thing, who flings herself at Heathcliff's head and is devoured; her brother Edgar Linton, gentle and amiable, bewildered by his wife's infatuation; the wretched boy who is Heathcliff and Isabella's demoralized offspring; and the simple, rustic, honest-hearted Hareton, what Hindley may have been before he was brutalized by evil courses—they are distinct and lifelike, though not memorable on their own account. But Nelly Dean, old Joseph, and the younger Catherine do arrest attention; and even Lockwood, though criticism has disparaged him, is fully equal to the duty allotted him, which is not quite otiose. He has the first as well as the last word; and the temptation which he resists to fall in love with Catherine Linton is a touch that brings that sprightly creature nearer, and with its tag of irony for him, Hareton's good luck, lets the story down gently to the mundane level. But the phlegmatic Mrs Dean, whose original was Tabby Brown, an old servant at the parsonage, with her obtuseness to all the glamour, is much livelier and racier, and also a better medium for a story that may leap in a moment from the common earth to somewhere between heaven and hell. Emily Brontë has been reproached for the clumsiness of this complicated mode of narration. But much is to be said for her choice of the indirect method, though it was overdoing it perhaps to begin with the epilogue, Catherine having already departed this stormy life when the story opens, and Heathcliff

---

or Vegetation, is Finite & Temporal" ("Vision of the Last Judgment," *Poetry and Prose of William Blake*, ed. Geoffrey Keynes, 1927, pp. 830, 842). Any coincidence of thought is, of course, probably accidental; Emily had apparently never read Blake, though she was fairly well acquainted with German fiction and perhaps German philosophy. Somehow, at any rate, she arrived at a conception parallel to Blake's of the devils as redeemers—defenders of the "freedom of the natural soul." Blake, whether she knew of him or not, throws some light on the daring course taken by her imagination.

> What immortal hand and eye
> Dare frame thy fearful symmetry?

being about to follow. Yet could the drama possibly have unfolded itself with such impressiveness had it kept to the straightforward order of events? Its force is concentrated in a series of tremendous climaxes; the fire and fury of one scene gives momentum enough until the next. There are, it is true, intricate complications and obscurities in between; but, when the great moment arrives, the mental and moral situation is made clear enough by the actors themselves. Lucid order may be at a discount; but the lack of it is a trifling defect; for, as Swinburne pointed out, [1] the alleged "confusion or incoherence" is only "external and accidental," not "inward and spiritual." Better, however, not to dwell too minutely on the legal points involved in Heathcliff's inheritance of the two estates. A wide ignorance of the law may be condoned in a young woman's first novel. And, after all, what are such faults of execution in the light of the almost superhuman conception realized with such power? That the would-be clever hand of Branwell Brontë is traceable in the first two chapters, with their over-literary phraseology and strained facetiousness, may perhaps be conceded to Emily's many scholiasts. [2] But a chapter follows at once which ushers in

---

[1] *Miscellanies*—"Emily Brontë," 266.

[2] These concessions to the prevalent mode of novel-writing occur elsewhere in the book; Emily was not always at the full height of poetic inspiration. But these first two chapters are particularly stilted, and do suggest that there was another hand at work as well as Emily's. Branwell put forward various rather indefinite claims to the authorship of *Wuthering Heights*. The theory that he wrote it all is, of course, as silly as the idea that Charlotte Brontë wrote it, but has not been too monstrous to find exponents. But there is good reason to believe that he was in the secret when Emily was writing the book, that they discussed it together, even if they did not collaborate further, and thus portions written wholly or in part by him, such as these two chapters, were incorporated. The tale goes that Branwell, whilst drinking with some friends, pulled some sheets of paper from his hat, and read out what proved afterwards to be a part of *Wuthering Heights*, asserting that it was his own work. The sceptic might ask whether the fact that the papers were in Branwell's hat proved anything—he was looking there for some poetry he had written. Without branding him as an out-and-out liar, no one can deny that Branwell was a *poseur*, and, what is more troublesome to those in quest of facts, a self-deceiver. He was quite capable of deluding himself into the firm belief that he had written a book in which he had had the smallest finger. The question is summarized by Benson (168–179) and argued in more detail and with an intent to rehabilitate Branwell by Leyland (*The Brontë Sisters, passim*). The theory that Heathcliff was drawn from Branwell is another of the Old Aunt Sallies erected by eccentric admirers, and hardly worth while knocking down. "No doubt," say the editors of the *Shakespeare Head Brontë*, Messrs T. J. Wyse and J. Alexander Symington, "that Branwell's experiences and behaviour were the vital influences

admirably one of the great moments. It describes Lockwood's trying night in the quaint old bedroom at Wuthering Heights, his nightmare after reading Jabes Branderham's sermon, and the worse than nightmare of the fingers clutching through the lattice and the voice sobbing "Let me in—let me in!" Catherine is there. To use her phrase about the children's plays at Haworth, Emily has "established" her tragedy. If it was clumsy to take the last events first, it was assuredly the clumsiness of genius.[1]

It is unlikely that the two novels of Anne Brontë (1820– *Anne* 1849) would be remembered to-day, or indeed that they would *Brontë* ever have been written, had she not been the sister of Charlotte and Emily. A gentle, quiet, affectionate being, she took her

---

which resulted in the conception and creation of *Wuthering Heights*" (ii. 57). But that Branwell may have been the suggester, intentionally or the reverse, of such things as the dare-devil sentiments, and the violent outbursts of imprecation, is a totally different matter. One of the most grotesque of the Old Aunt Sallies was Dr William Wright's pretence, pulverized by A. M. Mackay (*The Brontës: Fact and Fiction*), that *Wuthering Heights* was a version of Brontë ancestral history in Ireland —an apocrypha originating in delusion rather than deliberate fraud, or what is almost as bad, the rage for original discovery—of mares' nests. Mr Benson's statement that "the intention to make a *motif* out of Catherine's beauty and Lockwood's complacent susceptibility" "was scrapped" is hardly true. As already noted, it gives a little touch of beauty to the close, when Lockwood realizes the chance he has missed (see above, p. 75). Lockwood does not "drop out " (Benson, 175), but utters the thoughts which make such a fine ending.

[1] It is astounding to hear very superior folk talk about the "sentimental" ending of *Wuthering Heights*: they must have got the word on the brain without being quite clear what it means. Sentimentality is non-existent in the story of Catherine and Heathcliff; that is one of its supreme glories. Heathcliff is actuated by two passionate motives, revenge on Hindley and all belonging to him, and the furious hunger for union with Catherine. In his last hours, he feels himself on the verge of attaining this final reunion, and the lesser impulse sinks into indifference. He has ceased to love or hate anything on earth but Catherine. Hence, Hareton and Catherine the second, whom he has despised rather than actively hated, as mere accidents in the path of his vengeance, are brushed aside as no longer of the least importance, and the tale comes naturally to the symmetrical close. Heathcliff and Catherine are united in death; the Earnshaws and the Lintons reunite in the present generation. Further, vengeance is shown again defeating itself, as Emily had already shown, in the baby Hareton's escape when Heathcliff involuntarily saves his life, and also in Hareton's unconquerable affection for Heathcliff. "Poor Hareton, the most wronged, was the only one who really suffered much. He sat by the corpse all night, weeping in bitter earnest. He pressed its hand, and kissed the sarcastic savage face that every one else shrank from contemplating." Heathcliff himself had said, "It is a poor conclusion . . . an absurd termination to my violent exertions." He had slaved like Hercules to demolish the two houses, and now the will to wreak his revenge had vanished. "But where is the use? I don't care for striking; I can't take the trouble to raise my hand!" Emily wrote this, which is a sufficient reply to such fatuity.

modest part in the literary activities of the household, noting in her diary in 1845 that she had finished the third volume of "Passages in the Life of an Individual," which meant that when the sisters resolved to try their fortunes with a novel apiece she had the material ready. *Agnes Grey* was published as a third volume with *Wuthering Heights* (1847). It is a *Jane Eyre* in embryo, without the strange love-affair. Anne also had been a governess (1839–1845), and was wounded by the folly and indifference of parents who spoilt their children and treated the conscientious, hard-working teacher as a menial. She bore it with resignation; she had none of Charlotte's fierce resentment; but she ingenuously hoped that a plain story of what she had gone through would be a lesson to thoughtless parents. Agnes Grey and her sister are the two left alive of the six children of a clergyman in straitened circumstances. It is practically Anne's own case. In her first situation, she has to bear with an ill-conditioned boy, "the flower of the flock," as his mother calls him, and a set of backward girls, conceited about their good looks. A cantankerous father, a pharisaical and capricious granny, and a bumptious uncle, who "was not above the foppery of stays" and easily convinces Miss Grey that he was "no gentleman," complete the circle of empty-headed, overbearing people, all of whom think themselves very much her betters. But when she finds herself in a wealthier and more pretentious family, she has to put up with the same drudgery and worse insolence: they are savages beneath the skin. Anne was as clear-sighted as her sister.[1] All three saw through the placid, smug, prudish mentality of most middle-class people then, whose daughters they had to teach the elements of useful knowledge and deportment, and they did their duty by telling the candid truth, instead of subscribing to the amiable fiction current at the circulating libraries. Satire was not their object, though

---

[1] Agnes says—it is when she is thinking about the new clergyman, Mr Weston, who eventually rescues her from her trials and makes her his wife—"I began this book with the intention of concealing nothing; that those who liked might have the benefit of perusing a fellow-creature's heart: but we have *some* thoughts that all the angels in heaven are welcome to behold, but not our brother-men—not even the best and kindest amongst them". (chap. xiii.). There speaks the sister of Charlotte and Emily.

Charlotte occasionally digressed, and was so caustic, for instance, in her picture of the genteel Sympsons and their two daughters, in *Shirley*, "two pattern young ladies, in pattern attire, with pattern deportment," as to excite suspicions of a personal grievance. Even Emily performed her part in smashing illusions. What could be more unlike the usual Arcadian version of rustic life than *Wuthering Heights*? Emily gave the facts, so far as she knew them. Similarly, Charlotte demolished the idyll of the modest, bashful, and demure young lady's love-affairs, by putting something truer and more interesting in place of it. Anne abstained from satire, which may indeed be one of the useful arts when it helps to kill or cure a social nuisance, but is usually read by the wrong people, those who do not need it. She wrote more in sorrow than in anger; but *Agnes Grey*, benevolently didactic in intention, is an honest bit of realism, and as good a document as the relevant portions of her sisters' books.[1] They were all three strong enough to contemplate sordid and inane realities at close quarters, yet expound with confidence their own finer vision and their trust in human nature.

In her other and longer novel, *The Tenant of Wildfell Hall* "*The Tenant of Wildfell Hall*" (1848), Anne is supposed, on the authority of Charlotte Brontë herself,[2] to have made up the story of Arthur Huntingdon out of her unhappy experience of the misdoings and ultimate demoralization of Branwell, her degenerate brother. Charlotte disliked the book, and was as hard on it as she was upon Branwell, who, in actual fact, was no more a Huntingdon than he was a Heathcliff. She might just as well have seen his counterpart in the imaginary narrator, Gilbert Markham, who falls in love with Huntingdon's ill-used wife, and when she becomes a widow marries her.[3] That it is indirectly the history

---

[1] It is desirable in considering the Brontës to bear in mind the dates of contemporary works dealing with social and economic evils, absurdities, and distresses—the great "condition of England question"—*e.g.* Carlyle's *Chartism* (1839) and *Past and Present* (1843), Disraeli's *Sybil* (1845), Kingsley's *Yeast* (1851), Dickens's *Hard Times* (1854), Tennyson's *Maud* (1855), and Reade's novels a little later, *e.g. Never Too Late to Mend* (1857). We shall come to Mrs Gaskell's in a moment.

[2] Gaskell, xvi.

[3] Shorter remarks that Gilbert's mother "is obviously a picture of Miss Branwell, who used to pet her nephew in the same way" (*Charlotte Brontë*, 92–93). It is curious, also, that the situation of the young man (Markham, not Huntingdon) in

of Branwell has been repeated ever since, by people who could, surely, never have looked into the novel to see if this was even possible.   Huntingdon is not a weak, ineffectual creature, who gives way to temptation though spasmodically struggling against it.   He is the full-blown reprobate of fiction, a resolute libertine and drunkard, cynically glorying in his profligacy, and taunting his wife with her jealousy of his boasted amours. This is not Branwell.[1]   Anne was, it is true, brought into contact with the seamy side of life by watching Branwell's lapses; she may have learned from his tuition what novelists call her local colour.   But more likely she acquired her very hazy knowledge of fast society and devil-may-care licence from such sources as the novels which she and Charlotte read to improve their French.   It is an odd book to come from the innocent Anne, though she manages somehow to make it edifying.   Strange that anyone could have thought it was a novel from the same hand as *Jane Eyre*—or as *Wuthering Heights*!   Yet that was the bruit, believed in by many readers and by an American publishing house, which made Charlotte and Anne take their celebrated journey to London to demonstrate physically that "Currer Bell" and "Acton Bell" were not one but two persons.[2]   It was thoroughly like them! And it would not be possible to imagine "Ellis Bell" doing such a thing.

love with the unhappy wife is on all fours with that alleged to have existed between Branwell and the wife of his employer, Mr Robinson.
  [1] "A careful study of the question has, indeed, convinced me, not only that Huntingdon is no portrait of Branwell Brontë, but that he is distinctly and designedly his very antitype."   That is the view of one who may not be always reliable, but at all events knew what he was talking about, for he was a friend of Branwell's, F. A. Leyland, the sculptor (*The Brontë Family*, ii. 226).
  [2] Gaskell, xvi.   The incident confutes some of the preposterous theories about the respective authorships which have provided comic relief (shall we say?) to the study of the Brontë sisters.

CHAPTER III

MRS GASKELL AND OTHER WOMEN
NOVELISTS

THE first impression of those who have read only the finest *Mrs* things of Mrs Gaskell, *Cranford* and the Cranford-like full- *Gaskell* length of *My Lady Ludlow*, or that affecting little study of *noblesse oblige*, *My French Master*, or *Wives and Daughters*, with its sly exposure of insincerity in Mrs Gibson and anatomy of something more elusive in her daughter Cynthia, may well be that they have found a lesser and homelier and kinder Jane Austen. The delicacy of feeling and of workmanship, and a gift for natural gossipy talk and scenes exactly like ordinary humdrum life but tense with dramatic meaning, are rare enough to warrant even such a high comparison. And it is eminently so again in that loveliest idyll, *Cousin Phillis*, another of the Cranford jewels, even though the pastoral touch might not have fascinated the author of *Emma* and *Mansfield Park*. Second thoughts, however, and further reading soon correct this hasty generalization. The refined workmanship is not sustained; it is intermittent. And Mrs Gaskell is far from sharing the lucid, penetrating, almost infallible intelligence of her great predecessor, who was always as sure of her aim and as undeviating in reaching it as if she were demonstrating a theorem. Mrs Gaskell, with all her charm, continually betrays fitfulness and uncertainty. She can spin a story for half its length upon one motive, and end on one entirely different. Even her humour, one of the most genuine things about her, does not always flow as limpidly as it should. Thus in a coarser example of the Cranford manner, *Mr Harrison's Confessions*, on which she is known to have spent much pains, the comedy degenerates into downright farce, the mere drollery of a magazine story. Jane Austen's thrice-refined irony and Mrs Gaskell's susceptible fondling of human eccentricities are two radically different things. Jane Austen, who saw so unerringly the under side of everything going on around her, held herself aloof; she seemed to regard it all from a pinnacle near omniscience, never disturbed, never sentimental, never in the least didactic. Never in the world would she have gone down into the market-place to champion a Mary Barton or a Ruth. Her world was a small and restricted one in comparison with Mrs Gaskell's, narrow as was the latter's when Dickens and Thackeray are thought of beside her. But the span and grip of her understanding, its piercing clarity, the insight of the highest comedy, were so far beyond Mrs Gaskell's that even in catholicity she is immensely superior. It is entirely untrue that Mrs Gaskell saw deeper, though she changed the focus and was alive to other interests. Like the Brontës, she had the romantic outlook, and her characters have souls to be saved as well as infirmities and infatuations to be anatomized for the world's amusement. She was not afraid of the passions any more than Charlotte Brontë was, though she knew so little about them that they usually led her into melodrama; and in the atlas of literary affinities she must be placed at a considerable distance from the demurely ironical Jane, and at least as near the Brontë sisters as to George Eliot, to whose stern philosophic scrutiny her commiserating interest in wrongdoers and the wronged, and her earnest desire to make the world wiser and better, gave her a superficial resemblance. Fiction had recently been widening its scope; without letting go its hold of the individual and his domestic relationships, it now embraced all the miscellaneous interests of the world at large: it was becoming panoramic. This suited Mrs Gaskell exactly when she made her début in fiction by taking up the cause of the poverty-stricken mill-hands, whose wrongs she had witnessed at close range in Manchester. It was the very thing for the problem novel, which, by dint of what purported to be unbiased and veracious realism, sought to make a more convincing appeal than abstract argument, or Carlyle's fierce denunciations, to the public conscience. It was propagandist

fiction that she began with, and not until she had become an
established writer did she bethink herself of her youthful
memories and give her readers *Cranford.* Her work, in fact,
goes roughly, and not with entire exclusiveness, into two
categories, the character of each set from the beginning by the
character and circumstances of her two successive homes—
Knutsford where she spent her childhood, and Manchester
the scene of her strenuous married life. The vein of early
impressions was worked later; it was the one that suited her
talent best. But the sterner subsequent experience had such
lasting effects upon her mind that it blended continually with
the other, the tragedies of actual life which had passed before
her eyes being responsible for the graver note sounded in
Lizzie Leigh and *Sylvia's Lovers,* as well as in a number of her
slighter tales.

Elizabeth Cleghorn Gaskell (1810–1865) was a year or two *Circum-*
the senior of Dickens and Thackeray, and six years older than *stances*
Charlotte Brontë, whom she outlived by ten years and whose *make her*
biography she was to write, a work as distinguished as any but *a novelist*
the very best of her novels and stories. Her father, William
Stevenson, a lowland Scot and a writer of many-sided learning,
was at one time a Unitarian minister, and then took up farming
in combination with teaching, something like "Minister"
Holman, in *Phillis,* one of the genuine worthies who figure in
her pages and like the rest of them demonstrably taken from the
life. He became keeper of the Treasury Records, and thus
Elizabeth was born a Londoner, seeing the light at Chelsea.
She lost her mother soon after, and was sent to Knutsford, in
Cheshire, to be brought up by her mother's elder sister, Mrs
Lumb. Knutsford is Mr Harrison's Duncombe, the Eltham
of *Cousin Phillis,* and, of course, Cranford of *Cranford.* It is
also the Hollingford of *Wives and Daughters.* Here her
grandfather Samuel Holland owned the fine old house of
Sandlebridge, the Hope Farm so lovingly portrayed as the
home of Cousin Phillis. The little girl used to go the rounds
with her uncle, Dr Peter Holland, who is perhaps to be recognized in Dr Gibson of *Wives and Daughters.* Mrs Gaskell
was always safe on matters of medical etiquette and the

routine of a country practitioner's life: take for instance the two partners in *Mr Harrison's Confessions*. She painted her *émigré*, in *My French Master*, whose courtliness and intrinsic nobility realize the old ideals of his order, from the M. Rogier who taught her French and dancing. Points enough of identity have been established between her stories and her experience to show that no one ever drew from the life more transparently. She went to school at Stratford-on-Avon; and then her life amid rural tranquillities came to an end; at the age of twenty-two she married, and settled in Manchester. Her husband was the Rev. William Gaskell, Unitarian minister, and professor at the training college there for clergy of that persuasion. A new era in her life commenced. It was the year of the Reform Act. The industrial revolution was beginning. Distress and discontent were raging in all the manufacturing districts, of which Manchester was one of the most afflicted. The Gaskells were leading workers among the poor, labouring on the spot in the cause for which Sadler, Ashley, and their comrades were fighting in Parliament. The Chartist agitation was in full swing, and Mrs Gaskell saw it from the inside. Hence, when she was stricken to the ground by the loss of her little son, she found an outlet for her misery in writing a tragic story, depicting in harrowing colours the state of the working classes in a city where housing was neglected to a degree now almost incredible, and where feeling between the employers and the factory-hands was at boiling-point. Disraeli's *Sybil*, which appeared in 1845, the year she began her novel, is a doctrinaire and abstract study in comparison with such well-informed realism. Dickens, also, was without the advantages of a witness on the spot, when he wrote *Hard Times* a few years later, and knew even better than his critics that it was a missfire.

"*Mary Barton*" *Mary Barton, a Tale of Manchester Life*, was finished in 1847; but Mrs Gaskell had the greatest difficulty in finding a publisher, and it was not till 1848 that it was brought out by the firm who published the works of Dickens, Chapman & Hall. It had the usual reception of controversial books, especially those in the form of fiction. The *Manchester Guardian* was not unjust in pointing out that the realism was not impartial, though to call her sympathy for the starving operatives morbid and to charge her with unfairness to the industrialists, who were pushing the doctrine of competition to its fatal logical extremes, was hard on a well-meaning lady. But she had had to take sides. At this time of day, it may perhaps be regretted that she ever wrote her sociological novels, at any rate this one and *Ruth*, in both of which her feelings spoke but not her genius. *North and South* was less overweighted; she had acquired experience and learned to look on both sides; and yet its value is now chiefly historical. *Mary Barton* is, at most, a telling contemporary gloss on the denunciations and manifestos poured out by Carlyle. Mary's father, driven to frenzy by the wrongs of his class, commits a crime at the behest of the workers' committee, and her lover is wrongly charged with the murder. Remorse preys upon John's mind, and after an affecting interview with the father of his victim he dies. But even a realistic novel with such a definite appeal must have its love-story. The man shot was one of the employing class, who had been pursuing Mary Barton; and the reader is asked to believe that she would have married him, though she was deeply in love with Jem Wilson, who is suspected to have done the deed out of jealousy. For this gratuitous melodrama, Mary's self-consistency is sacrificed; and the intervention of her aunt Esther, a woman of sin, brings in other cross-motives, adding nothing to the inherent strength of the book and running counter to its ulterior purpose. Plot was not Mrs Gaskell's forte; it has no place in her best stories. When she dragged it in, instead of letting characters and circumstances shape events, she falsified what ought to have been as plain as gospel truth.

The Moorland Cottage (1850) is a slight affair, the only "*The* interest of which is that Edward and Maggie Brown anticipate *Moorland* the temperamental opposition of George Eliot's Tom and *Cottage*" Maggie Tulliver, the weak and fretful mother in either story *and "Ruth"* being another point of likeness. But the author of *The Mill on the Floss* had her own recollections to work upon, and as likely

as not never read this.[1] Mrs Gaskell was naturally a warm
admirer of Charlotte Brontë, and wrote to her enthusiastically
after reading *Shirley*. Charlotte thought Mrs Gaskell's nature
showed "a remote affinity" to her sister Emily's; but a closer
affinity was to herself. Already in *Mary Barton*, and now more
explicitly in *Ruth*, Mrs Gaskell is seen handling feminine
problems with the courage of a Charlotte Brontë, and with
less of the prudery of that day than Thackeray showed when
he made his abject apology for not telling the whole truth
about his young men.[2] In several of her large-scale portraits
of women she asserted the right of the sex to full personal
development, intellect included, which, to judge by her erudite
Cousin Phillis, she did not think women's weak point. *Ruth*
(1853) is a plea for the woman betrayed. It has had a large
progeny, from Trollope's *Dr Thorne* to Hardy's *Tess*, and
others still later; yet it is only another instance of Mrs Gaskell's
feelings overriding both truth and logic. The seduced girl is
represented as too innocent and ignorant of the world for
anyone but the simplest inhabitant of Cranford. By a pious
fraud she brings up her child respectably, and is aided and
abetted in so doing by a friendly minister, who is found out,
and brings on his own head obloquy and even material
retribution. Mrs Gaskell demanded the same moral standards
for men and women, and inevitably raised an outcry from the
Pharisees, who saw in the charitable conduct of the minister
only an aggravation of the offence.

"*North and South*"   Her third sociological novel, *North and South* (1855), was not
written till after *Lizzie Leigh* and *Cranford*, but may as well
be summarized along with the others. It pleads more persuasively for understanding and sympathy between capital and
labour; and the object being conciliation Mrs Gaskell tried
not to overcharge her picture of human misery and the callous-
ness of the money-maker, as in *Mary Barton*. But she could
not forget what had wrung her heart. She knew too well
what "clemming" meant; and this outcry of a poor father

---

[1] It was eulogized by Swinburne as a contrast to the third volume of *The Mill
on the Floss*, which he regarded as a deplorable debacle after the first two (*Note on
Charlotte Bronte*, 34).
[2] See Volume VII. 361–362.

during the strike is more telling even as propaganda than the cumulative pathos of the earlier book:

"It's no use, Higgins. Hoo cannot live long a' this'n. Hoo's just sinking away—not for want o' meat hersel'—but because hoo cannot stand th' sight o' the little ones clemming. Ay, clemming! Five shilling a week may do well enough for thee, wi' but two mouths to fill, and one on 'em a wench who can welly earn her own meat. But it's clemming to us. An' I tell thee plain—if hoo dies, as I'm 'feard hoo will afore we've getten th' five per cent, I'll fling th' money back i' th' master's face, and say, 'Be domned to yo'; be domned to th' whole cruel world o' yo'; that could na leave me th' best wife that ever bore childer to a man!' An' look thee, lad, I'll hate thee, and th' whole pack o' th' Union. Ay, an' chase yo' through heaven wi' my hatred—I will, lad! I will—if yo're leading me astray i' this matter. Thou saidst, Nicholas, on Wednesday sennight—and it's now Tuesday i' th' second week—that afore a fortnight we'd ha' the masters coming a-begging to us to take back our work, at our own wage—and time's nearly up—and there's our lile Jack lying a-bed, too weak to cry, but just now and then sobbing up his heart for want o' food—our lile Jack, I tell thee, lad!· Hoo's never looked up sin' he were born, and hoo loves him as if he were her very life—as he is—for I reckon he'll ha' cost me that precious price—our lile Jack, who wakened me each morn wi' putting his sweet little lips to my great rough fou' face, a-seeking a smooth place to kiss—an' he lies clemming." [1]

As the title implies, *North and South* tries to put the rights of the case by drawing a contrast between the patriarchal landed gentry of the agricultural south and the aristocrats of money in the industrial north. The accommodating policy of the Corn Laws is pitted against the doctrine of *laissez faire*. Mrs Gaskell did not see very far into the economics of the situation; but she could touch the feelings and shatter indifference, which was an invaluable service at the moment. She must have had Charlotte Brontë's *Shirley* running in her head all the time she was writing *North and South*. Her just and philanthropic manufacturer, or would-be just and philanthropic,

[1] Chap. xix.

is a Robert Moore who has had his eyes opened to his social responsibilities. Like Dickens in *Hard Times* and Charles Reade later on in *Put Yourself in his Place*, she wanted to bridge the gulf between employer and employed; and the victory over blind selfishness takes place in the bosom of John Thornton. Almost a replica of Shirley herself appears in Margaret Hale, whom he loves and who rejects his suit in a parley inevitably recalling the scene in Charlotte Brontë's novel between Shirley and Moore.[1] But Mrs Gaskell over-does her Diana, who as good as tells her high-spirited lover that he is no gentleman. Evidently, she exaggerated their antagonism, antagonism hingeing mainly on the strike, to render their ultimate reconcilation more dramatic; but she strained the character-drawing in the ill-advised attempt. Her Higgins, trade unionist and atheist, is as good, however, as any in the little band of malcontents who make things hot for Robert Moore, in *Shirley*. Another fine character is the Rev. Mr Hale, as fine at least as her distinctly feminine talent could make him, whose act in throwing up his living because of his doubts—his alleged doubts, for, unfortunately, what they are is never explained, as of several famous persons at that date—seems mere quixotry to the time-serving lawyer, Mr Lennox. Some kinship with the Brontës, and some presage of George Eliot's tragic realism idealized by human charity and devotion, are discernible in a story of the Rochdale moors and Manchester, which appeared first in a magazine and then gave a title to *Lizzie Leigh, and other Stories* (1855). *Lizzie Leigh* is a novel compressed into a short tale of a mother's indefatigable quest for a daughter led astray. Its brevity makes the reader kick against such a catalogue of unmitigated disaster. As usual, Mrs Gaskell shows her weakness for co-incidence, contriving that Will Leigh the brother should meet and fall in love with Susan, the saviour of Lizzie's child.

"*Cran-ford*"   Among other early short stories, the best is the afore-mentioned *Mr Harrison's Confessions* (1851), an amusing sketch of a spinster-ridden township, where a young doctor's efforts at an ingratiating manner result in his becoming affianced, by

---

[1] Chap. xxv., cp. *Shirley*, xxx.

gossip, to three ladies at once, and all but losing the girl he loves. There are many things in it which give a foretaste of *Cranford*: for instance, the ill-omened arrival of Mr Harrison's old chum, Jack Marshland, who flusters Miss Tomkinson and the rest of the dovecot with his loud behaviour, and manages to leave everybody firmly convinced that poor Harrison was once a bad lot and has been in gaol. Engaged by Dickens to contribute to *Household Words* (1851–1853), Mrs Gaskell explored her Knutsford memories further, and the result was the series of sketches which she afterwards rounded off into a book, *Cranford* (1853), one of the minor masterpieces of English literature. *Cranford*, happily perhaps, is not a novel; she might have said of it, as her mouthpiece says of *My Lady Ludlow*, "It is no story: it has, as I said, neither beginning, middle, nor end." From first to last, the writer is simply miniaturing still life, and spinning indulgent comedy from the interplay and byplay of quaint idiosyncrasy in her little bevy of womenfolk of the polite class. There is but the faintest touch of irony or satire; playful extravagance there is, but it is the drollery of a heart that loves the very foibles of these simple, homely, even ignorant people, none of them clownish or unrefined, though the refinement is that of a gentle soul, an unselfish nature, not of the intellect. Mrs Gaskell could find truly humble characters among such modest gentlefolk, the needy genteel, as well as among peasants and farmers and her Lancashire working-people. She is Wordsworthian in her regard for sterling worth in the poor and lowly, and in her love of the simplicities.[1] Her best achievement, after her lifelike rendering of manners and her evocation of a most fragrant atmosphere of pure integrity and lovingkindness, is to have left on record such gracious beings as Miss Matty, Lady Ludlow, Cousin Phillis, and Molly Gibson, of *Wives and Daughters*. *Cranford* is just a succession of scenes and episodes, hardly more closely connected than the Coverley papers in the *Spectator*; calling up, however, the mild spirit of Goldsmith

---

[1] It was an event for her when Crabb Robinson brought Wordsworth to see the Gaskells, at their holiday home in the Lake District (1849). Cowper, Crabbe, and Burns of the "Cottar's Saturday Night" must also have been among her teachers and inspirers.

rather than that of Addison. They are incidents in the placid life of Miss Matty and her friends: the autumnal revival of her old love-affair with Mr Holbrook, the burglar scare, the escapade and flight of poor Peter—a reminiscence of her brother, John Gaskell, who mysteriously disappeared, which does not fit chronologically—the bank smash, the Signor Brunoni business, the misalliance of Lady Glenmire and Dr Hoggins, and the return of Peter as the Aga Jenkyns. The mere fooling is delicious: the discursus on the prefix Fitz, which at any rate meant something aristocratic, and the superciliousness of the lady and gentleman who spelt their names with two small f's, the debate on the Grand Lama, and the question whether llamas were carnivorous or graminivorous, Miss Matty's pangs of conscience in selling green tea, and the adventure of the cat that swallowed the cream with the priceless old lace in it. The quiet strokes of humour are inimitable, as when the widowed Mrs Fitz-Adam reappears in rustling black silk, "so soon after her husband's death that poor Miss Jenkyns was justified in the remark she made, that 'bombazine would have shown a deeper sense of her loss.'" [1]

" Lady Ludlow " and " Cousin Phillis " Nearest in matter and manner to *Cranford* are two shortish stories, *My Lady Ludlow*, which appeared in *Round the Sofa* (1859), and *Cousin Phillis* (1865). The one is the portrait of an exquisite old dowager, with her handmaidens grouped around her, like a sainted feudal lady in her bower, drawn by her one-time servitor, now an old woman. She is an inimitable mixture of wisdom and prejudice, shrewdness and obstinacy— a portrait no man could have painted. Incidents there are in it, but it can hardly be called a story. There are other characters: the parson, Mr Gray, Mr Horner, Captain James, and the sectary, Mr Brooke. But the men shine only in their half-feminine traits: Mr Gray with his devotion and moral courage, who persists in his district-visiting in spite of a bad cough, for which the ladies send him gruel and bottles of medicine; and the reserved old steward, Mr Horner, who dies a martyr to

---

[1] There are many passages of domestic incident related in a mildly humorous manner in Miss Martineau's *Deerbrook*, which might possibly have suggested the accidental and slightly pictorial plan of *Cranford* (see A. Stanton Whitfield's *Mrs Gaskell*, 134–135).

duty, obviously because he had no woman to look after him. There is the free-spoken Miss Galindo, who might be a first sketch for Mrs Poyser,[1] with her strong views on marriage:

"Indeed, my lady, I have long left off trying to conjecture what makes Jack fancy Gill, or Gill Jack. It's best to sit down quiet under the belief that marriages are made for us, somewhere out of this world, and out of the range of this world's reason and laws. I'm not so sure that I should settle it down that they were made in heaven; t'other place seems to me as likely a workshop."

But the immortal scene is the tea-drinking at the Hall when Mrs Brooke, who has never been in such company before, spreads a bandanna handkerchief over her best silk gown. Even John Footman was on the grin—

"I wonder how long it is since he was own brother to a scarecrow, only not so decently dressed—and Mrs Parsoness of Headleigh—I forget her name, and it's no matter, for she's an ill-bred creature, I hope Bessy will behave herself better —was right-down bursting with laughter, and as near a hee-haw as ever a donkey was, when what does my lady do? Ay! there's my own dear Lady Ludlow, God bless her! She takes out her own pocket-handkerchief, all snowy cambric, and lays it softly down on her velvet lap, for all the world as if she did it every day of her life, just like Mrs Brooke, the baker's wife; and when the one got up to shake the crumbs into the fireplace, the other did just the same. But with such a grace! and such a look at us all! Tom Diggles went red all over; and Mrs Parsoness of Headleigh scarce spoke for the rest of the evening; and the tears came into my old silly eyes; and Mr Gray, who was before silent and awkward in a way which I will tell Bessy she must cure him of, was made so happy by this pretty action of my lady's, that he talked away all the rest of the evening, and was the life of the company."

As a lover of fair old things, Mrs Gaskell is often another Charles Lamb. She is too emotional, too fond of death-beds and lovers' partings; her humour often fails through her over-seriousness. And it is a pity, and another sign of inherent weakness, that she kept her comedy and her tragedy for separate

[1] *Adam Bede* appeared the same year, 1859.

tales. One of the beauties of that perfect idyll *Cousin Phillis*
is that the humour and the pathos are not put in different
compartments. The humour is a specific against her liability
to sentimentalism, but leaves the tenderness unimpaired. As
the fickle lover puts it, Phillis is a character "as unusual and
rare as her beauty. God bless her! God keep her in her
high tranquillity, her pure innocence!" The strong, sensitive,
virginal heart frankly accepts a pledge never put in words but
spoken only with the eyes. The heartbreak when it dawns
upon her that the pledge has been forgotten, and the remorse
of the boy who had believed in his friend and confirmed her
belief, have the pathos that skirts tragedy. Mrs Gaskell was
content this time not to elaborate unduly. It is a true idyll,
most poetic in its running pastoral accompaniment, and most
classic in its beautiful and reticent close. In reading *My
Lady Ludlow*, one seems to be listening to a Haydn symphony;
this is like a perfect sonata.

"*Sylvia's
Lovers*" *Sylvia's Lovers* (1863), which appeared whilst she was writing
Cousin Phillis, sins by the lack of this simplicity. It is semi-
historical, the date being 1796–1800, and the principal scene
Monkshaven, which is Whitby, during the French war. The
Dutch painting of quiet domestic life amid the storm-swept
moorlands and the wave-washed cliffs is that of a junior George
Eliot; and the moralistic intention of a plot always threatening
tragedy also suggests that writer, who, of course, had by this
time published her first and best work. So, too, the humour,
which goes hand in hand with the pathos: there is nothing that
can be called comedy. Hear old Daniel Robson: "Come in,
Harry, come in, and talk a bit o' sense to me, for a've been
shut up wi' woman these four days, and a'm a'most a nateral
by this time." Or the people who listened unperturbed to
parson preaching:

They did not recognize their daily faults or temptations
under the grand aliases befitting their appearance from a
preacher's mouth.

Notice, also, that the humour is strikingly didactic; take the
hit at the procrastinating Corneys:

Why the fruit was not gathered, as it was evidently ripe, would have puzzled anyone not acquainted with the Corney family to say; but to them it was always a maxim in practice, if not in precept, "Do nothing to-day that you can put off till to-morrow"; and accordingly the apples dropped from the trees at any little gust of wind, and lay rotting on the ground till the "lads" wanted a supply of pies for supper.

The estimable but over-timid and over-taciturn Philip Hepburn loves Sylvia, a creature of such charm and spirit that it detracts nothing from her beauty, or from her dignity, that she can neither read nor write; and he is cut out by the dashing "specksioneer" (harpooner) Kinraid. The press-gang kidnaps the successful lover, and Philip is the only witness of the occurrence. He holds his peace, and fails to convey Kinraid's message of unchangeable loyalty to Sylvia. Presently, her father gets mixed up in an attack on the press-gang, and is hanged at York. Her feeble old mother and herself being thrown on Philip's hands, she at length consents to marry him. Then Kinraid returns, now an officer in the Navy. Sylvia is already a mother; but she turns on her husband and vows never to forgive him. So far the story has carried conviction. The minds of Philip and Sylvia, and of the Quaker-bred Harriet, who has silently loved Philip but resigned herself to the hests of Providence, have been laid bare in pages of moving drama. Philip and Sylvia have long been estranged; his mind half-paralysed by the guilt of his betrayal, hers as yet unaware of this, but congenitally unable to love him: Mrs Gaskell's analysis of the mental situation before the reappearance of Kinraid is sensitively done. Perhaps that return, as if from the dead, is out of key. At any rate, what follows—Philip's flight and enlistment and his rescue of Kinraid in the danger-zone outside Acre—is too much. All this is designed to provide the required atonement, but is none the less melodrama for being turned to edifying uses.

Mrs Gaskell died on the eve of finishing what is, neverthe-less, her fullest and ripest novel, *Wives and Daughters* (1866); but the end is so clearly foreshadowed that the few pages

"Wives and Daugh-ters"

missing are no serious loss. It was the realization of all she had been aiming at, unless a masculine portrayal of men was one of those aims. But the title permits the male characters to be dismissed in a few words. Mr Gibson is important, but only as a shrewd onlooker and very plain-spoken comforter; Squire Hamley and his sons, whose relations with the two young women bring out what these ambiguous creatures are made of, and Lord Cumnor, who is in a minority of one in a houseful of aristocratic femininity, are all subsidiary to the wives and daughters. As to the bland, pushful, sinister Preston, he is plausible in the melodramatic but not the psychological sense. But three of her most complete characterizations of women entirely overshadow these routine figures. In *Wives and Daughters*, Mrs Gaskell built, if not better than she knew, at least better than she intended. Mrs Gibson, whose "superficial and flimsy" character, she said, was conceived almost in the spirit of a lampoon, is as true as she is entertaining. And, by a most fortunate miscalculation, there are two heroines, or at least two young women in whom interest inevitably centres: one all goodness, the sterling but somewhat dull goodness which the Victorians prized; the other, meant to be the black sheep, whose blackness turned the most fascinating colours of the rainbow. This reprehensible Cynthia Kirkpatrick, Mrs Gibson's elder daughter, is Elizabeth Gaskell's most delicate and delectable creation. To describe the three would be to tell the story, which is as it should be. Mrs Gibson cannot open her lips without betraying her sleepless, scheming, calculating selfishness. How in the world did the hard-headed and sceptical Mr Gibson come to marry her? Where was his famous penetration then?

Three nicely differentiated women Both the heavier and the lighter forms of snobbery had been gently satirized in *Cranford*, in the Hon. Mrs Jamieson, Miss Pole, and others. Snobbishness shows itself here in the diverse shades of arrogance in members of the house of Cumnor; whilst in Mrs Gibson, the erstwhile governess, it is but a minor foible through which her ingrained insincerity is brought into clearer daylight. During a call at the Towers, she had been patronized or frankly snubbed; but when she told the tale at home, "rose-colour was the medium through which" the facts were seen.

"There are many visitors staying at the Towers—oh, yes! a great many: the duchess and Lady Alice, and Mr and Mrs Grey, and Lord Albert Monson and his sister, and my old friend, Captain James of the Blues—many more in fact. But of course I preferred going to Lady Cumnor's own room, where I could see her and Lady Harriet quietly, and where we were not disturbed by the bustle downstairs."

But Molly must not presume; she must not even repay the frank and easy courtesy of her betters with the sprightliness of a buoyant young girl:

"Molly, I cannot have you speaking so to Lady Harriet," said Mrs Gibson, as soon as she was left alone with her step-daughter. "You would never have known her at all, if it had not been for me, and don't be always putting yourself into our conversation."

"But I must speak if she asks me questions," pleaded Molly.

"Well! if you must, you must, I acknowledge. I'm candid about that at any rate. But there's no need to set up to have an opinion at your age."

"I don't know how to help it," said Molly.

"She's such a whimsical person; look there, if she's not talking to Miss Phœbe; and Miss Phœbe is so weak she'll be easily led away into fancying she's hand and glove with Lady Harriet. If there is one thing I hate more than another, it's the trying to make out an intimacy with great people."

Molly, if she seems staid or even dull beside the irrepressible Cynthia, is almost a Wordsworthian figure, with her unconscious goodness and intuitive wisdom; yet puzzled by the worldliness of her stepsister and turning elsewhere for sympathy, her nature ripening all the while by cruel experience. *Shirley* may have been running in her author's head again, for the shock when Molly hears that Roger Hamley is making love to Cynthia is like that which overwhelmed poor Caroline Helstone when she thought she was to lose Robert Moore. But Molly bears it more quietly. Transports and agonies were outside Mrs Gaskell's range. Molly has hardly realized till now that she herself is in love; and what does Mrs Gibson care? That lady's face was "mysterious and radiant."

"I've been watching for you, dear. Don't go upstairs into the drawing-room, love! It might be a little interruption just now. Roger Hamley is there with Cynthia; and I've reason to think—in fact I did open the door unawares, but I shut it again softly, and I don't think they heard me. Isn't it charming? Young love, you know, ah, how sweet it is!"

"Do you mean that Roger has proposed to Cynthia?" asked Molly.

"Not exactly that. But I don't know; of course I know nothing. Only I did hear him say, that he had meant to leave England without speaking of his love, but the temptation of see- ing her alone had been too great for him. It was symptomatic, was it not, my dear? And all I wanted was, to let him come to a crisis without interruption. So I've been watching for you, to prevent your going in and disturbing them."

"But I may go to my room, mayn't I?" pleaded Molly.

"Of course," said Mrs Gibson, a little testily. "Only I had expected sympathy from you at such an interesting moment."

Molly escapes, and tries to understand it all; but what could she understand? "For a few minutes, her brain seemed in too great a whirl to comprehend anything but that she was being carried on in earth's diurnal course, with rocks, and stones, and trees, with as little volition on her part as if she had been dead." The words are Wordsworth's; but Mrs Gaskell is revealing herself as the natural complement to the Brontës, and yet a contrast in her serenity to their passionate discontent. She could not create a Jane Eyre or a Lucy Snowe; but she has the same high regard for personality, a like belief in the marriage of true minds. But she is a saner critic of life, because she has the saving sense of humour, and because she can hold herself aloof, instead of being too much in the conflict. Charlotte Brontë was not sure of herself in drawing Caroline, who often looks like the average sentimental miss; there is nothing of that in Molly Gibson. Cynthia is more complex, more artificial; she is her mother's child, but refined and subtilized,

her self-love redeemed by generous impulses and finer perceptions. She has fascinations that never fail; and she knows
herself, no one better.

Cynthia herself appeared extremely indifferent upon the
subject, and took very little notice of her mother's constant
talk about the gaieties that were possible, and the gaieties
that were impossible, in Hollingford. She exerted herself
just as much to charm the two Miss Brownings as she would
have done to delight Osborne Hamley, or any other young
heir. That is to say, she used no exertion, but simply followed
her own nature, which was to attract every one of those she was
thrown amongst. . . . One day Cynthia read Molly's thought.
"I'm not good, and I told you so. Somehow, I cannot
forgive her for her neglect of me as a child, when I would
have clung to her. Besides, I hardly ever heard from her when
I was at school. And I know she put a stop to my coming over
to her wedding. I saw the letter she wrote to Madame Lefèbre.
A child should be brought up with its parents, if it is to think
them infallible when it grows up."
"But, though it may know that there must be faults,"
replied Molly, "it ought to cover them over and try to forget
their existence."
"It ought. But, don't you see, I have grown up outside
the pale of duty and 'oughts.' Love me as I am, sweet one;
for I shall never be better."

It is a finished, though apparently a light-handed and careless image of the frivolous, fickle, pleasure-loving young woman,
who has good impulses yet no comprehension whatever of the
point of honour or of rectitude, but charms even those who see
right through her. The reader falls in love with the portrait,
whilst praying never to come under the spells of such an
enchantress. To Molly falls the pleasant task of explaining to
Roger, whom she loves, that Cynthia is not the girl for him.
She returns to her stepsister:

"Was he very terrible?" asked Cynthia, as she sat with
Molly in the stillness of Mrs Gibson's dressing-room.
"Oh, Cynthia, it was such pain to see him, he suffered so!"
"I don't like people of deep feelings," said Cynthia, pouting.

"They don't suit me. Why couldn't he let me go without this fuss? I'm not worth his caring for!"

"You've the happy gift of making people love you. Remember Mr Preston—he too wouldn't give up hope."

"Now, I won't have you classing Roger Hamley and Mr Preston together in the same sentence. One was as much too bad for me as the other is too good. Now I hope that man in the garden [Mr Henderson, the third lover] is the *juste milieu*—I'm that myself; for I don't think I'm vicious, and I know I'm not virtuous."

Mrs Gaskell's affinities The literary life of Mrs Gaskell measured less than twenty years, and her work seems to be all of a piece, except for the difference between her propagandist novels and those in which her modest genius moved unfettered. But on a closer inspection minute differences are discernible, gradual changes and ripenings, which illustrate the way in which fiction in general was moving. Her contacts with the Brontë sisters, that is with Charlotte and Anne, have been noted. She was like Charlotte in the way they both turned out more or less lifelike characters. Both began by taking notes of people's mannerisms. Both were sometimes able to produce characters that were not only self-consistent, not merely finished composites, but seemed as alive as life, possessed of that spontaneity, that full artistic integrity, to which some passing whim of inconsistency is not fatal. And yet in both cases the difference jumps to the eye between these true scions of the imagination and the merely observed, the bundles of no doubt authentic attributes from which personality has managed to escape. It is possible to draw too directly from life: that was a failing of Charlotte Brontë and Anne, and also of Mrs Gaskell. Her frequent approximation to the moralistic procedure of George Eliot has likewise been noted. But George Eliot was not only a greater novelist, she was a serious and methodical thinker. Often the impression left by her fiction is of a moral philosopher anatomizing life, seeing the whole of it, from birth to death and from the humblest actor to the highest, in the light of one comprehensive truth. Mrs Gaskell, in comparison, is only a story-teller who is glad to bring out the lesson which she saw implied in a tale of wrong-doing, as an admonition to the frail and erring. Philip Hepburn, in *Sylvia's Lovers*, is put through one of those ordeals which purify or consume, such as form the central theme in *The Mill on the Floss* and *Middlemarch*. But George Eliot would never have meddled with the romantic farrago on which Mrs Gaskell had to fall back before she could make an ending. Yet Sylvia herself and some others of her hard-used women would not have discredited the more thoroughgoing moral psychologist. It is a fact, however, not without significance that four of the Barchester novels appeared before *Wives and Daughters* was written. This is not to imply that she imitated or competed with Trollope, but only that they were in the field together and were absorbed by the same interests. Both Trollope and Mrs Gaskell were connoisseurs of character, "character-mongers" in the same sense as Dr Johnson applied the phrase to Fanny Burney. And Trollope was as good at fashioning a woman or a young girl as at bringing forward an inexhaustible variety of men. Numbers of his female creations are complicated mixtures of good and bad. He compassed the obliquity of a Lizzie Eustace as successfully as the ingenuous magnanimity of a Grace Crawley. Some of his young women would not be in the least out of place at Mansfield Park or among the acquaintances of Emma Woodhouse; they would be thoroughly eligible companions for Molly Gibson and Sylvia Kirkpatrick. And they alter and develop and grow up; although Lily Dale, the one whose growth is followed through the largest number of volumes, is notable for not changing her mind, though she does grow from girlhood to mature womanhood. In this case, Trollope had made up his mind not to let her deviate from her first resolve, and he had to confess to himself that by so doing he had made her a prig. In short, she is the exception that proves the rule: his women are as complex, and grow and change as much, as his men. And it is with Trollope's young women, and some of his older women too, that Mrs Gaskell's are very closely akin. To be sure, she was a woman, with the finer perceptions of her sex. His are women seen by the experienced man of the world; but they are not a man's women in the sense that her male characters are a woman's men. Thus, if Mrs Gaskell shows definite links with Charlotte Brontë and other links with George Eliot, she has even more in common with Anthony Trollope, on that very side in which he comes nearest to Jane Austen.

The short stories   Mrs Gaskell published many short stories besides those already mentioned, often along with the more concise of her novels; they had usually appeared first in *Household Words*, *Cornhill*, or some other periodical. As often as not, humorous tales relieved pairs of sad ones, these latter dealing with crimes of passion or lack of self-control which bring down their fatal retribution. But they also present stoical ideals of duty and devotion, which make life endurable and even lovely and happy. One of the darkest and most relentless is *The Crooked Branch*, the tragedy of a beloved son who goes astray and wantonly robs his aged parents. *The Grey Woman* is a half-legendary story of the Rhine and Neckar at the time of the ferocious bands of robbers known as the Chauffeurs. It is noticeable that the domestic pathos dear to Mrs Gaskell overrides the romance: the true heroine is not the Grey Woman but the brave and devoted maidservant, who puts on man's clothes, and disguised as her fugitive mistress's husband redeems the crude gothicism. *Lois the Witch* was a tale of the crusade against witchcraft in Salem, and may have been inspired by Hawthorne. Mrs Gaskell was always attracted by the supernatural, and both the historical circumstance and the local colour are used with remarkable dramatic effect. *A Dark Night's Work* (1863) displays her as a rather prosy George Eliot—this was the year of *Romola*. A plot hingeing upon a murder dissembles the relationship. It is another story of long-deferred nemesis; tragedy is hinted at all through, and there is more psychological analysis than was her wont. A country solicitor, an irascible fellow, with a partner whom he detests, one night in a fit of exasperation strikes him, and the man drops dead. With the aid of a faithful coachman, the corpse is buried in the shrubbery, and what has become of Dunster remains a mystery. The person in whom sympathies centre is the daughter, who is soon left an orphan, and who has been jilted by the young barrister Corbet, who suspects some dark secret. Years later, a railway is cut through the grounds; the body is discovered, and Dixon, the coachman, falls under suspicion and is put on trial. Ellinor rushes home from Italy to find him awaiting execution. She goes to Judge Corbet, and succeeds in obtaining a reprieve. Corbet has long been a married man; and one of the incidents emphasized is that whilst Ellinor is waiting in the hall, presently down the stairs, with slow deliberate dignity, came the handsome Lady Corbet, in her rustling silks and ample petticoats, carrying her fine boy, and followed by her majestic nurse. By pure accident, long before, the unhappy Ellinor had been a spectator of Corbet's wedding. She had caught sight of him from her window going to the deanery for his bride; and thought to herself, why not be present at the church? There she watched it all from behind a pillar. It is more like the sentimental Mrs Inchbald than George Eliot; and perhaps the famous tale of the girl sentenced to death by the man who seduced her suggested the painful situation of the one-time lover trying Dixon, the wretched scapegoat for Ellinor's dead father. But the motive for these coincidences was obviously moralistic. If Mrs Gaskell studied Hawthorne, as *Lois* seems to show, she did not observe how much better it is to employ moral situations only as apt material for the artist in human nature, without taking sides even with virtue; to stand aloof, as in the dramatizing of any other conflict. Her rooted predisposition to didacticism was encouraged by the prevailing attitudes of her time, and by the practice of other novelists. Even Thackeray, in *The Newcomes* and indeed in most of his novels, cannot refrain from sermonizing. *Sylvia's Lovers* and various short stories still more heavily charged came after *Adam Bede* and *The Mill on the Floss*. George Eliot insists so much on the weakness and wickedness of Arthur Donnithorne and Hetty Sorrel, and the ruinous consequences of Maggie Tulliver's giving way to a gust of passion, that it is evident her interest was not the calm, contemplative neutrality of the artist. Mrs Gaskell had gone astray at the very beginning, in her novels of purpose; and the propensity grew upon her, in

novels with no overt thesis. Most of the numerous women who
at this period took up domestic fiction followed the same path.
Charlotte Mrs Gaskell won notoriety with *Mary Barton* and *Ruth*, and
Yonge then emancipated herself from what may be called applied
fiction; and discovered her true genius in *Cranford*, *Lady
Ludlow*, and *Phillis*. All Charlotte Yonge's, on the other hand,
might be described as novels with a purpose; they are all
directly or indirectly didactic, whether they take the shape of
family chronicles, stories of the day, or historical novels. She
was a cultivated woman who loved picturing the life around her,
and she had a gift for story-telling. But she was also a woman
of ardent religious convictions, who in everything she did had
in view the higher purpose of serving the kingdom of heaven
on earth. Whatever she looked at, the moral and spiritual
aspect lay uppermost; however the tale went, this was the
all-important interest. If a bad character trespassed on the
scene, he must be shown up; the final outcome of habits,
feelings, and actions had to be conscientiously traced, as a
warning or an example; above all, characters and lives worthy
of emulation must be presented in every book with all the
attractiveness at her command. She had strong views on the
results of "mischievous reading," and deplored the encouragement given to this by the old-fashioned circulating libraries.
In her autobiography she describes a system of private book-
clubs in vogue among certain families of her acquaintance,
enabling parents and vigilant friends to exercise a "guiding
power." [1] Spiritual child of the saintly John Keble, who
prepared her for confirmation, she inculcated and illustrated
the principles of the Oxford movement, in fiction, history,
and biography. She was read with enthusiasm by those of her
way of thinking, including such men as Morris and Rossetti,
this appeal to the Pre-Raphaelites testifying to her close
kinship with the Romantics. Her first asset was the soundness
of her character-drawing, always consistent, always clear-cut.

---

[1] Christabel Coleridge's *Charlotte Mary Yonge*, pp. 111–112. The Rev. Thomas
Bowdler who was a friend of the Yonges at Cambridge was not the Thomas Bowdler
immortalized in the verb "bowdlerize," but his nephew. But Charlotte's views
on mischievous reading were not so very different from those of the expurgator of
Shakespeare.

Her mastery of the art of conversation was a valuable but more doubtful one, inasmuch as it led her far too often to tell the story by means of dialogue; and, however lively a way that may be at right times and seasons, it can easily be overdone, and a too scanty allowance of straightforward narrative may put a strain on both writer and reader. A story ought not to be like a play written out, with mere stage-directions. She had a habit as a girl of writing down conversations which she had listened to or been engaged in with her friends and relations; some of them have been preserved. They interested her, not for the views interchanged, but as "the ordinary chit and chatter of clever young people." Intentionally or not, it was part of her training for authorship. Faithful realism was her object, with the ulterior purposes already mentioned. Her "prime literary affection," she said, must ever be for Sir Walter, and she delighted in Lockhart's *Life of Scott*. There are stray allusions in her letters to Jane Austen, Charlotte Brontë, Mrs Gaskell, and, later on, George Eliot, [1] Trollope, and Mrs Oliphant, showing that she had the familiarity of any educated person with their works; and she cherished a special admiration for Miss Mitford. But she had more to say about such writers for the young as Elizabeth Sewell, Mrs Alfred Gatty, and her daughter Mrs Ewing, who put mental and moral improvement in the forefront of their aims. The poets whom she knew best were Wordsworth and Southey, George Herbert and Cowper, and her contemporaries Tennyson and Keble. In brief, she took domestic fiction as it had been shaped by Miss Edgeworth, Charlotte and Anne Brontë, and Mrs Gaskell, and wrote it with a vigilant eye for moral values, and for the influence of religious convictions or the reverse on character, conduct, and the general tenor of a man's or a woman's life.

Whilst contributing all sorts, including her *Cameos from English History*, to a religious and educational magazine, the *Monthly Packet*, which she edited, where Mrs Gatty and Mrs· Ewing, and also Margaret Roberts, author of *Mademoiselle*

---

[1] She remarked of George Eliot, not without prejudice but not without acuteness: "It seems to me that she could represent but not create, and that when she had lived with a world she did not really know, her ideals were absurd, as in *Deronda*" (Coleridge, 340).

"The
Heir of
Red-
clyffe"
and "The
Daisy
Chain"

Mori and *The Atelier du Lys*, afterwards figured, Charlotte
Mary Yonge (1823–1901) sprang into fame with that "sweet
youthful tragedy of piety and devotion," *The Heir of Redclyffe*
(1853), still the best-known of her works, though not her
finest. There was almost a craze at that time for earnestness
and the cult of a saintly life; and it was read with ardour,
not only by young girls, but also by young officers in the army,
undergraduates at Oxford, and thoughtful people of all ages.
The theme of expiation of wrongs heedlessly committed and
of self-rehabilitation is pursued to illogical extremes; but it
furnished casuistical points for and against Guy or Philip which
readers eagerly debated, and which were threshed out anew
by the novelist in her letters. The chivalry and inherent
goodness of the masculine characters and the sweetness of the
Flaxman heroine were rendered irresistible by the pathos and
heart-searching which accompanied them. Whilst she was
writing, Charlotte lived with her creations, and it is eloquent
of the way she surrendered herself to her imagination to read
such phrases in her letters as "I have found out what the
offence was that made Guy bang the door." She threw herself
with the same enjoyment into another novel of her own day,
Heartsease, or the Brother's Wife (1854). Then, after two
historical tales for children, *The Little Duke* (1854) and *The
Lances of Lynwood* (1855), came the first of her family chronicles,
The Daisy Chain, or Aspirations (1856), which began as a series
of sketches, says the preface, but grew into a novel. The
characters also grew into a large crowd, foremost among them
the Mays, children of Dr May and his wife. They are at the
plastic age, for this is a study of those years of early life "when
the character is chiefly formed," "an endeavour to trace the
effects of those aspirations which are a part of every youthful
nature." Little is omitted of the normal history of childhood
and youth; but one incident might perhaps have been better
placed among the antecedent circumstances, rather than dwelt
on so tearfully in the first few chapters. This is the death of
Mrs May in a driving accident, for which her husband was not
entirely blameless. But Charlotte Yonge loved pathos for its
own sake; and the hospital atmosphere, the lingering death,

and the funeral, are fully detailed, and strike a gloomy note
which is out of key with the rest.   It is a history of young
minds developing, in a household and among circles where
"earnest goodness" is the quality and attitude to be cultivated.
Slovenly ways must be eradicated, girls must be ladylike, as well
as dutiful and unselfish.   Life must be lived according to the
Prayer Book; and there is much about church services, christen-
ings, confirmations, ordinations, and missions.   Leading to the
altar is genuinely a religious rite, in short, the most critical and
exalted moment in this terrestrial life, which is lived in the sure
and certain hope of a fuller life hereafter.   The evangelizing
of Cocksmoor and the establishment of a new church there are
one of the big episodes.   But it would be very unfair to call
the book dull, for Charlotte Yonge knew how to excite keen
interest in such events, and the narrative is refreshed with
humour, though "unbecoming levity" is severely reprehended.
There was a supplement to this in *The Trial, more links in the
Daisy Chain* (1868), which is a murder story; the innocent
hero is imprisoned for years before being exonerated.

Dynevor Terrace (1858) and *The Young Stepmother* (1861) *Other*
were more like ordinary novels, inspired, however, with *novels*
Miss Yonge's usual fervour.   *The Clever Woman of the Family*
(1865) is a new departure, in which she discreetly sinks
the didactic and moralistic plan and tries satire.   With dry
humour, she tells the story of a conceited but well-meaning
young lady, cursed with a zeal for putting everybody right.
After a series of mishaps, the poor thing is taken in by an
impostor who trades upon her philanthropic ambitions, and the
end is a comic tragedy.   In the fraud and its unmasking, Miss
Yonge had evidently learned a good deal from Wilkie Collins,
not least in her handling of the element of suspense.   Many
of her historical novels were able stories written for children.
The Dove in the Eagle's Nest (1866), however, was a more
painstaking study, based on Freytag's *Bilder*, of Ulm and
Swabia under Frederick III and that extraordinary character
Maximilian I.[1]   In *The Chaplet of Pearls, or the White and*

[1] Christina's prophetic dream of her wounded brother's return and the visit of
the Emperor Maximilian disguised as a knight was dreamed by Charlotte Yonge

Black Ribaumont (1868), she addressed herself again to the younger generation; and, inspired in some measure by Millais' pictures of the Huguenot and the Inquisition, painted a vivid picture of the times of the massacre of St Bartholomew. She sought to avoid the charge that her stories were controversial; but she cannot get away from the nineteenth-century point of view, and is of course as devout and as didactic as ever. *The Caged Lion* (1870) was a very romantic tale of King James of Scotland as a captive in England, and his friendship with Henry V; the preface makes a clean breast of her licences and inaccuracies. But she went on with the same conscientious but highly questionable stuff, telling of Mary Queen of Scots in England, in *Unknown to History* (1882), returning to the Ribaumonts in *Stray Pearls* (1883), and re-interpreting history in some half-dozen further novels or romances. But the spiritual glory investing the most humdrum existence dedicated to worthy purposes was equally the mark of her semi-historical stories and those of her own time. Her long family chronicle, *The Pillars of the House* (1875), is as good as *The Daisy Chain*, if not better. To her, the people in it were all beloved friends, and she was apt to make them mouthpieces of her opinions, as well as exemplars of her lofty but not impossible ideals. Her last novel, *Modern Broods, or Developments unlooked for* (1900), was chiefly interesting for the puzzled views and anxious criticism of an elder sister in charge of four modern girls. She had outlived her epoch. The day of the lay preacher in the guise of novelist, seconding the efforts of ·those ordained to the apostolic mission of interpreting divine truths, was passing away.

Minor novelists —Emily Eden   The crowd of women who pampered their vanity by writing novels, or found in this an occupation that paid more or less, are of more interest to the student of social psychology who wants to know who read them than to the literary historian. They were already numerous. Of late, several whom time had apparently eliminated have been rescued and reprinted, one of the forgotten but worth remembering being the Hon.

herself. She often waited for such directions from her brooding imagination, and took them for supernatural promptings (Coleridge, 226).

Emily Eden (1797–1869), whose two novels, *The Semi-attached Couple* and *The Semi-detached House*, the former written in the thirties and both published in 1860, have appeared in the "Rescue" series (1928). Miss Eden, a daughter of the first Lord Auckland and granddaughter of the Earl of Minto, belonged to that exalted Whig society whose image has been perpetuated in the *Greville Memoirs*. She was a pupil of Jane Austen moving in higher circles, with a pretty talent, well shown in the first, for disclosing the jealousy and pangs and frictions between a pair who have made what the world thinks a most eligible match, but are a long time settling down to mutual trust and harmony. The other novel—both are short —has none of this emotional interest; but is just as lively in the ironical touches with which the human ways of these patricians are hit off by an observer at close quarters.

Catherine Crowe (*née* Stevens, 1800–1876) and Caroline Archer Clive (*née* Meysey-Wigley, 1801–1873) were, in comparison, of the tribe of hack-writers. Mrs Crowe was a pioneer of the lowliest sort of domestic fiction, though it was the sensationalism of her best novel, *Susan Hopley, or the Adventures of a Maidservant* (1841), that enthralled her readers. *Lilly Dawson* (1847) and *Linny Lockwood* (1854) are truer to the type. Lilly is brought up in a family of smugglers, but sees better days and tries to be a fine lady, marrying, however, the lover of her humble beginnings. Linny, betrayed by her husband, finds herself the servant of his deserted mistress, whom she nurses in her last hours. Mrs Crowe was a champion of her sex, and protested against the inferior education conceded them. She was best known, however, for a collection of ghost-stories and creepy anecdotes of warnings and hauntings, *The Night Side of Nature* (1848), which claimed to be authentic and worth taking with the most philosophic seriousness, though their only difference from the tales in Wilkie Collins's *After Dark* (1856) is that she apparently accepted them as gospel truth. Mrs Clive was also a pioneer, but in psychological fiction, which was a novelty then. She wrote a curious pair of novels, *Paul Ferroll* (1855) and *Why Paul Ferroll killed his Wife* (1860), the latter being, not a sequel, but a sort of key to the other.

Mrs Crowe and Mrs Clive

Paul marries the wrong woman, whilst in love with another who responds to his passion. Hence he has some reason for detesting his wife; and, being a man of resolute will, he eventually gets rid of her. It is not melodrama: thoughts, motives, conversations are retailed in the most natural way, with no straining after effect. It is something new, this unsensational treatment of a provocative theme; it is good, sound realism. A telling bit of true insight is Paul Ferroll's hurried return to the room which he will never enter again, when he is about to face his fellow-magistrates and confess the deed of which another is under suspicion.

Holding and pressing her hand a moment, he went away. In a minute more he came back, and stood looking into the room.

"Have you lost something? Do you want anything?"

"No, I had forgotten how that picture hung; I should have been tormented if it had not been clear to my mind's eye. Farewell."

The daughter said nothing, she knew nothing, but she could not help being frightened.[1] With other names, though all else is parallel, the novelist, who was also a poetess, submits a case in the second novel which she pleads would explain why a man such as Paul Ferroll would kill his wife. A young man loves a convent girl, who consents to a secret engagement. But a wealthy young woman, whose impulses are of the predatory rather than any warmer kind, sets herself to divide them, and at the moment when he is only half-recovered from brain fever, on the plea that he has compromised her, prevails upon him to marry her. Too late he finds out the truth. No very searching analysis is displayed in this statement of the case; but the characters, at any rate, are not animated dummies. Mrs Clive's are certainly superior to most of the commodities manufactured for the circulating libraries, then and now. Time has certainly been kinder to them than to the works of Mrs Anne Marsh (*née* Caldwell, 1791–1874), one of the regular producers of what was known as "standard novels." *Two*

---

[1] *Paul Ferroll* was resuscitated and republished by the Scholartis Press (1929).

Old Men's Tales: the Deformed and the Admiral's Daughter (1834), *Tales of the Woods and Fields* (1836), and *Emilia Wyndham* (1846) are probably the best of a miscellaneous output which she kept going down to the sixties.   Those of Lady Georgiana Fullerton (1812–1885), *Ellen Middleton* and *Constance Sherwood* (1865), may be bracketed with Charlotte Yonge's; she was a slightly earlier exponent of High Church principles.

The novels of two Irishwomen, Julia Kavanagh (1824–1877) *Two* and the Hon. Caroline Norton (1808–1877), were also fondly *Irish* supposed to be superior, but they have not survived the century *novelists* in which they were read with admiration.   Miss Kavanagh lived part of her life abroad, and was one of the first to put into fiction the observations and experiences which usually go into records of travel.   But, unlike so many who have made the Continent the scene of the most incontinent adventures, she tended to idealize both her young girls and their lovers, whether they were French or Italian or English people residing in a foreign land.   *Madeleine* (1848) is a pretty love-tale of Auvergne, *Adèle* (1857) presents a charming Norman heroine, the wilful young thing who gives the title to *Silvia* is a winning and estimable Italian, and so it is with the rest.   Miss Kavanagh could paint character and manners, and had a knack for agreeable comedy, or at any rate farce.   Mrs Norton, who was born a Sheridan, does survive, but as the original of a character in a novel not her own.   Meredith's Diana of the Crossways is her portrait, glorified to what extent who shall say? [1]   Mrs Norton's *Stuart of Dunleath* (1851) was a pathetic, long-drawn, very old-fashioned novel, though subtitled "a story of modern times," in which she is supposed to have inserted much autobiography; *Lost and Saved* (1863), a society novel, making an appeal on behalf of the woman wronged; and *Old Sir Douglas* (1868), the presentment of a chivalrous old gentleman, whose weak good nature is rewarded with sorrow and ingratitude. Some of the by-characters are pungently drawn, but the satire has now lost its flavour.

[1] The story, so far as it concerned her, was literally true enough to the facts, at any rate, to induce Lord Dufferin, Mrs Norton's kinsman, to persuade the novelist to deny the truth of the incident in which the fictitious lady sells a political secret to *The Times*.

Other old stagers   One of the domestic novelists who had a very long innings during the latter half of the century, but of whose works probably only one is now in print, the famous *John Halifax, Gentleman* (1856), was Mrs Craik, known at least as well by her maiden name, Dinah Maria Mulock (1826–1887). She was as industrious and as prolific as the devoted Mrs Oliphant, though she did not live long enough to produce more than half the hundred novels left by her younger colleague. *The Ogilvies* (1849), *Olive* (1850), the problem novel *A Life for a Life* (1859), *Mistress and Maid* (1862), *The Woman's Kingdom* (1868), and many more, drew character, at least feminine character, with some mastery, but were prized rather for their sentiments and wholesome ideals, and the infectious pathos, than for qualities pertaining to literature as distinguished from a tract. *John Halifax* was long regarded by the faithful as a classic of the literature whose chief object is to do readers good. Its subject is the career of an able and God-fearing man who rises from poverty to wealth, and maintains his integrity throughout. The story goes so far back that a glimpse is afforded of Lady Hamilton, and it comes down to the age of steam and the riots occasioned by the introduction of machinery among the hand-workers.[1] Two younger writers, Amelia Blandford Edwardes (1831–1892) and Matilda Betham Edwards (1836–1919), are now as little read, perhaps less, although the latter was still writing in the first years of the present century, and one of her novels, *The Lord of the Harvest* (1919), is among the "World's Classics." Amelia Edwardes was a scholar and a traveller, and a distinguished Egyptologist, whose six or eight novels deal with foreigners or the experiences of English people abroad. *Barbara's History* (1864) has scenes in a German college, *Debenham's Vow* (1870) exciting occurrences in the American Civil War, *Lord Brackenbury* (1880) mingles pleasant views of country life in Cheshire with the recollections

---

[1] The present writer can remember listening as a boy to at least one semi-religious, semi-political discourse by Handel Cossham, the self-made colliery-owner who was the reputed original of John Halifax. At his house on the outskirts of Bath he had a lecture-hall built; and here he held what would now be called "Pleasant Sunday afternoons," largely for the purpose of impressing working-men with his views, not only of religion, but of the general situation.

of an acute and friendly observer of foreign ways. Miss Betham Edwards also began with a German novel strong in portraiture, *Dr Jacob* (1868), anatomizing the complexities of a "noble but oblique" character, at Frankfurt. One French province after another was the scene of various subsequent novels, one or two semi-historical, before the novelist settled down to the congenial task of depicting rural life in Suffolk at the time of the repeal of the Corn Laws. The international novel was well in view, if it had not yet arrived. George Borrow, much earlier than this, had led his readers through Spain and Portugal as far as Morocco, and Borrow wrote fiction if he is only in a limited sense a novelist.[1] It was as if the novelist had set out to annex half the countries in the world. But this cosmopolitanism, though constantly recurring, was only a digression. Fiction makes its conquests in other ways; its real advance is on internal lines. Trollope was beginning to deal with every side of English life, as methodically as if he had mapped out the ground with a theodolite; George Eliot was about to explore deeper than anyone yet into the inner man; Mrs Oliphant, Miss Thackeray, as well as Miss Yonge, with a crowd of the more ephemeral, were to maintain an abundant supply of domestic fiction, showing the reactions of thoughts and feelings on conduct and character within that homely but vital sphere. And then the two Kingsleys, Thomas Hughes, Cardinal Newman, and even G. A. Lawrence and Charles Reade in their more violent ways, were to attack the social, economic, and religious problems of the day to much better purpose than Dickens and Disraeli and Mrs Gaskell had done before them.

[1] Such brief mention of such a great imaginative writer as George Borrow is sufficient in a history of fiction, not because he does not deserve more, but simply because he is not really a novelist, but only an autobiographer adopting the forms and accomplishments of fiction, for the reason that they happened to suit his curious mind. It may be objected that *The Sentimental Journey* was not excluded, and it must be admitted that the border-line is very difficult to lay down. In Borrow's case, as in Sterne's, the manner and the mannerisms have been closely imitated by writers who cannot be denied the name of novelists.

CHAPTER IV

TROLLOPE

Anthony's mother, Frances Trollope TURNING from the Brontës and Mrs Gaskell to Trollope is to come to one who was outwardly the least romantic and most prosaic of all the Victorian novelists of any eminence, more so even than Thackeray, whom he venerated as a man, and also as his criterion of the kind of fiction which he himself would like to write, so far as it lay within his powers. He was the younger of the two novelist sons of Frances Trollope,[1] author of the notorious *Domestic Manners of the Americans*, of the Widow Barnaby series, and of several fighting novels in which she took up the quarrel of the oppressed factory-hands, besides a mass of undistinguished fiction turned out for the market. Frances Trollope was a character, and one as singular, as robust, and on the whole as estimable as any of those owing their literary paternity to her son. An only too outspoken denouncer and satirist of what she held to be follies, vices, or absurdities, she did not stick at exaggeration or even calumny, or refrain from Billingsgate, when she honestly thought the object ought to be ridiculed out of existence or when she simply wanted to keep her readers in a state of hilarity. She was as sincere a critic as ever worked herself or himself into a fury of invective; but she was also, assuredly, one of those who are much too ready to see the worst side of everything they look at. Her husband, Anthony's father, made an extraordinary mess of his affairs, through an easy-going optimism that often seemed to border on insanity. He died, practically insolvent, four years after the never - to - be - forgotten adventure of the fancy - goods bazaar in Cincinnati, from which he and his family came back ruined but unashamed, with the materials for her vengeance

[1] See also Volume VII. 225-226.

on the Americans already simmering in Mrs Trollope's brain. *Her Domestic Manners of the Americans* (1832) appeared early next year; and now this indomitable woman of fifty-two, with an invalid husband and a family of children, settled down to a life of hard literary labour, in the three decades which remained to her producing well over a hundred separate works.   Most of her children died in infancy or youth; but she contrived that her sturdier sons, Thomas Adolphus and Anthony, should have as good an education as her means and their differing abilities could secure; Adolphus went to Winchester and took his degree at Oxford; the duller Anthony had to put up with a more haphazard schooling at Harrow and Winchester and then back again at Harrow, but appears to have picked up more scholarship of a miscellaneous but not unsound kind than he would ever have admitted in cold blood.   He was always inimitable at self-depreciation.   Mrs Trollope now turned herself into a book-maker of all sorts, doing occasional articles for magazines, writing novels, and compiling books on most of the western countries of Europe, some of them practical guides for travellers, works of popular biography, and chit-chat on English society past and present; in short, anything that would bring grist to the mill.   Her industry was amazing; yet she enjoyed life, made friends, and was idolized by the children who were left to her.   She won popularity, she won abuse, and made some sort of a hit with the major part of her output.   It was nearly all written abroad, for she settled at Bruges in 1834, where Thomas Trollope died, and spent the rest of her days almost continuously on the Continent, her last home being Florence, where she died in 1863.

novels and other work

Little need be said of Anthony's elder brother, Thomas Adolphus Trollope (1810–1892).   Though five years older, he outlived his brother.   He was of a milder and less exuberant temperament, but evidently quite as tough and resistant, for he was equally capable of hard and sustained work, like their mother.   He lived with her until his marriage in 1848; in fact, in his miscellaneousness if in nothing else he is another Frances Trollope, with better claims to both seriousness and decorum.   Long residence at Florence and then at Rome,

Thomas Adolphus Trollope

where he was correspondent for the *Standard*, qualified him to write feelingly of the Italian peasants and apply accurate shades of local colour to novels of Florence, such as *La Beata, a Tuscan Romeo and Juliet* (1861), and *Marietta* (1862); of the Romagna, *Beppo the Conscript* (1864); Ravenna, *The Siren* (1870); and rural Tuscany, *Diamond cut Diamond* (1875) and other stories. Aggressively Protestant, he tried to show up the evils of priestcraft. But he was a sentimentalist, and his peasant heroines are mere idealisms emblematic of his crusade for better moral standards. Adolphus Trollope was a good hand at plot, as his murder novel, *The Siren*, attests, with its ingenious riddle, who did it? He is supposed to have furnished Anthony with the plot of *Dr Thorne*, which presumably means the idea of the self-made man beginning life as an artisan, and surprising the heroine, in love with a gentleman who must marry money, and unaware that she has a flesh-and-blood uncle, with the bequest of his vast fortune. Like his mother, Adolphus turned out quantities of biographical and semi-historical literature, of which a joint work with his wife, Frances Eleanor, also a novelist, *Homes and Haunts of Italian Poets* (1881), was the favourite. And he left an autobiography, *What I remember* (1887). A bibliography of all the Trollopes would be a voluminous affair.

Anthony Trollope's beginnings   In a more famous and probably the most candid and disillusioning autobiography ever penned, his brother Anthony depicted himself. He was a distinguished dolt at Harrow and Winchester; he was bullied and reviled by masters and schoolfellows for his shabbiness and alleged uncleanness; throughout boyhood and hobbledehoyhood he was awkward, loutish, and miserably shy. He suffered the pangs of Ishmael, but felt no more resentment than he was to show towards the puppets of his imagination, even when they harboured vices and evil tendencies that he detested. When Trollope had absorbed all the education that could be instilled in his rambling course of schooling, he managed to get into the Post Office, after the farcical apology for an examination which, he says, is "accurately" described in Charley Tudor's experiences, in *The Three Clerks*. It was probably the only one he could have passed.

The pay was slender, and he found what he considered his idle lot at headquarters boring; hence, after seven years, he was glad to be transferred from London to a postal surveyor's office in Ireland. He remained in that country from 1841 to 1859, with a break in 1851–1853 when he held a roving inspectorship in the west of England. At length he had full scope for his energies. Trollope revelled in hard work, and yet found ample time and opportunity for amusement, especially hunting. Personally, he was a big, bluff John Bull, talking like a northeaster and glorying in his Philistinism. There was a breezy manliness about him; he had the doggedness of his father without the wrongheadedness that terminated in ruin. Trollope married in 1844, about a year after the little experience that gave birth to his first novel. He relates in the *Autobiography* how, as he and a friend were brooding over the ruins of a country house somewhere in Leitrim, the melancholy visage of the old dwelling-place seized his imagination. Whilst they strolled among the tumbledown walls, wondering what was its history, he "fabricated" the story of *The Macdermots of Ballycloran* (1847). It was, of course, a tragic tale, such a tale as Carleton or one of the Banims would have told. Needless to say, Trollope had read them and the rest of the Irish novelists; Carleton he read and reread, Lever he knew personally. He thought his plot rather a good one. Feemy Macdermot, sister of a squireen, is madly in love with a revenue officer, who is killed by her brother in the act of abducting her. She dies in giving birth to a fatherless child; and her brother Thady, after the first and longest of many trials in Anthony Trollope's novels, dies on the gallows. Unfortunately, the plot takes the author himself in hand: the tale is over-elaborated. Except that it shows his thoroughness in drawing a variety of characters, true to the time and country, *The Macdermots* is hardly an earnest of his future creativeness. He was to lay it down later that "The object of a novel should be to instruct in morals while it amuses." [1] There is too much instruction, and too much information: this novel is enough of itself to throw doubt on such an unfortunate dogma. Nor was there

[1] His monograph on *Thackeray* (Men of Letters series), p. 109.

much more promise in *The Kellys and the O'Kellys* (1848), a more cheerful book, with, however, as thoroughbred and consistent a scoundrel in it, in Barry Lynch, as he ever created. Long after, Trollope returned to Irish subjects in *Castle Richmond* (1860), dealing with the famine years of 1846–1847 which he had witnessed on the spot, and again in *The Land Leaguers* (1883), left unfinished and published after his death; but both these novels, though the work of his maturity, display next to nothing of the genuine Trollope. And a story of the French Revolution, *La Vendée* (1859), prompted by the events of 1848, is negligible except as evidence that even in the well-trod realm of historical fiction he was sure to be honest and matter-of-fact, unromantic and unsentimental.

The novels that count

His early efforts were failures; but Trollope was convinced that he could write novels, and he persevered. It was during the spell of surveying English postal services that he had the experience, in 1851, of looking on a very different scene from the gloomy old house in Leitrim, when a very different sort of story shaped itself in his mind. He states in the *Autobiography* that it was whilst sauntering in Salisbury Close that he had his first glimpse of the little world of cathedral dignitaries which was the germ of the Barchester novels.[1] The germ quickly ripened. He began *The Warden* in the summer of 1852 and finished it in the autumn of the next year. It appeared in January 1855, and he started at once upon the continuation, *Barchester Towers*, his first success and as good a novel as he ever wrote. At the time when Mr Harding dawned upon his imagination, Trollope's mind was full of recent scandals concerning the misapplication of old endowments; several cases, including that of the Holy Cross hospital at Winchester, were before the public. Thus he had an extraneous motive in writing *The Warden*; in fact, this controversial element first drew attention to the book, it was this which interested the reviewers. But, at all events, Trollope's imagination had lighted upon two of his finest and

[1] Barset is Somerset; but Barchester was evidently a dream-city made up of memories of Winchester, rather than Salisbury, with certain features borrowed elsewhere, from Wells, for instance, and perhaps even from Canterbury (see Sadleir, 151–155, on "the Barsetshire riddle").

most serviceable characters, in Mr Harding and his son-in-law, Archdeacon Grantly; they were the nuclei round which a great company was soon to collect. An imposing group of cathedral buildings may originate in a modest edifice. So, *Barchester Towers* (1857) was added to *The Warden*, and *Doctor Thorne* to *Barchester Towers*, as the little knot of clerical personages and their families expanded in Trollope's mind to the whole society of the episcopal town, then took in the neighbouring gentry and country people, and eventually the territorial magnates and all the rank and file of provincial life; in short, a fat slice of contemporary England, with its natural features and towns, villages, country houses, and railways, all so clearly visualized that he could draw a map of it, and tell exactly how long it would take to get from Mr So-and-so's door to someone else's. His realism was matter-of-fact and methodical. He first cut out a small segment of English life, then added other segments, letting the picture extend to right and left, until it was a panorama of a certain limited range. But he was very leisurely about it; there is no reason to suppose that Trollope saw at once all the possibilities opening out, or had any scheme for a comprehensive survey of rural England. He was not a Balzac. Even before *Doctor Thorne*, he had digressed in *The Three Clerks* (1857), in which he let fly at another grievance, the "much loathed scheme of competitive examination" for public offices, and pilloried its great apostle, Sir Charles Trevelyan, as Sir Gregory Hardlines. It was the chequered love-tale of three clerks in the Civil Service, one of whom, Charley Tudor, although, or because, he stands in some sense for Trollope himself, is curiously reminiscent now of Tom Jones and now of Captain Booth. But there is far more of Dickens than of Fielding in a more arrogant personage, Lawyer Chaffanbrass, who here makes his first appearance. If, however, there is a great deal of autobiography embedded in this one, the Barsetshire novel that followed, *Framley Parsonage* (1861), was much more like a return to his own people. Trollope played truant again in *Orley Farm* (1861–1862) and *Rachel Ray* (1863); the one the history of a law case which just misses greatness, although Chaffanbrass bulks large in it; the other a mild satire on the straitlaced and scandal-mongering and the snobs in a petty country town, with pages in it that bring Jane Austen to mind. Then, after another pleasant sojourn at home, in *The Small House at Allington* (1864), he went off on other paths in *Can You Forgive Her?* (1864–1865), an attempt to "novelize" his unsuccessful play, "The Noble Jilt," with more than a glimpse of the world of politics which was soon to be the subject of a new series of novels, and in *The Belton Estate* (1866), one of his quietly efficient studies of a sensitive woman who has to decide between two eligible suitors of entirely opposite natures. And now he wound up all his Barsetshire sub-plots and incorporated them with a story bordering upon tragedy, in *The Last Chronicle of Barset* (1867); and even extended his territory into neighbouring shires, in *The Claverings* (1867), a novel that falls little short of the Barsetshire standard. Trollope was by this time settled in England again. *The Warden* had been finished at Belfast, and *Barchester Towers* was written in Ireland. He was abroad, visiting his mother and proceeding on a postal mission to Egypt, when he wrote *Doctor Thorne*. But in 1859 his desire to be given an appointment on this side of the Irish Sea was gratified; and from now till 1867, when he resigned from the Post Office, and indeed to still later, for he was entrusted with official missions and had many other irons in the fire, he led a life that would have killed an ordinary man. Without ever neglecting his duties, and never missing a hunt or even a seasonable game of whist, he worked steadily at his novels, and also edited or contributed to various magazines. "Few men, I think," he says in the *Autobiography*, "ever lived a fuller life," and no one, he believed, made a larger contribution, in that length of time, to English letters, or, at any rate, written matter. But his greatest work had now been done. He was over fifty. In the first of a pair of novels, *Phineas Finn* (1869), he drew political society with some approach to the urbane realism of the Barsetshire series and occasional links with the old plots; and he followed this up with *Ralph the Heir* (1871), *Phineas Redux* (1874), a sequel better than its precursor, *The Prime Minister* (1876), and *The*

Duke's Children (1880). In between, came a capital story of rural but not rustic life, *The Vicar of Bullhampton* (1870); a moving tragedy of mistaken love, *Sir Harry Hotspur of Humble-thwaite* (1871), one of his best-constructed stories; and an odd but brilliant sort of detective novel, *The Eustace Diamonds* (1872), which is also a sort of social satire, and, confessedly, to a certain extent, Trollope's attempt at a *Vanity Fair*. But his most devastating satire, the one in which he turned on the younger contemporaries who scoffed at his good-natured portraiture of a world that had all but vanished, was *The Way We Live Now* (1875); it is the only one of his novels in which there are characters who have not a single redeeming feature. *The Bertrams* (1859) and *Miss Mackenzie* (1865) were earlier satires that scarcely hit their mark. This cannot be said of the sardonic irony of the posthumous *Mr Scarborough's Family* (1883). From time to time, he wrote novels that were more persistently analytical than was his wont. In the domestic tragedy, *He Knew he was Right* (1869), he was almost pathological; and the position of the young man in *An Eye for an Eye* (1879), who wants to get rid of his mistress decently, also affects the psychological method, not brilliantly. *Is he Popenjoy?* (1878) has one of his cleverest plots; the double plot of *Ayala's Angel* (1881), on the other hand, tends to miss-fire, though Ayala Dormer is one of his most seducing young women. *Dr Wortle's School* (1881) is notable for the tart sarcasm with which the theme of scandal and social ostracism is treated, and also for Dr Wortle himself, a good characterization of at least one side of his author. Trollope made the experiment in *Nina Balatka* (1867) and *Linda Tressel* (1868) of writing anonymously of foreign scenes and in a style of fiction foreign to him; he did not escape detection, but, as he admitted, the works were too slight for this to be of any importance. Nor need much be said of *Harry Heathcote of Gangoil* (1874) and *John Caldigate* (1879), fruits of his visit to Australia to see his son.

Trollope thought *Pride and Prejudice* the finest novel in English [1]; but he never quite fathomed the secret of Jane

Trollope's realism

[1] He "partially withdrew" this opinion after a second reading of *Ivanhoe*, "and did not completely bestow it elsewhere till *Esmond* was written" (*Autobiography*, iii.).

Austen's art. Her delicate yet deadly irony escaped him; he relied on heavier-handed methods, when he approached irony at all. In his rather inept book on Thackeray, after reiterating the opinion that a novel should convey a wholesome lesson—"in matter it should be moral and amusing"—he discusses realism in style, and observes,

"And yet in very truth the realistic must not be true—but just as far removed from truth as to suit the erroneous idea of truth which the reader may be supposed to entertain." [1]

It is the conversations that he is talking about; but, of course, if this is a sound principle here it must be sound there and everywhere in fiction. On the next page he speaks of "the realistic, by which we mean that which shall seem to be real." It is a compromise with actuality; lying, he says, between the two, that is, between a literal reproduction of ordinary talk and the literary version which pleases by its superior pith, point, and shapeliness.[2] Trollope was well aware that his own realistic fiction was much more than a literal rendering of what he saw and heard. But he came nearer to putting his finger on the all-important function of the novelist's mind in ordering experience and rendering it as intelligible and significant as it would appear after exhaustive scrutiny, comparison, and reflection, in his advice to Kate Field, which consisted of various glosses on the text, "You must exercise your mind upon

---

[1] *Thackeray* (English Men of Letters), 185–186.

[2] He gives a sample in *Dr Thorne* (chap. vii.) of what ordinary "educated" people would actually say in making and receiving a declaration, remarking "that these matters are not always discussed by mortal lovers in the poetically-passionate phraseology" generally thought appropriate.

Gentleman. "Well, Miss—, the long and the short of it is this: here I am; you can take me or leave me."

Lady,—scratching a gutter on the sand with her parasol, so as to allow a little salt water to run out of one hole into another. "Of course, I know that's all nonsense."

Gentleman. "Nonsense! By Jove, it isn't nonsense at all; come, Jane, here I am; at any rate you can say something."

Lady. "Yes, I suppose I can say something."

Gentleman. "Well, which is it to be; take me or leave me?"

Lady,—very slowly, and with a voice perhaps hardly articulate, carrying on, at the same time, her engineering works on a wider scale. "Well, I don't exactly want to leave you."

That was the realism on which he thought his "compromise" was a decided and legitimate improvement.

it." [1] His own characters look exactly like truth; yet Trollope's
private stamp is on every one of them. But no novelist
ever attained a more apparent actuality, even by sticking to
the crude truth, which was not Trollope's object. He lived so
intimately with his characters before he turned them out into
the world, that they are not only recognizable as his familiar
friends, or his familiar foes, he seems to put the reader on
visiting terms with them. In his day-dreaming, he saw and
heard them as vividly as he saw and heard the people about
him. They were making history, and the history they made
must not be altered. Hence he could never manage drastic
changes in a plot successfully: once he had clearly realized
what such and such personages would do in the circumstances,
this was an ascertained fact that he dare not falsify. The
character, or the group of characters, was the first essential;
then came the plot. With his characters clearly defined to
himself and grouped in the right posture, set in such relation
to each other that something dramatic was bound to happen,
plot was simply the studied resultant of the parallelogram of
human forces. [2] At times, however, he did have some attitude
or situation in his head to begin with, and the problem then
was to show this arising naturally from the friction or collision
of different minds and temperaments: in such cases, the
characters and the crucial circumstances suggested themselves
together; they must have done so, for instance, in *The Warden*.
But that "day-dreaming" of his, the preliminary gestation,
was as important a process and probably occupied him as
busily as the writing, which was in good sooth a mechanical
affair, being only the swift transference to sheets of paper of all
that had matured in his brain. For the supposedly mechanical
nature of his fiction has become a byword quite erroneously.
He was indeed a pattern of industry. He used to rise at
5.30 A.M., and write two hundred and fifty words every quarter
of an hour. He rivalled Scott, if he did not outdo him. Yet
it was Trollope who observed, "There is no way of writing well

<hr />

[1] Quoted by Sadleir, 275-276.
[2] This is not contradicted by his own words, "The plot is but the vehicle for
all this" (*Autobiography*, vii.). Too many plot-novels are what he calls "the vehicle
without the passengers" (*Ibid.*).

and also writing easily." [1]   When all his achievements in breaking the record for speed of composition were recounted in cold blood in the *Autobiography*, in the dreamy days of the Æsthetes too, it sounded scandalous.   But the only thing to make a fuss about was the freshness of his mind and its powers of endurance.   When he sat down to his desk, he had everything ready; he only had to make his report.

Normal life, not idealized
He let fall some pertinent observations on the kind of life he chose to depict, and his determination not to idealize, in *The Eustace Diamonds*:

> There arose at one time a school of art which delighted to paint the human face as perfect in beauty; and from that time to this we are discontented unless every woman is drawn for us as a Venus, or, at least, a Madonna.   I do not know that we have gained much by this untrue portraiture, either in beauty or in art.

He meant to deliver a likeness of reality, however dull, and even if it was ugly:

> And yet in real life we are content with oats that are really middling, are very glad to have a useful horse, and know that if we drink port at all we must drink some that is neither good nor sound.   In those delineations of life and character which we call novels a similarly superlative vein is desired. Our own friends around us are not always merry and wise, nor, alas! always honest and true.   They are often cross and foolish, and sometimes treacherous and false.   They are so, and we are angry.   Then we forgive them, not without a consciousness of imperfection on our own part.   And we know—or, at least, believe—that though they be sometimes treacherous and false, there is a balance of good.   We cannot have heroes to dine with us.   There are none.   And were these heroes to be had, we should not like them.   But neither are our friends villains—whose every aspiration is for evil, and whose every moment is a struggle for some achievement worthy of the devil.
>
> The persons whom you cannot care for in a novel, because they are so bad, are the very same that you so dearly love in your

---

[1] *Barchester Towers*, xx.

life, because they are so good. To make them and ourselves
somewhat better—not by one spring heavenwards to perfection,
because we cannot so use our legs—but by slow climbing, is,
we may presume, the object of all teachers, leaders, legislators,
spiritual pastors, and masters. He who writes tales such as
this, probably also has, very humbly, some such object distantly
before him. A picture of surpassing godlike nobleness—a
picture of a King Arthur among men, may perhaps do much.
But such pictures cannot do all. When such a picture is
painted, as intending to show what a man should be, it is
true. If painted to show what men are, it is false. The true
picture of life as it is, if it could be adequately painted, would
show men what they are, and how they might rise, not, indeed,
to perfection, but one step first, and then another on the
ladder.[1]

Licentiousness and the fouler vices do not come into
Trollope's purview; if they are mentioned or hinted at, they
are left unspecified, for example, in *The Macdermots*, or in the
case of the Hon. John or Lord Porlock, in *The Small House at
Allington*. Sheer rascality lurks in the background, until in
The Eustace Diamonds and in that indignant satire, *The Way
We Live Now*, he drags it to the front. There is no need to
suppose that he distorted anything out of his wish to be wholesome and improving. For it is obvious that his desire to do
good was only a secondary thing, just any honest person's wish
not to do anybody any harm: his real motive was to amuse,
as he himself was amused, with the spectacle of life.

In *The Warden* and *Barchester Towers*, and the rest of the *The Bar-*
Barsetshire series, he found exactly the right subject, the right *chester*
sphere, the social conjunctions and oppositions, and the assort- *novels*
ment of characters that suited him. The technical mastery
which he attained in writing this group of novels never deserted
him; but only at times and places in his later work did he rise
to the Barchester standard of creative resource. *Orley Farm,
Can You Forgive Her, The Claverings, The Eustace Diamonds,*
and *Dr Wortle's School* are perhaps the ones that sustain the
comparison best. Trollope was forty when *The Warden*

---

[1] Chap. xxxv.

appeared, two years after writing the first chapter of his first novel; he was over fifty when he wrote *The Last Chronicle of Barset*; so there is nothing surprising in this fact. All but one of the other best half-dozen belonged to the same period of his life. His habit was to start on a fresh novel the morning after finishing the last. But he took his own time over the Barsetshire set; the others that appeared whilst this was in hand were mere parerga, which could be thrown off at leisure whilst more important matters were preparing in his mind. His very first novel had been written in the established Irish style; and its only distinction was the way his paramount interest in character made him heedfully depict the world in which the characters move and have their being. *The Kellys and the O'Kellys* which followed was less absorbing as a story, but much more like the delineations of character and manners which supervened. Murder and arson were not in his line; with rare exceptions, he stuck to normal life, the world as it goes on the average, with no romance or heroics or improbable adventures. "The trivial round, the common task" furnished all that he was inclined to ask. Yet improbabilities do occur in ordinary life; it may be that Trollope was too drastic in excluding the exceptional, which often gives an extra dash of vitality to the ordinary. Yet he does show that ordinary life can be interesting in all its ordinariness, as interesting to look at as it is to those who are living it. In Barsetshire, he cut off a big piece of the existing world, and made it a microcosm, though by no means a universe, and not such a re-creation of the actuality everyone knows as emerges from the works of Dickens and Thackeray. Trollope's procedure was the converse of theirs. He did not sit down to write, like Dickens or Thackeray, George Eliot, Meredith or Hardy, with a definite view of reality that cried out to be expressed, a view of the human world that we know and of the universe that we do not know, such a personal view as must have coloured and characterized and probably modified the features of everything they looked at. He was no thinker; he had no fixed attitude or point of view, no philosophic idea, no deep-seated impulse to analyse, criticize, or expound; he simply enjoyed, and wanted

to make others enjoy, the humours, the pathos, and the variety
and incessant novelty of human nature in the act of living.
The spectacle entertained him, and he reproduced it with
the minimum—his minimum—of comment and explanation,
to entertain his readers. Even with the ripening of experience,
he never attained the comprehensive vision of a Thackeray;
nor was he a George Eliot, sounding the depths of character
and conscience. He certainly had no inclination to evolve a
world out of his day-dreaming and put it in place of the real
one; he makes one of his characters observe that "Dickens had
manufactured a kind of life that never had existed, and never
could exist." [1] Perhaps it will turn out that Trollope was only
an absolutely first-rate journeyman, who, when he hit upon the
right subject and kept to the right level, achieved what looks
the equivalent of genius. But who shall define and strictly
demarcate genius?

The little world of which Trollope had glimpses in strolling *Bar-*
about Salisbury Close was nothing extraordinary, and it was *chester*
pre-eminently a quiet world, though he knew very well that *and*
there must be elements of disturbance latent there as every- *Barset—*
where else. But it was a world conspicuously marked with those *classes*
class gradations which he recognized as the dominating feature *versus*
of the English social landscape. These class distinctions strike *individu-*
the eye more glaringly in the provinces than in London; *ality*
which was why Trollope, whom they interested, went only on
occasional trips to the metropolis for a subject. In cathedral
towns they are, as it were, underlined. In such as are county
towns as well, the ecclesiastical dignitaries of various grades,
with their differences of worldly wealth, and the parallel distinctions of rank among the laity which seem to gain emphasis
by the juxtaposition, especially the gap between the plain old
landed gentry and the full-blown aristocrats, or the new
moneyed grandees, provide all the materials for the social
drama of caste, wealth, birth, and manners, and full play for
such motives as arrogance and exclusiveness, envy and ambition,
even were hatred and malice finally eliminated. Gossip and
tittle-tattle, scandal and calumny, are, at least to the novelist,

---

[1] Miss Marrable (*Vicar of Bullhampton*, ix.).

the staple products of such a state of things. Snobbishness, in its diversified shapes, is a by-product; but this is not so much to the fore in Trollope, who at any rate does not specialize in it, like Thackeray, but simply takes it as it comes. One important result of his choice of such a social world is the semi-public character of many of his stories. The clerical and the higher lay society of Barsetshire, with the De Courcys, Greshams, Thornes, Luftons, and Grantlys, as prominent as the bishops and deans, is everybody's study, like politics or the leading events of the London season. Everyone knows everyone else; and such affairs as the jilting of Lily Dale, the corporal punishment administered to Mr Crosbie or Mr Moffat, Mr Crawley's supposed theft, Lady Glencora's love-affair, or the disappearance of Lizzie Eustace's diamonds, are all public property. Other things that Trollope was good at catching were professional mannerisms and the stamp of groups and sects; his parsons and lawyers and lawyers' clerks have all the marks of their orders, which may cut across other social distinctions, and at the same time are balanced discerningly with the more general human instincts and the more personal motives. But Trollope's interest in the class system was not that of a sociologist; he relished it for its effects on character, and for the comedy it provided. His social perspective was a great deal wider than that of the Brontës, Mrs Gaskell, or Charlotte Yonge; but it had nothing like the scope of Dickens's and Thackeray's. A good many classes are ignored because they had no interest for Trollope. He thought of classes as collections of interesting individuals whose manners and ways of living were fairly uniform, aspects of minor interest to the sociologist. Idiosyncrasy was the prey he was always after. When Frederic Harrison remarked upon the "thorough knowledge of the organism of English society which specially distinguished Trollope," [1] he was a little misleading; organisms and organization are the main concern of the sociologist, not of a Trollope. One elementary proceeding of the sociologist, a primary and indispensable act, is to classify. Trollope was less of a classifier than Thackeray or

---

[1] *Early Victorian Literature*—"Anthony Trollope."

even Dickens. Though he was fond of bestowing designations
which are labels rather than names upon the undistinguished
crowd, such as Miss Gushing, Major Fiasco, Sir Abraham
Haphazard, Dr Fillgrave, Mr Bold, Mr Love, Mr Kissing—
who afforded the Commissioners their little joke that "Kissing,
they feared, went by favour, and that Love would still be lord
of all"—the lawyers Fidus Neverbend and Gitemthruet, or
the election agents, Mr Nearthewinde, Mr Closerstil, and Mr
Reddypalm—a clear sign that these are generic specimens
rather than odd individuals or eccentrics—yet his more distinctive characters are very far indeed from being mere varia-
tions of a few types. A character out of Trollope means
rather such people as Mr Harding, Mrs Proudie, Archdeacon
Grantly, Dr Thorne, Plantagenet Palliser, John Eames, the
Signora Neroni, Miss Dunstable, Mary Thorne, or Grace
Crawley, people who cannot be summarily thrown into the
common categories of saints, snobs, fortune-hunters, flirts,
wiseacres or nincompoops, or mere eccentrics. Dickens cari-
catured, and in so doing provided the classifier with unmistakable earmarks. Even Thackeray, the inventor of Major
Pendennis and Colonel Newcome, and of how many others
who would be recognized anywhere and could not be taken for
anyone else, to a very large extent classified mankind, offering
types, representatives of breeds and sets, for our inspection,
at any rate inviting the reader to classify. He was more of
a moralist, and much more of a satirist, with his snobs, his
blacklegs, and his truckling hypocrites, all busily though
unconsciously anatomizing themselves in the public eye.
Trollope, on the contrary, was bent on showing off the infinite
differences and the inexhaustible comedy of men's peculiarities
of temperament, temper, and mentality, and selfish or generous
outlook. He was all for differentiating between people,
whether of the same sex, station, and type, or otherwise. *The
Book of Snobs* is the natural history of a genus; Trollope's
snobs are all the miscellaneous people whom the reader can
sift out as stamped with this particular foible, among the
traits that assimilate them to or distinguish them from the
rest of the crowd. The same range of variation can be looked

for and found in his rogues, or his lovers, or his parsons, politicians, or other representatives of parts, vices, professions, or social orders: they are all first and foremost individuals. Even his young women and maturing girls, the most likely to be true to sex, age, and position, are very far from being merely true to life. The De Courcy sisters, to take only one instance, have more individuality than the De Courcy brothers. No novelist was a greater contrast than Trollope to those of his profession who were mere machines for turning out articles of a stamp that hardly varied, with the same trade-mark on characters, sentiments, and story.

"The Warden" and "Barchester Towers" After his various false starts, Trollope found himself on the right road at last. *The Warden* (1855), though a minor novel in length, was to lead straight on to the broad and ample and richly diversified comedy of Barsetshire. It was a sort of entrance lodge to *Barchester Towers* (1857), where everybody is intimate with everybody who is anybody in a large neighbourhood. Brief as it was and still tentative, there was quite enough in it for Trollope to find and give full assurance of his power to handle such a group of characters as the gentle, generous, and too-scrupulous Mr Harding; the pig-headed denouncer of his rapacity, Mr Bold; his blustering son-in-law, Archdeacon Grantly; Tom Towers, and the rest of those mixed up more or less with the anomalous affair of the sinecure held by the innocent old precentor. In some points, the case is like certain later ones of disturbed and tormented minds. The heart-searchings of the persecuted warden are almost as distressing as those of Mr Crawley, when he is unable to account for the cheque supposed to be stolen, or even the agonies of Lady Mason brooding over her guilt, in *Orley Farm*. There is, indeed, a superficial parallel to the cases of conscience analysed a little later by George Eliot. But, although Mr Harding does talk and think about his conscience, it is rather his sensitive shrinking from public odium and his doubts of the formal legality of his position that worry him at last into his act of self-renunciation. Trollope could not quite keep clear of controversial bias, though he regarded the warden with so much tenderness; the question was one calling out his polemical

instincts, just as a few years later, in *Orley Farm*, he could not
restrain himself from vituperating the lawyers for defending
cases which they knew to be unsound.[1] But he scrambled
back to an attitude of impartiality; and the reader is left free
to enjoy the bickering of the archdeacon and other defenders,
the love-dilemma of Bold, who marries the daughter of the man
whom, as he avers, out of pure public spirit, he is compelled to
attack, the parodying of Carlyle and a magisterial Press in the
fulminations of Mr Anticant and the *Jupiter*, and all the byplay of the pensioners, the mild old bishop, and other onlookers,
each with his private views, disinterested or otherwise, on the
whole affair. Mr Harding is no hero; yet he proves himself
worthy of appearing in every one of the Barchester novels;
and so does his opposite in disposition, the archdeacon, of
figuring in nearly all. Bold also was probably meant for
further service; but Trollope killed him off, leaving Mrs
Bold as a widow to be the nominal "heroine" of the subsequent book, little as she deserves it. With other newcomers,
Trollope's finest pair of protagonists now enter on the scene:
Mrs Proudie, wife of "the most hen-pecked man on the
episcopal bench," and Mr Slope, a character drawn almost
spitefully and yet not exactly a caricature—perhaps the nearest
approach to the sour malignancy of Smollett's realistic portraiture to be found anywhere. After enumerating his large
mouth, with thin and bloodless lips, the prominent eyes, and
the big nose, of a spongy texture, "as though it had been
cleverly formed out of a red coloured cork," Trollope breaks
in himself,

I never could endure to shake hands with Mr Slope. A
cold, clammy perspiration always exudes from him; the small
drops are ever to be seen standing on his brow, and his friendly
grasp is unpleasant.

It seems hardly fair for the novelist to interpose like that with
his personal dislike, though it was a habit of which Trollope

[1] "There were five lawyers concerned, not one of whom gave to the course of
justice credit that it would ascertain the truth, and not one of whom wished that
the truth should be ascertained. Surely, had they been honest-minded in their
profession," etc., etc. (*Orley Farm*, lvi.).

never tried to break himself; but as an illicit stroke of sheer
actuality it is murderously effective: no one can disbelieve in
Mr Slope after that, and everyone watches with bloodthirsty
delight the guerrilla warfare between him and Mrs Proudie.
That lady achieves the honours of both sexes, notably in the
scene where she turns on Mr Slope with her "Do you bandy
words with me, you ungrateful man?" and summons her
spouse to do his duty as head of the diocese. She remains
undiscomfited until the parallel scene in *The Last Chronicle*,
when Mr Crawley rebukes her with his "Peace, woman;
you should not interfere in these matters. You simply debase
your husband's high office. The distaff were more fitting for
you." But, as Trollope points out, "she was not all devil."
Mrs Proudie had some sort of a heart within her stiff-ribbed
bodice, and was touched by the woes of Mrs Quiverful, whose
expectations of an appointment she would not allow to be
cozened away "by the treachery of Mr Slope and the weakness
of her husband." Trollope's charity is never-failing, even for
his scamps or his ogres. He is entirely on her side, and he
enlists the reader with him, in the Medea passage, when the
bishop proposes to make Mr Slope dean of Barchester. "Dean
of Barchester, indeed! I'll dean him." "The hyena laughed
out."

Medea, when she describes the customs of her native
country,—I am quoting from Robson's edition—assures her
astonished auditor that in her land captives, when taken, are
eaten. "You pardon them?" says Medea. "We do indeed,"
says the mild Grecian. "We eat them!" says she of Colchis,
with terrific energy. Mrs Proudie was the Medea of
Barchester. She had no idea of not eating Mr Slope. Pardon
him! merely get rid of him! make a dean of him! It was not
so they did with their captives in her country, among people
of her sort! Mr Slope had no such mercy to expect. She
would pick him to the very last bone.

But, though Trollope compels the reader to take sides here
with the exasperated fury, his charity, not to say his regard for
verisimilitude, will not let him do more injustice to Mr Slope's
remarkable abilities than he will do presently to the Stanhopes,

whose great family characteristic was heartlessness, which want of feeling was "accompanied by so great an amount of good nature as to make itself but little noticeable to the world." *Barchester Towers* contains several of his most memorable scenes, besides the one just quoted; pitched battles, they might be called. There is the one in which Mrs Bold slaps the face of the too-presuming Mr Slope, and the earlier scene in which Mr Slope is too much even for Mrs Proudie, which will be quoted presently as an example of Trollope's efficient dialogue. And, as to the wickedest of the naughty but ingratiating Stanhopes, there is the accident to Mrs Proudie's lace train and that irate lady's "Unhand it, sir!" to the irreverent Ethelbert, with the sequel that goes one better:

"It's not me; it's the cursed sofa," said Bertie, looking imploringly in her face, and holding up both his hands to show that he was not touching her belongings, but still remaining on his knees.

Hereupon the Signora laughed; not loud, indeed, but yet audibly. And as the tigress bereft of her young will turn with equal anger on any within reach, so did Mrs Proudie turn upon her female guest.

"Madam!" she said—and it is beyond the power of prose to tell of the fire which flashed from her eyes.

The Signora stared her full in the face for a moment, and then turning to her brother said, playfully, "Bertie, you idiot, get up."

The Signora Neroni is not much more than a sketch, but it is a sketch masterly enough to hang among the choicest performances in Trollope's gallery. He never did anything subtler or more complex, even with many more strokes. To say that the Stanhope good nature redeems her would be feeble and not strictly true, though she electrifies the virtuous Mrs Bold when she takes up the cudgels for the absent Mr Arabin:

"Do you love him, love him with all your heart and soul, with all the love your bosom can feel? For I can tell you that he loves you, adores you, worships you, thinks of you and nothing else, is now thinking of you as he attempts to write his sermon for next Sunday's preaching. What would

I not give to be loved in such a way by such a man—that is, if I were an object fit for any man to love!"

Not too often can it be said of Trollope's characters that one would gladly see a great deal more of them; but it is true of the Stanhopes. The lady has that with which Trollope can endow even the unlikeliest of his creations, magnanimity, which he can withhold even from such patterns of excellence as Mrs Bold.

"Doctor Thorne" —Trollope's handling of plot

The next of the series (1858) has Trollope's most flawless heroine, and a plot, not his own, which among other things ensures the happy mean between the diffused, the Barsetshire interest, and the personal, the suspense in which Mary's fate and the happiness of Dr Thorne, who is more to her than a father, hang trembling, as they should in a good story, before the symmetrical close. The windows look out on Barset, and the neighbouring great house is that of the chief commoner of the shire, whose heir is in love with Mary. On this very question of suspense, Trollope delivered his views candidly and at some length in *Barchester Towers*:

Here, perhaps, it may be allowed to the novelist to explain his views on a very important point in the art of telling tales. He ventures to reprobate that system which goes so far to violate all proper confidence between the author and his readers, by maintaining nearly to the end of the third volume a mystery as to the fate of their favourite personage. Nay, more, and worse than this, is too frequently done. Have not often the profoundest efforts of genius been used to baffle the aspirations of the reader, to raise false hopes and false fears, and to give rise to expectations which are never to be realized? . . . Our doctrine is, that the author and the reader should move along together in full confidence with each other. Let the personages of the drama undergo ever so complete a comedy of errors among themselves, but let the spectator never mistake the Syracusan for the Ephesian. Otherwise he is one of the dupes, and the part of a dupe is never dignified.[1]

And he says in the first few pages here, with regard to Frank Gresham, "I am too old now to be a hard-hearted author, and

[1] Chap. xv.

so it is probable that he may not die of a broken heart." In fact, whatever the hints received from Adolphus Trollope may have amounted to, the plot worked out here is simply the resultant of a set of given factors, with a new one introduced a little later. The element of surprise, mystery, or suspense is reduced to what the sympathetic reader can stand without protest. His history is implicit in a man's character, as George Eliot was to insist with philosophic solemnity. Here the end can be roughly forecast from the characters and their situation with regard to each other. Frank is faced with the alternative, Mary or money. He is young enough and disinterested enough to vote for the former, but is faced with the paternal fiat, no money, no Mary. But at this point the reader is let into the secret that Frank may after all be able to marry her and have both. For the present, no one else, neither Frank nor Mary, nor even Dr Thorne, realizes the altered circumstances. Only the doctor is aware even that the man from the backwoods with the colossal fortune, who eventually secures a mortgage on most of Frank's father's estate, is actually Mary's uncle. But the reader who knows his Trollope can now breathe freely; he guesses pretty nearly what will happen, and has the pleasures without the pangs of suspense. He can watch the interplay of motive, and enjoy the attempts on Frank's constancy, and such incidents as his proposal to that shrewdest and merriest of bluestockings, Miss Dunstable, without fearing that there is no escape for the lovers, short of a miracle. Trollope, in brief, is offering the novel-reader a new bill of fare. He has removed the heavier dishes and the grosser stimulants, and provided something more savoury for the real epicure. And he is like a motherly waiter in his zeal for pointing out the merits of the chief dainties. Trollope always plays the part of showman, and there is no stint of authorial comment, to underline the fine points and all that is at stake. Read the many stage-directions in the chapter of talk on "Matrimonial Prospects"; and note also how Trollope overdoes his solicitude when, between the receipt of Mary's last letter and the reply in which Frank clinches his loyalty, he observes, "Perhaps it was well for Mary's happiness that he had seen Miss Dunstable in the interval." This was casting an unjust slur on her lover's stanchness.

"Fram-
ley Par-
sonage"
—the
social
comedy
He went farther afield in the next novel (1861), which rambles all over both East and West Barsetshire, and brings in not only the Thornes, Greshams, and De Courcys, and the cathedral clique, but also the Luftons, the Dales, Sowerby of Chaldicotes, and the great Duke of Omnium, who gives a famous dinner to the mob of parasites, and the few whose mind was their own, at Gatherum Castle. It is the most comprehensive survey of this chosen world of Trollope's, and serious comedy on the whole; approximating to Jane Austen's in such side-issues as that of Lucy Robarts, generously subduing her affection for Lord Lufton; growing almost tragic when it touches on such things as the Crawley affairs; but relieved with any amount of lighter comedy, and such drolleries of caricature as Mr Harold Smith's lecture, punctuated with Mrs Proudie's interruptions, or the wordless encounter of Lady Lufton and the Duke. The political business is treated with a flippancy that sounds almost like scoffs at Disraeli, whose earlier political novels were by now only a legend but were still awaiting their sequels in *Lothair* and *Endymion*. More probably, however, Trollope had no definite butt. He used to swear, at this date, that he did not understand politics.[1] But politics and all the other miscellaneous interests are dovetailed into each other; and they do dovetail. As yet Trollope had not caught the mania for interlacing a number of odd-come-short stories into a mere pretence at unity, as if there was a competition to see how many different tales could be told at a time. The matrimonial schemes for uniting Lord Lufton and Griselda Grantly, who frustrates Lady Lufton by securing the higher prize of Lord Dumbello, set off Lufton's real love-affair with Lucy Robarts, and go not incongruously with the unfortunate monetary affairs of the Rev. Mark Robarts and his dealings with Mr Sowerby, the fluttering of the fortune-hunters round the Dunstable flame, and the covert envy, hatred, and malice

[1] See, for instance, his impatient account of Mr Gresham's politics (in *Doctor Thorne*, xv.). He speaks of the coquetting of the Conservatives with the Manchester school, "through some inscrutable twists in modern politics which are quite unintelligible to the minds of ordinary men outside the circle."

between Lady Lufton and Mrs Grantly, Lady Lufton and the Duke, or Mrs Proudie and any chance offender against Broad Church decorum. The leading characters sustain their parts with perfect lifelikeness, or rather, the comedy in which they perform arises in the most lifelike way from their natural dispositions and contacts. Lady Lufton is worthy of Jane Austen; so is the loving and self-suppressing and courageous Lucy Robarts, and so are those delightful anomalies, the Earl and Lady Julia de Guest, in the *Small House* which followed. The immaculate Lord Lufton, the statuesque but not insipid Griselda Grantly,[1] her impassive bridegroom, Lord Dumbello, "whose muteness was his most eloquent mode of expression," that irresistible rogue, Mr Sowerby, with his victim, Mark Robarts, form an omnium gatherum rich in comic possibilities. Lady Arabella is still on show, and hard-headed and caustic Miss Dunstable is still always coming in with the downright sense that her name historically betokens. Trollope revives the old cony-catching tradition in the seducing Sowerby, seducing in a double sense, for his bonhomie and cool impudence capture the reader as well as the Reverend Mark. "As a clergyman it would be wrong of me," said Robarts, when Mr Sowerby asks him to write "Accepted" across the bill.

"As a clergyman! Come, Mark! If you don't like to do as much as that for a friend, say so; but don't let us have that sort of humbug. If there be one class of men whose names would be found more frequent on the bills in the provincial banks than another, clergymen are that class. Come, old fellow, you won't throw me over when I am so hard pushed." Mark Robarts took the pen and signed the bill. It was the first time in his life that he had ever done such an act. Sowerby then shook him cordially by the hand, and he walked off to his own bedroom a wretched man.

The dialogue which comes to the point at once and gets something done, a difference patched up, a war to the knife

---

[1] Archdeacon Grantly always insisted that Griselda was "clever": "Griselda not clever! Good heavens!" Griselda's letter to her mamma, which she diplomatically shows to Lord Dumbello, after Plantagenet Palliser's cautious essay at love-making (*Small House*, ii., chap. xxv.), is a masterpiece of unruffled innocence that should convince the most sceptical.

launched, a blunder or other mischancy act committed on which fatal issues will presently hinge, is the best possible instrument for comedy. Plentiful use had been made of it in *Barchester Towers*, for instance, in the little episode, to be read and read again, when Mrs Proudie turns on Mr Slope and is herself overthrown.

"Mr Slope," she repeated, "I wish to be alone with my lord."

"His lordship has summoned me on a most important diocesan business," said Mr Slope, glancing with uneasy eye at Dr Proudie. He felt that he must trust something to the bishop, and yet that trust was woefully ill-placed. "My leaving him at the present moment is, I fear, impossible."

"Do you bandy words with me, you ungrateful man?" said she. "My lord, will you do me the favour to beg Mr Slope to leave the room?" My lord scratched his head, but for the moment said nothing. This was as much as Mr Slope expected from him, and was, for him, an active exercise of marital rights. "My lord," said the lady, "is Mr Slope to leave this room, or am I?"

Here Mrs Proudie made a false step. She should not have alluded to the possibility of retreat on her part. She should not have expressed the idea that her order for Mr Slope's expulsion could be treated otherwise than by immediate obedience. In answer to such a question the bishop naturally said in his own mind, that as it was necessary that one should leave the room, perhaps it might be as well that Mrs Proudie did so. He did say so in his own mind, but externally he again scratched his head and again twiddled his thumbs.

Mrs Proudie was boiling over with wrath. Alas, alas! could she but have kept her temper as her enemy did, she would have conquered as she had ever conquered. But divine anger got the better of her, as it had done of other heroines, and she fell.

"My lord," said she, "am I to be vouchsafed an answer or am I not?"

At last he broke his deep silence and proclaimed himself a Slopeite. "Why, my dear," said he, "Mr Slope and I are very busy."

That was all. There was nothing more necessary. He had gone to the battle-field, stood the dust and heat of the day, encountered the fury of the foe, and won the victory. How easy is success to those who will only be true to themselves!

It will be noticed that the showman is on duty all the time; Trollope did not think novels should be written like plays, with the barest minimum of stage signs. Certainly, the contrary method pays in this case. So again in the ironical situation when Mrs Grantly breaks the news to Lady Lufton that her daughter and Lord Dumbello are going to make a match of it.

"Poor dear Griselda!" said Mrs Grantly, almost with a sigh. "I need not tell you, Lady Lufton, what my hopes were regarding her."

"Has she told you anything--anything that——"

"She would have spoken to you at once—and it was due to you that she should have done so—but she was timid; and not unnaturally so. And then it was right that she should see her father and me before she quite made up her own mind. But I may say that it is settled now."

"What is settled?" asked Lady Lufton.

"Of course it is impossible for anyone to tell beforehand how these things will turn out," continued Mrs Grantly, beating about the bush rather more than was necessary. "The dearest wish of my heart was to see her married to Lord Lufton. I should so much have wished to have her in the same county with me, and such a match as that would have fully satisfied my ambition."

"Well, I should rather think it might!" Lady Lufton did not say this our loud, but she thought it. ... .

"Dear Mrs Grantly," she said, "I have foreseen for the last few days that our mutual hopes in this respect would not be gratified. Lord Lufton, I think;—but perhaps it is not necessary to explain—— Had you not come up to town I should have written to you—probably to-day. Whatever may be dear Griselda's fate in life, I sincerely hope that she may be happy."

"I think she will," said Mrs Grantly, in a tone that expressed much satisfaction.

"Has—has anything——"

"Lord Dumbello proposed to Griselda the other night, at Miss Dunstable's party," said Mrs Grantly, with her eyes fixed upon the floor, and assuming on the sudden much meekness in her manner; "and his lordship was with the archdeacon yesterday, and again this morning. I fancy he is in Mount Street at the present moment.

"Oh, indeed!" said Lady Lufton. She would have given worlds to have possessed at the moment sufficient self-command to have enabled her to express in her tone and manner unqualified satisfaction at the tidings. But she had not such self-command, and was painfully aware of her own deficiency.

"Yes," said Mrs Grantly. "And as it is all so far settled, and as I know you are so kindly anxious about dear Griselda, I thought it right to let you know at once. Nothing can be more upright, honourable, and generous, than Lord Dumbello's conduct; and, on the whole, the match is one with which I and the archdeacon cannot but be contented."

"It is certainly a great match," said Lady Lufton. "Have you seen Lady Hartletop yet?"

Now Lady Hartletop could not be regarded as an agreeable connexion, but this was the only word which escaped from Lady Lufton that could be considered in any way disparaging, and, on the whole, I think that she behaved well.

"The Small House" and "The Last Chronicle"

Some other novels and two gatherings of hunting and travelling sketches intervened between the two final numbers of the Barsetshire series, *The Small House at Allington* (1864) and *The Last Chronicle of Barset* (1867). The focusing-points in these two are the jilting of Lily Dale, with Crosbie's dismal expiation, and the terrible ado over Mr Crawley and the mysterious cheque. But in both Trollope gave way to the lust for sub-plots, and the *Last Chronicle* especially is full of loosely-connected affairs not all properly rounded off. It is an enormously crowded canvas, most of the Barsetshire worthies appearing and delivering the upshot of their several stories, and Mrs Proudie signalizing the event by dying, though Trollope had once said that she ought to live for ever. No doubt, he meant something when he called the first of the pair *The Small House.* You are to turn, he seems to say, from the buying and selling and the insidious flirtations of Courcy Castle, and contrast society love-making with the all-absorbing affection of a Lily Dale, or the staid and honourable marriage of Bell and Dr Crofts. The misalliances of the De Courcys and the surreptitious profligacy of the Honourable John cannot stand such a comparison. True, the pretty idyll of the Allington Lily comes to a sad end; but she and the Small House do keep faith; and life there is better to look at, even after their chastening, than the hollow garishness of the big mansion. There is, indeed, as full a measure of moral expatiation in these two as in any of Trollope's novels. Even the spiteful neighbours, Mrs Boyce and her daughters, talk pharisaically about the lesson to be learned from Mrs Dale's family misfortunes: "Bell and Lily were about to have a fall in the world," so "they were to be treated accordingly," in other words, with the condescending pity of those who were now demonstrably their betters. Crosbie is formally judged, after being chastised by John Eames and still more severely by Lady Alexandrina's domestic discipline; though Trollope tempers the sentence with his usual forbearance. The fact is, though he took special pains with Crosbie, this character is not quite consistent from first to last; or perhaps it would be nearer the mark to say that there is a sort of foreshortening just where it ought to have been made perfectly clear that the Crosbie who fascinates Lily Dale is veritably the Crosbie who succumbs to the wiles of Alexandrina. Whether Lily would ever have fallen in love so precipitately with the man about town is another matter. But, though he wrestles with his conscience for pages on pages, and the duel in which Lady Alexandrina brings him down is Trollope's dialogue at its very best, this sudden collapse of the newly affianced of Lily is not thoroughly substantiated. Crosbie, however, is only of secondary importance; he is merely the false lover required in the story of a heroine true till death. Trollope might have been competing with the hyperbolic tales of woman's constancy in old French romance. Lily is at first a bewitching, and then a pathetic figure, but in the long run only an offering to sentimentalism—or to Trollope's own obstinacy. She tired even him out at last, and in the *Autobiography* he had to admit "she was somewhat of a French prig." But he might reasonably have pointed out that she shared the well-known obstinacy of the Dales, like Bernard and the stern old squire. Obstinacy was not an attitude of mind that came natural to Trollope, nor was it one he would naturally bestow on an admired heroine, even under the name of steadfastness. Both these novels provide some curious questions for our modern psychoanalysts. The strange case of the perpetual curate of Hogglestock is obviously one to delight them; but this of John Eames and Lily Dale opens up side-issues quite as abstruse. John is more than a chip of the author's own block. Trollope had made use of certain personal facts in the history of Charley Tudor, in *The Three Clerks*; in John Eames, and in different ways in Phineas Finn, Ralph the Heir, and Dr Wortle, he projected bits at least of his own character and mental experiences, exactly how much it is impossible to say. Maybe he was not fully aware of what he was doing; Trollope was no introvert. But there is certainly much self-betrayal in John Eames, if only a half-betrayal, and this entirely apart from John's entanglement with "Ameliar," which was his author's own plight.[1] The humiliations endured in Trollope's schooldays left a deposit at the bottom of his consciousness which sometimes came to the top. They account more than any natural predisposition for the diffidence and shyness to which he always remained prone, his boisterous optimism and blustering self-assertion being simply the attitudes instinctively adopted in self-defence, or self-defiance. There must be something in the theory of "inferiority complexes," in spite of the infamous English in which it is expounded. A good deal of sheer bravado must be discounted in that buoyant *Autobiography* of his. John Eames is just such another mingling of opposites; and the contradictions in him, with the uncertainties that he excites in some critics, are surely to be explained by the view that his shyness and hesitations, the want of tact at trying moments, and the noisy good nature and jollity, are Trollope himself. Both the author and this favourite character are self-distrustful, both all but succeed in dissembling these infirmities even to themselves. To fulfil Trollope's first resolve, Lily Dale had to remain inflexible,

[1] "Anthony Trollope, when are you going to marry my daughter?" (*Autobiography*, iii.).

though she can offer no better apology than that she once "liked somebody else better," or, as the writer himself put it, "A man of such a character, known by a girl from his boyhood as John Eames had been known by Lily Dale, was likely to find more favour as a friend than as a lover." Perhaps some old, half-forgotten experience, some personal disillusionment, lurked at the back of Trollope's mind, when he stiffened himself never to give L.D. to J.E.

Trollope thoroughly enjoyed himself in the *Last Chronicle*, and was not too careful of lucidity and perfect coherence. He had no business to drag in so many fresh motives which are mere erratic excursions. He loved to recall characters from other books; several here were to appear yet again. It was out of sheer delight in their amiable eccentricities; and one at first welcomes them back, in spite of the ceremonious introduction thought necessary every time. But when they go on parading the same old foibles, the reader, like the characters, becomes exhausted. Mr Crawley's misfortunes had been given in an abridged form in *Framley Parsonage*; and the principal new dish is the philandering of John Eames and Madalina Desmolines, and of that abandoned sentimentalist, Mrs Dobbs Broughton, and Conway Dalrymple, which sails nearer the wind than Trollope usually ventures. The Crawley affair is often cited as an example of our author's tragic power.[1] Tragic power is certainly exhibited, but the case itself is not tragedy. Mr Crawley is not a man hounded by his wrongs and by utter despair into the commission of a felony. He is guilty of no crime, only of a strange but perfectly intelligible lapse of memory. It brings agonies upon his own head, and intense suffering to his family. Terrible are the "black moods" into which his and their misery leads him:

> What she most dreaded was that he should sit idle over the fire and do nothing. When he was so seated she could read his mind, as though it was open to her as a book. She had been quite right when she had accused him of over-indulgence

Tragi-comedy and some idealism

[1] A well-known clergyman was so impressed by Trollope's realism that during the suspense created by the *Last Chronicle* he included the name of the Rev. Josiah Crawley among the persons to be especially remembered in the prayer for "all those who are any ways afflicted, or distressed, in mind, body, or estate."

in his grief. He did give way to it till it became a luxury to him—a luxury which she would not have had the heart to deny him had she not felt it to be of all luxuries the most pernicious. During these long hours, in which he would sit speechless, doing nothing, he was telling himself from minute to minute that of all God's creatures he was the most heavily afflicted, and was revelling in the sense of the injustice done to him.[1]

Yet his wife's and his friends' belief in him relieves the anguish, for the sympathetic reader, and yields that exaltation of feeling which ought to be experienced from the contemplation of tragic life. And there is another sort of sublimity in Grace Crawley's unselfconscious self-devotion, in the great scene between her and the archdeacon, in which that man of the world also attains something like sublimity. The archdeacon had been remonstrating with Grace on what he called his son's behalf.

"Now, Miss Crawley, pray listen to me. I will speak to you very openly. I must speak to you openly, because it is my duty on my son's behalf;—but I will endeavour to speak to you kindly also. Of yourself I have heard nothing but what is favourable, and there is no reason as yet why I should not respect and esteem you." Grace told herself that she would do nothing which ought to forfeit his respect and esteem, but that she did not care two straws whether his respect and esteem were bestowed or not. She was striving after something very different from that. "If my son were to marry you, he would greatly injure himself, and would very greatly injure his child. . . . Now, Miss Crawley, of course I cannot wish to say a word that shall hurt your feelings. But there are reasons——"

"I know," said she, interrupting him. "Papa is accused of stealing money. He did not steal it, but people think he did. And then we are so very poor."

---

[1] Cp. *Framley Parsonage* (chap. xv.): "He had always at his heart a feeling that he and his had been ill-used, and he often solaced himself, at the Devil's bidding, with the conviction that eternity would make equal that which life in this world had made so unequal; the last bait that with which the Devil angles after those who are struggling to elude his rod and line."

"You do understand me then,—and I feel grateful; I do indeed."

"I don't think our being poor ought to signify a bit," said Grace. "Papa is a gentleman and a clergyman, and mamma is a lady."

"But, my dear——"

"I know I ought not to be your son's wife as long as people think that papa stole the money. If he had stolen it, I ought never to be Major Grantly's wife—or anybody's wife. I know that very well. And as for Edith—I would sooner die than do anything that would be bad to her."

The archdeacon had now left the rug, and advanced till he was almost close to the chair on which Grace was sitting. "My dear," he said, "what you say does you very much honour—very much honour indeed." Now that he was close to her, he could look into her eyes, and he could see the exact form of her features, and could understand—could not help understanding—the character of her countenance. It was a noble face, having in it nothing that was poor, nothing that was mean, nothing that was shapeless. It was a face that promised infinite beauty, with a promise that was just on the very verge of fulfilment. There was a play about her mouth as she spoke, and a curl in her nostril as the eager words came from her, which almost made the selfish father give way. Why had they not told him that she was such a one as this? Why had not Henry himself spoken of the speciality of her beauty? No man in England knew better than the archdeacon the difference between beauty of one kind and beauty of another kind in a woman's face—the one beauty, which comes from health and youth and animal spirits, and which belongs to the miller's daughter, and the other beauty, which shows itself in fine lines and a noble spirit—the beauty which comes from breeding. "What you say does you very much honour indeed," said the archdeacon.

"I should not mind at all about being poor," said Grace.

"No; no; no," said the archdeacon.

"Poor as we are—and no clergyman, I think, ever was so poor—I should have done as your son asked me at once, if it had been only that—because I love him."

"If you love him you will not wish to injure him."

"I will not injure him. Sir, there is my promise." And

now as she spoke she rose from her chair, and standing close to the archdeacon, laid her hand very lightly on the sleeve of his coat. "There is my promise. As long as people say that papa stole the money, I will never marry your son. There." The archdeacon was still looking down at her, and feeling the slight touch of her fingers, raised his arm a little as though to welcome the pressure. He looked into her eyes, which were turned eagerly towards his, and when doing so was quite sure that the promise would be kept. It would have been sacrilege—he felt that it would have been sacrilege—to doubt such a promise. He almost relented. His soft heart, which was never very well under his own control, gave way so far that he was nearly moved to tell her that, on his son's behalf, he acquitted her of the promise. What could any man's son do better than have such a woman for his wife?

Two tears trickled down his old nose; and who can read this scene without being moved to tears by the sheer beauty of it? Nor is that beauty marred by Mrs Grantly's dry comment, when her husband tells her how it is he has come to take a very different view of his son's love-affair. Humour is fatal to sentimentalism; it cannot hurt that which is genuine and noble. Superficially the least romantic of all Victorian novelists, Trollope was not, after all, utterly devoid of the finer romance. He read the poets, he said, with reverence, which meant, with a somewhat distant respect for them and for those who understood them; but it was his inveterate diffidence, his doubt whether he fully appreciated poetry, that deterred him from quitting the path of well-trod realities. The crucial evidence, however, for any poetry there was in him, any romance, any idealism, is in the generous feelings and self-abnegating motives that he regards as perfectly natural, as the reverse of surprising and extraordinary, in such as Mr Harding, Grace Crawley and her father, Dr Thorne in all the beauty of his devotion to Mary,[1] Sir Peregrine and Mrs Orme, the one with his quixotism, the other with her unchangeable

[1] There is a piquant contrast between the passage in *Dr Thorne* (xiii.—"The Two Uncles"), where the old doctor is outraged by the coarsely benevolent sentiments of Sir Roger Scatcherd towards his precious Mary, and the gross pecuniary motives that throw Miss Gresham into the arms of Mr Moffat in the subsequent chapter. "Beauty is truth"; but truth is sometimes the very opposite.

affection for the guilty Lady Mason, in *Orley Farm*; or in such acts as Plantagenet Palliser's when he refuses the offer of the Chancellorship to try to make up to Lady Glencora for a loveless marriage, in *Can You Forgive Her?*; or the goodness of the unhappy Burgo Fitzgerald, in the same novel, to the poor street-walker:

He took her to a public-house and gave her bread and meat and beer, and stood by her while she ate it. She was shy with him then, and would fain have taken it to a corner by herself, had he allowed her. He perceived this, and turned his back to her, but still spoke to her a word or two as she ate. The woman at the bar who served him looked at him wonderingly, staring into his face; and the potboy woke himself thoroughly that he might look at Burgo; and the waterman from the cab-stand stared at him; and women who came in for gin looked almost lovingly up into his eyes. He regarded them all not at all, showing no feeling of disgrace at his position, and no desire to carry himself as a ruffler. He quietly paid what was due when the girl had finished her meal, and then walked with her out of the shop. "And now," said he, "what must I do with you? If I give you a shilling can you get a bed?" She told him that she could get a bed for sixpence. "Then keep the other sixpence for your breakfast," said he. "But you must promise me that you will buy no gin to-night." She promised him, and then he gave her his hand as he wished her good-night—his hand, which it had been the dearest wish of Lady Glencora to call her own. She took it and pressed it to her lips. "I wish I might once see you again," she said, "because you are so good and so beautiful." He laughed again cheerily, and walked on, crossing the street towards Cavendish Square. She stood looking at him till he was out of sight, and then as she moved away—let us hope to the bed which his bounty had provided, and not to a gin-shop —she exclaimed to herself again and again—"Gracious, how beautiful he was!" "He's a good un," the woman at the public-house had said as soon as he left it; "but my! did you ever see a man's face handsome as that fellow's?"

The poetry is not so much in the sudden impulse, as in the sudden clear revelation of all it meant to that little knot of human creatures. Trollope's easy-going attitude to sinners led to charges of worldliness, moral indifference, and even cynicism. But such instances as these show what he believed our nature is capable of. His Mary Thorne, Lily Dale—all the more that she errs on the right side—Grace Crawley, and many a lesser actor in the social drama who is an example of pure integrity, are proof enough that his belief in mankind's potentialities was neither cynical nor prosaic.

Novels of political life   At the end of the *Last Chronicle*, Trollope explains why in the Barsetshire novels, which deal so largely with clergymen, there is hardly a word about religion or the Church as a spiritual entity. His ecclesiastics are like any other members of the upper classes, not particularly religious, at any rate in their personal and social relations, but rather of the world worldly. They take their part regularly in social amusements; they hunt, some of them bet and gamble; and, apart from the formal Sabbath-keeping of such as Lady Gazebee and a perfunctory condemnation of dancing by Mrs Proudie, no one thinks any special strictness of life or a good example incumbent on them as a class. How differently such a writer as Hawthorne would have handled the themes naturally arising; how altogether otherwise George Eliot was about to do so! Trollope was far too reserved and diffident to touch such questions, except in such exceptional cases as Mr Harding's, Mr Crawley's, or that of Mark Robarts, where the black coat and clerical collar laid the wearer open, rather more than the man in the street, to remarks on his behaviour. The world of politics and the political arena were only another tract of country which offered Trollope similar opportunities. His novels in this next group are not political in the way Disraeli's were, though he read up the subject beforehand, and stood as Liberal candidate for Beverley in 1868. Many slips have been pointed out in his allusions to parliamentary procedure, due to his reliance on second-hand information: he had no serious interest in politics. The subject, or object, is again character, or rather characters. The politics in question are the party game, which was as good a sport as whist or hunting. For some, it is a career, as with Phineas Finn, the chief but not the most

interesting figure in the novel named after him (1866) and its
sequel, *Phineas Redux* (1874). The series had already been
started in *Can You Forgive Her?* (1864–1865); *Ralph the Heir*
(1871) came between the two Phineas stories, and the sequence
was continued in *The Prime Minister* (1876) and *The Duke's
Children* (1880). In the first, the marital drama between
Plantagenet Palliser and Lady Glencora gives a sharp personal
interest to these two which saves them from ever lapsing into
mere figureheads. They are leading characters right to the end,
and characters whose personality develops; hence Trollope's
anxiety that these novels should be read as a sequence. He
thought Palliser his best picture of a great gentleman, and
Lady Glencora, with all her faults, a very woman. "Taking
him altogether," he said, "I think that Plantagenet Palliser
stands more firmly on the ground than any other personage I
have created."[1] As to Phineas Finn, it is not by any means
obvious at a glance whether he is a Liberal or a Tory, nor does
it much matter. He wanted to get into Parliament, as he
thought it a field in which he could display ability and creep
into office, so evading the drudgery of a barrister's life in
Dublin. An axiom of the time-serving Barrington Erle was
men not measures; "when he was told of any man, that that
man intended to look to measures and not to men, he regarded
that man as being both unstable as water and dishonest as the
wind." And even Lady Laura, whom Phineas regards as his
mentor, lays no stress on a political conscience: "A political
leader is so sure of support and so sure of attack, that it is hardly
necessary for him to be even anxious to be right."

In many, perhaps in most, of Trollope's novels he sticks to *Bent for*
the common order of things, the even tenor, the situations that *psycho-*
are always recurring, and is content to show that these are not *logical*
so commonplace as they are usually supposed, and to reveal *analysis*
depths and delicacies of heart and mind which are quite
unexpected, with of course the emotions experienced by
everyone at the crises of existence. But he was growing more
and more interested in exceptional natures, motives not so
easy to account for, bizarre relationships between people, and

[1] *Autobiography*, x.

faults out of the common order. In *Orley Farm*, he had
thought of one of those strange acts which stirred his imagination and set him improvising; and in *Can You Forgive Her?*,
Phineas Redux, *The Claverings*, and *He Knew he was Right*, he
tried to solve some of the more perplexing problems which now
and then confront the individual in the ups and downs of life.
Phineas Finn, as has been said, is far from being the one person
who engrosses attention in the two novels bearing his name.
The interest centres rather in Violet Effingham, whom he loves,
in "that red devil," Lord Chiltern, a seasonable example of
Matthew Arnold's "barbarians" and of the muscular hero of
the day, like Kingsley's berserks; and in Lady Laura, in love
with Phineas, yet obliged to lend a patient ear to his sighs for
Violet Effingham. Another exotic character is Madame Max
Goesler, to whom the senile Duke of Omnium offers his hand
when she declines to be his mistress.

No great A growing psychological curiosity is shown again in Trollope's
complexity study of the chill remorseless marital tyranny of Robert
or pro- Kenneby, and the rancorous, though unconfessed and perhaps
fundity only half-conscious, jealousy which in the second novel drives
him stark mad—like the monomaniac husband in *He Knew he
was Right*. Phineas and Lady Laura try to be confidants; yet
her mind and his are beyond a certain limit impenetrable to
each other. Then, another fine point, the rivalry of Chiltern
and Phineas is prolonged by the very fact that Violet Effingham
"could treat her rejected lovers as dear familiar friends immediately after her rejection of them." In *Orley Farm*, Trollope
did not explore far into the depths. For one thing, he kept
too near the ordinary commercial pattern of serial fiction, with
its alternations of grave and gay, serious and assuaging; he
introduced sub-plots and intertwined love-stories, as if it
were not sufficient to tell a tale, he must relate a whole batch
under one. There are only too many complications in *Orley
Farm*; but the gist of it, Lady Mason's culpability and her
shame, is the simple sequence of crime, remorse, and the dread
conflict with herself which is more tragic than the legal exposure.
Trollope here achieves the truest pathos; and among those
poignant ironies which herald tragedy is the incident in which

the stricken woman's son eagerly assures her of his faith in her innocence, whilst she is borne down by the knowledge of her guilt and the consciousness that the poor boy must be told, and by whom if not by herself? There are tragic sides to the serio-comedy of *Can You Forgive Her?* apart from the unhappy imbroglio of Lady Glencora and her husband. The lady referred to in the title does not endear herself by her virtues, nor does the man who gives her up to a man who had previously left her, but returns to her at last. And he who is twice rejected forfeits any sympathy by his sheer rascality and glaring lack of chivalry. But this novel is at any rate a sound example of Trollope's grounding of everything in character; character is the whole foundation, and character is the mainspring and the test of everything that happens. Chance is thrown overboard. It is the same, and more pleasingly, in the quiet little story of a small town in Devon, *Rachel Ray* (1863), as quietly humorous as one of Jane Austen's domestic dramas, in which Trollope indulges in some mild satire of scandal-mongering gossips, and pokes fun at the Nonconformist conscience, as a sly retort to the "unco guid," hated by his mother. It was not solely on account of the stir about Rachel's going to the dance that Norman Macleod refused it for *Good Words*; or did Trollope barb it more pointedly after the rejection? Mrs Prime and Mr Prong are the chief media of the satire; the latter is almost caricature. Here once more Trollope is seen making the most ordinary things interesting, and for the time being absolutely absorbing. The young man, and the young woman too, are shown from the inside, in their most private thoughts; but they have no esoteric thoughts or feelings; they are healthy, normal young people of the right stamp, more interesting than the average in being scrupulous and self-respecting, and possessed of minds, though not in the least complicated ones. It is an admirable bit of commonplace truth.

Straightforward, unheightened and unexciting, but absorb- *Studies of* ing realism is again the stuff of which *The Belton Estate* (1866) *other* and *The Claverings* (1867) are composed. They each deal with *dilemmas* the quandary of one more or less in love with two persons, and puzzled which to fix upon, in the first case as husband, in the second as wife. Clara Amedroz has to make up her mind between the cold-hearted, conventional, and probably insincere Captain Aylmer, who from the worldly point of view is the more eligible, and that rough diamond, the bluff and impulsive Will Belton. Her predicament is complicated by the question whether the latter will inherit Belton Castle as male heir, the Amedroz family losing it on the death of Clara's father. There are other complications, such as the scandal when the immaculate Aylmers hear that Clara is intimate with the compromised Mrs Askerton, the lady who had run away from a brutal husband and actually lived with her rescuer before she was free to marry him. Clara rejects Will Belton, being secretly in love with the captain, until she has glimpses into the heart of him—"a cold-blooded fish of a man, who thinks of nothing in the world but being respectable!" "Engaged to her! Oh damn him!" says Will, and Will is right. She had accepted him too quickly.

Captain Aylmer, when he heard the hearty tone of the girl's answer, already began almost to doubt whether it was wise on his part to devote the innermost bin of his cellar to wine that was so cheap. Not that he had any idea of receding. Principle, if not love, prevented that. . . . "When you asked me, I could but tell you the truth," she said, smiling at him. The truth is very well, but he would have liked it better had the truth come to him by slow degrees.

Clara's enlightenment comes by slow degrees: she presently realizes that it had been her fate "to love the thinner and meaner of the two men."

The putting right of mistakes is never pleasant; and in this case it was so unpleasant that she could not bring herself to acknowledge that it must be done. And yet, I think that, by this time, she was aware of the necessity.

Super-
fluous
explana-
tions

Trollope the showman is speaking; but such trite annotation is superfluous; the story speaks for itself, and at this stage the end is obvious. But after the Barchester series, the habit was growing on Trollope of stopping to point out the lie of the land, as each critical moment approached, and explaining what everyone was thinking or going to say. It was all very well to withhold nothing from the reader, to keep no secrets up his sleeve; that is the right policy in fiction which has a higher appeal than common melodrama. But he so underrated ordinary intelligence, and so carefully eschewed mere hints and innuendoes, the finer shades of suggestion and the still finer implications of irony, with all the eloquent resources of reticence, that much of his writing falls below the level of literature. Often the dialogue approximates to the phonographic reproduction of ordinary dullness which he had himself condemned.[1] The decline in Trollope's quality which is vaguely perceived after the *Last Chronicle* must be put down to these growing faults of manner rather than to any positive falling off in his creative power. But the result in such a novel as *The Claverings* (1867) is that the main story, the part in which he was most patient and conscientious, the story of Harry Clavering and his prolonged hesitation between his old love, the widowed Lady Ongar, and the plain, unromantic, but true-hearted Florence, fails to interest as much as that which was purely incidental, the humours of Captain Boodle, Sophie Gardeloup, the Russian spy, and her brother, Count Pateroff. Trollope was right to congratulate himself on the "genuine fun" they provide.[2] Otherwise, *The Claverings* is a variation on the Belton theme, with the sex of the rival loves reversed; and in all respects it is enormously better than Disraeli's novel, *Henrietta Temple*, dealing with a similar problem. Disraeli could not have risen to, or descended to, such an incident as Harry's discovery in Theodore Burton, who dusted his boots with his handkerchief, of a man of fine feelings who never did a mean thing in his life; or the affair of the awkward curate, Mr Saul, another plain and even grotesque exterior hiding a modest and refined nature. Harry's sister Fanny is a bit of odd comedy that prettily relieves the tension, as do also the cattish exchange of amenities between some of the women, and the bickering of Sir Hugh and most of the people he has much to do with. Irony of course has full play, though it is of a

---

[1] See above, 120, note 2.   [2] *Autobiography*, xi.

coarse texture. Madame Gardeloup has plenty of the more
malicious kind, when she condescendingly pockets Archie
Clavering's bribes, without the least intention of helping him
with the rich widow, and in the farcical abduction of Captain
Boodle, whom she carries off in triumph when England has
grown too hot to hold her. There is irony again in the neat
bit of dialogue, the Devil quoting Scripture, when Sir Hugh
exhorts Archie to make up to Lady Ongar, in spite of her being
under a cloud.

"I don't suppose there was anything really wrong, eh?"
"Can't say, I'm sure," said Sir Hugh.
"Because I wouldn't like——"
"If I were you, I wouldn't trouble myself about that.
Judge not, that you be not judged."
"Yes, that's true, to be sure," said Archie; and on that
point he went forth satisfied.

Trollope as satirist Satire was not very congenial to Trollope; he often remains
almost neutral where Thackeray would have hit his hardest.
The inimitable portrait of Mr Slope is not a skit or a caricature;
the impression it leaves is of the candid likeness of a disagreeable
person whose vices and absurdities are extremely amusing to
the intelligent onlooker. That of the pompous, overbearing
Lord Trowbridge, in *The Vicar of Bullhampton* (1869), is done
in the same way, though it cannot vie with the masterpiece:

The Marquis was a man nearer seventy than sixty, but very
hale, and with few signs of age. He was short and plump,
with hardly any beard on his face, and short grey hair, of
which nothing could be seen when he wore his hat. His
countenance would not have been bad, had not the weight of
his marquisate always been there; nor would his heart have
been bad, had it not been similarly burdened. But he was a
silly, weak, ignorant man, whose own capacity would hardly
have procured bread for him in any trade or profession, had
bread not been so adequately provided for him by his fathers
before him.

Trollope talks almost like a Radical with a grievance who
knows his man. He had grievances in *The Three Clerks* and in

The Warden, but, fortunately, he was half-hearted about them. In this new novel he takes a harrowing problem of social ethics, that of the unfortunate woman whom he describes as a "castaway," and treats it with a boldness and a humanity extremely commendable at that date. Otherwise, *The Vicar of Bullhampton*, with its fighting parson, and a woman's dilemma between the lover whom she had accepted and the one she had loved but rejected when he was too poor to marry, is of the same class as *The Belton Estate* and *The Claverings*, with one distinction, its drawing of rustic folk and especially of crusty old Farmer Brattle. A grievance that Trollope hugged, the wickedness of lawyers who defend through thick and thin clients that they know to be guilty, is canvassed at large in *Orley Farm*, mostly in terms of mere protestation.

We may say that all the persons most concerned were convinced, or nearly convinced, of Lady Mason's guilt. Among her own friends Mr Furnival had no doubt of it, and Mr Chaffanbrass and Mr Aram but very little; whereas Sir Peregrine and Mrs Orme of course had none. On the other side Mr Mason and Mr Dockwrath were both very sure of the truth, and the two Rounds, father and son, were quite of the same mind. And yet, except with Dockwrath and Sir Peregrine, the most honest and the most dishonest of the lot, the opinion was that she would escape.

Later he censures the legal world in the most solemn way for finding no fault with Mr Furnival, "conceiving that he had done his duty by his client in a manner becoming an English barrister and an English gentleman." The satire in the chapter entitled "The State of Public Opinion," where Kenneby and Smiler discuss Moulder's proposition, "Look you here, John; if you're paid to bring a man off not guilty, won't you bring him off if you can?" is legitimate, it is comedy. The would-be legal reformer has returned to his proper business, humour, even if he has not perceived the absurdity of his recent trespass into pamphleteering diatribe. For Trollope was essentially a humorist; mirth, not derision, was his proper aim. He might criticise and protest and expose; but in his heart he would not have the existing scheme of things altered, or deprive himself of his bores and humbugs and black sheep, and the other rare and exquisitely preposterous specimens collected with a connoisseur's delight in absurdity. His satire, if it can be called satire, was directed at the delightfully ridiculous, not at the monstrous and detestable, except in the one instance, *The Way We Live Now*, which proves the rule. Vice, baseness, falsehood, unmitigated selfishness, he branded in other ways. Though his realism kept clear of those repulsive matters which some later novelists have regarded as compulsory tests of their competence, he was more honest than Thackeray, and invariably said what he meant. Though he might veil under a generalizing phrase or polite allusiveness the ugly and evil things which inevitably crop up, the base and sordid acts, the nefarious, underhand, unscrupulous, or brutal characters, he did not beat about the bush, or pretend they were nothing of the sort; they are clearly specified, though with due regard for social decency. Some, as already noted, have discerned in this unblinking perception of the world as it is, combined with his refusal to carry out to the bitter end any harsh doctrine of nemesis, symptoms of a careless, cynical heart. It may be a proof of the contrary. It may have been due to his instinctive faith that the good in human nature will on the whole have the best of it. Trollope was too genial, too charitable, for satire. He cannot keep it up, without painful effort, unless he has been exasperated, which is a rare thing with Trollope. That in *The Eustace Diamonds* (1872) is only incidental; when he tried to be sardonic throughout, as in *Miss Mackenzie* (1865) and *Mr Scarborough's Family* (1883), he is forced and artificial, or else guilty of a rather gruesome frolic, with his wicked old scoffer who will not die, in spite of doctors and should-be fatal operations, and the piquant stratagem of the two wills held over the heads of the two ill-conditioned sons. He kept clear of satire, and he kept clear of plot, enigmas, and surprises, for none of which had he any relish, in the short and simple *Dr Wortle's School* (1881), which is a mild and mellow half-counterpart to *The Warden*.

In the first few pages of the epic of Lizzie Eustace, Trollope speaks of her as "that opulent and aristocratic Beckie Sharpe," evidently having some idea of trying at a Thackerayan heroine, "*The* though he forgot how the original spelt her name. Lizzie is *Eustace* not an unworthy rival. She is covetous and rapacious; "of *Diamonds*" all the heartless creatures in the world," says her aunt, Lady Linlithgow, "she is the most heartless." Another good authority pronounces her "the greatest liar about London." Yet it is impossible to detest Lizzie Eustace. Partly, it is because the author of her being endowed her with some of his own bonhomie; partly, because of her little human weaknesses, as when she plays the fool with her cousin, and when she is paralysed by the theft of the casket, supposed by the police and everyone else to have contained the diamonds, which had all the time been safe under her pillow. She is a perfect actress, as the author shows by word and example, and an actress even to herself. Else she could not have doubled up the hesitating Lord Fawn with her dignified appeal to the patrician friends who hardly knew her:

"Let us name someone to decide between us which of us has been wrong. Lady Glencora Palliser is a friend of yours, and her husband is in the Government. Shall we name her? It is true, indeed, that her uncle, the Duke of Omnium, the grandest and greatest of English noblemen, is specially interested on my behalf." This was very fine in Lizzie. The Duke of Omnium she had never seen; but his name had been mentioned to her by Lady Glencora, and she was quick to use it.

But Lizzie should have been drawn with unswerving Thackerayan irony, to have made a Becky Sharp of her and a *Vanity Fair* of her history. And then there are the diamonds. With the diamonds and the owner of the diamonds in jeopardy for chapter after chapter, satire has to go into abeyance. For merely as a detective novel it is a thrilling story, related with sustained sprightliness, and as much dramatic suspense as if the narrator had not "scorned to have a secret between himself and his readers." And the humour is up to Trollope's old standards, sometimes, at any rate. Go back to Lord Fawn's original proposal to Lizzie, the predatory female and the dull, conventional, penniless peer, humbugging each other about their disinterested motives—what a love-scene! On the other hand, the diamonds are responsible for most of the comedy: all the world is staggered and absorbed by the case; the political parties, even the Government, take sides; whilst the theft that failed, and the police theories on "the got-up plant," are all the more diverting from our being in the secret. The satire of the fastest society, and the lurid exposure of the underworld of criminals and detectives, are of secondary interest; and the sub-plot of Mrs Carbuncle and Lucinda Roanoke, the tragic misery of the woman sold for cash, is slurred over and degenerates into melodrama.

"The Way We Live Now" But in *The Way We Live Now* (1875), in which Trollope rounded on the young contemporaries who sneered at him, he flung out a savage pasquinade as different as possible from the mild satire in his previous novels. By concentrating all his realism on a picture of social corruption, he made the world which had depreciated his urbane creations look both sordid and ridiculous—"a horde of swindlers" and their dupes, as foolish as they were repulsive. The whole of society comes into the picture: cringing, sycophantic authors, venal publishers, truckling and spiteful editors, the politicians, the Church, with its Romanizing antics and congregations to whom religion is only a social observance that pays; but, above all, the frivolous, toadying, gambling and cheating, pretentious and extravagant Belgravia of that day, with the financiers who preyed upon it, money versus land again, personified in the Carburys, Longestaffes, Primeros, and the bogus nobility of the Monograms, and the sinister Melmotte, who swindles them all, a greater Merdle, though Trollope when he drew his colossal speculator had not read *Little Dorrit*. The young bloods who had laughed at Trollope look like sucking criminals; all are depraved and odious together. It is a caricature made formidably realistic; these incredible excesses are to be taken literally—the negation of all that he had previously written, and yet all substantiated with his usual cunning. The most abject of the lot is the son of a she-novelist, Lady Carbury, who flatters and sponges on editors and publishers, for the

sake of this worthless scion. The hiding he gets from John Crumb, whose sweetheart he feebly tries to seduce, is an episode awaited only too long by the outraged reader. Even the arch-scoundrel Melmotte is not so loathsome as this; he is indeed grandiose in a Miltonic or Dantesque way, with his will-power and courage, as when at bay he stalks out of the House with the nonchalance of supreme audacity. "It was thus that Augustus Melmotte wrapped his toga around him before his death." It is a bitter satire, and Trollope cannot even keep his disgust under at the changes of taste in women's beauty and women's dress.

In these days men regard the form and outward lines of a woman's face and figure more than either the colour or the expression, and women fit themselves to men's eyes. With padding and false hair without limit a figure may be constructed of almost any dimensions. The sculptors who construct them, male and female, hairdressers and milliners, are very skilful, and figures are constructed of noble dimensions, sometimes with voluptuous expansion, sometimes with classic reticence, sometimes with dishevelled negligence which becomes very dishevelled indeed when long out of the sculptor's hands. Colours indeed are added, but not the colours which we used to love. The taste for flesh and blood has for the day given place to an appetite for horsehair and pearl-powder.

All the other novelists of any account in this period, even the Kingsleys, Reade, and Wilkie Collins, did something to enlarge or vary the compass of fiction; they did not leave the novel exactly as it was when they adopted it as their vocation or the organ of their humanitarian views. Not so Trollope. *Trollope's strength and his limitations* He did not alter the fabric or change the content. So far as he was concerned, the art of fiction stood still: he might have been a survivor from the eighteenth century. He found the novel as developed by Fielding, Fanny Burney, and Jane Austen, which Thackeray had used as the keyboard of his irony, the form so precisely suited to his talents that his knowledge of the world he lived in, and the characters, situations, and events which he devised to match what he saw going on around him, fell naturally into this framework. And he was such a faithful craftsman, so incapable of wandering off the track of actual experience, that his novels are a lucid, undistorting mirror for a wide span of the social life of his day. Though he had not the vision essential to great creative art, in the sphere marked out by his superlative craftsmanship this degree of artlessness was a positive asset. His limitations have come to light repeatedly in the foregoing survey. No one had a wider or more intimate acquaintance with those sections of society then termed "the governing classes," which were the backbone of Victorian England; outside that range he was not so well-informed, and of "the masses" he knew next to nothing. No one understood better the sentiments and traditions that gave those classes their solidarity, or the pride and arrogance, the envy, spites, and humiliations, the snobbery and flunkeyism, which are the eternal adjuncts of class distinctions. His interest always centred in the individual, and the individual's relations to the social scheme, not in abnormal incidents and adventures. His well-stocked imagination easily and spontaneously turned out any number of live characters the very image of those whom he had watched with curiosity, amusement, or friendly appreciation. He struck no pose of moral superiority over the people he observed or those he created; he was not their master, organizing them into a new world as a criticism of the existing one; he was simply and solely the observer, with no definite attitude towards them beyond sympathy or antipathy, and the gusto of the humorist. Trollope's was no deep-searching intellect: he had neither the comprehensive vision of the man of genius, nor the penetration which goes to the core of things, elucidating apparent inconsistencies and contradictions, that imaginative light which floods the dark places of character and motive as by a sort of divination. He was too apt to rely on intuition, and shirk the hard thinking which corrects and supplements first impressions. Rarely did he ask himself why people were like this or like that, or perceive the need to isolate the fundamental passion or weakness which explained what seemed inconsistent or contradictory. A number of his characters, in short, were left unfinished; they were not studied with the thoroughness

required for a complete portrait. His insight was shrewd but
not unerring, from this failure to sift his observations and
ascertain all they implied. This, too, in spite of his complacent
small talk about what was not very recondite, the lengthy
explanations which might have been condensed into a stroke
of irony. Few if any of his characters are really complex;
there is nothing very enigmatic in the tormented Mr Crawley
or in Lady Glencora, any more than in Mrs Proudie or Miss
Dunstable. Any novel of Jane Austen or Thackeray presents
figures of more subtle and complicated texture. Yet such
beings as Violet Effingham, Lord Chiltern, Lily Dale, Mr
Crosbie, or the Signora Neroni evidently remained for him
unsolved paradoxes, or at any rate examples of odd caprice and
amusing inconsistency. They were either people whom he
had known, or characters that had become real to him, and so
were not to be meddled with. As to explaining their aberrations as the result of some original twist, the need for such an
effort never occurred to him. He took them as they came,
and they grew so substantial and interesting that he could not
help talking about them and discussing their idiosyncrasies.
He was the child of his age, the moralistic age of Browning
and George Eliot, and so his comments are usually of a kind
to improve the occasion, though his plots are by no means all
based on the favourite principle of poetic justice. So, for
instance, he sermonizes on the misdeeds of Mark Robarts, in
Framley Parsonage, or on the incidence of providential punish-
ments on the "vain and foolish," in *The Small House.*[1] Yet
his philosophy of life consisted merely of the common sense of
a man of the world, dropping off-hand remarks on what was
going on under his eye. And it was not in his nature to be
very severe. He vouchsafes more sympathy, or at least winks
at the reader's toleration, for his rascally heroine Lizzie Eustace
than Thackeray ever conceded to her prototype. He is kind
to everyone, including the rogues, if not the humbugs, in spite
of his falcon-eyed detection of motive and his distrust of

[1] He is very wordy on "the teaching of novels," in the *Autobiography* (xii.). "A
vast proportion of the teaching of the day—greater probably than many of us have
acknowledged to ourselves—comes from these books, which are in the hands of all
readers. It is from them that girls learn what is expected from them," etc., etc.

appearances. Even such a wretched fraud as Lady Carbury, the trashy and sycophantic author, in *The Way We Live Now*, has "good in her, false though she was," for she would endure anything for her idolized son. This soft-heartedness was only another symptom of the temperamental nonchalance shown in the lack of any passionate earnestness in his drawing of character, even when at grips with some tragic issue. The intensity with which his fellow-novelists conceived and etched in trenchant lines a Jane Eyre or a Rochester, a Heathcliff, a Pecksniff, Fagin, Quilp, or Micawber, a Becky Sharp, Barnes Newcome, or Old Campaigner, was the very opposite of his tranquil, easy-going delineation of people that one would love to meet.

CHAPTER V

THE KINGSLEYS, WILKIE COLLINS,
READE, AND OTHERS

WHATEVER cohesion there was in the group of novelists most *New de-* conspicuous in the eighteen-fifties and sixties derived from *partures* their violent revulsion from quiet domestic fiction and almost everything represented by Trollope. They demanded more excitement; they also claimed to be interested in things of vastly greater importance than manners and personal idiosyncrasy, though they thought of themselves still as creators of character. Their novels commonly had definite subjects, which were illustrated and debated, the author not standing too pedantically aloof but usually being ready, as it were, with the casting vote. Moral and religious, social, economic, and political reforms were the objects at which they aimed. Incidentally, their protests and propaganda brought in idealistic elements that gave a certain exaltation to this new romanticism. For, though they would have called themselves realistic novelists, their realism was only a means of enforcing their view of personal and social regeneration or of reinforcing sensations of wonder and suspense, terror and revolt. Really it is two groups that are in question, though as malcontents and innovators they were at one, and individuals might alternate between one group and the other. Charles Kingsley, Thomas Hughes, and G. A. Lawrence were the exponents of certain moral ideals, put forward at an hour of crisis as the cure for national ill-health; Wilkie Collins and Charles Reade, whilst they were only too ready to canvass grievances and propose remedies, turning the novel wholly or in part into a bellicose pamphlet, were in eager pursuit of those literary effects which are commonly accepted as romantic. They were the apostles of a renovated Gothicism, belated successors of Horace Walpole, Mrs Radcliffe, "Monk" Lewis, and Maturin. All alike prided themselves on being good descriptive novelists. Highly coloured description, "word-painting" as it was called, of natural scenery and other picturesque accompaniments of what they related was much in favour. They considered the setting not less important than the drama, and doubled the part of playwright with that of scene-painter. Novels were written to depict little-known phases of life. Reade showed how the fisher-folk in a Scottish village slaved and strove with adversity. He took immense pains to make himself familiar with the technique of tool-making and the unscrupulous tactics of the craft-unions in a place like Sheffield, with law business, banking operations, the routine between decks on an ocean tramp, life at the Australian gold-diggings, and so on; and after filling a library of notebooks emptied out his observations into his novels. Kingsley also attempted realistic descriptions of industrial conditions and the miseries of sweated operatives, but had not the same command of technical details. He made great capital, on the other hand, out of his attainments in natural history, when he had the opportunity to paint an impressive landscape or seascape with words as pigments. As to his brother, Henry Kingsley's biographer continually quotes long passages from the novels to illustrate the novelist's actual experience of knockabout life—a curious reversal of ordinary procedure.[1] This descriptive element in fiction developed later on so far that thousands were supposed to read novels for the sake of the light they shed on unfamiliar aspects of human existence at home or abroad, and novelists catered for them by getting up out-of-the-way subjects. Most of the group could be described as amateurs—men of letters or men of leisure who took to the novel as a handy form or a combination of amusement and outlet for their convictions. Kingsley was a country parson with strong views on the state of the poor, on the land question, and some other matters; G. A. Lawrence dabbled in many pursuits before he wrote his novels as illustrations of the physical force doctrine; Reade

[1] See S. M. Ellis, *Henry Kingsley*, *passim*.

was a barrister who had made a hit with a couple of plays, and wrote novels which were subsequently transferred to the boards. Wilkie Collins was the most regular professional among them, and he oscillated between the theatre and theatrical fiction. Though they all broke with a great deal of the past, they none of them broke with Dickens. It is only perhaps in observing how much these and other novelists owe to his example that one comes to realize the astounding versatility of this great master. He had shown how to describe with the knowledge of an expert and the vividness of a magician all sorts and conditions of life, without having to work up a knowledge for the occasion. And in this particular direction, the theatrical character of his plots, his great scenes, and histrionic performers, he had given such a lead, that, when Reade and Collins began writing novels easily adaptable to the stage or plays that could be readily turned into novels, they were recognized, and were proud to recognize themselves, as Dickensians. This group, at any rate, did not leave the novel where they found it. Though not gifted with the faculty for living portraiture of their fellow-beings that was inborn in Trollope, though they were novelists by choice or by policy rather than by nature, they had ideas which they put in practice in fiction, sometimes to its detriment as an art, sometimes quite otherwise. They were helped enormously, both in their propagandist activities and in their transfer to fiction of much that had hitherto been consecrated to the stage, by recent changes in the methods of publishing books read for entertainment. It was now customary to bring out a novel first of all as a serial in the magazines, or in shilling numbers. Cheap editions appeared soon after, or sometimes in place of, the three-volume issue. All this led to an immense increase of the reading public, and classes were reached which had hardly ever seen a novel before. Such lower strata of the population actually became the goal of the novelist's effort, and to an appreciable extent the arbiters of taste whom he had to keep in his mind's eye if he was to make sure of the rapidly increasing reward of popular authorship. The result of the reaction between readers in their thousands and the novelist himself was an overbearing tendency to what always thrills the crowd, that is, to melodrama. This was the great age of sensational fiction, particularly of that fine art of maintaining suspense which Gaboriau had recently applied to the novel of crime and detection. As most novels that promised big returns to the publisher were put through the magazines or issued in weekly numbers, the novelist began to cultivate various devices, such as the manipulation of climaxes and the trick of breaking off at a critical moment, which would leave the reader. anxious for more. The formula laid down by Wilkie Collins has often been quoted: "Make 'em laugh; make 'em cry; make 'em wait."[1]

A time of new movements The world presented in the novels of Trollope is a static world; but all the time he was writing, and he kept going till his death in 1882, the actual world was stirred by many afflicting questions which few novelists could ignore. For much more than a decade from the turn of the century onwards, minds were in a state of intellectual and spiritual ferment, agitated by all sorts of mental and moral questionings, public controversies, and organized movements. To all these vexatious matters Trollope remained sublimely indifferent; merely from reading his novels no one would suspect their existence. His brother-novelists were not so impercipient, not even those who confined themselves to the domestic sphere. Not only in such a novel of protest as *Hard Times* (1854), but also in *Oliver Twist* (1838), *Little Dorrit* (1857), and many a page of his other novels and stories, Dickens showed himself fully alive to the urgency of the condition of England question, and burning with reformatory zeal. Mrs Gaskell had begun with a poignant study of the social problem, *Mary Barton*, in 1848, and returned to the subject in one of her latest novels, *North and South*, in 1855. Charlotte Yonge, who went on writing till the end of the century, was chiefly engrossed by the religious question; she was an expositor of Tractarian principles to the young and susceptible. The poets were by no means

---

[1] See Walter C. Phillips: *Dickens, Reade, and Collins, sensation novelists: a study in the conditions and theories of novel-writing in Victorian England* (1919); a mine of information for any who wish to pursue these reactions in detail.

indifferent. Mrs Browning, who has obvious affinities with
the more thoughtful among the domestic novelists, continually
breaks out in anguish at the state of things around her, as
in *Casa Guidi Windows* (1851) and *Aurora Leigh* (1857).
Tennyson and Browning were not blind to what was going on.
Tennyson sometimes, as in *Maud* (1855), rushed into violent
lyrical outbursts on the mammonism and irreligion of the age;
Browning, the creator of Blougram and Mr Sludge the Medium,
looked at contemporary questions, though he interested himself
solely in those that were of all time. Even that odd poetic
aphorist Coventry Patmore, in *The Angel in the House* (1854)
and its various sequels down to 1863, often roused himself to
complaint and admonition. Among the minor poets, many
wrote eloquently on public issues; the Crimean War and the
Indian Mutiny were specially fertile, transforming such as
Gerald Massey, Sydney Dobell, and Alexander Smith, for the
nonce, into something like greatness. The Oxford Movement,
which began in 1833 with *Tracts for the Times*, reached its
height as a disturbing force among English churchmen during
the eighteen-forties, simultaneously with the dissensions in the
Scottish Kirk that led to the Great Disruption. Coming into
collision with the scientific movement, it had for sequel the
long conflict of faith and rationalism. Newman, Pusey, and
F. D. Maurice were writing now. Froude's *Nemesis of Faith*
(1848) and the manifesto of "the doubting school," *Essays and
Reviews* (1860), made a great noise, though they are now but
historical landmarks and taken as read. The same may be
said of the future George Eliot's translations of Strauss's *Life
of Jesus* (1846) and of Feuerbach's *Essence of Christianity*
(1853), works now as defunct as Bishop Colenso's arithmetical
challenge to the literal authenticity of the scriptural record.
But more permanent foundations for the new thought were
presently laid by Herbert Spencer, in *Social Statics* (1851) and
Principles of Psychology (1855), and then by Darwin, in *The
Origin of Species* (1859), and his follower and expounder, Huxley.
It is pertinent here to notice Newman's two novels, the
expository *Loss and Gain* (1848), and *Callista* (1856), the story
of a martyr in the third century, and also Cardinal Wiseman's

Fabiola (1854), a story of the Church in the Catacombs, though they are of small literary importance. The very year when Kingsley began his career as a novelist with the publication of *Yeast* in *Fraser's Magazine* (1848) was signalized by several occurrences in England, literary and other, as well as by the revolutionary events on the Continent which roused opinion here, especially when this country became the home of swarms of refugees. Besides some already mentioned, Mrs Gaskell's *Mary Barton* appeared that year, and also Thackeray's *Vanity Fair*, Mill's *Political Economy*, the first volumes of Macaulay's *History*, and Clough's *Bothie*. Further, it was the year of the foundation of the Pre-Raphaelite Brotherhood; *The Germ* made its unobtrusive appearance in 1850. Clough's dilettante scepticism, which was further expounded in *Dipsychus* (1850), made little impression; but it was otherwise with his friend Matthew Arnold's championship of unbiased thought and more deliberate and better-directed attacks on dogmatism. All this time, Carlyle was still watching events; though his great days were over, he stepped now and then down into the arena, and something like his old energy blazed up again in *Chartism* (1840), and *Latter-day Pamphlets* (1850). He remained an inspiration, not only to Kingsley and his fellows, but also to Meredith, whose first regular novel, *Richard Feverel*, appeared in 1859, and whose seventh, *Beauchamp's Career* (1876), is full of Carlyle. Ruskin, also, was bringing out *Modern Painters* volume by volume from 1843 to 1860, and meanwhile publishing *The Seven Lamps of Architecture* (1849), *Pre-Raphaelitism* (1850), and *Stones of Venice* (1851–1853), after which came the first of his tractates on moral and social reform, *Unto this Last* (1862).

Charles Kingsley   This bare catalogue is enough to indicate where Kingsley and his comrades stood, at the middle of the century, in the struggle for the enlightenment and the social betterment of the people. They adopted the programme of Christian Socialism which Frederick Denison Maurice had endeavoured to put in action during his residence in London; and with this object Kingsley joined Maurice, Ludlow, Vansittart Neale, Thomas Hughes, and others, in founding the Society for the Promotion of Working Men's Associations (1849). It was the personal

magnetism of Maurice, whom he reverenced only second—if
second—to Carlyle, that dominated Kingsley, a man of fervid
sentiment and ardent religious instincts, but no deep thinker;
he accepted the master's Christian rationalism, and aspired to
be his popular interpreter. Charles Kingsley (1819–1875) was
a Devon man, son of the rector of Clovelly; a lover of nature,
with enough scientific training to write excellent elementary
works on natural history and geology, and sufficient scholarship
to acquit himself to the satisfaction of his time as professor of
modern history at Cambridge; a man of numerous interests,
a sportsman, one with practical views on agriculture, a stimulating preacher, and a poet, with some of the best songs in
English to his credit, besides some fair achievements of a more
ambitious kind. In his contributions as "Parson Lot" to
Politics for the People (1848) and to *The Christian Socialist*
(1850–1851) he made a strong appeal for sympathy with the
victims of industrial greed and of unlimited competition,
denouncing the orthodox political economy of that day.
Yeast, which first appeared in *Fraser's Magazine* (1848), to be
published separately in 1851, is a manifesto as much as a novel,
or more so. In *The Saint's Tragedy* (1848) he made a social
drama out of the story of Elizabeth of Hungary, and attacked
Romish priestcraft and the doctrine of celibacy. In *Yeast* and
in *Alton Locke* (1850), as in his published volumes of sermons,
he appears as the eulogist of country life and hater of the slums,
the apostle of social hygiene in all senses of the term, and,
whilst a disciple of the idealism of Coleridge and Carlyle, a
fierce Protestant and the declared adversary of Pusey and
Newman. In his Hampshire parish of Eversley he antagonized
the old-fashioned squirearchy with his sermons on rural
drunkenness and lawlessness, his agitation for schools, and
denunciation of insanitary housing. He was as optimistic and
at least as pugnacious as Dickens, in his attacks on the new poor
law and other evils. He believed progress to be inevitable:
make it Christian! He called himself a Liberal and a democrat,
though by birth and temper he was a strong individualist.[1]

---

[1] "Comme Dickens, il oscillera entre l'idée égalitaire et le sentiment des inégalités
bienfaisantes" (Cazamian: *Le Roman social en Angleterre*, 169).

He would invoke the Church as the ordained antagonist of the shopkeepers and the Manchester School—the Mammonites.

His first novels— "Yeast" and "Alton Locke"

Alton Locke (1850), *Yeast* (1851), and *Hypatia* (1853) are all expositions of the social and spiritual doctrines which Kingsley so passionately held, though the last of the three is a story of Egypt in the fifth century. Its sub-title ran, "New Foes with an Old Face." The title of *Yeast* refers of course to the ferment of ideas then raging. It is a vehement, impulsive, ill-digested book; yet powerful, and not so laboured as *Alton Locke*. Apparently, Kingsley did not read *Mary Barton* till later, though that also appeared in 1848; and it was not till afterwards that he read *Coningsby*, though he could hardly have been unacquainted with Disraeli's *Sybil* (1845). Nowadays, it would be called a discussion novel, since it contains a good deal of debate, the revolutionary Chartism of the previous decade being condemned, in favour of a moral and philanthropic Chartism—the name "Christian Socialism" had not yet been adopted. But it is written with a zest and enthusiasm which are very infectious: it is a summons, a war-cry. Of story there is almost nothing. The new gospel is hammered out in the impact and interaction of a handful of characters, who if they are not in love with each other are more or less at blows. Two heroes are among the number, Lancelot Smith and the gamekeeper Tregarva, who indoctrinates Smith with his knowledge of the state of the poor, and the iniquity of game-laws, landlordism, and insanitation, enlisting him in the social crusade; and a heroine, Argemone, who writes elegies to Sappho and inspires Smith with her spirituality and idealism. Lord Minchampstead represents efficient individualism; he is a rich industrialist, a strong man and a benevolent—Carlyle's doctrine of work shown in action. Lord Vieuxbois is a fine old gentleman, benevolent by disposition, but frightened by the current abuse of Chartism and trade-unionism. The mysterious Barnakill, who looks like a reminiscence of Sidonia, as the exponent of the theology of F. D. Maurice, converts Lancelot, and reveals to him the kingdom of Prester John, the New Jerusalem of Christian Socialism. Then there is Luke, the Tractarian, and Claude Mellot, the pagan artist, who wastes his time painting nymphs and the like. Barnakill implores him to do landscape and portraits, preaching a Ruskinian cult of the beautiful and the true before Kingsley had actually read Ruskin. A number of these people were to make a second appearance in *Two Years Ago* (1857). Barnakill calls upon Lancelot and those who think with him to give a national lead in the questions now pressing upon the age: "It has been England's privilege hitherto to solve all political questions as they arise for the rest of the world; it is her duty now." *Alton Locke* (1850), the first of Kingsley's novels to appear as a separate book, came after the cholera epidemic of 1849 and an exposure of the evils of sweating, by the *Morning Chronicle*, the same year. Both these events moved him deeply, and turned his attention to the urban problem, which was brought before his eyes again in his father's London parish. This is the autobiography of a converted Chartist, who incidentally gives a history of the movement; and it may have been suggested by the career of one or the other or of both of two working-men, Thomas Cooper, author of *The Purgatory of Suicides* (1845), and William Lovett, who wrote the very able book *Chartism, a New Organization of the People* (1841), and was the great advocate of moral force. After the defeat of Chartism, Alton accepts Kingsley's alternative, moral persuasion, and renounces the idea of using force to bring about a democratic revolution. But the raciest character in the novel is Carlyle's disciple, Sandy Mackaye, whose ideas are, however, condemned as unpractical or merely negative. After listening in grumbling fashion to the Emersonian sermon of Mr Windrush, Sandy lets himself go in his native lingo on some of the more high-flown sentiments:

"Intellect—intellect!" rejoined he, according to his fashion, catching one up at a word, and playing on that in order to answer, not what one said, but what one's words led to. "I'm sick o' all the talk anent intellect I hear noo. An' what's the use o' intellect? 'Aristocracy o' intellect,' they cry. Curse a' aristocracies—intellectual anes, as well as anes o' birth, or rank, or money! What! will I ca' a man my superior, because he's cleverer than mysel?—will I boo down

to a bit o' brains, ony mair than to a stock or a stane? Let a
man prove himsel' better than me, my laddie—honester,
humbler, kinder, wi' mair sense o' the duty o' man, an' the
weakness o' man—and that man I'll acknowledge—that man's
my king, my leader, though he war as stupid as Eppe Dalgleish,
that could na count five on her fingers, and yet keepit her
drucken father by her ain hands' labour for twenty-three
years."

"Hy-
patia"
Thus *Alton Locke* teaches the value of an aristocracy of
morals, manners, and culture. It all ends in a cosmic vision
of the progress of life from the mollusc to the reformed and
illuminated man. In *Hypatia*, on the other hand, Kingsley
attempted a supremely difficult if not impossible feat, to
project the representative mental and moral types of his day
into a far historical environment, and to weave their feelings
and actions into an interesting novel, a novel, not a romance,
with all the modern paraphernalia of love at cross-purposes and
complicated intrigue prized at the circulating libraries. Up
to a point, he was successful. Many scenes and descriptive
pages are brilliantly done, though the historic perspective is
inevitably falsified. If to us, nowadays, his Alexandria in
the time of the Goths looks like a Chicago terrorized by
gangsters, Kingsley might plead that human nature is always
the same. At any rate, he showed his mastery here and in
Westward Ho! of those realistic arts which are of priceless
service to sensationalism. The reader thoroughly enjoys
himself when Philammon gets the dagger home: it is not
the hero alone that holds his breath "in fearful suspense."
Alexandria, with its mingling of primitive Christianity and
paganism, of order and mob-law, of profligacy and murder and
philosophic calm, is a pandemonium looking out on paradise.
Various races, various forms of polytheism, various forms of
Judaism, and various Christian sects are quarrelling together
and expounding their tenets. But the result of identifying
these ancient antagonisms with those of his own day is that the
modern reader, having a sense of humour that Kingsley never
possessed, amuses himself with recognizing the author himself
in Bishop Synesius, the blasé West-Ender in Raphael Ben-

Ezra, the Jewish hag of Adelphi melodrama in Miriam, and
Kingsley's stock characters in the rest, notably Argemone
Lavington in Hypatia. It is a novel to be read when one is
young and enthusiastic, when even shallow psychology goes
a long way, and mere figures seem to be characters; when
eloquence—and Kingsley is often eloquent, especially in
objurgation—never falls flat, and the orgy of sentimentality in
which the book ends—poor apologetics even for the bloodthirsty Christians—seems impressive.[1]

Between this novel and the next, *Westward Ho!*, an event *The*
took place which had profound effects upon Kingsley and *Muscular*
many other novelists and men of letters, though Trollope *novel*
showed little sign of being perturbed. The Crimean War was
not one of the most glorious episodes in our national annals,
yet it bulks larger in literature than almost any other war before
the one of a few years ago. It came to England as a tremendous
moral awakening. There were optimists who looked on
Waterloo as the blow that had ended war. Peace, however,
had not brought the social millennium; Tennyson's fierce
lines in *Maud* (1855) sound like an echo of *Yeast* and *Alton
Locke*:

Peace sitting under her olive, and slurring the days gone by,
When the poor are hovell'd and hustled together, each sex,
    like swine,
When only the ledger lives, and when only not all men lie;
Peace in her vineyard—yes!—but a company forges the wine.

After a catalogue of rascalities and injustices such as Kingsley
would have dittoed, Tennyson glances at the war, which may
offer a cure for his hero's despair:

For I trust if an enemy's fleet came yonder round by the hill,
And the rushing battle-bolt sang from the three-decker out of
    the foam,

---

[1] A funny instance of how Kingsley forces the note may be found in chapter xxii.,
where he describes the entry of the elephant, in the pageant of mighty beasts: "On
he paced solemnly, while the whole theatre resounded to his heavy tread." An
elephant padding along on the solid floor of a vast ancient theatre would have struck
the observer then as now with the majestic silence of his march.

That the smooth-faced snub-nosed rogue would leap from his
counter and till,
And strike, if he could, were it but with his cheating yardwand,
home.

For Kingsley and many soberer thinkers war came in 1854 to
show "what the realities of life are." It enters as a redeeming
catastrophe into the most interesting of his novels, *Two Years
Ago* (1857), the title of which alludes to the war-time. "There
are nobler elements under the crust," says the fine old soldier
to the society girl who was to experience her awakening with
the rest, "which will come out all the purer from the fire;
and we shall have heroes and heroines among us as of old,
sincere and earnest, ready to face their work, and to call all
things by their right names once more." G. A. Lawrence,
whose first and most notorious novel, *Guy Livingstone, or
Thorough*, came out the same year, is never tired of dilating on
this theme in the most impressive language at his command:

That was a time that we all remember right well; when,
without note of preparation, the war-trumpets sounded from
the East and the North; when Europe woke up, like a giant
refreshed, from the slumber of a forty years' peace, and took
down disused weapons from the wall and donned a rusty
armour.

It is not straining the point to trace some of the most striking
contrasts between the literature before and after the eighteen-
fifties to the immense moral force of this event. The note of
strenuousness, the sense of struggle, the feeling of the deep
significance of action, are conspicuous by their absence from
the prose and poetry of the earlier period. What was more
characteristic of our most representative poets and novelists
for some time after? The novel is peculiarly the autobiography
of feeling and opinion. The day of the novel of manners was
passing, that of the novel of character and action was about
to be.

*Muscular
bris-
anity* "It is better to fight for the good than to rail at the ill,"
says Tennyson in *Maud*, published while Sebastopol was
besieged. He had been made Poet Laureate in 1850, and

in 1854 had written "The Charge of the Light Brigade." In *Tom Brown's Schooldays* (1856) the idea of "Muscular Christianity" is seen maturing. "Something to try the muscles of men's bodies, and the endurance of their hearts, to make them rejoice in their strength," declares the author, is better than education; and if it is left out, "your great Mechanics' Institutes end in intellectual priggism, and your Christian Young Men's Societies in religious Pharisaism." A year or two later "Muscular Christianity" had become a catchword, and Lawrence began frankly to preach the "Physical Force doctrine," without the Christianity. It soon became a topic of controversy, and in due course the object of a violent reaction. Nevertheless, freed from the exaggerations and crudeness of its first exponents, it had far too much healthy vitality to be suppressed, and never was it taught with more acceptance than with the advent of Kipling. For many reasons, *Maud* did not at first increase the popularity that *The Princess* and *In Memoriam* had secured. But the voice that condemned it in the sternest accents was the voice of the moralist, Mr Gladstone, who left critical considerations on one side, but fell harshly upon Tennyson's doctrine of the purifying influence of war. He admitted that peace has its moral perils and temptations for degenerate man, and that "amidst the clash of arms, the noblest forms of character may be reared, and the highest acts of duty done." "The love of country receives a powerful and generous stimulus from the bloody strife."

But this is as the furious cruelty of Pharaoh made place for the benign virtue of his daughter; as the butchering sentence of Herod raised without doubt many a mother's love into heroic sublimity; as plague, as famine, as fire, as flood, as every curse and every scourge that is wielded by an angry Providence for the chastisement of man, is an appointed instrument for tempering human souls in the seven-times-heated furnace of affliction, up to the standard of angelic and archangelic virtue.

The censor went on to condemn the recommendation of war "as a specific for the particular evil of Mammon-worship."

He made amends later for ignoring the lyrical beauty of the poem, in a note appended to a reprint of his article.

"West-ward Ho!" and "Two Years Ago"

Kingsley's *Westward Ho!* (1855) and *The Heroes, or Greek Fairy Tales for my Children* (1856), were products of the war-time. In the year of Balaclava and Inkermann he wrote to F. D. Maurice, "This war would have made me half mad, if I had let it. It seemed so dreadful to hear of those Alma heights being taken and not to be there; but God knows best, and I suppose I am not fit for such brave work, but only like Camille Desmoulins, 'une pauvre créature, née pour faire des vers.' But I can fight still (I don't mean in controversy—I am sick of that) . . . but in writing books which will make others fight. This one is called *Westward Ho!*" Here Kingsley tried to mirror the Elizabethan era as the sagas mirrored the great epoch when the Norsemen explored the Arctic and Atlantic, discovered America, and subjugated Britain. It is a saga of English enterprise and adventure, with a band of viking heroes: at a later date it would have been called a Jingo romance.[1] Amyas Leigh, epitome of all those heroes, came straight out of the sagas:

Why are all eyes fixed with greedy admiration on those four weather-beaten mariners, decked out with knots and ribbons by loving hands; and yet more on that gigantic figure who walks before them, a beardless boy, and yet with the frame and stature of a Hercules, towering, like Saul of old, a head and shoulders above all the congregation, with his golden locks flowing down over his shoulders?

Amyas and the other young gentlemen have the muscles and valour of berserks, kept in check by the scrupulous delicacy of a well-trained Anglican schoolboy. This is muscular Christianity, not quite the same thing as the Elizabethan spirit, nor an exact reproduction of that of the Norsemen. In *The Heroes* he retold the stories of Perseus and Andromeda, the Argonauts, and Theseus, as a modern tale of adventure,

---

[1] Whilst writing it Kingsley had his mind on the war then going on, as involuntary allusions show. Amyas "had no time to be sick while his men were sick, a valid and sufficient reason (as many a noble soul in the Crimea had known too well)" (chap. xxi.).

put into a simple, straightforward style intelligible to children. Then came *Two Years Ago* (1857), the incidents of which are dated 1854–1855, coincidently with the war. It is thus almost an autobiography of the genesis of the Physical Force doctrine. In Tom Thurnall, said to be a study of his brother George, Kingsley portrayed the muscular hero all complete, except that he is not a Christian hero. On the contrary, Thurnall is a professed Agnostic, with unconquerable faith in himself and in science, and little otherwise in either man or God; the other characters are exponents of the gospel of strength, struggle, and self-sacrifice, either directly or by way of contrast, such as the village schoolmistress, the mystic who sees visions and gets into trouble with the High Church parson for going to chapel. She is secretly in love with Tom, who stupidly suspects her of complicity in a theft. The parson, though a formulist, shows himself a hero when cholera ravages the village, and the society girl proves a heroine. The old Indian soldier, Major Campbell, and his servant Bowie, who stands six feet four without his shoes, and has summary methods with any who come philandering after his ladies, are also among the characters typifying strength. On the other side are various weak-kneed persons, most contemptible of all the poet, Elsley Vavasour, *alias* Briggs, married to the woman whom Campbell Byronically loves. To these people comes the war, and they hastily throw over their diverse interests and misunderstandings. One goes out as a chaplain, one as a nurse, others as soldiers. Thurnall departs on a mysterious journey into Central Asia, where his wonderful knowledge of languages and of men can be utilized. "And now two years and more have passed and gone, and all whose lot it was have come Westward Ho! once more, sadder and wiser men to their lives' end, save one or two, from whom not even Solomon's pestle and mortar and discipline would pound out the innate folly." Note the echo of Carlyle's style, whose teaching received a fresh impetus from the events of that time. Thurnall makes his mark as a general practitioner in the village where misfortune drops him, not only during the cholera, but also as a reforming influence on weaklings and reprobates. He inculcates sanitation, one of Kingsley's own crusades, in face of violent prejudice. The poet is beyond redemption. But the drunken Cornish squire, Trebooze of Trebooze, is persuaded to take a commission in the militia, and six months at Aldershot turn him into a self-respecting man. Thurnall recovers the belt containing his savings, lost in the wreck, and the schoolmistress is exonerated. After the war he reappears, his spirit tamed by a Tartar prison.

And so the old heart passed away from Thomas Thurnall; and instead of it grew up a heart like his father's, even the heart of a little child.

Kingsley was not a realist, and fails to authenticate such a complete transformation. Muscular fiction emanated from sentimentalism, not from any sound moral philosophy; Kingsley's did, at any rate, however much it owed to Carlyle's new valuations of manliness, courage, and the capacity for doing things. Its sources were in the eighteenth-century novel of sentiment, which likewise aped at times the epical strain. Kingsley saw his own likeness in Henry Brooke (1703–1783), and brought out a modern edition of *The Fool of Quality*, with an admiring character-study of the author.[1] In his Vindex Brimblecombe, of *Westward Ho!*, he reproduced Brooke's Mr Vindex from *The Fool of Quality*, simply Devonizing the name.

"*Tom Brown's School-days*"

The year peace was declared, Thomas Hughes (1823–1897) published *Tom Brown's Schooldays* (1856), a book of the first importance in the history of the Muscular novel. It has its weak points, but romanticism and writing for effect—charges that may justly be laid against Kingsley—are not among them. There are no false notes in the book; it is sincere from beginning to end, whether regarded as a biographical study, a story conveying a sermon, or the expression of Judge Hughes's ideals in the spontaneous form of a picture of life. It was written out of the fullness of his heart by one who had a lofty lesson to teach, and who would have smiled at anyone who accused him of being didactic. He would, no doubt, have measured

[1] See Volume V. 114–117.

its success by its power to influence and inspire. Yet *Tom Brown's Schooldays* is a very fine story, and that not merely in the way the Parables are, because they attain their end by simplicity and directness. To put it bluntly, every novel of the Muscular school is liable to this charge of didacticism. They were all written by men of strong views, who could not, if they would, have given an unbiased portrayal of life as it is. But they did not wilfully falsify the issues, although both Kingsley and the intractable Lawrence, self-constituted champion of what soon came to be called "Muscular Black-guardism," often fell into the tone of controversy, inviting the critic to question the doctrine as well as appraise the story. Tom Hughes's tirades were pardonable as the irrepressible remarks of a very outspoken mind. It is unfair to say of *Tom Brown's Schooldays* that the real hero is Dr Arnold of Rugby. Tom is the hero right enough, though the great headmaster stands behind him like the god in a Greek play, a presence embodying the spiritual meaning of the story. This figure of Arnold, drawn with rare taste and reverence, represents the emotional and ideal element ordinarily lacking when a tale is not a love-story. In the creed enunciated, he stands for the finer, the spiritual side of the doctrine of strength. Without this beautiful portrait, the author's downright, unqualified assertion of the Physical Force doctrine might have sounded not only crude but unconvincing.

Hughes was as truculent in his good-humoured way as *Carlyle's* Lawrence. His hero is a fighter by race and by nurture. *influence*

The Browns are a fighting family. One may question their wisdom, or wit, or beauty, but about their fight there can be no question. Wherever hard knocks of any kind, visible or invisible, are going, there the Brown who is nearest must shove in his carcase. . . . Most other folk get tired of such work. The old Browns, with red faces, white whiskers, and bald heads, go on believing and fighting to a green old age. . . . After all, what would life be without fighting? From the cradle to the grave, fighting, rightly understood, is the business, the real highest, honestest business of every son of man. Everyone who is worth his salt has his enemies, who must be

beaten, be they evil thoughts and habits in himself, or spiritual
wickedness in high places, or Russians, or Border-ruffians, or
Bill, Tom, or Harry, who will not let him live his life in quiet
till he has thrashed them. It is no good for Quakers, or any
other body of men, to uplift their voices against fighting.
Human nature is too strong for them, and they don't follow
their own precepts. Every soul of them is doing his own piece
of fighting, somehow and somewhere. The world might be a
better world without fighting, for anything I know, but it
wouldn't be our world; and therefore I am dead against crying
peace when there is no peace, and isn't meant to be.

Notice how the sentiments, and even the phrases and ring
of the sentences, chime in with Carlyle's homilies on the gospel
of work, the function of the hero, the doer, the fighter, in
human affairs. Carlyle had grown up amid the storm and
stress of the Napoleonic wars. He was twenty when Waterloo
was fought. The social disturbances of the next decades
deepened his earnestness of character and the sternness of his
teaching. Hughes and Kingsley found in *Chartism* (1840),
On Heroes (1841), and *Past and Present* (1843) views on their
own ethical and social problems that appealed to their temperaments. Carlyle's optimism, his equation of right and might,
and glorification of the "savage fighting Heptarchies," gave
the support of a vigorous though incoherent thinker to their
instinctive combativeness. Sandy Mackaye is always quoting
Carlyle, and adopting his manner of apocalyptic denunciation.
The novelist seized and developed the philosopher's ideas, and
in the heat of the war-fever he found a responsive public.

The saga-spirit There is another literary influence, one that fascinated and
left its mark on Carlyle, which is easy to trace, not only in the
ideas of the Muscular novelists, but in their actual words and
phrases. At this time, the Icelandic sagas were in a fair way
of becoming known to every well-read person in Europe.
Carlyle's praise of the *Heimskringla* and of Olaf Tryggvason,
"the wildly beautifullest man, in body and soul, that one has
ever heard of in the North," had helped to spread their fame.
Scott had paraphrased the *Eyrbyggia Saga*. Mallet's *Northern
Antiquities* was an old book even in his time. Müller's

Sagabibliothek appeared in Copenhagen in 1817–1830. But the general resurrection of the sagas began with the splendid translations published by Dasent about the turn of the century. The saga-spirit was in the air; men talked about it at college, and wrote about it in magazines. Words like "berserk" and "viking" became generally current at this date, and writers found meanings for them in the life they had to describe. In general lines, the saga-hero was much like other primitive heroes, but certain traits were curiously exaggerated. Will, self-reliance, independence, impatience of wrong were developed in the Icelander to the degree of vices; and the complementary passions of savage individualism, ungovernable obstinacy, and bloodthirsty revenge furnish all the villainy necessary to the most bloodthirsty of plots. Though public opinion in Iceland branded the rabid fury of the berserk as a detestable thing, and the most reverenced figure in the whole literature is the wise old lawgiver Nial, whose hands were unstained with blood, the sagas, by the sheer vividness of their portrayal, exalted violence to a dangerous pitch. They depict a state of society in which the strong arm, in spite of complicated legal checks, is actually supreme. This almost Nietzschean individualism is reproduced in Lawrence's heroes, while the finer spirit of the sagas is implicit in Kingsley. Among the Lawrentian heroes it is easy to find counterparts to Murdering Glum, who had fits of laughter when the appetite for killing came upon him, and of the irascible Grettir, with his incorrigible weakness for getting into scrapes and slaying men illegally. Kingsley painted a lifelike berserk in Salvation Yeo, the cunning old slayer of the Philistines, and there are still more direct traces of the viking rage and "shape-strength" in *Hereward*. "I never on earth met him whom I feared, and why should I fear him in heaven? If I met Odin, I would fight with Odin. If Odin were the stronger, he would slay me; if I were the stronger, I would slay him." He succeeded best in resuscitating the northern ideal in *Hereward the Wake* (1866), which has a similar ground-plan to that of the epical *Olaf Tryggvason*. Though Kingsley's sub-title was "The Last of the English," he regards Hereward as a Norseman, a viking, a free adventurer, fighting for his own hand and owing no man fealty. Britain belongs to the Scandinavian world; England is the former conquest of Canute, and now the prize of another Norseman, William the Conqueror. Hereward runs the conventional career of a saga-hero, is outlawed, wins distinction in foreign parts, and comes home to fight for his patrimony. He is selfish, brutal, and immoral; a slave to passion, a bully who drives his wife to a nunnery, a bravo who lets his country go to ruin rather than subdue his Danish pride to fight under the West Saxon Harold. This is his evil side. His virtues are indomitable courage, self-reliance, and a lordly generosity. Even his vices have the epic grandeur so unfailing in the tragic heroes of the sagas.

G. A. Lawrence The salient characteristics of the Muscular novel were exaggerated to a ludicrous degree by George Alfred Lawrence (1827-1876), author of *Guy Livingstone*, in which, as well as in his later novels, the war and the saga-spirit jump to the eye as the inspiring ideas. Lawrence was a graduate of New Inn Hall, and was entered at the Middle Temple; but in 1857, owing to the sensation made by *Guy Livingstone*, he gave up law for literature. He held a commission in the militia, and was commonly known as Major Lawrence. During the American Civil War he sympathized with the South—who could doubt it after reading his novels? He sailed to the States with the intention of joining the Confederate army, but before he reached their lines was captured by the Federals, and released from durance only at the British Ambassador's intercession and on the express understanding that he should return at once to England. Lawrence published nine novels and *A Bundle of Ballads*, the bare titles giving an inkling of their nature—*Sword and Gown, Barren Honour, Sans Merci, Breaking a Butterfly, Brakespeare*. He came into his popularity on the crest of the wave, and went on writing defiant idealizations of muscularity when public opinion had tired of it. By the time he came to *Sword and Gown* he observes:

"There is a heavy run just now against the Physical Force Doctrine. It is true there are some writers, not the weakest, who still cling to the old-fashioned mould. Putting Lancelot

and Amyas Leigh out of the question, I think I would sooner
have stood up to most heroes of romance than to sturdy Adam
Bede.[1] It can't be a question of religion or morality; for
'Muscular Christianity' is the stock sarcasm of the opposite
party; it must be a question of good taste. Well, ancient
Greece is supposed to have had some floating ideas on *that*
subject, and she deified Strength. It is perfectly true that to
thrash a prize-fighter unnecessarily is not a virtuous or glorious
action; but I contend that the *capability* of doing so is an
admirable and enviable attribute. There are grades of physical
as well as of moral perfection; and, after all, the same Hand
created both."

This sort of stuff would be hailed as very crude Nietzschean-
ism to-day, and Lawrence's anticipations of the superman as
bad caricature. His heroes were described by those who loved
them not as a mixture of libertine and prize-fighter. Their
leader, Guy Livingstone, reappears in successive novels with
differences of period and costume, and, in one case at least, of
sex. He is endowed with prodigious bodily strength, with a
savage temper masked by imperturbable calm; he is haughty,
domineering, and contemptuous of everybody and everything
not belonging to his own order, for every character of Lawrence's
whom he treats with the slightest respect is "thoroughbred."
One can hardly conceive how even the omnivorous borrower
from the circulating library could tolerate such a creation,
except as a recoil from the type of smug, genteel hero
which had brightened the pages of Mrs Gore and Lady
Georgiana Fullerton. Still, there was a time when Lara and
the Giaour had crowds of worshippers all over Europe, and
Lawrence wielded a vigorous, arrogant style which fascinated
the sort of reader who afterwards fell a victim to the blandishments of Ouida.

Guy Livingstone, or Thorough, has the simple plot of a memoir "*Guy*
by an admiring crony. Guy flirts with the society beauty *Living*
Flora Bellasys, and spoils her reputation, but brings ample *stone*"
retribution on his own head by breaking the heart of the
woman he really loves. After this life is a burden, and he

[1] *Adam Bede* had appeared that same year (1859).

meets his death in the hunting-field with a serene disregard of danger. There are numerous scenes illustrating Guy's ruthlessness and prowess, some of them pretty gory. Bret Harte's cruel burlesque, "Guy Heavystone,"[1] depicts him in the final scene, armed with sabre and his landing-net for salmon, taking part in the defence of a country house against Irish peasants.

A howl was heard from without, and a party of fifty or sixty armed men precipitated themselves against the door.

Suddenly the window opened. With the rapidity of lightning, Guy Heavystone cast the net over the head of the ringleader, ejaculated "*Habet!*" and with a back stroke of the cavalry sabre severed the member from its trunk, and drawing the net back again, cast the gory head upon the floor, saying quietly:

"One."

Again the net was cast, the steel flashed, the net was withdrawn, and the ominous "Two!" accompanied the head as it rolled on the floor.

"Do you remember what Pliny says of the gladiator?" said Guy, calmly wiping his sabre. "How graphic is that passage commencing: '*Inter nos, etc.*'" The sport continued until the heads of twenty desperadoes had been gathered in. The rest seemed inclined to disperse. Guy incautiously showed himself at the door; a ringing shot was heard, and he staggered back pierced through the heart. Grasping the door-post in the last unconscious throes of his mighty frame, the whole side of the house yielded to that earthquake tremor, and we had barely time to escape before the whole building fell in ruins. I thought of Samson, the Giant Judge, etc., etc.; but all was over.

Guy Heavystone had died as he had lived—*hard*.

"*Sword and Gown*" The ancient blood, the superb physique, the intractable will, and the prowess among the ladies, that distinguished Guy, were inherited by Major Royston, in *Sword and Gown* (1859). What attracted readers to Lawrence was his trick of putting a barbarian hero from the dark ages in a modern environment. At all events, when he placed his berserk in what should have

[1] *Sensation Novels Condensed* (1870), included in the *Select Works of Bret Harte* (1872).

been a more congenial sphere among the knights of Chandos
and Du Guesclin, as he does in *Brakespeare,* a tale of the
Hundred Years War, he was not so successful. Yet this is a
rousing story, with no lack of Homeric combats. Of course,
he inveighs at large on the abolition of duelling, that touchstone of gentility. "Prudent and polite Prussia," he says, in
language that shows what the Muscular doctrine was leading
to, "under the rule of the most Christian of all monarchs,
ordains these matters differently. If hand be laid on the
sacred uniform," etc.

Reaction was inevitable. Everyone knows how it was *The re-*
voiced in Matthew Arnold's *Culture and Anarchy* (1869) and *action—*
Friendship's Garland (1871), and the immortal subdivision of *Matthew*
the British people into Barbarians, Philistines, and Populace. *Arnold*
But a different sort of book that had considerable though *Wilkie*
ephemeral effect was *Man and Wife* (1870), by Wilkie Collins. *Collins*
It was admittedly written for a purpose, or rather two purposes,
to show up the defects of the marriage laws, and to denounce
"the present mania for athletic sports." Granted that a
story framed to expose what the writer considers a corrupt
state of things may be styled a novel, *Man and Wife* is a good
one; at any rate, it is constructed with the author's well-known
mastery of craftsmanship, and is uniformly interesting. Wilkie
Collins combines his two grievances, first depicting a nation
absorbed, to the exclusion of any higher interests, in the cult
of athletic sports, and then showing the effect upon their
attitude towards women.

There is far too much glorification in England, just now, of
the mere physical qualities which an Englishman shares with
the savage and the brute. And the ill results are beginning
to show themselves already. We are readier than we ever
were to practise all that is rough in our national customs, and
to excuse all that is violent and brutish in our national acts.
Read the popular books; attend the popular amusements—
and you will find at the bottom of them all a lessening regard
for the gentler graces of civilized life, and a growing admiration
for the virtues of the aboriginal Britons.

Had he been reading Kingsley's opening paragraphs in

Hereward, where the virtues of primitive times, of the era of the Norman Conquest, for instance, are contrasted with the vices of "incivilization"? Collins hits out with both fists. Argument he puts in the mouth of a sensible and satirical old gentleman, Sir Patrick Lundie, who cannot put up with the present generation of young men, nor they with him. But his frontal attack is with the awful example, in the person of Geoffrey Delamayn, son of Lord Holchester, and champion of all England as runner and boxer—marvellous combination! Delamayn, who unites many incompatible propensities, an insatiable thirst for beer, addiction to tobacco, and a Guy Livingstone's zest for the sport of woman-hunting, with devotion to the prize-ring, the foot-race, and the Spartan training necessary for pre-eminence in these accomplishments, is the monster whose villainies serve to exhibit the abuses of the marriage laws, and whose brutality and well-merited fate show what the craze for athletic sports can bring an educated gentleman to. He drives one unfortunate woman to the verge of suicide and another to crime, and brings himself to a disgraceful end in the act of attempting murder. Lawrence let the cat out of the bag when he praised Prussia for keeping up the duello, in the same breath as he glorified the "Physical Force Doctrine." Let the author of *Man and Wife* have a say on such methods of preparing young men for their social responsibilities:

The savage element in humanity—let the modern optimists who doubt its existence look at any uncultivated man (no matter how muscular), woman (no matter how beautiful), or child (no matter how young)—began to show itself furtively in his eyes, to utter itself furtively in his voice. Was he to blame for the manner in which he looked at her, and spoke to her? Not he! What had there been in the training of *his* life (at school or at college) to soften and subdue the savage element in him? About as much as there had been in the training of his ancestors (without the school or the college) five hundred years since.

The Muscular novel is not of great importance in the history of literature. As usual, war had its effects upon writers and readers, but did not evoke any imaginative creation of surpassing merit or permanence. It is in reference to the educational question, in its widest aspects, that the Muscular novel is significant; each of the writers now under consideration was virtually engaged in expressing his ideas on that problem.

Tennyson regarded war as an educating and refining experience. This is the thesis also of *Two Years Ago*; all Kingsley's novels, indeed, from *Yeast* to *Hereward*, enunciate definite views on the proper ideal for England and English character and the means of attaining it. Hughes set out, from a practical account of education at school and university, to discourse at large on the methods then adopted for educating the masses. Following the lead of Kingsley, whom he admired without any real sympathy, Lawrence propounded his own ideal, crude and reactionary as it was. Collins in *Man and Wife* wrote more as a social critic than in his accustomed rôle. Muscular heroes became a fashion; they were always appearing. Charles Reade's Alfred Hardie and David and Edward Dodd, in *Hard Cash*, are examples, and Lytton's Kenelm Chillingly is another, more belated.[1]

That rolling stone, Henry Kingsley (1830–1876), much the younger brother of Charles, who did not love him, was at one time a fine example of athleticism and muscularity himself, though he never went out of his way to preach it as a doctrine. His literary career was a brief one, beginning with *Geoffrey Hamlyn* (1859), culminating in his next novel, *Ravenshoe* (1862), and falling away gradually to the posthumous *Mystery of the Island* (1877). Neither of the Kingsleys was a man of genius; they belonged to the inferior yet honourable order that comes a little below the great. Charles, as a fashionable preacher in the days of Tractarianism and the Church Militant, a propagandist in the social and political field, lived in the glare of publicity whilst his brother wandered in backwoods and back streets. But that is not the whole reason why in the literary world he managed to eclipse his brother, who in some respects was a better novelist, in the production of lifelike characters, at any rate. The popular novelist, preacher, or

Henry Kingsley

---

[1] See Volume VII. 201.

after-dinner orator is the man who can tell a story. Admirable character-drawing never made a novelist dear to the multitude without the gift of absorbing narrative. Charles Kingsley had that gift, as well as a talent for embodying ideas and ideals then much before the public in characters that did things even if they were not remarkable human creations in themselves. Some of Henry's episodes are unforgettably thrilling. But it is as a delineator of virile, sterling, but not brilliant human figures, a portrayer of happy, ordinary family life, with an atmosphere of mellow, bracing, and often hilarious feeling, that the younger Kingsley makes his appeal. He was in various ways a contrast to his famous brother, who achieved that grand object of the modern Englishman's terrestrial existence, success. Henry was an ineffectual kind of man. He took no degree at Oxford, but took himself off to the Australian gold-fields, whence he returned after some years of hardship, not a millionaire, to find his brother at the zenith of his brilliant career.

"Geoffrey Hamlyn" In a year's time he published his first novel, *Geoffrey Hamlyn*, which like many first novels was constructed of autobiographical material. It opens amid the scenes of his boyhood in Devon; but the early incidents are only the prelude to a fascinating narrative of life on the big cattle-stations of New South Wales, which the author sometimes advertises in the style of an emigration prospectus. After a few chapters, the villain of the piece, one George Hawker, is transported for forgery to Van Diemen's Land, and the circle of friends and relations already introduced are found settled on vast estates along the Snowy River, amidst the glorious scenery of Gippsland. It is managed very artlessly, how all these delightful people gravitate together, some by chance, some by design; grow rich and happy together; and in the course of years, when old memories revive the spell of the motherland, moneyed uncles die, fortunes and landed estates are opportunely bequeathed, titles and grand old Devon castles inherited, and even the delectable Dr Mulhaus, who is really an exiled baron in disguise, is recalled to high office under the king in his native Germany. But clumsiness

in the plot escapes attention whilst the reader is as it were talking with this charming company of English men and women, and sympathizing with their joys and troubles as if they were his own kin. Henry Kingsley is optimism incarnate. "The good people in the world outnumber the bad, ten to one, and the ticket for this sort of belief is 'optimist.'" Like the rest of his novels, it is a noble eulogy of friendship and high character, and there is not a false note in it. But into this golden atmosphere of health and happiness come the thunder-clouds of life; the temper of the young race of heroes must be tried by storm and tragedy. The terrible Hawker, whose hereditary profligacy had brought himself and others to ruin, long ago in Devon, escapes to the mainland with a band of convicts, and is suddenly heard of as the captain of a gang of bushrangers who have committed fearful crimes and are the terror of the country. Few episodes in English fiction surpass the paralysing tension of fear and suspense in the chapters telling how these desperadoes are foiled in their attack on the stations, hunted down by settlers and mounted police, and shot or captured in a beautiful defile of the Snowy Mountains. The romance of circumstance and the romance of incident are surpassingly combined in Hawker's ride and last stand under Mount Kosciusko, near the springs of the Murray. The younger Kingsley had a magical gift for description, whether it is the solitudes of the Australian bush with its giant trees, vast plains and rivers and solemn mountains, the moors and grand ancestral parks of the west country, in *Ravenshoe*, or the scenery of the Hebrid Isles, in *Austin Elliot*. And he did it with a careless ease, with strokes of life not art, so to speak, that are as graphic, or more so, as the studied and elaborate effects of his brother's word-painting. And it is not mere physical adventure with no concern for the things of the spirit. How beautiful is the epilogue to the story of the little boy who strayed across the river to the wonderful forbidden country, and wandered on up the mountain till he died! Beside his body, which they are the first to find, Sam Buckley and Cecil Mayford unbosom themselves of their rival passion, and swear an honourable truce, like two paladins of old romance. The

reader parts very reluctantly with bluff Tom Troubridge, fine
old Major Buckley, and the athletic dean, Frank Maberley,
one of the muscular parsons of that era, who comes on the scene
as the hero of a rat-hunt, and jumps five-barred gates at middle
age to show that he is not getting flabby.

"Ravens-
hoe" Yet in the next novel, *Ravenshoe* (1862), the reader finds himself in the midst of a still larger crowd of not less attractive
people. Ravenshoe is an ancient priest-ridden house on the
edge of Exmoor, or somewhere like it in north Devon overlooking the sea. Cuthbert Ravenshoe, the ruling squire, is the
hero's brother, or half-brother, or a changeling innocently
claiming to be such—the mystery is so involved that the
reader yields himself to it and asks no questions. But the
plot is of small interest; it is the people, from the somewhat
enigmatic Cuthbert, a recluse with many fine traits, down to
the delightful if too precocious children, the servants, fishermen,
and other West Country folk, who make a galaxy of diversified
and captivating figures. Cuthbert's tutelary genius, the
domineering priest Mackworth, is a villain, but a man for all
that, and one that cannot but be liked. Henry Kingsley loved
his villains; he could not help allowing them some relics of
fallen nobility; they are never mean, cold-hearted, despicable
—it is the result of his incurable optimism and inexhaustible
benevolence. Yet they are truly villainous; their wickedness
is so genuine because they are so thoroughly human. Hence,
for example, the curious fascination of such a creature as the
young Lord Welter, blackleg and bully and rather stupid as
he is; though his guilt is glozed over by no sentimentality, he
keeps his bonhomie and some generous impulses to the last.
Then Lady Ascot and the other dowagers, old Humby, a most
humorous figure of a Devonshire squire, and, best of them all,
Lord Saltire, representative of the grand seigneurs who by
twenty years of no surrender saved Europe from Napoleon, are
creations that stick to the memory when plot and story are in
the limbo of forgotten things. Henry Kingsley never mastered
the art of construction. The story as a whole may be naught,
yet the scenes remain vivid, and single episodes often seem
matchless pieces of narrative. Such are the wreck of the

Warren Hastings—"a-sunk beneath the briny waves, my
darling; and all aboard of her, being good sailors and brave
soldiers, is doubtless at this moment in glory!"—and the hunting of the Black Hare, believed to be a witch—"They all came
round the corner pell-mell. Here stood the dogs, panting and
looking foolishly about them, while, in front of them, a few
yards distant, stood Father Mackworth, looking disturbed and
flushed, as though he had been running."

In *Austin Elliot* (1863), again, the tale is of small account, *His other*
the gallery of characters everything. For pictures of child- *novels*
life, young manhood, and ·healthy, unaffected friendship
between father and son, the book is charming. The love-story
takes a subordinate place to the friendship of Austin and Charles
Barty, its happy springtide and fatal culmination. The love-
affair, in truth, is really an idealized friendship, beginning with
the betrothal of the boy and girl, the growing boy telling the
girl of his frequent loves, until there is one serious passion
which he omits to confess. Then respect and affection grow
with the increase of years and wisdom, till Austin realizes that
the girl who loves him is the best woman in the world. Inchoate
as anything he wrote, *The Hillyars and the Burtons: a Story of
Two Families* (1865), is also as charming, particularly in its
reminiscences of the family life of the Kingsleys in the old
Chelsea rectory where Henry spent his boyhood. He pursues
the fortunes of different members of the two families, from
Chelsea to Australia, and the pictures of life and scenery in
the new country are coloured with his usual high spirits and
enthusiasm. The characters are as fine a set of honest, manly,
and affectionate people as he ever drew. *Silcote of Silcotes*
(1867) is another family chronicle, with a troop of children
who talk too much like their seniors, and the note of tragic
irony and disillusionment in their subsequent lives is forced
and unconvincing. Kingsley often ruined his effects by his
habit of delivering judgment on everybody and everything as
he went along; the characters do the same, with regard to
each other, which inevitably provokes the reader to vote some
of them prigs. But there is power in the old berserk Silcote,
the bullying but engaging "dark Squire"; and the terse,

critical, sarcastic dialogue is in tune, even if the situations are too monotonously charged with dramatic irony.

Sketches of character

Kingsley was good at bringing out family traits, without slurring strong personal differences. Arthur, the Puseyite, built like his stubborn old father, but an idealist, and, in truth, not free from priggism; Algernon, the forsaken son, with his indomitable pride, of which a proud humility is a chief constituent; the half-mad princess, obstinate and utterly irresponsible; the frank, clear-eyed Dora; the wayward, ungovernable Anne, and the wild viking Tom, are a set of strong, masterful, clashing characters taken in the act of development. The Silcotes are souls of fire, not men of clay; they are the peers of Charles Kingsley's Heroes: their strength, courage, magnanimity, their viking hearts, enthrall, and quickly relieve the reader's mind of any suspicion of their pure spontaneity. But Henry Kingsley does not here so much as elsewhere seem the precursor of William de Morgan, in the tender humanity which invests so many of the latter's characters, tempting the reader to fall in love with them and wish their family annals to go on for ever.[1] The Italian war of liberation cuts the thread of several destinies, and the battlefields of Montebello and Palestro are described with military details learned, not on the spot, but from personal observation of the French army manœuvres of 1866. Kingsley often makes a show of censuring sentimentality; but neither he nor such a creation as Aunt Eleanor, in *Stretton* (1869), is quite weatherproof, and there is plenty of sentiment in the relations of the young men. "I gave it all up to come to you, and you don't care for me," says one young man to his friend. "I care for you more than any living being, Edward," is the rejoinder. "Hush, man, I know you do." This lack of customary English reticence in Henry Kingsley's friendships should not, however, be condemned; but the rubbish about a philtre to make Ethel and Roland fall in love and marry is a different matter, and an illicit device even if he is right in talking about that "slight

---

[1] I remember long ago talking about this to "E. Nesbit," the late Mrs Bland, but cannot remember which of us first confessed to be struck by the affinity which we both sensed between authors in many ways so different.

caricature of life which we call fiction." [1]   Like Silcote, *Stretton*
is semi-historical, the Indian Mutiny being dragged in, and
that clumsily, for the ends of poetic justice.   His *Mademoiselle
Mathilde* (1868) had been a very creditable study of the Reign
of Terror, and now *Old Margaret* (1871) was as good on Antwerp
in the time of Philip the Good of Burgundy and the Van Eycks.
Valentin (1872) was "a French boy's story of Sedan," but a
sad come-down from the vigour and vividness of *Geoffrey
Hamlyn* and *Ravenshoe*.   In the family history of *The Harveys*
(1872), a very Bohemian family, published just before, he
almost recaptured, however, the leisurely charm of his earlier
domestic novels.[2]

Rather as a couple of friends who wrote in a manner that he *"The
School of
Dickens"
—Wilkie
Collins
and
Reade*
approved for the magazines run by the master, than as thoroughgoing imitators, William Wilkie Collins (1824–1889) and Charles
Reade (1814–1884) are sometimes described as constituting a
"School of Dickens."   They could rival and outrival the
author of *Oliver Twist* and *Bleak House, Great Expectations*
and *Edwin Drood*, in sensationalism and the manipulation of
theatrical plots; and they imitated him at a greater distance
in a number of picturesque and serio-comic characters.   They
were men of great natural talent rather than genius; but as
expert craftsmen they stood the comparison brilliantly.   Reade
plumed himself on being first and foremost a playwright, and
desired that the word "dramatist" should precede that of
"novelist" on his tombstone.   A number of his plays had been
produced, and he had made a great hit at the Haymarket
with *Masks and Faces* (1852), before he converted this into
his first novel, *Peg Woffington* (1853).   Wilkie Collins, son of
the painter William Collins, with a biography of whom he
commenced authorship (1848) and whose example he so far
followed as to have a picture hung at the Academy (1847),
first wrote novels which were afterwards dramatized, by his

[1] S. M. Ellis (*Henry Kingsley*, 84–85) scouts the suggestion that *Stretton* contains
any self-parody, and attributes its absurdities to Henry's financial worries, which
led him to the verge of distraction just then.

[2] Kingsley witnessed Sedan, and there was a legend that he was the first Englishman to enter the captured town; but he was far more vivid in his accounts of the
Italian war, in *Silcote*, and of the Reign of Terror, in *Mademoiselle Mathilde*.   "But
his power with the pen was now weakening," as Ellis observes (p. 94).

own or other hands. As a youth, he was articled to a firm of tea-merchants; then he studied law, and was called to the Bar (1851), but speedily applied himself wholly to letters. In his early teens he had been taken to Rome by his parents, and his first novel was the very creditable essay in an old-established style, *Antonina* (1850), a story of Alaric in Rome, the picturesque staging done with a sense of atmosphere which was always to stand him in good stead. He met Dickens shortly after, and his next novel was read by the master himself. This was *Basil* (1852), a gloomy "story of modern life," which gave a better foretaste of the realistic stories of the present day, with an undercurrent of tragedy, that followed. Before long, Dickens had him contributing to *Household Words*, and later on to *All the Year Round*. The two went on a tour to Switzerland and Italy, with Augustus Egg (1855), as Forster amusingly recounts in the life of Dickens; they also paid several visits to Paris together. Dickens frequently had theatricals at his house, and on one memorable occasion a melodrama in two acts by Collins, entitled *The Lighthouse*, was followed by *Mr Nightingale's Diary* by himself. A tour they made together in the northern counties was punctuated by some alarming incidents, and furnished Collins with scenic impressions for *The Woman in White*.[1] The fact is, the function of impressive surroundings in a drama of character, as well as the art of manipulating plot, was a side of his work in which the older hand definitely acquired something from the younger. Dickens took part with Collins in various performances of *The Frozen Deep*,[2] by Collins; and their collaboration in *No Thoroughfare* (1867),[3] a novel speedily dramatized, was so close that it is not easy to reach any safe conclusion on their respective shares. They worked hand in glove on some of the Christmas numbers for the two magazines; and *Bleak House* (1853), *Little Dorrit* (1857), and *A Tale of Two Cities* (1859) show the effect of their

[1] They told their tale of this expedition in *The Lazy Tour of Two Idle Apprentices* (*Household Words*, October, 1857).
[2] *The Frozen Deep* was turned into a novel, which is carefully examined as typifying Collins's insistence upon the "coincidences, resemblances, and surprises of life" by Mr T. S. Eliot (*Selected Essays*—"Wilkie Collins and Dickens," 414-415).
[3] See Volume VII. 325.

collaboration on Dickens. Though Reade first made his mark as a playwright, he was already a popular novelist, chiefly on the strength of his *Never Too Late to Mend* (1856), when he contributed *Hard Cash* (1863) to *All the Year Round*. It was Lytton who had introduced him to Dickens, and the latter would gladly have had Reade on the staff of his magazine. But Reade had a public of his own, which evidently was not quite identical with that of Dickens. He and Collins were great friends, much more so than Reade and Dickens ever were. The master did not see eye to eye with Reade, and the serial publication of *Hard Cash* did not mend matters, for it seems to have reduced the circulation of the magazine by three thousand copies.[1] Collins, on the contrary, was a pillar of strength, and wrote *After Dark* and *The Dead Secret* for *Household Words*, and *The Woman in White, No Name*, and *The Moonstone* for *All the Year Round*. It was the great era of the popular magazine largely alimented with fiction. Thackeray, Trollope, George Eliot, and Meredith, as well as Wilkie Collins and Reade, had serials in the *Cornhill Magazine*; *Blackwood's* had Lytton, *Macmillan's* Tom Hughes, *Fraser's* some of Thackeray's and Kingsley's novels. Mrs Gaskell wrote regularly for *Household Words*. Collins was on the staff of Dickens's two magazines; Reade was only a contributor, and a rare one at that. He was busy writing plays as well as novels to the end of his life, and his fiction always savours more or less of the theatre. Careful examination, indeed, shows that the art of managing climax and curtain, which the two learned in writing for the stage, proved just as useful in the treatment of stories for serial publication. The separate instalments of *Armadale* and *Hard Cash*, for instance, can still be recognized by the terminal incidents, the "curtain lines," which left the reader aghast, and in a state of eager suspense for the sequel. Reade was particularly addicted to this device, though it was Collins who formulated the injunction, "Let 'em wait." [2] The opposite results of having to fill three volumes are similarly

[1] Phillips, 115.
[2] Both wrote several of their best-known novels as serials in the *Argosy* or the *Cornhill Magazine*.

observable in the leisurely gait and occasional padding in work meant for publication in that form. And fiction of that kind relied far less on what was Collins's and Reade's speciality, plot. These two, in fact, did not aim at a stereotyped length, and their novels are anything but uniform in this respect.

Wilkie
Collins
—early
novels

Already, in the preface to *Basil*, Wilkie Collins had affirmed his view "that the novel and the play are twin sisters in the family of fiction." Melodrama was the sort of play he had in mind; and the novel that followed, *Hide and Seek* (1854), with its secret long withheld, "The Yellow Mask" and the other tales comprised in *After Dark* (1856), and his Cornish story, *The Dead Secret* (1857), with which he took his place as the master of ingenious plot-work and of the art of holding the reader in a trance of expectation, mark clear stages in the development of such theatrical fiction. A typical Wilkie Collins novel has three main ingredients: an intricate puzzle-plot, some amusing characterization in the Dickens style, and a love-tale interwoven. Long after his day and Reade's, the modern detective novel was evolved, in which the plot is the business, and these other factors are at a discount, even if there is an ostentatious regard for the psychology of motive as distinct from character; the intellectual problem is given full scope. Collins was determined to let his readers have their full money's worth, to satisfy all tastes; and subscribers to the circulating libraries insisted on having their love-story, what was roughly labelled humour, and plot. Thus the intellectual scheme was clogged up with extraneous interests, and Collins and Reade are not always free from padding. In *The Dead Secret* the main concern is the gradual disclosure of the secret to the reader, which secret is darkly conveyed in a letter handed to the chief character on the death-bed of the chief delinquent, in the initial chapter. To construe this, the novel must be read to the end. Thus the whole fabric of mystification depends upon a trick, the novelist withholding a piece of information, and then letting the reader fathom it bit by bit, whilst those vitally concerned have to find it out. In a sense, it is only elaborate make-believe, the æsthetic qualities, apart from this inversion of the torments of Tantalus, arising from the dramatic tension of fear and suspense, in the characters, and the cunning manipulation for the reader's benefit of such theatrical effects as curiosity, hope, and surprise. The misanthropic uncle, Andrew Trevanion, and his crusty henchman, Squelch, are Dickensian eccentrics, who furnish some comedy, and are skilfully employed as pivots to the underlying scheme. There had been a moral purpose in *Hide and Seek*: to show how the life of a deaf-mute might be made happy. In a later novel, *Poor Miss Finch*,[1] the heroine is a blind girl, and Collins has blind characters elsewhere. Warm humanitarian feelings no doubt account sufficiently for these and other victims of the world's injustice who are frequent in his novels. As he was now collaborating with Dickens, it is not strange that such a figure as Uncle Joseph and also the children are drawn with a humour and a delight in life's oddities savouring strongly of his adopted father in art. But the plot interest, which continually overrides the purely human interest, holding the reader magnetized till the secret is fully disclosed, surpasses any of his great senior's performances in the same particular line, even after the latter had learned dexterity from his junior's example.

Next to a composite volume, *The Queen of Hearts* (1859), "*The Woman in White*" notable for a first-class tale of terror, "Brother Morgan's Story of the Dead Hand," came *The Woman in White* (1860), which must compete with *Armadale* and *The Moonstone* for first place with devotees of Collins. It is a complication of intrigue, concealed crime to be exposed, and counterplotting of the villains and the honest people, all hingeing on coincidence —that is, on the existence of a double, so like the heroine, Lady Glyde, that the nefarious baronet can pass her off as his wife, bury her, and claim the fortune, whilst he locks up his real wife in an asylum as the madwoman, her very image. At the outset, the man who tells the story has not yet met the beautiful woman about to become Lady Glyde, whom later he is to fall in love with, and in the upshot rescue and marry. This

[1] *Poor Miss Finch* and *No Name* are to a large extent novels of purpose, like *Man and Wife* (see above, p. 183). So too are *The New Magdalen* (1873), which records the tragic redemption of a camp-follower, and *Heart and Science* (1883), attacking vivisection.

innocent gentleman encounters the Woman in White, the famous double, on Hampstead Heath, and is thus accidentally involved in the whole mysterious business the day before he goes to Cumberland to take the post of drawing-master to the future Lady Glyde. This, for the reader, is the starting-point. The complications go on steadily growing in intricacy, with gleams of illumination from time to time, down to the last chapter. Then it comes out that the mysterious double is the illegitimate sister of Lady Glyde; that the baronet is not a baronet at all, but illegitimate; and that he has been scheming all along, with the aid of a more accomplished villain, Count Fosco, to get hold of the money urgently required to save him from ruin. The pseudo-baronet is accidentally burned to death while tampering with a church register. Count Fosco, his brother-in-law, is an Italian spy who has played traitor to his compatriots; cool, audacious, polished in manners, utterly unscrupulous, not sticking at murder, but externally a very attractive person. Sir Percival is a paltry scoundrel in comparison, so much so as to raise the question, did Collins make Fosco too pleasing? One purpose was to furnish the usual comic relief and picturesque diversity to the grimmer elements. Collins went further; but it can hardly be objected that he makes anyone in love with crime, however much Fosco fascinates for a while with his white mice, his cockatoo, and canary-birds. No objection on this score, at all events, lies against the other great character, Marian Halcombe, "the good angel of our lives," as the chief raconteur calls her at the end. Collins surpassed himself in describing this lady:

She had not heard my entrance into the room. . . . She turned towards me immediately. The easy elegance of every movement of her limbs and body, as soon as she began to advance from the far end of the room, set me in a flutter of expectation to see her face clearly. She left the window— and I said to myself, The lady is dark. She moved forward a few steps—and I said to myself, The lady is young. She approached nearer, and I said to myself (with a sense of surprise which words fail me to express), The lady is ugly!

The others are little more than puppets with names attached. It is a defect in a representation of human nature; but, after all, in a plot-novel plot is the thing. Characters are mere abstracts or generalizations in the works of such story-tellers as Poe and the French melodramatists, differentiated into such broad categories as angels, demons, and animated waxworks. Collins, at all events, made his villains picturesque: Fosco, Trevanion, Squelch, Sergeant Cuff, Betteredge, Miss Clack, and the rest, may be manufactured articles; but the pattern is interesting, and they are well made, as much after Dickens as Collins could achieve. The valid objection would be that as characters, as something more than figures in the action, they are described and depicted rather than dramatized; they are automata with interesting outsides. Dickens applied plot to character; Collins added character to plot, and made it fit as best he could. The method of *The Woman in White* approximates to that of a trial, the depositions of various witnesses being submitted as if the readers were a jury. He said in the preface that he had been coached by a solicitor of great experience, who guided his steps "whenever the course of the narrative led me into the labyrinth of the Law." The solution of the mystery is circumstantial enough, however complicated. But such intricate concatenations of circumstance do not occur in life with the frequency postulated by the sensational novelist, who must however employ them freely to hold his structure together. Sir Percival's expensive plotting, with his crowd of servants, spies, myrmidon lawyers, and the like, is somewhat difficult to reconcile with his impecuniosity, for he is supposed to be all the time on the verge of bankruptcy; and his suspicious ways and moodiness are enough to arouse distrust. But a much more serious improbability is that of Mr Fairlie's refusal to acknowledge his own niece, who has lived with him for years. And this might be considered the pivot on which everything turns. The public, however, did not mind, if it noticed such weak points; in six months *The Woman in White* ran through more than as many editions, and an adaptation for the stage was inevitable, though an authorized dramatic version was not presented till

1871, twelve years after the first instalment had appeared in *All the Year Round.*

In the novel that followed, *No Name* (1862), in which the marriage laws are challenged on behalf of a girl who finds herself illegitimate, Collins reduplicated the complications of a veritable puzzle-plot and wrung their full sentimental value out of melancholy landscapes on the coast of Suffolk. He obviously got suggestions for the most prominent characters from Dickens; the swindler, Captain Wragge, and his wife, Miss Garth the governess, and perhaps Magdalen Vanstone, may be entered to that account. The craftsmanship is faultless, but there are as it were only rare accidents of inspiration. *Armadale* (1866) is brilliant in comparison; here Collins has not hampered himself with any controversial thesis, though in a curious apology he pleads guilty of having overstepped "in more than one direction" the narrow limits readers would put to the development of modern fiction. His quack doctor at the Hampstead sanatorium gives notice:

"The English novelist who enters my house (no foreign novelist will be admitted) must understand his art as the healthy-minded English reader understands it in our time. He must know that our purer modern taste, our higher modern morality, limits him to doing exactly two things for us, when he writes a book. All we want of him is—occasionally to make us laugh, and invariably to make us comfortable."

Is it to the villainies shown up that he is alluding—the murder of Ingleby in the water-logged ship, and the forgeries, poisonings, and bigamies of Miss Gwilt, not to mention Manuel, Mrs Oldershaw, the beauty specialist, and some others of a very black lot, or to the Dickensian gardener, Abraham Sage? Wilkie Collins never surpassed the eeriness of the scene-painting in this novel—the waters that wrecked the derelict ship off the Calf of Man, and the meres and creeks of East Anglia in the later chapters. He was never more a master of suggestive atmosphere. The machinery in this case is in full view, but that does not detract in the least from the compulsive interest with which the reader watches it moving.

"Arma-dale"

He goes so far, now and then, as to discuss the position, which is tantamount to canvassing the effects employed; and even this does not disenchant. The ingenuity and close-fitting elaboration are of his best; surprises and other theatrical strokes are all properly prepared and authenticated; there are cautious identifications, corroboration of evidence by experts; the improbabilities are honestly faced and justified. Hence, though the impression conveyed is that in this world nothing occurs but coincidences, even this is vindicated by the theory of chance as destiny, the obverse of Conrad's theme in *Chance*, half-a-century later. When Allan tosses to decide whether he shall accept Major Milroy or the family solicitor as his tenant, Midwinter observes: "I was wondering . . . whether there is such a thing as chance." When Allan and the seventeen-year-old Miss Milroy are debating an elopement at the very hour when Miss Gwilt has consented to marry Midwinter, the novelist interprets:

Here again, in this, as in all other human instances, the widely discordant elements of the grotesque and the terrible were forced together by that subtle law of contrast which is one of the laws of moral life. Amid all the thickening complications now impending over their heads—with the shadow of meditated murder stealing towards one of them already, from the lurking-place that hid Miss Gwilt—the two sat down, unconscious of the future, with the book between them (Blackstone's *Commentaries*); and applied themselves to the law of marriage, with a grave resolution to understand, which in two such students was nothing less than a burlesque in itself.

And so the deponent protests, when pious Mr Decimus Brock tries to reason him out of his superstitious sense of fate, that it is "encouraging him to trample down his own imagination, with an Englishman's ready distrust of the noblest of the human faculties." Mr Brock is one of the select figures carefully individualized in order to provide guide-posts, as well as to interest in themselves. In a plot-novel, heavy demands are made on the reader's powers of concentration and retention; it may be difficult to keep count of the various actors, to hold the terms of a complex equation clear in the mind. In a novel of Scott or of Dickens, it is impossible to forget the characters, who are never mere counters or abstract terms, though they may be absurdities. Foremost among those characters who have better reasons for their existence stands Miss Gwilt, not an entire monstrosity; for, though she is prepared in the last chapter to murder Allan Armadale, and benefit by the sum bequeathed to his widow, as which she is ready to pass though actually the wife of Ozias Midwinter, she yet trembles with remorse, and saves Midwinter before her own suicide. But the foolish, impulsive Allan, the vile Mother Oldershaw, turned pious, the jealous Mrs Milroy, and the infatuated old Bashwood, who runs eagerly after Miss Gwilt though he knows her whole history, equal to the situation as their idiosyncrasies consistently make them, are only skin-deep characterizations. It is amusing and edifying to compare Miss Gwilt with the far less culpable Becky Sharp.[1]

"The Moon- stone"
In *The Moonstone* (1868),[2] the method of converging depositions by a crowd of witnesses was applied with the utmost rigour. Eight separate narratives are devoted to "the Discovery of the Truth," which is the problem and the title of the largest section of the book. These successive reports are summarized, and certain inscrutable incidents are cleared up, at the end. Eight centuries ago, the jewel was looted from the Indian idol; and now, after infinite patience, heroism, and cunning, three Brahmins steal the well-guarded jewel and flee with it to India. Their adventures are desperate and complicated enough; but that is not the theme. It is the mystery and the haunting terror emanating from the operations of the three Indians in the background that absorb the reader and hold him spellbound. It is romance, romance of here and now, and as true an example of "matter-of-fact romance" as any of Reade's, who loved that phrase. It is romance of the authentic Radcliffian stamp, too, though at times it proceeds from a mouth in which it certainly sounds falsetto, as when

---

[1] *Armadale* was dramatized by Collins as *Miss Gwilt* (1875).
[2] Dramatized under the same title, and produced at the Olympic (1877). *The New Magdalen* appeared there too, and was a great success.

that admirable steward, Mr Betteredge, delivers himself of such a sensitive bit of meditative feeling as this, whilst he goes the rounds of the house towards midnight:

"The night was still and close, and the moon was at the full in the heavens. It was so silent out of doors, that I heard from time to time, very faint and low, the fall of the sea, as the ground-swell heaved it on the sand-bank near the mouth of our little bay. As the house stood, the terrace side was the dark side; but the broad moonlight showed fair on the gravel walk that ran along the next side to the terrace. Looking this way, after looking up at the sky, I saw the shadow of a person in the moonlight thrown forward from behind the corner of the house."

Betteredge is more in character with his *Sortes Virgilianæ* from *Robinson Crusoe*. He is one of the Dickensian figures, like that formidable policeman, Inspector Cuff, and Miss Clack, a feminine Chadband. But Wilkie Collins was not born a humorist; he believed that "the two qualities which hold the highest place" in the public estimation were character and humour,[1] and he forced himself to provide what was wanted. And this straining after something which did not come natural, however much it helped for the moment to individualize figures that otherwise might have seemed automata, in the absence of any searching exposure of motive, left even his most sensational evildoers far less concrete and impressive than those who occur in unsensational chronicles of normal life. Miss Gwilt could never compare with Becky Sharp, and looks simply factitious beside a masterpiece in the same genre, Lady Eustace, the heroine of the diamonds.[2]

[1] Preface to *Heart and Science* (1883.)

[2] Trollope expressed his high admiration, but had to avow that much of the work of Wilkie Collins was "very much lost upon me individually." "When I sit down to write a novel I do not at all know, and I do not very much care, how it is to end. Wilkie Collins seems so to construct his that he not only, before writing, plans everything on, down to the minutest detail, from the beginning to the end; but then plots it all back again, to see that there is no piece of necessary dovetailing which does not dovetail with absolute accuracy. The construction is most minute and most wonderful. But I can never lose the taste of the construction. The author seems always to be warning me that something happened at exactly half-past two o'clock on Tuesday morning; or that a woman disappeared from the road just fifteen yards beyond the fourth milestone. One is constrained by mysteries and

Charles
Reade

Charles Reade (1814–1884), ten years the senior of Wilkie Collins, was the youngest son of an Oxfordshire squire of old family, and an Oxford man who was elected fellow and subsequently vice-president of Magdalen. He entered Lincoln's Inn and was called to the Bar, speedily however turning his main attention to the theatre. He retained his college fellowship all his life. Reade's first play, *The Ladies' Battle*, was an adaptation from Scribe and Legouvé; produced at the Olympic (1851), it was quickly followed by others, a number of them in collaboration with Tom Taylor. His first great hit was the two-act comedy, *Masks and Faces* (1852), in partnership with Taylor; out of it he manufactured his first novel, *Peg Woffington* (1853). He was now in his fortieth year, and was to publish eighteen in all. Play after play followed, all of the melodramatic sort, some of the most popular based on his novels, *Never Too Late to Mend* (1865), for instance, and *Foul Play* (1868).[1] His novels inevitably took their prevailing colour from his early training in theatrical methods, and easily adapted themselves to the stage. Reade was never such an adept at the mechanics of plot as Collins; but he was by no means less addicted to the sensational, and with him likewise characterization drops to a subordinate level; he has few memorable human creations to his account, and these few are what they are rather by situation than intrinsically. They are products of the drama, not the converse. In the same comparison again, suspense and surprise in his stories are relatively less important elements in the rush of adventure, the deeds of violence perpetrated, and the perils and calamities into which he plunges his heroes and heroines and other martyrs of circumstance. He rarely indulged, like Collins, in elaborate mystifications. The dramatic situations which he carefully

hemmed in by difficulties, knowing, however, that the mysteries will be made clear, and the difficulties overcome at the end of the third volume. Such work gives me no pleasure. I am, however, quite prepared to acknowledge that the want of pleasure comes from fault of my intellect" (*Autobiography* (1883), ii. 81–82). It is like kicking the novelist upstairs. Trollope had no deep-rooted dislike for sensational incident, though he never sought it for its own sake, just taking it serenely if it came in his way.

[1] His play, *The Double Marriage* (1867), was made from the novel, *White Lies* (1857).

prepared are presented as the outcome of overwhelming clashes of events, rather than of surprising revelations and discoveries. He proclaimed himself, and was, a conscientious and thorough-going realist. A scholar, trained in the methods of research, he put himself through an arduous course of preparation for writing each of his novels, collecting the literature of the subject, visiting prisons, private lunatic asylums, and the like, to study the routine and the inmates, storing masses of information and steeping himself in it to give pith and colour to and authenticate his account of things or people or events. His encyclopædic notebooks are as famous as Zola's, who was not so much his junior but that Reade was to turn one of his novels, *L'Assommoir*, into a play, *Drink* (1879), his greatest success on the boards. Reade owed not a little to the French. Certain of his plays were broad adaptations from Scribe and from Molière. In fiction, he often believed he was competing with Dumas, though it was rather Eugène Sue, Gaboriau, and sometimes Victor Hugo, that he actually rivalled at times.[1] It would be vain to compare him with Balzac. If no genuine creator of character, Reade was a brilliant story-teller. Time has not ratified his confidence in pronouncing himself a great dramatist. But his perpetual stage-effects in both narrative and dialogue do, at all events, give an essentially theatrical air to most of his fiction. Drama, in short, was what he aimed at, in the swift recurrence of tense situations, the curt, racy, energetic, if need be violent, run of his dialogue, and the vivid, staccato, animated style of the rest. He kept mere description at a minimum, though he was always primed with special information, and was inferior to none when description was wanted. Even into this he infused something akin to drama, as witness, for instance, what nowadays might be termed his kinematograph of boat-racing at Henley, in *Hard Cash*. Background and surroundings he evoked with deft touches that avouched thorough familiarity; and the result, when he sought to create impressive atmosphere, was that he stood unsurpassed by any Gothic romancer of his own or any other day. But

---

[1] Swinburne's critical comparison of Reade with Dumas and other French novelists is excellent (*Miscellanies*—"Charles Reade," 73-74).

his stage experience brought him back incessantly to dialogue, as the way of rendering action and indirectly motive in which he was most at home, and his dialogue was extraordinarily efficient. He could tell a story almost entirely in lifelike speech; Dickens and Wilkie Collins knew that art, but were not equal to Reade, whose only rival was the elder Dumas. Hence the brevity of so many of his novels. He was quick at getting to the point; he never dawdled over inessentials. And when the chief vehicle was a series of dialogues between the characters engaged, with the least possible allowance of description and comment, he produced novels almost as brief and compact as the text of a play.[1]

Reade's first novels   *Peg Woffington* (1853) was a hasty transmutation of the comedy *Masks and Faces* into the form of a novel, and his free and lively portrait of the famous Irish actress almost atones for the clumsy stage-trick of the animated picture. Most of his women are better and more sensitively drawn than his men. This and *White Lies* (1857), afterwards dramatized as *The Double Marriage* (1867), have the highest percentage of words put in the mouth of the characters.[2] Reade took more pains with *Christie Johnstone* (1853), made from the play *Fish, Flesh, and Good Red Herring*, though the jerky, ejaculatory style often sounds like a travesty of Victor Hugo, or even of Rabelais. His sense of humour was defective, and he ran fearful risks when he attempted drollery. Here he inculcates the return to nature; and Christie is real womanhood, a confutation of the affected, the fashionable, the snobbish, of shams of all sorts. The fisher-folk of the east coast of Scotland are drawn with a vivacity that makes good the lesson of realism and charity to the blasé nobleman who goes among them and has an adventure which calls out his manhood. Now came Reade's boasted example of a "matter-of-fact romance," *It is Never Too Late to Mend* (1856). It was an attack on two evils of the day, the prison system and the gold mania. The horrifying pictures of what was perpetrated under a so-called humanitarian regime

---

[1] See Phillips (204), who is wrong, however, in supposing *White Lies* to have been made out of a play.

[2] See Phillips (204) on the percentage of speech to narrative in various novels of Reade's.

were taken from an actual case, Winston Green gaol, near Birmingham. This episode, however, only loosely attached, upsets the balance of the novel, and is nearer to journalism than to literature, especially when Reade schedules his notes in parallel columns, and indulges in other freaks befitting a modern advertising expert. Apart from the pamphleteering, which no doubt had more effect than it ever would have had in a more legitimate place and form, this is a huge melodrama of roguery, crime, and heterogeneous adventure, from the first scene on the Berkshire farm to the episodes at the Australian diggings, with a love-story woven in. The excitement never relaxes. Reade's inventiveness is ever on the stretch, and many of the incidents are blood-curdling to an extreme. His graphic pen was equal to anything in the presentment of sinister characters, of the horrors of the bush, of the savagery of the miners' camps. He thought himself an adept at characterization, of a rough-and-ready stamp, at least; but all he achieves is a rendering that looks lifelike of strong, simple, bluff Englishmen, with no niceties of sense or feeling, nothing that is worth calling personality. But the terse, blunt, elliptical style is incomparably vivid; it is a style so clear that a fool cannot mistake the meaning, and so plain that it is sometimes as crude and ungentle as a bludgeon; often it has the effect of a series of violent shocks. It makes the thing go, whatever the matter in hand. And Reade could always fall back upon his gift of dialogue, although this is not exercised so much as usual here, except in the combative chapters on prison reform. He lifted out his *Autobiography of a Thief* (1858) from chapter twenty-two of this novel. It is the criminal record of an Edinburgh student, who seduces a girl and runs away, is caught thieving, and joins a gang of coiners in London. Still hoping for a chance of leading an honest life, he falls into the hands of the police, is transported for ten years, and in his "Prison Thoughts" declares himself an enemy of mankind.

In *Hard Cash* (1863), *Griffith Gaunt* (1866), and *Foul Play* (1869) the novel becomes a pocket theatre, everything being enacted before the reader's eyes. He hears, and it is not Reade's fault if he does not see. Perhaps it is not literature,

pure literature, to use the consecrated phrase; Reade would
not have cared twopence. All he wanted was to give the
reader, by any means, legitimate or illegitimate according to
artistic canons, the very sensations of seeing and hearing,
feeling and shuddering, and of understanding what he saw and
heard as he would understand or be momentarily perplexed
by the actualities he witnessed. The method was well developed in *Griffith Gaunt* and other books; but *Hard Cash*
may be taken as the typical Reade novel. When all this
patent apparatus of actualism was applied to historical fiction
the result was *The Cloister and the Hearth* (1861), which stands
probably unique in its kind. But in this instance Reade did
not restrict himself to his special devices; thus, he did not ban
description; it is vividly pictorial; from beginning to end it
is not only full of adventures, in breathless succession; it glows
with picturesque and diversified scenes, and the tone and
temper is a brotherly feeling for human nature in its manifold
phases. As the reconstruction of an epoch, the fifteenth
century in the Netherlands, Germany, France, and Italy, it is
a brilliant exposition of the notebook system. Reade must
have saturated himself in the literature and the historical
records, and thrown himself into his task this time with a
warmth of enthusiasm that may well be called inspiration.
But, though certainly the greatest, this is not the most characteristic of his novels. Rather is it as if he had accepted
for the time being a self-denying ordinance, not to indulge
in his customary self-denial, not to eschew word-painting,
interpretative comment, and everything else that must
necessarily be denied to the playwright. The best of the
characters, further, are as good flesh and blood as any he ever
evolved. Gerard, the assumed father of Erasmus, his partner
Denys, his sometime servitor, the merry vagabond Cul de
Jatte, and the much-enduring Margaret, do not look like
figures painfully exhumed from books and broadsheets. Reade
whilst he was writing lived in the literature and the records;
hence the picturing of manners and usages is as vivid as if the
result of actual contact. Probably the excellence of *The
Cloister and the Hearth* was owing to Reade's having thought

it over more than once or twice, since a bit of it had appeared
as "A Good Fight" in *Once a Week* (1859), and now he devoted
"more than a year's very hard labour" to developing this
germ and avoiding certain previous deviations from history
that he regretted.[1]

"*Hard Cash*," says the preface, "like *The Cloister and the* "*Hard
Hearth*, is a matter-of-fact Romance—that is, a fiction built of *Cash*"
truths," which truths were gathered from innumerable sources,
including Blue books, newspapers, letters, manuscripts, and
living people, with Reade's customary unflinching industry.
The extra-literary object on this occasion was to expose the
malpractices of private lunatic asylums and the imbecility of
our lunacy laws, one fertile in sensational incident. But *Hard
Cash* was also the sequel to *Love Me Little, Love Me Long*
(1859), a tale of courtship that highly delighted Swinburne, in
which the simple, chivalrous sailor, David Dodd, and the
Diana-like Lucy Fountain, and also the egotistical Mrs Bazal-
gette are introduced, to reappear in the more famous story.
The case is got up like a barrister's brief, a vast amount of
technical information being assimilated and handled with
consummate ease. But the same familiar knowledge and the
same knack of conveying it are shown in scenes of University
life at Oxford, and such incidents as the boat-race, a tea-
clipper taking in cargo, the voyage, with exhaustive nautical
details, an exciting fight with pirates, a bank smash, feverish
speculation in Old Turks, and so on—it often looks like realism
for its own sake. In an attack on the medical profession, of
which the gifted practitioner Sampson is the champion who
slays Goliath, the professional minutiæ are flung about with a
lavish hand, even prescriptions being given in full Chinese,
with burlesque translations. Crowds of doctors figure,
especially alienists. David Dodd goes mad after being swindled
out of his fourteen thousand. Alfred Hardie, sane, is imprisoned in three different institutions. Old Maxley becomes
a raving idiot, and kills Hardie's sister. It is even suggested,
as a plea for letting off the villain lightly, that he too is a
monomaniac. Reade does nothing by halves. Coincidence

[1] Preface.

cuts the knot with unblushing frequency. For example, Dodd and his would-be son-in-law find themselves in the same madhouse, and in the same room when the place is on fire; and Dodd's stalwart son, now a fireman, rescues both. Reade had a weakness for trial scenes; they showed off his pithy, dramatic, and, if need be, truculent dialogue. One is given here, in amplest detail; and it is none the worse for the comic intervention of the Yankee Fullalove and his negro friend Vespasian, who, with David and the sarcastic medical reformer Sampson, of the unruly tongue, are the most amusing and interesting characters.[1]

"Griffith Gaunt" *Griffith Gaunt, or Jealousy* (1866), was criticized by Swinburne with a gravity appropriate to Elizabethan drama. He objected to the sub-title, alleging that the motive for Griffith's act of treachery in offering himself to poor Mercy Vint, being already tied to his wife Kate, was envy, not jealousy. This may be conceded; but the tempest in Griffith's soul which drove him from his home, and all but impelled him to crime, was jealousy of his wife and her idolized priest. In this novel, Reade tried to be psychological and to exhibit motive; it is his nearest approach to that sphere of the true realist. But, whilst the two women are clearly drawn, and their actions are always rational if largely the result of high-wrought feeling,

---

[1] It is in *Hard Cash* (chap. xlviii.) that Reade pauses to expound his view of narrative in the novel, and his effort to "restore, in the reader's judgment, that just balance of 'the sensational' and the 'soporific,' which all writers, that have readers, disturb." He says, "No life was ever yet a play: I mean, an unbroken sequence of dramatic incidents. Calms will come; unfortunately for the readers, happily for the read. And I remember seeing it objected to novelists, by a young gentleman just putting his foot for the first time into 'Criticism,' that the writers aforesaid suppress the small intermediate matters which in real life come by the score between each brilliant event: and so present the ordinary and the extraordinary parts of life in false proportions. Now, if this remark had been offered by way of contrast between events themselves and all mortal attempts to reproduce them upon paper or the stage, it would have been philosophical; but it was a strange error to denounce the practice as distinctive of fiction: for it happens to be the one trait the novelist and dramatist have in common with the evangelist. The Gospels skip fifteen years of the most interesting life Creation has witnessed, relating Christ's birth in full, and hurrying from His boyhood to the more stirring events of His thirtieth and subsequent years. And all the inspired histories do much the same thing. The truth is, that epics, dramas, novels, histories, chronicles, reports of trials at law, in a word, all narratives true or fictitious, except those which, true or fictitious, nobody reads, abridge the uninteresting facts as Nature never did, and dwell as Nature never did on the interesting ones."

the man is nothing but a creature of instinct and impulse. He is a very barbaric barbarian, such a thrall to violent gusts of passion as some of the weaker vessels of the cruder Elizabethan drama. Griffith Gaunt is not worth so much powder and shot. The one character that does shine is the lowly innkeeper's daughter, Mercy. Once again, Reade achieved a splendid melodrama, but failed in the attempt at something superior. Is this searching analysis? Is there not far too much taken for granted?

When he left Mercy Leicester, he was a bigamist in law, but not at heart. Kate was dead to him; he had given her up for ever, and was constant and true to his new wife.

But now he was false to Mercy, yet not true to Kate; and, curiously enough, it was a day or two passed with his lawful wife that had demoralized him. His unlawful wife had hitherto done nothing but improve his character.

But a great fault once committed is often the first link in a chain of acts that look like crimes, but are, strictly speaking, consequences.

This man, blinded at first by his own foible, and, after that, the sport of circumstances, was single-hearted by nature; and his conscience was not hardened. He desired earnestly to free himself and both his wives from the cruel situation; but, to do this, one of them he saw must be abandoned entirely; and his heart bled for her.

A villain or a fool would have relished the situation; many men would have dallied with it; but, to do this erring man justice, he writhed and sorrowed under it, and sincerely desired to end it.[1]

Ship-knackers and the wicked business in coffin ships were *More* the burden of the denunciatory *Foul Play* (1869), and rattening *novels of* and other underhand practices of the trade-unions that of *purpose* *Put Yourself in his Place* (1870). The scuttling of ships for the sake of the insurance money was a topic calculated to bring out all Reade's powers of melodrama. It does not fail to bring out also his versatility and the inexhaustible fund of special information amassed for the purpose. Ships are

---

[1] *Griffith Gaunt* was censored in the United States as demoralizing. Reade replied to this and other attacks in "The Prurient Prude."

descried getting under way, and steering across the Pacific from Sydney, homeward bound. A lady goes into raptures over the method of finding latitude and longitude by the chronometer in mid-ocean. This was the year of the panic in the City (1866), and the suspension of payment by Overend & Gurney, which of course does not escape the attention which is its due. ·The love-business and the attempt at an idyll on· a desert island is contemptible mawkishness in comparison. The subject brought up as one of the most urgent questions of the day in *Put Yourself in his Place* (1870), and illustrated with detailed evidence in a "report," is the ruining of tools and machinery by discontented operatives. The hero is a workman of mechanical genius in advance of his time; and, as he earns three times as much as his comrades, they band together to destroy his tools, and even to blind, maim, and slaughter himself. The exposure is eked out with the romantic paraphernalia of hand-to-hand combats, murderous assaults, blood-curdling frights, and such events as a catastrophic flood due to the collapse of a dam, into the usual exciting melodrama. An ancient derelict church, workers of alleged magic, and a preposterous old squire with an ineradicable grudge against trade and industry might all be reckoned among the heirlooms of Radcliffian romance. And if Jael Dence is pleasing as one of Reade's humbler heroines, the raging, tearing love-tale is melodrama again.

More melo-drama Reade put himself into *A Terrible Temptation: a Story of the Day* (1871), in the man of letters, Rolfe, who piles up an enormous collection of documents, and is consulted by the heroine as the best conceivable adviser in the dilemma in which she is involved; the outspoken realism was no doubt meant to be provocative and did not fail to excite protest. An American reviewer stigmatized it as "carrion literature," and he and his like were duly stigmatized by Swinburne, who considered this "one of the very best and truest in study of character, most rich in humour and interest," of all Reade's fictions, a verdict which may be accepted so long as the comparison is kept within those limits. But what Swinburne called the "vehemence" with which the story is told is really brute violence, and the reader can have no more sympathy for the blackguard hero than for the blackguard villain. Richard Bassett claims to have been cheated out of the Bassett entail by Sir Charles Bassett, whom he opposes and thwarts and annoys, and by a slander tries to prevent from marrying. When Lady Bassett's little one dies, her maidservant foists off her child as the son and heir, succumbing to the "terrible temptation." Years later, the young fellow in a frolic breaks into Richard's house, and Richard maliciously puts pressure on Sir Charles as a magistrate to commit the youth to prison. And then the old maidservant reveals that the boy is hers, and the illegitimate son of Richard Bassett. The scene is in Reade's regular stage-manner:

When they were gone Mary turned to Richard Bassett, and said, "Why do you want him sent to prison? to spite Sir Charles here, to stab his heart through his son?"

Sir Charles groaned aloud.

The woman heard, and thought of many things. She flung herself on her knees, and seized his hand. "Don't you cry, my dear old master; mine is the only heart shall bleed. HE IS NOT YOUR SON."

"What!" cried Sir Charles, in a terrible voice.

"That is no news to me," said Richard. "He is more like the parson than Sir Charles Bassett."

"For shame! for shame!" cried Mary Meyrick. "Oh, it becomes you to give fathers to children—when you don't know your own flesh and blood. HE IS YOUR SON, RICHARD BASSETT."

"*My* son!" roared Bassett, in utter amazement.

"Ay, I should know, FOR I AM HIS MOTHER."

This astounding statement was uttered with all the majesty of truth; and when she said, "I am his mother," the voice turned tender all in a moment.

They were all paralysed, and, absorbed in this strange revelation, did not hear a tottering footstep; a woman, pale as a corpse, and with eyes glaring large, stood amongst them all in a moment, as if a ghost had risen from the earth.

It was Lady Bassett.

At sight of her Sir Charles awoke from the confusion and amazement into which Mary had thrown him, and said, "Ah!

—Bella, do you hear what she says—that he is not our son? What, then, have you agreed with your servant to deceive your husband?"

Lady Bassett gasped, and tried to speak; but before the words would come the sight of her corpse-like face and miserable agony moved Mary Wells, and she snatched the words out of her mouth.

"What is the use questioning *her*? She knows no more than you do. I done it all—and done it for the best. My lady's child died; I hid that from her, for I knew it would kill her and keep you in a madhouse. I done it for the best; I put my live child by her side, and she knew no better. As time went on, and the boy so dark, she suspected; but know it she couldn't till now. My lady, I am his mother, and there stands his cruel father—cruel to me and cruel to him. But don't you dare to harm him! I've got all your letters, promising me marriage. I'll take them to your wife and daughter, and they shall know it is your own flesh and blood you are sending to prison. Oh, I am mad to threaten him! My darling, speak him fair, he is your father; he may have a bit of nature in his heart somewhere, though I could never find it." [1]

Of two novels published in one year (1873), *A Simpleton* half atones for dullness in the earlier chapters by the excitement in those which follow; and Reade was opportunist enough to seize public preoccupation with the Tichborne case and exploit it with a novel, *The Wandering Heir*, based on the parallel Annesley case of 1743. This was dedicated to Miss Braddon, who was now coming into her own, or, rather, into the more domesticated portion of the Reade estate. *A Woman Hater* (1877) was another novel of protest, at the insanitary conditions of village life, as illustrated by a hamlet on Reade's brother's property at Ipsden. *The Perilous Secret*, *Singleheart and Doubleface*, and *The Jilt, and Other Stories* (1884) were posthumous novels of the regular sensational stamp, the first founded on the play, *Love and Marriage*, by himself and H. Pettitt, and the second on one entitled *Single Heart and Double Face*, his own last dramatic work, which had been presented the year previous.

[1] *A Terrible Temptation*, xliv.

Besides his incessant crusades against public and private *Reade's* abuses and injustices, Reade had plenty of quarrels as a result *character* of his irascible and contentious disposition. There was *and* something almost heroic about Reade; yet he was egotistic, *influence* pedantic, dogmatic, sarcastic, and often enough eccentric; and, with his many foes, these were all "sticks" to beat him with. With Trollope he had a famous row; and before and after it he looked upon Trollope as "mediocrity incarnate." In the *Autobiography*, that novelist, whose fiction was the very antipodes of Reade's, speaks more warily on the subject than he had upon Wilkie Collins. No writer had puzzled him so much "by his eccentricities, impracticabilities, and capabilities."

"I look upon him as endowed almost with genius, but as one who has not been gifted by nature with ordinary powers of reasoning. . . . In the common affairs of life he cannot see what is right or wrong; and as he is altogether unwilling to be guided by the opinion of others, he is constantly making mistakes in his literary career, and subjecting himself to reproach which he hardly deserves."

Trollope cites various instances of what ordinary persons would call plagiarism, which are now only of interest as illustrating Reade's oblivion of every scruple, artistic or moral, in his pursuit of the one object, to thrill and fascinate his reader.

"In story-telling he has occasionally been almost great. Among his novels I would especially recommend *The Cloister and the Hearth*. I do not know that in this work, or in any other, he has left a character that will remain; but he has written some of his scenes so brightly that to read them would always be a pleasure."[1]

This is from Trollope's survey of the chief novelists of his own day and his yesterday, and it probably represents the mean between the opinion of Reade's multitudinous devotees, mostly inarticulate, and the indifference of those who preferred Thackeray, Mrs Gaskell, George Eliot, and Trollope himself. Both Reade and Wilkie Collins had a powerful influence on those schools of novelists who do not quite mix with these

[1] Chap. xiii.

great ones, on Miss Braddon (1837–1915),[1] Mrs Henry Wood (1814–1887),[2] James Payn (1830–1898),[3] Benjamin Leopold Farjeon (1838–1903),[4] the egregious "Ouida" (1865), and a host of others, many of whom must be left unnamed even, in a history, not of popular taste, but of a literary species.

"Ouida" The last-named calls for some notice as a literary phenomenon of an age of cheap books, when, as in the case of the Scoto-Italian, Marie Corelli, two decades later, appeals to mass sentiment and mediocre intelligence may excite a world-wide response. Marie Louise de la Rame (who afterwards spelt her name "Ramée"), best known by her pen-name "Ouida" (1840–1908), had a French father and an English mother. As

---

[1] Mary Elizabeth Braddon (1837–1915), who became Mrs John Maxwell, was the most notorious of those who tried to emulate Collins's and Reade's sensationalism and plot-work, though the realism was beyond their powers—or their inclinations. She tried at something like *The Woman in White* in *Lady Audley's Secret* (1862), and her success with an enormous public was such that she went on with a considerable yearly output until her death. Her very first novel had been *The Trail of the Serpent* (1861). *Aurora Floyd* (1863) was an effort in the *Madame Bovary* vein. *Eleanor's Victory* (1863), *Henry Dunbar* (1864), and *Joshua Haggard's Daughter* (1876) may be considered fair samples of her work. She started a series of historical romances with *Ishmael* (1884), the plot of which is laid in Paris under the Third Empire. As to *Lady Audley's Secret*, "A significant fact which has apparently largely escaped attention is that Mrs Maxwell's story was dedicated to Bulwer-Lytton, 'in grateful acknowledgment of literary advice generously given'" (Phillips, 28).

[2] Mrs Henry Wood, whose maiden name was Ellen Price, gave pleasure and edification to some with a temperance novel, *Danesbury House* (1860), but made her hit with *East Lynne* (1861). She too had a countless following, and was only less prolific than Miss Braddon. Half-a-century ago, *Roland Yorke* and its sequel, *The Channings* (1862–1869), were recommended to young people as studies of life and character decidedly above the average of circulating-library goods; not exactly equal to the very serious George Eliot, but in a higher category altogether than the sensational stuff of Wilkie Collins. Yet *The Shadow of Ashlydyat* (1863) is typical of a group in which Mrs Wood tried to perform the Wilkie Collins trick, encumbering herself, however, with the domestic history in which she was more at home. It is interesting to know that Harrison Ainsworth pressed for further consideration of *East Lynne* when Meredith advised Chapman & Hall to reject it. Bentley published the book after a second refusal.

[3] Payn followed Trollope as a delineator of pleasant, loyal-hearted people and their opposites, but at too great a distance to engross the reader without the allurements of a plot in the fashion of Wilkie Collins. *Lost Sir Massingberd* (1864) is probably the best-remembered of his plot-novels; *By Proxy* (1878) and *The Canon's Ward* (1884) may indicate how far he came short of his other model.

[4] Farjeon went to Australia when he was seventeen, and then settled in New Zealand, where he jointly owned and edited a daily paper. He came back to England after making a stir with *Grif: a Story of Australian Life* (1866), the picaresque tale of a street arab at the diggings in the time of the gold rush. In his detective stories, and the like, it is hard to distinguish the Wilkie Collins strain from that of Gaboriau.

a girl, she wrote for *Colburn's Magazine*, and she gave the world her first novel, *Held in Bondage* (1863), when she was twenty-three. Harrison Ainsworth is said to have acted as a sort of literary godfather, and welcomed her to the pages of the *Monthly Magazine*.[1] *Strathmore* (1865), *Chandos* (1866), *Under Two Flags* (1867), *Puck* (1870), *Two Little Wooden Shoes* (1874), *Ariadne* (1877), *Moths* (1880), and a good many more followed. Utterly unlike Wilkie Collins and Charles Reade in temper and outlook, she adopted the melodramatic framework as a mould ready provided into which to pour the emotions of an impressionable soul, and the view of the life around her which she had formed through garishly tinted spectacles. The Byronic hero, who had had his avatars in Charlotte Brontë's Rochester, David Copperfield's Steerforth, and Le Fanu's Uncle Silas, she also adopted out of hand. He is the invincible Strathmore, who marries the daughter of the friend whom he shot in a duel; he is the dashing libertine in *Chandos* and *Under Two Flags*, and the brigand of *In Maremma*. They said that her imagination dwelt in a world of demigods and demi-reps. She loved the gorgeous, the sumptuous, the audacious, and could not distinguish the sterling from the meretricious. Her complacent and exuberant descriptions out-Braddon Braddon, and the pose of cheap cynicism is simply that of a clever child. Critical admonishment and ridicule in the comic papers she disdained, and went on her wilful way serenely, writing at the end as gushingly as at the beginning. But she was a good story-teller, and her sincerity was transparent. A worshipper of flowers and romantic scenery, of animals and such human creatures, Italian peasants and the like, as she loved to call children of Nature, she expressed them and her feelings for them in semi-lyrical accents which are often touching and eloquent. In later life she took up social and even political causes; she had long pleaded for kindness to animals, as in *A Dog of Flanders* (1872). *A Village Commune* (1881) and *The Waters of Edera* (1900) are studies of primitive rights and customs in Italian village communities threatened by the modern regime. And she wrote articles on conscription,

[1] Phillips, 30.

socialism, marriage, and the new woman, as outspoken as her novels.

Le Fanu   Lever was not the only Irish novelist. Joseph Sheridan Le Fanu (1814–1873), an Irishman of Huguenot descent, a great-grandson of the famous Sheridan's father, wrote a number of novels and stories, largely of mystery and the supernatural, which showed familiar knowledge of the people, but, so far as they have survived, are interesting as a variant of the sensational plot-work of Wilkie Collins, and at the same time a modernization of the Gothic romance of Mrs Radcliffe and "Monk" Lewis. His peculiar qualification, combined with a talent bordering on genius for the kind of narrative that holds the reader as if in the grip of nightmare, was an almost scientific knowledge of popular legends and superstitions, demonology, witchcraft, vampirism, and everything related to the occult. At times he can be as true a humorist as Lever or Lover; but he is much more of an Irish Edgar Allan Poe. After leaving Trinity College, Dublin, Le Fanu was called to the Bar, but preferred journalism to law, and acquired the control of several newspapers. Many of his early tales appeared originally in the *Dublin University Magazine*, many others in *All the Year Round* and other English magazines; later on, the majority went into such gatherings of the uncanny as *In a Glass Darkly* (1872). His father was Dean of Emly, and Le Fanu went about among the peasantry of County Limerick and the neighbourhood almost as one of themselves, at a time when faction fights were frequent, outlaws lurked in the mountains, and superstitions were rife. He wrote many rousing ballads, "Shamus O'Brien" probably the most celebrated; and the legends and anecdotes and personal escapades remembered from this period were to be invaluable material when he turned novelist. Le Fanu had no success with two anonymous novels in the Waverley style, *The Cock and Anchor: a Tale of Old Dublin* (1845), and *The Fortunes of Colonel Torlogh O'Brien* (1847). But later on the shock of his young wife's death made him almost a recluse, and he employed himself in writing gloomy novels combining the regular stock-in-trade of love-affairs, scandals and duels, murder and mystery, of the

Wilkie Collins strain, with the psychic experiences, the hauntings, and the ominous dreams which were his speciality. He
was a master of the macabre. He loved to weave an atmosphere
of horror and dread in which the supernatural becomes concrete, as in the gruesome shape of the plump white hand that
appears on the child's pillow, the boy carried off by the spectre,
or the dogging footsteps of the "Watcher," who presently
becomes visible, in the tale of that name. Yet such palpable
ghastliness is actually outdone by the murders, in *Uncle Silas*,
for instance, and such scenes as when the poor niece, Maud
Ruthyn, looks out through the steel-hinged window and sees
a stooping figure at work in the yard: "Like a thunderbolt it
smote my brain. 'They are making my grave.'"

This sort of thing is skilfully combined with the everyday *"The
stuff of fiction in *The House by the Churchyard* (1863), a story *House by
of Chapelizod, the pleasant village on the outskirts of Dublin, *the
then—at the time of the French Revolution—inhabited by *Church-
officers of the Dublin garrison, clergymen, lawyers, and the *yard,"
like, with their womenkind. "I suppose there isn't so tattling, *Silas,"
prying, scandalous a little colony of Christians on earth." *and other
Duels, and worse, are of common occurrence. The hero *tales
Mervyn is a reserved, melancholy person with a secret. In due
course the mystery is resolved: he is the son and heir of
Lord Dunoran, who was convicted of murder. But it turns
out, after endless complications, that a certain Dangerfield, a
wealthy voluptuary, is "the dead and damned Charles Archer,"
who perpetrated the crime, and others too. There is a second
villain in Black Dillon, a surgeon "possessing the power of a
demigod, and the lusts of a swine." It is a fully appointed
novel of the admired circulating-library order, with this
gruesomeness and the rest of the Le Fanu seasoning of
hauntings, apparitions, and brooding menace. There are
connoisseurs who would put it first among his books; but *Uncle
Silas* (1864) ought to have been a still stronger antidote to
"the *Albums*, the *Souvenirs*, the *Keepsakes*, and all that flood
of Christmas-present lore which yearly irrigated England,
with pretty covers and engravings, and floods of elegant
twaddle," once admired by Maud Ruthyn. This is Le Fanu's

version of the hackneyed ordeal of the beautiful young heiress, entrapped by the wicked uncle, terrorized to the verge of insanity, and marked down for death. But this time the girl has courage and presence of mind; and, being warned of her danger, escapes the assassin; whilst the accomplice, only half in the villainous uncle's confidence, meets the fate intended for the girl. Uncle Silas is an awe-inspiring grotesque, kept artfully in the background; his agent, the spiteful Madame de la Rougierre, might be a figure out of Dickens, invested with the terrors that Le Fanu revelled in, and all the more dreadful to the poor young thing because she cannot make out whether this strange being is eccentric friend or secret foe. In this case, the ghosts and inexplicable omens are half rationalized, and yet more than half intensified, through being interpreted as Swedenborgian mysticism.

"Why do you look frightened?" says Dr Bryerly to Mrs Rusk, his lean figure sheathed in shining black cloth, his eyes glittering with a horrible sort of cunning: "Where is your faith? Don't you know that spirits are about us at all times? Why should you fear to be near the body? The spirit is everything; the flesh profiteth nothing."

Whether Le Fanu believed in them or not, he was deeply versed in Swedenborgian doctrines. The five stories from the diary of a German neuropath, which compose *In a Glass Darkly* (1872), make a banquet of horrors. In "Green Tea," a learned divine, writing a book and keeping himself awake with this beverage, is haunted by a loathsome familiar in the shape of a black monkey, which, without uttering a sound, at length penetrates his inmost consciousness, fills him with abominable ideas, and eventually impels him to suicide. "Carmilla" is a vampire story, staged in an ancient castle in Styria. Both in this and the other, Le Fanu seems so convinced of the truth of what he relates that he inspires conviction. Such an attitude is of more effect than even the admirable circumstantiality and picturesqueness. But a few disciples would hold the earlier tale, *Wylder's Hand* (1864), his masterpiece [1];

---

[1] Lever, for instance, and Le Fanu's critic, the late S. M. Ellis, author of *Wilkie Collins, Le Fanu, and Others* (1931).

and there is something to be said for the Radcliffian *Guy Deverell* (1865). These are matters of taste, in which the views of the initiate are likely to be at variance with ordinary preferences.

Though other fashions intervened, and Wilkie Collins was *Plot and* not immediately followed by a host of competitors in the *sensation* mechanics of plot and sensation, nor Charles Reade by a school *in later* of matter-of-fact romancers, it was impossible that the new *fiction* ways of doing things should be without effect upon their fellow-craftsmen, and that novelists should stick to the old-established paths. Many of those who profited by the example of Collins, as already noted, were below the line that divides mere commercial fiction from literature. But, later on, he was to provide the working-pattern for such writers as Grant Allen, Hugh Conway, Seton Merriman, and Conan Doyle, and the gifted technicians of the later detective novel were to beat him by making the problem more abstract, that is, more essentially intellectual. W. W. Jacobs, in "The Monkey's Paw" and some of the contents of *Sea Whispers* (1926), was to approach Le Fanu very near, especially in the knack of making the reader's nerves tingle. Bram Stoker also contrived to do this, and so did Kipling in "The Phantom Rickshaw" and many another realistic yarn. The two Irish girls who wrote together under the pen-name of "K. L. Montgomery" must certainly not be forgotten in this context. Reade's influence is much more difficult to separate and trace out in the complication of those which contributed to the development of realistic fiction; but now and then it seems to emerge pretty clearly. In the history of the art of historical fiction, *The Cloister and the Hearth* is certainly a landmark. This was a vast cartoon of the multitudinous life of western Europe in a great epoch, the group in the foreground melting imperceptibly into the general perspective of countless individuals. It was common, workaday life that he portrayed here, as in his romances of the present; for he did not, like most historical romancers, exert himself to interweave certain notable public events with the private affairs of invented personages. It was a matter-of-fact romance, though not an extreme example of his patent methods. George Eliot's *Romola* (1863) and Blackmore's *Lorna Doone* (1869), both of the same decade as Reade's masterpiece, owe not a little to such a victorious lead; and, later, the historical novels of Besant and Rice, and even the more romantic work of Stevenson, are in debt more or less remotely to Reade. Meredith, doubtless, who missed nothing of importance in the art and craftsmanship of fiction, knew and appraised at their proper value all Reade's innovations. Is it too fanciful to perceive even in the poetry of the famous dream of Captain Weisspriess, in his last moments after the duel in the Stelvio Pass, a sort of transposition of Reade's matter of fact to the mental sphere? Weisspriess is indeed such a matter-of-fact person, compendium of such a matter-of-fact race! The concrete evocation, in sharpest detail, of the veteran soldier's professional business and most familiar experience, the marching and deploying of troops for battle, seems an application of Reade's technique in a way he had not foreseen. Hardy would show other instances; but who among the more accomplished of the subsequent generation would not? They took what they found serviceable in those who had gone before them, and utilized it in ways that concealed their sources, perhaps even to themselves.

CHAPTER VI

GEORGE ELIOT

GEORGE ELIOT is as distinct a landmark in the history of the modern novel as the Brontë sisters are. Again and again it has been pointed out that fiction in her hands is no longer a mere entertainment; it strikes a new note of seriousness and even of sternness; it has turned into a searching review of the gravest as well as the pleasanter aspects of human existence, reassuming the reflective and discursive rights and duties pertaining to the novel at its beginnings, without however sacrificing any of the creative and dramatic qualities that had developed in the intervening centuries. Before George Eliot ever thought of making literature out of her oldest impressions of life in the Midlands she had been for years an earnest student of philosophy and psychology, well abreast of contemporary science, the friend and collaborator of the leading thinkers, and herself a writer on philosophical and social subjects. She had translated Strauss and Feuerbach, and was widely known as a free-thinker, with strong views especially on ethical questions. She was verging on middle age when, after long nursing the idea of utilizing her vivid recollections of childhood and youth, she wrote the first of her *Scenes of Clerical Life*, and was at once recognized as a novelist of extraordinary power and originality. In these and the subsequent stories and novels based upon her earliest experiences, the critical views of man and society which had by this time formulated themselves in her mind were necessarily a shaping factor. They coloured her outlook on the world presented to her maturity, and were naturally still more potent when the strength of these early influences began to wane, and she had to solve new problems and interpret new types of character or the products of new

The philosopher turns novelist

221

social conditions. Thus she brought to the novel the attitude and attainments of a systematic thinker, of a rationalist, saved from the abstractness which commonly incapacitates such a character for creative work by her intense human sympathies, her rich fund of experience, and a sense of humour. Her psychological studies had sharpened her insight into the inner sphere of man's life and activity; her preponderant interest in morals fixed her eye on the mental processes by which acts are engendered, and the chains of consequence by which what a man does or what a man is becomes the decisive factor in his destiny and in that of many who are perhaps but slenderly connected with him. If the novel is a mirror lighted up by mind, it was of no small moment that the mind now brought to bear was one inured to philosophic ways of seeing. Her sense of responsibility deepened, and her novels grew more and more introspective and even theoretic as time went on, until with the exhaustion of her earliest and most vivid impressions they were that and nothing else, and in her last, *Daniel Deronda*, she built upon a scaffolding of abstract thought.

Early pre- cedents
All this seemed an innovation when compared with the easy-going attitudes or sheer indifference of her predecessors and contemporaries, who did not aspire to any philosophy more profound than enlightened common sense, or pretend to construct their novels on a basis of coherent ideas, but rather on the acute insight of a wideawake genius. Historically, however, it was but the further development of what had been an integral element in English fiction from its origins in the conduct-books and the dissertations and commentaries on manners and morals, character and behaviour, of Tudor and Stuart days. [1] Most of the novelists had been wont never to miss a chance of improving the occasion, and clung to the privilege of moralizing in season and out of season. Some, who might have admitted that this was not their proper business, seemed to have told themselves that they might teach and preach with impunity so long as they were not caught doing it. Only a few kept strictly to the drama of characters in action, in intuitive obedience to æsthetic principles not yet

[1] See Volume II., chapter xii., "Fiction and Discursive Literature."

laid down. The novel has always been first cousin to the essay, the inventory of characteristics, the disquisition on life; it was loath to repudiate its kinship and regard the association as compromising to its integrity. Fielding put his general remarks into introductory essays; George Eliot put hers into the mouth of Mrs Poyser and other sayers of good things, without refraining, however, from authorial comment elsewhere. The principal difference was in her closer analysis of mind and motive and in her greater earnestness. Fielding's was a rationalist interpretation of life, Richardson's that of the man of feeling: the age of sensibility followed the age of reason. Jane Austen, Maria Edgeworth, and Scott reverted to the Fielding pose, and this was the one assumed by Thackeray and Trollope, whilst Dickens gave himself over to his humours and grotesques and to transports of sentimentalism that would have seemed excessive even to Richardson.[1]

George Eliot's passionate determination to speak the truth, without idealizing and without embellishment of any sort, as well as her rationalism, allied her with those of her colleagues who maintained the Fielding tradition. With certain special exceptions, all novelists claim to be truth-tellers, but they have different criteria of truth. To the average honest novel-writer truthfulness is like the common desire to get one's sums right. It was instinctive in the Brontë sisters; any tampering with it would have been a kind of moral suicide. In George Eliot, truth was a doctrine and a conviction, to which she held with religious devotion. Truth was the whole duty of the novelist, once he had realized what were the aspects of life worthy of faithful portrayal. She would doubtless have held that all the comments and passing homilies with which she interrupts the narrative of what is going on were justified

A rationalist subscribing to romanticism

---

[1] There were "improving" novels in plenty when George Eliot began writing. An article of hers in the *Westminster Review* (1856), entitled "Silly Novels by Lady Novelists," dealt with "the frothy, the prosy, the pious, or the pedantic," and was down especially on what Brunetière describes, "les romans moraux et un peu niais que publient par douzaines les filles de *clergymen* . . . la plaie de la littérature anglaise" (*Le Roman naturaliste*, 209). These are the "white-neck-cloth" species of novel produced for the sweet tooth of the Low Church young lady. Her scorn when she had as yet no notion that she would become a novelist was a pledge anyhow that it would not be a novelist of that persuasion.

because they give still more of the truth. The fullest statement of her artistic creed is in the opening to the second book of *Adam Bede*, where, after remarking that she would not, even if she had the choice, "be the clever novelist who could create a world so much better than this," she goes on:

So I am content to tell my simple story, without trying to make things seem better than they are; dreading nothing, indeed, but falsity, which, in spite of one's best efforts, there is reason to dread. Falsehood is so easy, truth so difficult. . . . Examine your words well, and you will find that even when you have no motive to be false, it is a very hard thing to say the exact truth, even about your own immediate feelings—much more than to say something fine about them which is *not* the exact truth. It is for this rare, precious quality of truthfulness that I delight in many Dutch paintings, which lofty-minded people despise. I find a source of delicious sympathy in these faithful pictures of a monotonous homely existence, which has been the fate of so many more among my fellow-mortals than a life of pomp or of absolute indigence, of tragic suffering or of world-stirring actions. I turn, without shrinking, from cloud-borne angels, from prophets, sibyls, and heroic warriors, to an old woman bending over her flower-pot, or eating her solitary dinner, while the noonday light, softened perhaps by a screen of leaves, falls on her mob-cap, and just touches the rim of her spinning-wheel, and her stone jug, and all those cheap common things which are the precious necessaries of life to her;—or I turn to that village wedding, kept between four brown walls, where an awkward bridegroom opens the dance with a high-shouldered, broad-faced bride, while elderly and middle-aged friends look on, with very irregular noses and lips, and probably with quart-pots in their hands, but with an expression of unmistakable contentment and goodwill. "Foh!" says my idealistic friend, "what vulgar details! What good is there in taking all these pains to give an exact likeness of old women and clowns? What a low phase of life!—what clumsy, ugly people!"

But here between the lines, and more explicitly on the following page, there are indications that George Eliot was far from content with the critical realism dating from Fielding.

Not for her to stand aloof as on a pinnacle, serene, superior, amused, unshaken by all the gusts of pity or indignation. Her most compelling traits, and the antidote to all her science, were the tenderness, the universal charity, the love and esteem for lowly worth, which rescue her sternest tragedies from the chilling austerity of such as Hawthorne's, otherwise so like hers. These were signs that she was of the same mind as the Brontës, that the true romantic vision had been revealed to her also. Like them, she believed in the spirituality of life, in the intrinsic value of personality, and the sovereign importance of those events which take place in the inner consciousness. Strong, assertive personalities themselves, Charlotte and Emily Brontë had discovered or evolved characters which were their own like, and with no regard whatever for the sensuous side of love had mated them in impassioned union with kindred beings. George Eliot was to write many similar love-stories, in which such aspiring souls as Dinah Morris, Maggie Tulliver, Romola, and Dorothea Casaubon were to find or to miss their spiritual counterparts, and so consummate or not their self-development. To her the highest possible development of personality was a religion; duty was the first article of her belief. She emancipated herself from the Evangelical creed in which she had been brought up, but she was always religious-minded. The phase of positivism through which she passed after abandoning the belief in heaven and hell of her Evangelical upbringing did not last long. Pantheism she found unsatisfying, and she resigned herself to the conviction that there is no answer to our cravings for a definite faith. But hundreds of passages in her novels imply that she could never eradicate a profound sense, not merely of divine immanence, but of divine transcendence. Her puritanism, her worship of duty, rested all her life upon the consciousness of an inner reality, which adherents to the creeds readily identified with the Divine.[1] The monitor within represented something

---

[1] Her husband, J. W. Cross, relates in his biography that she told him, "in all that she considered her best writing there was a 'not herself' which took possession of her, and that she felt her own personality to be merely the instrument through which this spirit, as it were, was acting."

higher than ourselves, whether of another order of being or simply the loftiest ideal conceivable to man. This latter question remains inscrutable; but the terms in which she constantly speaks of duty, and conscience, and "the Supreme Power" which fashioned us,[1] are the terms of one who could hardly help believing. Nothing could be more unlike the acerbity of the bigoted agnostic.

A moral philosophy based on "the laws of the human heart"

Yet, in strict parlance, George Eliot remained an agnostic, since her spiritual values were based on no general system of thought, but rather upon what she felt to be the laws written in the human heart. When she outgrew and forsook the Christian orthodoxy of her youth, she sought in vain an adequate substitute in the theoretic teachings of Spinoza, on the one hand, or, on the other, in the utilitarianism of her sceptical friends. She would eagerly have seized hold of a philosophy that seemed to be founded on truth and to correspond to the realities of human nature. But, when she found herself without a speculative basis for her ideals of individual excellence, she clung all the more resolutely to the principles instilled in her Evangelical upbringing, though she had abandoned the dogmas which gave them authority and sanctity. She erected those moral principles into a religion, which she believed to be established, ratified, and sanctified by the admonitions of life itself. Her philosophy was simply a moral philosophy; she dealt with the problem of knowledge in terms of ethical truth.[2] Wordsworth was the poet that she read as

---

[1] Prelude to *Middlemarch*.

[2] "Persuadée de connaître la vérité sur ce plan (le plan moral), et de posséder, convenablement liés entre eux, les principes essentiels qui règlent la vie humaine, elle tendait invinciblement à poser le problème de la connaissance en termes de vérité morale, c'est-à-dire à partir de celle-ci pour resoudre celle-là; ainsi la question philosophique par excellence est celle de la synthèse du savoir et de la sagesse, de la science et de la spiritualité, on peut entreprendre cette synthèse en partant de l'un ou de l'autre terme, le choix de la méthode étant déterminé par la tournure individuelle de l'esprit et par la nature de ses premières certitudes. Or, les premières certitudes de Miss Evans—soit sa philosophie du bonheur—formaient un tout systématique assez puissant pour qu'elle put se reposer dans la croyance qu'elle possédait la clef de tous les problèmes, et remettre à plus tard le soin d'interpréter et d'intégrer minutieusement dans le système général de sa pensée les résultats partiels et complexes de ses études. Il lui était donc loisible de donner libre jeu à sa curiosité intellectuelle et à sa passion de connaître, certaine de pouvoir, le moment voulu, surmonter le savoir universel et l'ordonner selon une rigoureuse dialectique interne" (*George Eliot: essai de biographie intellectuelle et morale*, par P. Bourl'honne, 1933, p. 89). This is by

a girl, and he remained the poet of her womanhood. His conception of human solidarity, "the unity of man," was the same as hers. If she could not share his "Faith in life endless," she would have assented to his doctrine of "intellectual love," working through imagination and "Reason in her most exalted mood." Many passages in the *Prelude*, that autobiography of a developing soul, are echoed in the language in which she unfolds spiritual problems. For her, too, had been "intertwined "

> The passions that build up our human soul,
> Not with the mean and vulgar works of man,
> But with high objects, with enduring things—
> With life and nature, purifying thus
> The elements of feeling and of thought,
> And sanctifying, by such discipline,
> Both pain and fear, until we recognize
> A grandeur in the beating of the heart.[1]

---

far the most penetrating study of the inner life of George Eliot and the stages of thought and feeling through which she arrived at the ethical philosophy set forth in her novels.   The author lays great stress on the moral revolution which she experienced with the shock of her father's death, and the remorse she felt for having embittered his last years by her abandonment of the creed in which he had brought up his children.   She had tried to live by her ideas of self-perfection and holiness: "elle est convaincue de se trouver dans un état voisin de la sainteté."   But one cannot live by ideas: "son erreur fut, non pas de réfléchir et d'avoir des idées, mais de s'en servir . . . à trop vouloir raisonner, on déraisonne."   She was attracted by Spinoza, and translated two of his works; but found herself unable to accept his general theory of nature and man.   Utilitarianism left her cold.   Her personal philosophy was a moral philosophy, "liée à la vie intérieure, et élaborée en vue de justifier une certaine forme d'action; c'est, si l'on veut, une mystique, ce n'est point une théorie rationnelle de l'univers . . . elle reste subordonnée au sentiment et à la conscience morale, et se plie à la considération exclusive des valeurs spirituelles."   "D'où l'indifférence de Miss Evans à l'égard de l'utilitarisme."   Thrown back on her youthful standards and ideals, but without a transcendental religion to support them, she strove desperately to discipline her will to the pursuit of disinterested values and love of humanity.   But this moral philosophy was entirely subjective, though she endeavoured to make it an absolute science.   She opts for altruism—"G. Eliot a opté pour l'altruisme et la morale du désintéressement parce qu'elle était généreuse et sensible, parce qu'elle aimait l'humanité, parce qu'elle était grande, ou plutôt parce qu'elle avait soif de grandeur morale, et que l'altruisme, compris comme nous venons de le voir, est une haute et pure doctrine; mais elle n'a pas réussi à justifier son choix, et elle ne le pouvait pas, un idéal moral étant en soi injustifiable et relevant des seules dispositions individuelles " (*Ibid.*, 140).   M. Bourl'honne is evidently a student of philosophy, and is much more interested in George Eliot's ideology and the process by which she arrived at it than in her art.   Nevertheless, his searching analysis throws such a flood of light on George Eliot herself and her mental attitude in each of her books that the nature and extent of the artistic problem is better elucidated than by most of the literary criticism usually applied.

[1] *Prelude* (1850), Book I., ll. 407-414.

Mary Anne or Marian Evans (1819–1880) was born two years after the death of Jane Austen, at Arbury Farm, near Chilvers Coton, in Warwickshire, and went to school successively at Attleborough, Nuneaton, and Coventry. Her father was agent to the Newdigate family, of Arbury Park, a man of sterling character, some of whose lineaments are recognizable in Caleb Garth, in *Middlemarch*, and in Adam Bede. He was twice married, his first wife having died leaving two children. Mary Ann was the youngest of a second brood, and had an elder sister Christiana and a brother Isaac. Her early fiction is full of portraits of kinsfolk and neighbours; Tom and Maggie Tulliver, in *The Mill on the Floss*, represent broadly her relations with Isaac, and Celia and Dorothea Brooke, in *Middlemarch*, those with Chrissey. "That central plain, watered at one extremity by the Avon, at the other by the Trent," as she was to describe it in the opening chapter of *Felix Holt*, with its meadows and homesteads, scattered hamlets and "trim cheerful villages," and placid bucolic tenor of life, was likewise to be the background of her earlier stories and novels. Marian was observant and had a most retentive memory, and was all the while busily though unconsciously gathering material for her future work. Actual incidents, more, doubtless, than are known not to be inventions, were to go in, along with true stories that she had heard, such as that which she refashioned as "The Sad Fortunes of the Rev. Amos Barton." It is hard to say whether the chief debt to these years in rural Warwickshire was in her perfect command of manners and general atmosphere or in the material she was storing up for a great variety of human figures. When her father, now a widower, retired, she went to live with him on the outskirts of Coventry, and a new chapter of her life began. She soon made friends with the Brays, a ribbon-manufacturer and his wife, and through them with the Hennells. Charles Bray, the brother-in-law of Charles and Mary Hennell, was a dabbler in Combe's phrenology and the socialism of Robert Owen. He was a sceptic; and Hennell, a Unitarian, was led by their discussions and a re-examination of the evidences to adopt a view of the origin and bases of Christianity very similar to that of Strauss. Marian was deeply influenced by her intercourse with the Brays and the Hennells. When her Methodist aunt, Mrs Samuel Evans, whom she loved and reverenced as a woman of rare saintliness and was to portray in Dinah Morris, came on a visit, the change in her niece's religious opinions was a cause of grief and estrangement. Miss Brabant, who presently became Mrs Hennell, had begun a translation of Strauss's *Life of Jesus*. This was taken over by Marian Evans, and published anonymously (1846). The death in 1849 of her father, whom she had distressed by her changed views on religion, caused her much heart-burning. She had nursed him to the end, and was for a while broken down in health and spirits. The Brays took her abroad, and at Geneva she gradually recovered calm, and began reading and thinking again. She came home to live with the Brays, and was soon busy writing for the *Westminster Review*, the organ of the Radical party, holding the important office of assistant editor for a time (1851–1853). This meant living in London, and brought her into close contact with such persons as John Chapman, editor of the review, W. R. Greg, Froude, the Martineaus, Herbert Spencer, and Francis Newman. Spencer introduced her to G. H. Lewes, then regarded as a very advanced thinker, who interested her deeply. Lewes was living apart from his wife, but could not obtain a divorce. Marian and he decided to throw in their lot together, and believed that their union was as sacred as a legal marriage.[1] They went to Germany (1854–1855), while he was working on the life of Goethe; and it was after their return that with

[1] She dedicated her books to him as "to my dear husband." M. Bourl'honne, who thinks she made great progress towards "liberté d'esprit" whilst with the *Westminster Review*, declares roundly, "Son union avec Lewes ramena Miss Evans au point d'où elle était partie, la plongea à nouveau dan l'incessante méditation du bien et du mal, du devoir et de la responsabilité, de la vie et de la mort. Car elle se trouva dès lors et plus sérieusement que jamais, du fait qu'elle s'était placée au point de vue social dans une situation exceptionnelle, portée à ressentir la gravité de l'existence et à mettre le problème moral au centre de ses préoccupations. . . . Miss Evans était arrivée, en 1853, au terme de son évolution intellectuelle et morale." After remarking that she ought to have reconstructed her philosophy of life, he goes on, "De sorte que la révolte de Miss Evans contre la société en 1853, loin d'être pour elle un principe de libération et de renouvellement intellectuel, marqua, comme nous l'avons dit, l'arrêt de sa pensée et le retour, après une brève éclipse de quatre années, de son idée fixe de jeunesse, l'obsession du problème moral" (*op. cit.*, 199–200).

his encouragement and his continuous help in clarifying her ideas she wrote her first work of fiction, "Amos Barton," which was published in *Blackwood* (1857), and was followed by "Mr Gilfil's Love Story" and "Janet's Repentance," and by the volume, *Scenes of Clerical Life*, containing all three. The name "George Eliot" was first assumed in connexion with the second story. She lived with Lewes till his death in 1878, residing in different parts of London and then at Witley, near Godalming, with long sojourns on the Continent. Not many months before her own death, she married her friend, John Walter Cross, who wrote her life (1884).

Her theory of fiction: "Scenes of Clerical Life" When George Eliot wrote *Scenes of Clerical Life* she had her theory of fiction complete in her mind; these simple tales of humble village folk and their trials and dilemmas and obscure tragedies are thus an epitome of the qualities to be exhibited on a larger scale thereafter. They show, for instance, at the very outset her singular power of seeing through shams and pretentious airs or the reserve of modest worth to the real truth of things, of revealing what ordeals and agonies, and it may be what remorse, are rankling in the hearts of those who show an impassive exterior or are too humble to open their bosom to the world. Her protagonists are very commonplace people; she could invest with tragic dignity the lowliest, the most prosaic, the least attractive person. Amos Barton is too complacent and too obtuse to see through the wiles of the pampered foreign countess who sponges on his overworked wife. When the faithful Milly has slaved and pinched for him and the children till she wears herself into the grave, he realizes what he has thrown away; but it is too late for atonement. The other parson, Mr Gilfil, is hail-fellow-well-met with the squire and his parishioners; but he can never live down the poignancy of his one romance. And who knew anything of the anguish of Caterina, who innocently gave her heart to a philanderer, and has her eyes suddenly opened to his callous indifference?

"But," she says to an imaginary reader who objects to such "utterly uninteresting" characters,

It is so very large a majority of your fellow-countrymen that are of this insignificant stamp. At least eighty out of a hundred of your adult male fellow-Britons returned in the last census are neither extraordinarily silly, nor extraordinarily wicked, nor extraordinarily wise; their eyes are neither deep and liquid with sentiment, nor sparkling with suppressed witticisms; they have probably had no hairbreadth escapes or thrilling adventures; their brains are certainly not pregnant with genius, and their passions have not manifested themselves at all after the fashion of a volcano. They are simply men of complexions more or less muddy, whose conversation is more or less bald and disjointed. Yet these commonplace people— many of them—bear a conscience, and have felt the sublime prompting to do the painful right; they have their unspoken sorrows, and their sacred joys; their hearts have perhaps gone out towards their first-born, and they have mourned over the irreclaimable dead. Nay, is there not a pathos in their very insignificance—in our comparison of their dim and narrow existence with the glorious possibilities of that human nature which they share?

The point of view is changed; she looks inside the minds of these uninteresting people, and shows them feeling, thinking, acting, and maybe repenting in shame and agony. It is so with Janet in the third story, though the brutal Dempster, who hounds his wife almost to suicide, is viewed from the outside. The poor thing in her despair becomes a drunkard, and is saved by the Rev. Mr Tryan, who thus shows the mettle of the Evangelicalism which had brought him unpopularity. Yet she had been one of the Anti-Tryanites when she said, "kindness is my religion." He enlarges on that text, and preaches to Janet a sermon on the Divine Pity. But George Eliot had preached a sermon in her own person, in an earlier chapter, where she numbered Mr Tryan among "the real heroes, of God's making," and congratulated herself on being "on the level and in the press with him, as he struggles his way along the stony road, through the crowd of unloving fellow-men." For, though George Eliot did not write for any other avowed purpose than to show life as she had seen it, she hoped for results, and, as she said elsewhere, trusted that those who read would be "better able to imagine and to feel the pains and the joys of those who differ from themselves in everything but the broad fact of being struggling, erring human creatures." She was oppressed by a sense of her responsibility, especially when later on she came to be prized by many as something superior to a mere novelist. And this in spite of the scandal created for many thousands by her irregular union with Lewes, the consciousness of which on her part may account to a large extent for her severity in applying the law of moral retribution, the reiterated doctrine that sins bring their wages.[1] "Nemesis is lame," she says here, "but she is of colossal stature, like the gods; and sometimes, while her sword is not yet unsheathed, she stretches out her huge left arm and grasps her victim." This is one of her proleptic hints of fate lying in ambush, like the allusion to the "malignant destiny" which was preparing to upset Mr Barton, little as he suspected it. More moving to both mind and feeling is the death of Dempster's mother, in "Janet's Repentance," for this was an event having consequences which everyone could see.

When the earth was thrown on Mamsey's coffin, and the son, in crape scarf and hatband, turned away homeward, his good angel, lingering with outstretched wing on the edge of the grave, cast one despairing look after him, and took flight for ever.

Her novels Having tested her theory and her abilities and found that they worked, she wrote in swift succession two full-length novels, *Adam Bede* (1859) and *The Mill on the Floss* (1860), and a short one, *Silas Marner* (1860), which is a gem with hardly a flaw; and then with greater deliberation four more, *Romola* (1863), *Felix Holt* (1866), *Middlemarch* (1871-1872), and *Daniel Deronda* (1876). There is universal disagreement

---

[1] Bourl'honne (161-163) is of opinion that Lewes exercised an important influence on George Eliot by leading her to insist on the dramatic part of sorrow and suffering in life, especially the life of women. He had already laid it down that personal suffering was the great source of inspiration in feminine literature; women find relief for their pangs by transferring them to the fictional sphere—poetry is like the pearl secreted by the oyster touched by disease. All George Eliot's heroines, Maggie, Romola, Esther Lyon, Dorothea, Gwendolen go through the difficulties and agonies and struggles that had been her own lot, and for the most part are left contemplating a hard-won wisdom and a life of solitude. Maggie is saved by the accident of death from such a fate.

as to which of all these is her masterpiece, but none on the claims of *Silas Marner* to a humbler pre-eminence. Every novel in turn has been pushed into the place of honour by its devotees, with the one exception of *Felix Holt*; even the exotic *Romola*, for its incomparable study of moral declension in Tito. *Daniel Deronda*, in which her powers were not only failing but were also misapplied, an intellectual and didactic tendency hitherto kept under some restraint here having it all its own way, was characteristically seized upon as a model by a New England school of Puritan novelists, who were better hands at moral casuistry and edification than at writing fiction.[1] What she had said in "Amos Barton" was by no means a full statement of her aims or of what she had accomplished in that story. She was too modest and diffident when she wrote, in addition to the sentences quoted already:

For, not having a lofty imagination, as you perceive, and being unable to invent thrilling incidents for your amusement, my only merit must lie in the truth with which I represent to you the humble experience of ordinary fellow-mortals. I wish to stir your sympathy with commonplace troubles—to win your tears for real sorrow, sorrow such as may live next door to you —such as walks neither in rags nor in velvet, but in very ordinary decent apparel.

George Eliot had shunned "loftiness," but she had exerted imagination in so reconstructing the little provincial world [2] in which the originals of Amos Barton, Mr Gilfil, and Janet Dempster moved and had their being that her version received fullest significance as a picture of human beings acting, striving, and suffering, with the reactions upon themselves and upon those about them. It was the lot of mankind on earth that was in question. She was not a philosopher for nothing, though the philosophy was kept subservient to its proper office, illumination of the mirror. That is what it does in the earlier

[1] An English writer, Charles Gardner (*The Inner Life of George Eliot*, 224), calls *Daniel Deronda* "George Eliot's supreme achievement," and suggests in his preface that all who think otherwise are "ephemeral faddists who deride but do not read her."

[2] She reproduced so many features of the locality, Griff and Chilvers Coton, that characters and places were recognized by those on the spot, and she excited some resentment by her freedom in dressing up well-known histories.

group of novels, and with certain exceptions all it does in *Middlemarch*. Only after *Silas Marner* was it ever allowed to predominate to such a point as to overwhelm the creative faculty. Poets and novelists ought to be philosophic; but that is one thing, to be philosophers is quite another. Art is a more natural thing than philosophy; it proceeds according to instinct, taking the normal route which philosophy reverses. It is a development of the primary way of experiencing, and then of conveying experience. Intuitions come before concepts, but philosophy sets out from concepts. Experience must be anterior to reflection, generalization, abstraction, and logical demonstration. The philosopher has done all this; he has elaborated his theory of life; and, if, being only a philosopher, he were so ill-advised as to write a novel, it could hardly escape being only a rearrangement or reconstruction of his abstracts of reality. Such, indeed, is a good deal of *Romola*; such *Daniel Deronda*. Such, happily, were not the novels that George Eliot wrote in the full current of reliving the experiences of her girlhood in the Midlands, even if these often betrayed the excessive gravity of the assistant editor of the *Westminster Review* and the translator of Strauss, and the heavy-handedness of the writer on psychological phenomena and Comtist sociology. She was over-erudite, over-thoughtful, over-critical, and rather afraid of her irrepressible sense of humour, which, like Mrs Gaskell, she was inclined to keep for appropriate occasions, and not let it mix with the serious business of life, much less with the tragedy. But, when she gave that humour and her abounding sympathy and enjoyment of life full play, she surpassed all women novelists, with the sole exception of Jane Austen.

Dramas of moral conflict —some remodelling of the medium Her full-length novels went deeper into the obscure places of human nature, and dealt more elaborately and in greater variety with the conflicts and moral disorders that unhinge the will and the lapses which bring ruin upon the individual and his fellows. The inexorable fate of the clerical tales reappears in every one. It is not the external, malicious Fate of Greek poetry; it is simply the logical results of moral causation. Each individual is the master or the victim of

the fate which he bears within him. George Eliot's sphere
was the inner man; she exposed the internal clockwork. Her
characters are not simply passive, and they do not stand still;
they are shown making their own history, continually changing
and developing or degenerating as their motives issue into acts,
and the acts become part of the circumstances that condition
motive and purify or demoralize the will. "Our deeds
determine us, as much as we determine our deeds." [1] Thus
she rationalizes life and character, bringing the obscure into
clear daylight, with her zeal for truth applying the most
rigorous logic to the resolution of each problem, working it
out with the accuracy and solemnity appropriate to a judicial
inquiry, and issuing verdicts as irrefragable as the results of a
scientific experiment. This was to view life tragically, and
the novel had to be reshaped to bear the stress of the new
conception. Her novels are all biographies; *Middlemarch*
interweaves the biographies of some fifty individuals. For
the merely historical part the loose epical plan that served
Thackeray and Dickens was not inadequate. But the action
invariably concentrates sooner or later into a crisis which
automatically manifests itself in drama. This is where the
implicit idea, the central theme, becomes clearly apparent; and
the clash of motives and inhibitions which is the working out
of the problem now goes on to the logical conclusion. Such
a novel is not dramatic in the sense that the action culminates
in great scenes, spectacular events; there is a striking paucity
of what usually constitutes incident in George Eliot's novels.
She rarely exhibits characters struggling together as on a stage.
The drama is internal, it is the drama of moral conflict. The
conflict is that of egocentric impulses, good or bad, with an
opposing environment, and the antagonistic forces take many

[1] In an admirable and famous passage of *Le Roman naturaliste* (229), Brunetière
wrote: "Si vous n'avez pas lu le roman d'*Adam Bede*, vous savez—pour l'avoir
entendu dire ou pour en avoir vu des exemples autour de vous—que les conséquences
d'une seule faute peuvent se compliquer jusqu'au crime, mais vous ne savez pas
comment cela se fait, par quelle sourde conspiration des circonstances, et par quel
subtil travail de perversion intérieure. Si vous n'avez pas lu *Silas Marner*, vous
pouvez savoir—d'une façon spéculative—qu'une passion en chasse une autre, et
qu'une brusque transformation peut s'accomplir dans une âme humaine, mais
vous ne savez pas *comment* cela se fait, et combien est petite, insignifiante, presque
nulle enfin la part de ce que vous appelez le hasard."

forms. Though a rationalist, George Eliot was a woman of strong feelings herself, and went as far as the Brontë sisters in recognizing the subversive force of a quite instinctive and even irrational passion in human life, particularly the life of women. Love is a foremost agent in all the discords and dissensions which are the themes of her various books, and it is usually love gone wrong. Only in one, however, which happens to be the most autobiographical of all, *The Mill on the Floss*, is it of the magnitude and the devastating energy of Brontëan passion. In the case of Hetty Sorrel, the humblest and commonest, it is simply the yielding of a weak and facile nature. In Romola, Dorothea, Gwendolen Harleth, and others, the love-drama is one representative phase of the moral disorder of a world in which circumstances or ignorance or weakness thwart the effort to live up to ideals. Nearly always, the subject is studied from the woman's point of view; the women are so vastly superior to their lovers that it is difficult for the reader to appreciate all that it means for them. Arthur Donnithorne and Stephen Guest are drawn with the most convincing art, but that only serves to lay bare their unworthiness. The estimable Philip Wakem, whose father is the regular woman's idea of the wicked person a successful lawyer must be, Felix Holt, said to be her portrait of Gerald Massey, and Tito Melema, who, as Leslie Stephen pointed out, is really a woman in man's things, are all evidently evolved as embodiments of the qualities that a woman would justifiably prize in the opposite sex; they are flagrant examples of a woman's man, much more so than Charlotte Brontë's Rochester and Paul Emanuel were. It is always hard to sympathize with another person's love-affairs; but unless the novelist compels the reader's liveliest fellow-feeling he fails of his effect. Such lay figures as Guest and Will Ladislaw can excite only a tepid interest, with the regret that Maggie and Dorothea were not more difficult to please. But to insist on such a view would be unfair to George Eliot, in whose conception of the tragedy of life the mistakes of those aiming at the loftiest ideals were a principal factor. Guest and Ladislaw, though drawn without that intimate understanding which she had of characters of her own sex, were just the sort of men that Maggie and Dorothea, yearning for what had hitherto been denied them, would fall in love with, and it is the generous and aspiring hearts of these two women that claim attention, as the arena of the dramatic conflict. This is the argument in her defence, though it is obvious that it cuts both ways.

Adam Bede appeared the same year as *The Ordeal of Richard* "Adam Feverel* (1859), a year after Trollope's *Dr Thorne* and two Bede" before *Framley Parsonage*. Browning, who likewise contemplated life as an affair of moral conflict, and gave an ethical bearing to everything in which he was interested, painting, music, and the like, had published *Men and Women* in 1855, and in the near future was to give the world his *Dramatis Personæ* (1864) and *The Ring and the Book* (1868–1869). Trollope was hardly less moralistic and didactic than George Eliot, though his administration of poetic justice was in comparison mildness itself. Browning was not far from identifying æsthetics with ethics, as if beauty were simply holiness. It would not be time thrown away to compare some passages in Trollope, say the dialogue between Sowerby and his worldly and clear-sighted sister on his chances with Miss Dunstable, and certain colloquies in Browning. George Eliot affords closer comparisons: her treatment of Bulstrode, for instance, in *Middlemarch*, with his of Sowerby, would bring out how carefully she avoided the least concession to sentiment. Trollope was not stern enough, and too cheerfully humorous, for tragedy; *The Warden* and the *Last Chronicle* are tragic only on the surface. But all three writers, like Carlyle, Ruskin, and others, illustrate in their several ways the predilection of the age for moral instances. Such as were brought to conclusions in *Adam Bede* were not intrinsically different from those in the clerical tales, though they were given a wider orbit. It was again, in general, the contest of personal desires, weaknesses of the flesh, passion, with the claims of duty. The basis of her plot was in the story told her by Mrs Evans, the Methodist aunt, of the girl hanged for child-murder. George Eliot makes this the centre of a more elaborate history by supposing her shrewd and upright Adam in love with the frail but fascinating damsel, who is seduced by the superior graces of the young squire. Hetty's aunt, Mrs Poyser, with her husband, Adam's old mother and his brother Seth, the rector, the squire, the schoolmaster, and various neighbours, complete the village circle, which includes, besides the incomparable Mrs Poyser, a small galaxy of rustic wiseacres, such as Bartle Massey, who enliven the story with their wit and humour, and, as it were, serve as the author's deputies in expounding her philosophy in pithy aphorisms. Tangential to the domestic circle comes in the inspired apostle of a loftier creed than their worldly wisdom, Dinah Morris, destined to be Adam's recompense for the eclipse of his first dream of happiness. The situation is roughly parallel to those in later books. Adam is disillusioned in Hetty, but finds a worthier goal in Dinah, as Maggie in Stephen Guest and Philip Wakem, Dorothea in Casaubon and Will Ladislaw, Gwendolen Harleth in Grandcourt and Daniel Deronda. Apart from *Silas Marner* and *Felix Holt*, which hardly count, it might even be said that this is the one novel in which there is a hero claiming first sympathies; in the other cases, a woman is in that position. Adam, who was drawn, perhaps involuntarily rather than deliberately, from George Eliot's father, of whom Caleb Garth, in *Middlemarch*, is a nearer likeness, was evidently meant to be the embodiment of her ideals of stanch, sensible, and upright manhood; he has that clear insight which was the foundation-stone of her own realistic vision:

"There's nothing but what's bearable as long as a man can work," he said to himself: "the natur o' things doesn't change, though it seems as if one's own life was nothing but change. The square o' four is sixteen, and you must lengthen your lever in proportion to your weight, is as true when a man's miserable as when he's happy; and the best o' working is, it gives you a grip hold o' things outside your own lot."

Mrs Poyser is said to owe something to George Eliot's mother, more faithfully portrayed in the Mrs Hackit of "Amos Barton"; but this is like seeking the prototype of Sam Weller outside the genius of Dickens. There is no doubt, however, that the angelic Dinah was shaped and much idealized from the village evangelist, Elizabeth Evans, whose memorial tablet is still extant on the wall of the Ebenezer chapel in Wirksworth. No doubt, many of the other worthies had originals in the flesh, who are now too remote for identification. How coolly G. A. Lawrence appropriated Adam Bede as an example of the muscular heroes has been noted already. Adam was meant, of course, to be the very antithesis of that doctrine. The fight with Arthur Donnithorne into which he was beguiled by jealous rage reduces him to shame and horror; and in the earlier talk between the two, which, as was George Eliot's wont, hinted proleptically at what was to befall, he makes his sentiments perfectly clear. The young squire had laughingly said that Adam would knock him "into next week" if ever it came to a battle between them.

"God forbid I should ever do that, sir," said Adam, looking round at Arthur, and smiling. "I used to fight for fun; but I've never done that since I was the cause o' poor Gil Tranter being laid up for a fortnight. I'll never fight any man again, only when he behaves like a scoundrel. If you get hold of a chap that's got no shame nor conscience to stop him, you must try what you can do by bunging his eyes up."

The seduction of Hetty is the moralized version of what *A story* was a commonplace in fiction. George Eliot liked to dwell on *moralized* such cases of evil deeds bringing their inevitable retribution, like the memory over which Mr Tryan secretly brooded, in "Janet's Repentance," of the girl whom he had ruined, and discovered long afterwards in the dead woman of the London streets. It bulks large in the history of Bede, since she had, not very wisely, given it catastrophic importance. Some have objected to the "moral pedantry" with which, here and elsewhere, George Eliot makes sin the agent of its own chastisement, not allowing any of the escapes or alleviations which circumstances often provide in the actual world.[1] But in

[1] See *Victorian Novelists* (93–94) by James Oliphant, who defends the author on the score that she had a lesson of self-restraint to enforce—obviously, from the standpoint of one brought up on the Lesser Catechism. A more legitimate criticism is that George Eliot's novels depict "a closed world," where the troubles and conflicts of the

tragedy the train of causes and effects must be simplified, and chances that might interfere eliminated, if there is no evasion of the probabilities. Nevertheless, Hetty's story is open to valid criticism. George Eliot's usual sympathy fails her in this instance; she treats the pretty frivolous thing as acrimoniously as if she were jealous of her empty-headed beauty. That long essay on the wiles and graces that befool the best of us sometimes, which precedes Mrs Poyser's racier summing up that "She's no better than a peacock, as 'ud strut about on the wall, and spread its tail when the sun shone if all the folks in the parish was dying"; or the later homily ending with the characteristic premonition that she was weaving a light web of folly which one day would close round and change all at once "her fluttering, trivial butterfly sensations into a life of deep human anguish," are not quite fair to Hetty: they leave the impression that she was not meant to have a chance. But a worse blemish is the much-canvassed episode, based on the fact related to George Eliot by her aunt, of the interview in the prison with the condemned girl, when Dinah wrings a confession from the poor sinner, with the laudable motive, no doubt, of bringing her to a sense of the divine grace. It is more in the spirit of a tract than of a novel, and has no bearing whatever on the story of Adam Bede. The only valid defence would be that the whole book is an illustration of George Eliot's central doctrine, of the influence of one soul upon another. But, for the matter of that, Dinah Morris, beautiful thing that she is in herself, is altogether an intrusion, an artistic excrescence, in the story of Adam Bede. True, she becomes his wife after Hetty's catastrophe, and so rounds off the tale in the conventional way, which to some looks like an anticlimax. But she does not save Adam from the awkward inconsistency of having been in love with a flimsy creature such as Hetty when he could eventually rise to the level of Dinah. It is difficult to picture him as one of a perfect pair with either. George Eliot looked for results, and converted

---

great outside world that we know are unheard: her moralistic dramas are curiously insulated on a stage of their own. It is, emphatically, the inner not the outer world that she depicts (see Haldane, 280, 293, and 309–310).

a tragic story into one that would appeal to the great majority, listening too readily to the advice of Lewes, who saw that the prison scene would make a first-rate climax. It can hardly be doubted that it was Hetty's tragedy and Dinah's sermonizing Dickens was thinking of when he said that the reading of *Adam Bede* was an epoch in his life.

More sterling merits

The book was one of the most powerful expositions of her ethical philosophy; but it was not this which made *Adam Bede* great. There are too many weak points in that exposition; as a story it is of indifferent merit. But George Eliot did well to emphasize her claims to truth of description, and extol the virtues of Dutch painting. As a rich and crowded canvas, a veracious picture of English rural life in times already now gone by, it is one of the most valued possessions of our mental gallery. In comparison with this, the story may even be regarded as subordinate. But not the characters, or the inimitable humours. Mrs Poyser has become one of our most treasured oracles; we know her sayings by heart, better, most of us, than those of Shakespeare's fools and sages. George Eliot must have poured a large accumulation of wit and wisdom into *Adam Bede*, for a large part of the dialogue consists of sententious dissertation, commentary, and epigram. It is a text-book of practical wisdom, so rich and varied that she has to assign much of it to such rivals of Mrs Poyser as that lady's husband, or the misogynist schoolmaster, Bartle Massey, or Adam Bede himself. When all of them are at the front of the stage together, as in the sparring about Dinah Morris, the war of wits is dazzling.

"What!" said Bartle, with an air of disgust. "Was there a woman concerned? Then I give you up, Adam."

"But it's a woman you'n spoke well on, Bartle," said Mr Poyser. "Come, now, you canna draw back; you said once as women wouldna ha' been a bad invention if they'd all been like Dinah."

"I meant her voice, man—I meant her voice, that was all," said Bartle. "I can bear to hear her speak without wanting to put wool in my ears. As for other things, I daresay she's like the rest o' the women—thinks two and two 'ull come to make five, if she cries and bothers enough about it."

"Ay, ay!" said Mrs Poyser; "one 'ud think, an' hear some folks talk, as the men war 'cute enough to count the corns in a bag o' wheat wi' only smelling at it. They can see through a barn-door, *they* can. Perhaps that's the reason they can see so little o' this side on't."

Martin Poyser shook with delighted laughter, and winked at Adam, as much as to say the schoolmaster was in for it now.

"Ah!" said Bartle, sneeringly, "the women are quick enough —they're quick enough. They know the rights of a story before they hear it, and can tell a man what his thoughts are before he knows 'em himself."

"Like enough," said Mrs Poyser; "for the men are mostly so slow, their thoughts overrun 'em, an' they can only catch 'em by the tail. I can count a stocking-top while a man's getting's tongue ready; an' when he outs wi' his speech at last, there's little broth to be made on't. It's your dead chicks take the longest hatchin'. Howiver, I'm not denyin' the women are foolish: God Almighty made 'em to match the men."

"Match!" said Bartle; "ay, as vinegar matches one's teeth. If a man says a word, his wife'll match it with a contradiction; if he's a mind for hot meat, his wife'll match it with cold bacon; if he laughs, she'll match him with whimpering. She's such a match as the horse-fly is to th' horse: she's got the right venom to sting him with—the right venom to sting him with."

"Yes," said Mrs Poyser, "I know what the men like—a poor soft, as 'ud simper at 'em like the pictur o' the sun, whether they did right or wrong, an' say thank you for a kick, an' pretend she didna know which end she stood uppermost, till her husband told her. That's what a man wants in a wife, mostly; he wants to make sure o' one fool as 'ull tell him he's wise. But there's some men can do wi'out that—they think so much o' themselves a'ready; an' that's how it is there's old bachelors."

"*The Mill on the Floss*" There is plenty of the same Dutch painting, plenty also of an equally good brand of humour, not quite so rich, however, in inspired wisdom, in *The Mill on the Floss*. The household friends who may be conceived as forming the rustic chorus to the tragic drama are a more prosaic group, and, designedly, no doubt, serve to accentuate the contrast of their practical sense and Maggie's flightiness. This time it is George Eliot who is hard on the women, the average rural housewife, at all events. Listen to the admirable dialogue between the Gleggs, admirable, though not more perfect as natural conversation than any piece selected at random from any of her novels. Mrs Glegg has sat down to breakfast without her fuzzy front of curls, for such extravagances were unnecessary till the morning was more advanced, and "the absence of that cloud only left it more apparent that the cloud of severity remained." Mr Glegg kept discreetly quiet, until silence was felt as an injury by his better half, and he heard himself apostrophized:

"Well, Mr Glegg! It's a poor return I get for making you the wife I've made you all these years. If this is the way I'm to be treated, I'd better ha' known it before my poor father died, and then, when I'd wanted a home, I should ha' gone elsewhere—as the choice was offered me."

Mr Glegg paused from his porridge and looked up—not with any new amazement, but simply with that quiet, habitual wonder with which we regard constant mysteries.

"Why, Mrs G., what have I done now?"

"Done now, Mr Glegg? *done now?* . . . I'm sorry for you."

Not seeing his way to any pertinent answer, Mr Glegg reverted to his porridge.

"There's husbands in the world," continued Mrs Glegg, after a pause, "as 'ud have known how to do something different to siding with everybody else against their own wives. Perhaps I'm wrong, and you can teach me better. But I've allays heard as it's the husband's place to stand by the wife, instead o' rejoicing and triumphing when folks insult her."

"Now, what call have you to say that?" said Mr Glegg, rather warmly, for though a kind man, he was not as meek as Moses. "When did I rejoice or triumph over you?"

"There's ways o' doing things worse than speaking out plain, Mr Glegg. I'd sooner you'd tell me to my face as you make light o' me, than try to make out as everybody's in the right but me, and come to your breakfast in the morning, as I've hardly slept an hour this night, and sulk at me as if I was the dirt under your feet."

"Sulk at you?" said Mr Glegg, in a tone of angry facetiousness.

"You're like a tipsy man as thinks everybody's had too much but himself."

"Don't lower yourself with using coarse language to *me*, Mr Glegg! It makes you look very small, though you can't see yourself," said Mrs Glegg, in a tone of energetic compassion. "A man in your place should set an example, and talk more sensible."

Mrs Glegg is a Dodson, like Mrs Pullet, and that brainless old hen, Mrs Tulliver, Maggie's mother. There is an historical chapter on what many would call the sordid life of the Tullivers and Dodsons—"irradiated by no sublime principles, no romantic visions, no active, self-renouncing faith—moved by none of those wild, uncontrollable passions which create the dark shadows of misery and crime—without that primitive rough simplicity of wants, that hard submissive ill-paid toil, that child-like spelling-out of what nature had written, which gives its poetry to peasant life." And no one can miss the Sophoclean irony of it in thinking of the pent-up poetry in Maggie's soul. But these dull folk depict themselves best, as once more in the bit of dialogue between Mrs Tulliver and Aunt Pullet, when the latter takes her sister and Maggie into the best room to view the new bonnet. Maggie felt disappointed when it was unrolled from sheet after sheet of silver paper. "But few things could have been more impressive to Mrs Tulliver."

She looked all round it in silence, and then said emphatically, "Well, sister, I'll never speak against the full crowns again!"

It was a great concession, and Mrs Pullet felt it: she felt something was due to it.

"You'd like to see it on, sister?" she said, sadly. "I'll open the shutter a bit further."

"Well, if you don't mind taking off your cap, sister," said Mrs Tulliver.

Mrs Pullet took off her cap, displaying the brown silk scalp with a jutting promontory of curls which was common to the more mature and judicious women of those times, and, placing the bonnet on her head, turned slowly round, like a draper's lay-figure, that Mrs Tulliver might miss no point of view.

"I've sometimes thought there's a loop too much o' ribbon on this left side, sister; what do you think?" said Mrs Pullet.

Mrs Tulliver looked earnestly at the point indicated, and turned her head on one side. "Well, I think it's best as it is; if you meddled with it, sister, you might repent."

"That's true," said aunt Pullet, taking off the bonnet and looking at it contemplatively.

"How much might she charge you for that bonnet, sister?" said Mrs Tulliver, whose mind was actively engaged on the possibility of getting a humble imitation of this *chef-d'œuvre* made from a piece of silk she had at home.

Mrs Pullet screwed up her mouth and shook her head, and then whispered, "Pullet pays for it; he said I was to have the best bonnet at Garum Church, let the next best be whose it would." She began slowly to adjust the trimmings in preparation for returning it to its place in the wardrobe, and her thoughts seemed to have taken a melancholy turn, for she shook her head. "Ah," she said at last, "I may never wear it twice, sister; who knows?"

"Don't talk o' that, sister," answered Mrs Tulliver. "I hope you'll have your health this summer."

"Ah! but there may come a death in the family, as there did soon after I had my green satin bonnet. Cousin Abbott may go, and we can't think o' wearing crape less nor half a year for him."

"That *would* be unlucky," said Mrs Tulliver, entering thoroughly into the possibility of an inopportune decease. "There's never so much pleasure i' wearing a bonnet the second year, especially when the crowns are so chancy—never two summers alike."

"Ah, it's the way i' this world," said Mrs Pullet, returning the bonnet to the wardrobe and locking it up. She maintained a silence characterized by head-shaking, until they had all issued from the solemn chamber and were in her own room again. Then, beginning to cry, she said, "Sister, if you should never see that bonnet again till I'm dead and gone, you'll remember I showed it you this day."

Such scenes, and the dull, monotonous environment, are not mere circumstance and surroundings, they are factors in the tragic problem, they are the things with which Maggie feels herself out of harmony. Her case would now be called one of repressed personality. She grows up a pagan at heart,

Maggie's rebelliousness

like former Tullivers perhaps, like the clever Ralph, who was a high liver, rode spirited horses, and ruined himself. At the very beginning, she is seen hammering nails into her fetish, the wooden doll; and now, in her young womanhood, a pagan mysticism haunts the back of her mind, a sense of some power outside her, thwarting her best endeavours. It is the same "sense of loneliness and utter privation of joy" felt by Charlotte Brontë's heroines. This is George Eliot's most searching study of the instinctive and impulsive self, which happened in this instance to be her very own self, not amenable to rationalist control, for she was well aware that our minds do not work invariably according to the rules of reason. Hence, whilst applying her standards of truth with the usual conscientious-ness, she found that mere prose and positivism would not suffice, and *The Mill on the Floss* goes over the brink of poetry oftener and further than any other of her stories. It is, no doubt, the poetic freedom with which she poured herself out in Maggie that renders this character the most magnetic of all her heroines. Maggie, as a child, lets her imagination run loose, weaving fancies and romances and little dramas in her haunts in the old mill, awed by "the resolute din, the unresting motion of the great stones," which gave her the feeling of "an uncontrollable force—the meal for ever pouring, pouring— the fine white powder softening all surfaces, and making the very spider-nets look like a faery lace-work." The spiders were a subject of speculation with her, and she wondered how a certain "fat and floury spider," when he visited his cousins, liked his flies when they were served up, not as he was accustomed "well dusted with meal," and whether the lady-spiders were shocked at each other's appearance. But there is a moralist even in the old mill. When she asks Luke, the head miller, about the elephants, and kangaroos, and the civet cat, and the sun-fish, mentioned in her story-books, and whether he would like to know them, he tells her,

"Nay, Miss, I'n got to keep count o' the flour an' corn— I can't do wi' knowin' so many things besides my work. That's what brings folks to the gallows—knowin' everything but what they'n got to get their bread by. An' they're mostly lies, I think, what's printed i' the books: them printed sheets are, anyhow, as the men cry i' the streets."

Maggie is bullied by her unimaginative brother Tom, a picture, perhaps a little hardened, of George Eliot's brother Isaac, with whom she spent a happy childhood at Griff. When, as she grows up, she finds a congenial friend, and ultimately a lover, in Philip Wakem, the crippled son of the lawyer whom the Tullivers blamed for their bankruptcy, Tom is furious. But worse is in store. Maggie is irresistibly attracted by the good-looking Stephen Guest, who is pledged to her cousin Lucy. George Eliot had dwelt too long on Maggie's childhood; and when she came to the tragedy that was preparing in that rebellious heart, there was not time, as she acknowledged, to develop it properly. This part of the story has been heavily criticized; Swinburne's indictment is the most severe,[1] but it must be dismissed. That Swinburne was not in love with Stephen Guest is no reason why Maggie should not have been. She yields for a moment to the spell against which she has struggled, and they drift out to sea in a boat. But Guest cannot prevail upon her to fly with him. She insists on returning, whatever reproaches must be faced. Her brother is obdurate. George Eliot felt that the situation was insoluble, and she invoked the catastrophe that cuts the knot, the great flood in which brother and sister perish. As Brunetière pointed out, it is this melodramatic contrivance, so foreign to George Eliot's ordinary usage, that weakens the finale, which even so is profoundly moving.[2] Maggie has freed herself; the conflict in her mind is stilled; and, as she rowed over the flood, "there was an undefined sense of reconcilement with her brother: what quarrel, what harshness, what unbelief in each other can subsist in the face of a great calamity, when all the artificial vesture of our life is gone, and we are all one with each other

[1] "My faith will not digest at once the first two volumes and the third volume of *The Mill on the Floss*; my conscience or credulity has not gorge enough for such a gulp" (*A Note on Charlotte Brontë* (1877)). Swinburne was incorrect in supposing that George Eliot actually owed anything to Mrs Gaskell's *Moorland Cottage*; the resemblances were accidental.

[2] "Le dénouement bizarre et presque extravagant du *Moulin sur la Floss*—une réconciliation de famille au milieu de la rivière débordée—que l'on voudrait pouvoir effacer de l'œuvre de George Eliot" (*Le Roman naturaliste*, 250).

in primitive mortal needs? Vaguely, Maggie felt this, in the strong resurgent love towards her brother that swept away all the later impressions of hard, cruel offence and misunderstanding, and left only the deep, underlying, unshakable memories of early union." It is a great tragedy, and there is no wonder that people began to compare George Eliot with Shakespeare.[1]

"Silas Marner" George Eliot went to Italy with Lewes in 1860, and at Florence the plan of *Romola* was conceived; but before setting to work upon it she turned once again to her Warwickshire memories, and wrote *Silas Marner*, the whole tone of which is so benign and genial that it might represent an interval of recreation before the harder task. In length and scope it is only a minor work, an idyll mingling tragedy and comedy in acceptable proportions. Poor, misshapen Silas, his faith in God and the reliance of an infirm and diffident nature on his fellow-beings shattered by the false accusation of theft, migrates from his home somewhere in the industrial north, to the village of Raveloe, and there carries on his trade of weaver, but keeps apart from his neighbours, being left with no object in life but to save and hoard and count his money. One night the treasure disappears, and the old miser rushes frantically into the parlour at the Rainbow Inn to tell the company gathered there of his loss. And then, as he wakes out of one of his epileptic fits, the first thing his eyes fall upon is a child's golden hair, and he almost thinks his gold has been restored. The little foundling who has crept into his cottage becomes the instrument of his redemption. She loves the hard-favoured man, and he cherishes her as his own.

No child was afraid of approaching Silas when Eppie was near him: there was no repulsion around him now, either for young or old; for the little child had come to link him once more with the whole world. There was love between him and the child that blent them into one, and there was love between the child and the world—from men and women with parental looks and tones, to the red lady-birds and the round pebbles.

[1] Charles Reade had already said of *Adam Bede*, "It is the finest thing since Shakespeare."

After many years the mystery is cleared up—the fugitive wife, the forsaken child, and the scapegrace brother drowned after stealing the gold, which he is found clutching in his dead fingers when the stone-pits are drained. It is melodrama used allegorically to inculcate the persistent lesson of the mutual influence of human souls. Nowhere, however, are the darker aspects of a story relieved with a sunnier humour, and nowhere does George Eliot show an easier mastery of the rich vernacular of the English peasant. Lovers of George Eliot have the conversation of the village worthies in the Rainbow, just before Silas comes with the news of the robbery, almost by heart. And that "comfortable woman," Dolly Winthrop, is one of her most lovable creations of that type. They all have their share in voicing the thought implicit in the story. It is Dolly who says:

"It allays comes into my head when I'm sorry for folks, and feel as I can't do a power to help 'em, not if I was to get up i' the middle o' the night—it comes into my head as Them above has got a deal tenderer heart nor what I've got—for I can't be anyways better nor Them as made me; and if anything looks hard to me, it's because there's things I don't know on; and for the matter o' that, there may be plenty o' things I don't know on, for it's little as I know—that it is. . . . And all as we've got to do is to trusten, Master Marner—to do the right thing as fur as we know, and to trusten. For if us as knows so little can see a bit o' good and rights, we may be sure as there's a good and a rights bigger nor what we can know—I feel it i' my own inside as it must be so. And if you could but ha' gone on trustening, Master Marner, you wouldn't ha' run away from your fellow-creaturs and been so lone."

"Ah, but that 'ud ha' been hard," said Silas, in an undertone; "it 'ud ha' been hard to trusten then."

"And so it would," said Dolly, almost with compunction; "them things are easier said nor done; and I'm partly ashamed o' talking.

"Nay, nay," said Silas, "you're i' the right, Mrs Winthrop—you're i' the right. There's good i' this world—I've a feeling o' that now; and it makes a man feel as there's a good more nor he can see, i' spite o' the trouble and the wickedness. That drawing o' the lots is dark; but the child was sent to me: there's dealings with us—there's dealings."

Even Godfrey comes to realize that he must reap where he has sown, and that he must resign the hope of ever having back the dear child who was lost through his folly.

"While I've been putting off and putting off, the trees have been growing—it's too late now. Marner was in the right in what he said about a man's turning away a blessing from his door: it falls to somebody else. I wanted to pass for childless once, Nancy—I shall pass for childless now against my wish."

How absurd to suppose that humour is necessarily facetious! Humour might almost be termed idiosyncrasy—it is idiosyncrasy stating its own perceptions. Here the most humorous passages are those most fraught with the pathos of human existence.

"*Romola*" *Romola* marks a turning-point in the life of George Eliot, and one almost as definite in the history of English realism. It was the first of her novels after the stock of experiences accumulated by an eager observation in the plastic age began to be used up, and she was thrown back on other mental resources. Circumstances and personal inclinations had made her a moral philosopher; and, though the zest of a born artist had hitherto prevailed over her bent for abstract thought, this now began to have the upper hand. *Romola*, *Middlemarch*, and finally *Daniel Deronda*, each approximate more and more to the Comtist definition of a work of art, the concrete realization of philosophic ideas. She had been the first great novelist to explore the dimmer regions of consciousness, to trace the inner phenomena of which character and deeds are the outward manifestation; and she was more and more weighed down henceforward by the seriousness of such an undertaking and her responsibilities as a teacher employing one of the most persuasive appeals to human nature. The task she had set herself was virtually same as Meredith's, to show men how to know themselves and their relations towards the universe.[1] He applied the same fundamental seriousness, but he did not

[1] *The Adventures of Harry Richmond*, conclusion.

adopt such a pose of unsmiling solemnity, of tortured anxiety. With her, moral casuistry and the dissection of gangrened consciences gradually gain the ascendancy, art and spontaneity tend to be submerged. Already she had shown her obsession with the moral problem, and an overbearing propensity to take life tragically. Even in childhood and youth she had suffered from a morbid sense of her faults and imperfections; and, whether or not her union with Lewes was responsible for her never rising superior to that tendency of her nature, it was now always the problem of evil and the conjunct problem of suffering that monopolized her attention.[1]

She prepared herself for the feat of writing *Romola* by filling *A great* her notebooks on the spot, and by an exhaustive course of *effort of* reading in the historians and the contemporary literature. *circum-stantial* Yet, in spite of her indefatigable efforts to get the right local *realism* and historical colour, the actual outcome was one of her regular studies of selfishness and weakness and the nemesis that dogs wrongdoing, transposed to a foreign setting; it is not a living resuscitation of Florence in the times of Lorenzo de' Medici, Savonarola, and Macchiavelli; the dramatis personæ are not Italians of the fifteenth century, but English people of the nineteenth dressed up to look the part. Flaubert a year before had employed the same methods of reconstruction in *Salammbô*, with very similar results. The effect upon other novelists ought to have been to discourage such laborious efforts to improve upon the purely imaginative procedure of Shakespeare and Sir Walter Scott in calling up figures and events from the remote past. The actual effect of this application of scientific

---

[1] Bourl'honne (p. 210) puts it finely: "Cependant, emportée par sa commisération pour l'humanité souffrante, elle touche souvent aux limites extrêmes du pathétique et éveille dangereusement, selon nous, le sens poignant du remords—émotion captieuse qui plonge l'homme dans la contemplation de ce qui aurait pu être ou du mal qu'il a causé autour de lui, et qui, à la limite, menace de lui ôter tout courage de vivre. Cette émotion, nous savons que G. Eliot l'éprouvait souvent et nous croyons en connaître les causes. Certes, elle était portée au doute et au découragement, ainsi que nous l'avons fait voir; elle manquait de confiance en elle-même et elle chercha longtemps dans la religion ou dans la philosophie une vue raisonnée de l'existence qui lui apportât la certitude dont elle avait besoin; mais elle aurait vraisemblablement fini par triompher de cette disposition facheuse après 1849, quand elle eut compris la vanité de sa vie et de ses aspirations spirituelles, si son union avec Lewes n'était venue ranimer l'inquiétude dans son esprit et fixer d'une manière définitive le sentiment juvenile qu'elle avait de ses 'fautes' et de son imperfection."

methods, whether to historical fiction or to the intensive
analysis of contemporary life, was to encourage the novel of
industrious research and conscientious reporting, the notebook style of novel, at the expense of imaginative creation.
Labour and study had to do the work of genius. For a long
while, the novel which focused critical attention, and which
cultivated readers looked upon as fulfilling the orthodox aims
of fiction, was the novel professing to be a systematic diagnosis
of society or a psychological inquiry into the individual and
his reactions to the world outside him. If they were to be
taken seriously, novels must be so firmly grounded on accurate
and verifiable observation that the conclusions arrived at would
be as authoritative as the census returns. This was a view of
fiction which played into the hands of those writing with some
ulterior purpose. All the novels with a thesis to propound,
ethical, religious, or sociological, owed an immense debt to
George Eliot, author of *Romola* and *Daniel Deronda*. Her
genius was beyond the reach of mere imitation; but the use of
scientific methods and the illustration of theoretic ideas in
fiction claiming to be an impartial picture of life, were within
the scope of any intelligent writer. George Eliot was a power
of the first magnitude in fiction, and the novel of ideas, the
novel with a theme in lieu of a plot, was her creation; but,
as will be clearly seen later, her influence on those who followed
was not always salutary.

*Tito, a
great
study of
moral
deterio-
ration*

If only another of her dramas of moral conflict, this is equal
in power to any of the foregoing. There is no better example
of the wonderful gift extolled by Brunetière in his account of
George Eliot's naturalism, the gift most delightfully exhibited
in *Silas Marner* and most tragically in *The Mill on the Floss*.
She excelled all other novelists in revealing "how one passion
may expel another passion, how a sudden transformation may
take place in a human soul; she makes you see how it comes
about, and how small and insignificant, almost null, is the part
in it of what we call chance." [1] Romola herself is near akin
to Maggie, with perhaps a touch of Dinah Morris in her aspiring
soul and capacity for self-devotion, an ingredient to be further

[1] *Le Roman naturaliste*, 229.

developed in Dorothea Casaubon, George Eliot's picture of a modern St Theresa. But the character that rivets attention is Tito Melema, a being endowed with capacities for all that is best, but his will subject to a constitutional debility, which is never cured or eradicated, but grows and develops unperceived, till the whole nature is corrupted. He wrongs his benefactor and betrays Romola. He thinks himself safe from the consequences; but the net of destiny closes round, and he meets the doom which he has unwarily challenged. It is a noble work, fiction grappling again with the most vital problem of moral psychology, and embodying its conceptions in figures of tragic grandeur and consistent truth. But, like *Adam Bede*, it is marred by the unwise concession of a happy ending; and it was a mistake to trick out a drama intrinsically so moving in the habiliments of other times and places, especially as this led to the foisting in of such a celebrity as Savonarola, brilliantly represented, but having nothing to do with the matters at stake.

Felix Holt the Radical, which followed three years later, is "*Felix* a minor novel, though judged by general standards it is a fine *Holt*" one. It deals with the people she had once known so familiarly in the Midlands; but it involved a retrospect, the period being that of the agitation for reform in the thirties, and George Eliot had to get up the subject from the newspapers and other records of the time. The preface is a graphic summary of conditions "five-and-thirty years ago." So far as she enters into the political issues, she shows decisively that she had little faith in an unregenerated democracy. Her attitude, indeed, is almost the opposite of Meredith's in *Beauchamp's Career*, ten years later. Characteristically, she insists on the need for moral and social rather than political reform, which had better wait for the other. But her agitator is so high-minded, or rather so obstinate in his idealistic zeal, that he fails as signally as the "rocket-mind" of Beauchamp. Contrary to her wont, she entwines the complications of a plot with the history of his political efforts; and at the end Esther Lyon, the lady of higher degree whom Felix loves, renounces the advantages of wealth to wed the man of her choice, like

Dorothea Casaubon, in the novel that followed. The lovers are interesting; but George Eliot's humour comes out best in the portrait of the old dissenter, the Rev. Rufus Lyon, and her tragic power in that of the conscience-stricken Mrs Transome.

"Middle-march" Though without the charming vivacity of her best earlier work, the next, which is her biggest novel, showed no falling off in strength; on the contrary, *Middlemarch*, that vast realistic cartoon, is the ripest and fullest exposition of her mind and philosophy. It is also the most modern in subject, as well as in manner and outlook. It takes in the whole complex life of a provincial town at the middle of the century, bringing on the scene half-a-hundred separate characters, of whom nearly a dozen are analysed to the depths, and shown developing or deteriorating, as they face circumstances honestly and discerningly or succumb to the internal weakness which corrupts motive and paralyses will. It is a characteristic study of human solidarity. Our interests are inextricably bound up together. All these lives touch at innumerable points; their motives and the consequences of their acts are interwoven to an unforeseeable and dumbfoundering extent. No member of human society can have an independent existence; everything he does affects the remainder. The novelist has once more been harnessed to the moral philosopher, and she groups together a series of life-histories illustrating a certain truth. It is a cross-section of modern society, in which a multiplicity of characters are ranged in one perspective, all acted upon by one and the same impulse, to live their life and realize what is in them. In other words, she gives the clue to her interpretation of the bewildering enigmas, the perplexing maze, by reducing her calculations to one denominator. The clue is her own version of Carlyle's doctrine of work and struggle; and, as in Carlyle's histories, it might be said that the Day of Judgment is continually going on. Each one has his own conception of happiness and success, and strives or fails to strive, succeeds or comes to grief, taking his reward or punishment before our eyes. Dorothea's vague and fruitless aspirations, Casaubon's wasted labour on the Key to all Mythologies, Lydgate's chosen mission to be a medical reformer·

and its stultification by a thoughtless marriage, Bulstrode's
compromise with evil, are all a parable of lost ideals. The
stumbles and self-recovery and renewed efforts of Fred Vincy,
who listens to advice and encouragement from those who
know better; and the quiet, steady, undemonstrative goodness
of Caleb and Mary Garth, are the contrasts which enforce
the lesson. Success or failure depends inexorably on character,
and character is ours to make or mar.

"But, my dear Mrs Casaubon," said Mr Farebrother, smiling
gently at her ardour, "character is not cut in marble—it is not
something solid and unalterable. It is something living and
changing, and may become diseased as our bodies do."

This is not the strict determinism of positivist science.
George Eliot would have granted that motives and actions are
the resultant of circumstances outside and of tendencies within,
rooted preferences and prejudices, abilities and disabilities;
and that, if the external and internal conditions were fully
known, the resultant could be calculated and the actions
predicted. But she was aware of an incalculable element in
the self, which can react against and change conditions.
Ultimately, the will is free. This is the whole basis of her
moral philosophy, and the ground for her insistence on moral
responsibility.

Hence, whilst a number of her characters, such as Mr Brooke, *The*
the curmudgeonly old Featherstone, or the sarcastic Mrs *signific-*
Cadwallader, are "characters" in the old-fashioned sense, *ant*
that is, they are interesting because of their peculiarities and *characters*
their differences from the ordinary run of mankind, those of
most importance in the drama are those who have most in
common with the rest of humanity, faults and passions which
may or may not be corrected, souls to be saved or damned,
in this world, if not in another. These are living persons;
they develop or the reverse, and what they do is of decisive
import. George Eliot's prelude makes clear that she meant
in Dorothea to show one with the strength and the desire to
live an epical life, in contrast with the materialistic beings
around her. Lydgate thought to himself, "This young

creature has a heart large enough for the Virgin Mary." She had one of those natures, "in which, if they love us, we are conscious of having a sort of baptism and consecration: they bind us over to rectitude and purity by their pure belief about us; and our sins become that worst kind of sacrilege which tears down the invisible altar of trust. 'If you are not good, none is good'—those little words may give a terrific meaning to responsibility, may hold a vitriolic intensity for remorse." Her nobility and absolute integrity are thus a criterion by which all the rest are tacitly measured. And what a voice she had! "It was like the voice of a soul that had once lived in an Æolian harp." Even when her wings had been clipped through her blunder in marrying Mr Casaubon, she was still like "an angel beguiled." All the poetry of *Middlemarch* is in Dorothea. Ladislaw says to her, "You *are* a poem—and that is to be the best part of a poet—what makes up the poet's consciousness in his best moods." [1] Otherwise, *Middlemarch* is the sternest prose of life. But the weak point of the book is that Dorothea finds no better consummation of all her soaring ideals, even after realizing the mistake she had committed in marrying Mr Casaubon, than to unite herself with Ladislaw. Ladislaw was one of George Eliot's miscalculations—he is a blunder, and a blot on the whole story. In the abstract, he is all very well—spirited, cultivated, full of fine ideas—and he has the curly hair which George Eliot adored. But he never touches the reader's heart-strings: as the peer of Dorothea he is a delusion. He never excites the same fellow-feeling as the rolling stone, poor, erring Fred Vincy: Fred is superior chiefly because he was not meant to be superior. Obviously, he was brought in only as an escape from her heroine's disillusionment, to provide the same sort of happy ending as impaired *Adam Bede* and *Romola*. Rosamond is a much better correlative to Lydgate, the one who after Dorothea fixes deepest sympathies. He is an able, public-spirited man,

---

[1] "To be a poet is to have a soul so quick to discern that no shade of quality escapes it, so quick to feel, that discernment is but a hand playing with finely-ordered variety on the chords of emotion—a soul in which knowledge passes instantaneously into feeling, and feeling flashes back as a new organ of knowledge." So Ladislaw tells Dorothea (chapter xxii.).

who, through not realizing the cardinal importance of marriage, ties himself to a shallow, pleasure-loving woman, who becomes a clog on all his fine schemes, brings him to the verge of ruin, and makes the unselfish career on which he had pinned his hopes a failure. She is a searing study of narrow egotism and total lack of imagination. In his attempts to make her understand the need for cutting down household expenses to avoid crippling themselves with debts and perhaps going bankrupt, Lydgate treats her with a tender forbearance. But her "quiet, elusive obstinacy" paralyses him; the resolution to which he was brought by logic and honourable pride begins to relax "under her torpedo contact."

"Why can you not put off having the inventory made? You can send the men away to-morrow when they come."

"I shall not send them away," said Lydgate, the peremptoriness rising again. Was it of any use to explain?

"If we left Middlemarch, there would of course be a sale, and that would do as well."

"But we are not going to leave Middlemarch."

"I am sure, Tertius, it would be much better to do so. Why can we not go to London? Or near Durham, where your family is known?"

"We can go nowhere without money, Rosamond."

"Your friends would not wish you to be without money. And surely these odious tradesmen might be made to understand that, and to wait, if you would make proper representations to them."

"This is idle, Rosamond," said Lydgate, angrily. "You must learn to take my judgment on questions you don't understand. I have made necessary arrangements, and they must be carried out. As to friends, I have no expectations whatever from them, and shall not ask them for anything."

Rosamond sat perfectly still. The thought in her mind was that if she had known how Lydgate would behave, she would never have married him.

"We have no time to waste on unnecessary words, dear," said Lydgate, trying to be gentle again. "There are some details that I want to consider with you. Dover says he will take a good deal of the plate back again, and any of the jewellery we like. He really behaves very well."

"Are we to go without spoons and forks then?" said Rosamond, whose very lips seemed to get thinner with the thinness of her utterance. She was determined to make no further resistance or suggestion.

"Oh no, dear!" said Lydgate. "But look here," he continued, drawing a paper from his pocket and opening it; "here is Dover's account. See, I have marked a number of articles, which if we returned them would reduce the amount by thirty pounds and more. I have not marked any of the jewellery." Lydgate had really felt this point of the jewellery very bitter to himself; but he had overcome the feeling by severe argument. He could not propose to Rosamond that she should return any particular present of his, but he had told himself that he was bound to put Dover's offer before her, and her inward prompting might make the affair easy.

"It is useless for me to look, Tertius," said Rosamond, calmly; "you will return what you please." She would not turn her eyes on the paper, and Lydgate, flushing up to the roots of his hair, drew it back and let it fall on his knee. Meanwhile Rosamond quietly went out of the room, leaving Lydgate helpless and wondering. It seemed that she had no more identified herself with him than if they had been creatures of different species and opposing interests. He tossed his head and thrust his hands deep into his pockets with a sort of vengeance. There was still science—there were still objects to work for. He must give a tug still—all the stronger because other satisfactions were going.

But the door opened and Rosamond re-entered. She carried the leather box containing the amethysts, and a tiny ornamental basket which contained other boxes, and laying them on the chair where she had been sitting, she said, with perfect propriety in her air—

"This is all the jewellery you ever gave me. You can return what you like of it, and of the plate also. You will not, of course, expect me to stay at home to-morrow. I shall go to papa's."

To many women the look Lydgate cast at her would have been more terrible than one of anger: it had in it a despairing acceptance of the distance she was placing between them.

"And when shall you come back again?" he said, with a bitter edge on his accent.

"Oh, in the evening. Of course I shall not mention the subject to mamma." Rosamond was convinced that no woman could behave more irreproachably than she was behaving; and she went to sit down at her work-table. Lydgate sat meditating a minute or·two, and the result was that he said, with some of the old emotion in his tone—

"Now we have been united, Rosy, you should not leave me to myself in the first trouble that has come."

"Certainly not," said Rosamond; "I shall do everything it becomes me to do."

"It is not right that the thing should be left to servants, or that I should have to speak to them about it. And I shall be obliged to go out—I don't know how early. I understand your shrinking from the humiliation of these money affairs. But, my dear Rosamond, as a question of pride, which I feel just as much as you can, it is surely better to manage the thing ourselves, and let the servants see as little of it as possible; and since you are my wife, there is no hindering your share in my disgraces—if there were disgraces."

Rosamond did not answer immediately, but at last she said, "Very well, I will stay at home."

"I shall not touch these jewels, Rosy. Take them away again. But I will write out a list of plate that we may return, and that can be packed up and sent at once."

"The servants will know *that*," said Rosamond, with the slightest touch of sarcasm.

"Well, we must meet some disagreeables as necessities. Where is the ink, I wonder?" said Lydgate, rising, and throwing the account on the larger table where he meant to write.

George Eliot comments, a few pages further on:

There are episodes in most men's lives in which their highest qualities can only cast a deterring shadow over the objects that fill their inward vision: Lydgate's tender-heartedness was present just then only as a dread lest he should offend against it, not as an emotion that swayed him to tenderness. For he was very miserable. Only those who know the supremacy of the intellectual life—the life which has a seed of ennobling thought and purpose within it—can understand the grief of one who falls from that serene activity into the absorbing soul-wasting struggle with worldly annoyances.

Casaubon and Bulstrode

Casaubon is nothing in himself; he is only the monster that would have devoured Andromeda. He is Dorothea's mistake, as Will Ladislaw was George Eliot's. Is he too gross a caricature? It is hard to make up one's mind; but at every re-reading of the egregious letter offering the post of wife and amanuensis to the trustful Dorothea one roars with louder laughter:

"For in the first hour of meeting you, I had an impression of your eminent and perhaps exclusive fitness to supply that need (connected, I may say, with such activity of the affections as even the preoccupations of a work too special to be abdicated could not uninterruptedly dissimulate); and each succeeding opportunity for observation has given the impression an added depth by convincing me more emphatically of that fitness which I had preconceived, and thus evoking more decisively those affections to which I have but now referred. . . . It was, I confess, beyond my hope to meet with this rare combination of elements both solid and attractive, adapted to supply aid to graver labours and to cast a charm over vacant hours; and but for the event of my introduction to you (which, let me again say, I trust not to be superficially coincident with foreshadowing needs, but providentially related thereto as stages towards the completion of a life's plan), I should presumably have gone on to the last without any attempt to lighten my solitariness by a matrimonial union."

Even the Key to all Mythologies could not have provided better reading. As to Bulstrode, the sanctimonious knave, hypocrite even to himself in his double-dealing with his conscience, the only misgiving is whether it would not have been sufficient to exhibit him and then leave him to fester in his own rottenness of heart, instead of making of him one of those symmetrical instances of wickedness bringing down material as well as moral chastisement. After all, the workers of iniquity do flourish, and apparently are not always afflicted with an ill conscience; as, on the other hand, peace and inward satisfaction are the only reward that can be guaranteed to their opposites. George Eliot was perhaps too insistent on a more spectacular justice. And in this case her anxiety to

underline the didactic bearings led her into the Raffles melodrama and the obscure imbroglio connecting Ladislaw with
Bulstrode's past. Most people have known a Bulstrode, he
is by no means a rare phenomenon; which makes his vivisection
the more absorbing. Tito was a subtler exposure of the secret
mechanism of self-deception and the atrophy of inner
restraints; but there are features in this study of a diseased
soul which throw light on still further obscurities.

A man vows, and yet will not cast away the means of breaking
his vow. Is it that he distinctly means to break it? Not at
all; but the desires that tend to break it are at work in him
dimly, and make their way into his imagination, and relax his
muscles in the very moments when he is telling himself over
again the reasons for his vow.

Or read this:

Early in the morning—about six—Mr Bulstrode rose and
spent some time in prayer. Does anyone suppose that private
prayer is necessarily candid—necessarily goes to the root of
action? Private prayer is inaudible speech, and speech is
representative: who can represent himself just as he is, even
in his own reflections! Bulstrode had not yet unravelled in his
thought the confused promptings of the last four-and-twenty
hours.

Compassion is impossible for Bulstrode; the pathos is
concentrated in the wife who had believed in and venerated
him, and now must share in the dishonour of his exposure.
It was "as bitter as it could be to any mortal."

But this imperfectly-taught woman, whose phrases and
habits were an odd patchwork, had a loyal spirit within her.
The man whose prosperity she had shared through nearly half
a life, and who had unvaryingly cherished her—now that
punishment had befallen him it was not possible for her in any
sense to forsake him. There is a forsaking which still sits at the
same board and lies on the same couch with the forsaken soul,
withering it the more by unloving proximity. She knew, when
she locked her door, that she should unlock it ready to go down
to her unhappy husband and espouse his sorrow, and say of his

guilt, I will mourn and not reproach. But she needed time to gather up her strength; she needed to sob out her farewell to all the gladness and pride of her life. When she had resolved to go down, she prepared herself by some little acts which might seem mere folly to a hard onlooker; they were her way of expressing to all spectators visible or invisible that she had begun a new life in which she embraced humiliation. She took off all her ornaments and put on a plain black gown, and instead of wearing her much-adorned cap and large bows of hair, she brushed her hair down and put on a plain bonnet-cap, which made her look suddenly like an early Methodist.

Middlemarch is a picture of sordid and ugly things, but is redeemed from any repulsiveness by such traits of human fellowship and ingenuous ideality. Reading it attentively is like listening to some vast and complex symphony, full of clashing harmonies and discords, in which the pure spirit of Dorothea and those unpretendingly akin to her furnish the celestial counterpoint.[1]

"*Daniel Deronda*" It could scarcely be said of the author of *Middlemarch* that she "saw life steadily and saw it whole"; it would sound absurd in relation to *Daniel Deronda*, in which, however, she unfolded some of her final conclusions on the laws of human life. There was something of the treatise in all her novels; this last one is all treatise. It was as if she had written herself out, so far as fiction is concerned. Here, instead of illuminating the life she has seen with the mellow radiance of a wise and tolerant philosophy which has become part of herself, she reverses the operation, and all that is left to admire is the power and dexterity with which she sets forth moral and social problems in characters evolved out of her own consciousness. Everything is serious and austere. Her insight into the complexities of personal relations and the subtleties of feeling and motive

[1] George Eliot apparently had an ear for music, but shared her contemporaries' philistinism as regards the plastic arts. Dorothea's impercipience is too caustically expressed not to have been that of her creatrix: she says at Rome, "I should be quite willing to enjoy the art here, but there is so much that I don't know the reason of—so much that seems to me a consecration of ugliness rather than beauty. The painting and sculpture may be wonderful, but the feeling is often low and brutal, and sometimes even ridiculous" (chapter xxii.). Give her credit, anyhow, for not pretending to admire what she was told to.

is as acute as ever; but it is employed to illustrate and substantiate theoretic points; the book is a piece of applied psychology rather than a novel. A large proportion of her characters had originated in ideas; she had said herself that her stories "always grow out of psychological conceptions of the dramatis personæ," [1] which is much the same thing. But nowhere is this so self-evident as here. Deronda is a pure idealization, the visionary Mordecai pure literature. It is only on Gwendolen Harleth and her struggles with her baser self and the recalcitrance of the world that the old genius pours itself out again. Gwendolen has resemblances to Maggie and Romola and even Dorothea, with more of the human admixture of weakness and error. Grandcourt, however, her Casaubon, it is almost impossible to believe in, in spite of his being so horribly alive. Is it only the name that seems to suggest a candid portrait, a parody which is also an unmasking, of Sir Charles Grandison, by an anti-Richardsonian who saw through that creation, and proceeded to show that all his virtues and graces were spurious and himself a whited sepulchre? Is Grandcourt a Grandison inverted? Both characters are oppressive to many. The reader is gladder if possible than Gwendolen when her dreadful husband drowns and she will not stretch out a hand to save him. Novel-readers inevitably wax bloodthirsty when the inner wickedness of a man is so ruthlessly exposed. His very love-making is like the blandishments of a boa-constrictor. It hardly provokes laughter; in fact, George Eliot's humour seems to have evaporated, and the forced facetiousness and galvanic liveliness with which she tries to make up for this are merely tricks of the expert professional.

In default of humour, however, George Eliot has developed *Her* a caustic irony, which certainly keeps the conversations from *latest* falling flat, and sometimes becomes double-edged and a very effec- *manner* tive mode of oblique satire. Unfortunately, she has to explain exactly what she is doing, in little asides like the following:

Gwendolen, who had a keen sense of absurdity in others, but was kindly disposed towards anyone who could make life

[1] Haldane, 117.

agreeable to her, meant to win Mrs Arrowpoint by giving her an interest and attention beyond what others were probably inclined to show. But self-confidence is apt to address itself to an imaginary dullness in others; as people who are well off speak in a cajoling tone to the poor, and those who are in the prime of life raise their voice and talk artificially to seniors, hastily conceiving them to be deaf and rather imbecile. Gwendolen, with all her cleverness and purpose to be agreeable, could not escape that form of stupidity: it followed in her mind, unreflectingly, that because Mrs Arrowpoint was ridiculous she was also likely to be wanting in penetration, and she went through her little scenes without suspicion that the various shades of her behaviour were all noted.

There follows a conversation, barbed with furtive repartee on Gwendolen's part, which admirably reveals the character of both. Mrs Arrowpoint congratulates Gwendolen on her love of books and music, in a tone that seems to the latter too patronizing. She answers, gracefully:

"It is I who am fortunate. Miss Arrowpoint will teach me what good music is: I shall be entirely a learner. I hear that she is a thorough musician."

"Catherine has certainly had every advantage. We have a first-rate musician in the house now—Herr Klesmer; perhaps you know all his compositions. You must allow me to introduce him to you. You sing, I believe. Catherine plays three instruments, but she does not sing. I hope you will let us hear you. I understand you are an accomplished singer."

"Oh no!—'die Kraft ist schwach, allein die Lust ist gross,' as Mephistopheles says."

"Ah, you are a student of Goethe. Young ladies are so advanced now. I suppose you have read everything."

"No, really. I shall be so glad if you will tell me what to read. I have been looking into all the books in the library at Offendene, but there is nothing readable. The leaves all stick together and smell musty. I wish I could write books to amuse myself, as you can! How delightful it must be to write books after one's own taste instead of reading other people's! Home-made books must be so nice."

For an instant Mrs Arrowpoint's glance was a little sharper, but the perilous resemblance to satire in the last sentence took the hue of girlish simplicity when Gwendolen added— "I would give anything to write a book!"

"And why should you not?" said Mrs Arrowpoint, encouragingly. "You have but to begin as I did. Pen, ink, and paper are at everybody's command. But I will send you all I have written with pleasure."

"Thanks. I shall be so glad to read your writings. Being acquainted with authors must give a peculiar understanding of their books: one would be able to tell then which parts were funny and which serious. I am sure I often laugh in the wrong place." Here Gwendolen herself became aware of danger, and added quickly, "In Shakespeare, you know, and other great writers that we can never see. But I always want to know more than there is in the books."

"If you are interested in any of my subjects I can lend you many extra sheets in manuscript," said Mrs Arrowpoint—while Gwendolen felt herself painfully in the position of the young lady who professed to like potted sprats. "These are things I daresay I shall publish eventually: several friends have urged me to do so, and one doesn't like to be obstinate. My Tasso, for example—I could have made it twice the size."

"I dote on Tasso," said Gwendolen.

"Well, you shall have all my papers, if you like. So many, you know, have written about Tasso; but they are all wrong. As to the particular nature of his madness, and his feelings for Leonora, and the real cause of his imprisonment, and the character of Leonora, who, in my opinion, was a cold-hearted woman, else she would have married him in spite of her brother —they are all wrong. I differ from everybody."

"How very interesting!" said Gwendolen. "I like to differ from everybody; I think it is so stupid to agree. That is the worst of writing your opinions; you make people agree with you."

This speech renewed a slight suspicion in Mrs Arrowpoint, and again her glance became for an instant examining. But Gwendolen looked very innocent, and continued with a docile air,

"I know nothing of Tasso except the *Gerusalemme Liberata*, which we read and learned by heart at school."

"Ah, his life is more interesting than his poetry. I have

constructed the early part of his life as a sort of romance. When one thinks of his father Bernardo, and so on, there is so much that must be true."

"Imagination is often truer than fact," said Gwendolen, decisively, though she could no more have explained these glib words than if they had been Coptic or Etruscan. "I shall be so glad to learn all about Tasso—and his madness especially. I suppose poets are always a little mad."

"To be sure—'the poet's eye in a fine frenzy rolling,' and somebody says of Marlowe—

> 'For that fine madness still he did maintain,
> Which always should possess the poet's brain.'"

"But it was not always found out, was it?" said Gwendolen, innocently. "I suppose some of them rolled their eyes in private. Mad people are often very cunning."

Again a shade flitted over Mrs Arrowpoint's face; but the entrance of the gentlemen prevented any immediate mischief between her and this quick young lady, who had over-acted her naïveté.

Charac-
teristic
self-
analysis

There are further passages of arms, even with the illustrious Herr Klesmer, who fires up in splendid style when somebody happens to talk about "mere musicians." But more like the familiar George Eliot are the mental soliloquies in which Gwendolen analyses her situation in regard to Grandcourt. Like Maggie, or Dorothea, she had been "looking along an inescapable path of repulsive monotony . . . and lo, now, a moment of choice was come." Her mother tells her that Grandcourt is evidently about to propose. "Was it triumph she felt most or terror?"

Impossible for Gwendolen not to feel some triumph in a tribute to her power at a time when she was first tasting the bitterness of insignificance: again she seemed to be getting a sort of empire over her own life. But how to use it? Here came the terror. Quick, quick, like pictures in a book beaten open with a sense of hurry, came back vividly, yet in fragments, all that she had gone through in relation to Grandcourt—the allurements, the vacillations, the resolve to accede, the final repulsion; the incisive face of that dark-eyed lady with the

lovely boy; her own pledge (was it a pledge not to marry him?)
—the new belief in the worth of men and things for which that
scene of disclosure had become a symbol. That unalterable
experience made a vision at which in the first agitated moment,
before tempering reflections could suggest themselves, her
native terror shrank.

She shrinks and temporizes, till at length she makes the
compromise with conscience.

"How can I help what other people have done? Things
would not come right if I were to turn round now and declare
that I would not marry Mr Grandcourt." And such turning
round was out of the question. The horses in the chariot she
had mounted were going at full speed.

And it is far too late when she receives the letter of reproach
from the dark-eyed lady to whom she wondered whether she
had given any pledge. It comes with the diamonds that had
been Grandcourt's gift, first to one and now to the other.

"These diamonds, which were once given with ardent love
to Lydia Glasher, she passes on to you. You have broken your
word to her, that you might possess what was hers. Perhaps
you think of being happy, as she once was, and of having beautiful children such as hers, who will thrust hers aside. God is too
just for that. The man you have married has a withered heart.
His best young love was mine; you could not take that from me
when you took the rest. It is dead; but I am the grave in
which your chance of happiness is buried as well as mine. You
had your warning. You have chosen to injure me and my
children. He had meant to marry me. He would have
married me at last, if you had not broken your word. You will
have your punishment. I desire it with all my soul.

"Will you give him this letter to set him against me and ruin
us more—me and my children? Shall you like to stand before
your husband with these diamonds on you, and these words of
mine in his thoughts and yours? Will he think you have any
right to complain when he has made you miserable? You took
him with your eyes open. The willing wrong you have done me
will be your curse."

It is true that the machinery in *Daniel Deronda* is only

too visible, and that Gwendolen—and not Gwendolen alone among the characters—is "deductively delineated" [1] ; but the old, recurrent problem is staged and played out with the same truth as ever, and with very little less of the power derived from George Eliot's impassioned morality. The book is peculiarly interesting, for an inferior work often reveals more of the author than a real masterpiece does: it gives away secrets. [2]

Approximations to the "roman expérimental"   In these latest novels of George Eliot, fiction often seems to be a veritable experimentation with life. Possibly, the novelist did sometimes feel as if she were trying out an imaginary case, seeing how it would work in all its multitudinous details, at least on paper. Fiction had become, as it were, an art dwelling in the flesh and testing itself by life. It sets forth a theory or states a problem, and draws conclusions which look as if they could be verified. Through its scrutiny of men and women in the act of living, it elucidates the laws of human life, and may seem to demonstrate them scientifically, basing a practical philosophy on an array of cases which appear as sound as observed facts. [3] It is the teaching of experience at one remove; but that remove is presumed to represent only the careful ordering of what would else be too confused and baffling. All this was, on the one hand, in full accord with the seriousness of the age, which loved to regard itself as a court of inquiry, contemplating fellow-creatures on trial, and listening to the solemn conclusions, admonitions, and sententious maxims of a venerated judge; and, on the other hand, it was a happy thought to approximate fiction to science. The next step would be to claim that the results of such a working out of a given case according to the rules of verisimilitude had scientific validity; and this is what was in fact claimed by the *roman*

[1] W. C. Brownell (in *Victorian Prose Masters*, 112–113).

[2] It is a pity, however, that uncritical theorists insist on singling out such artistic nonentities as Ezra, Deronda, Mordecai, etc., as examples of the root-principles of art, when they are only the blunders of George Eliot's effort to vitalize mere theorems.

[3] Is not this what M. Bourl'honne refers to when he remarks on her growing habit "à speculer sur la vie au lieu de vivre, à prendre l'existence du point de vue de la représentation qu'on peut s'en faire—représentation qui consiste évidemment en un système d'idées dont la clef se trouve dans les *a priori* de la raison ou de la conscience morale—et non du point de vue de l'action ou de l'expérience simplement vécue, qui est celui auquel se range en général la maturité"? (p. 142).

expérimental. George Eliot, however, separated herself from
any who put forward such claims by her admission of the
element of free will into the inner theatre of contending forces.[1]
Nevertheless, her novels were the finest example extant of the
thoroughgoing realism which came to be known as naturalism;
and, as Brunetière declared in a famous study, it was vastly
superior, being truer, than Flaubert's, because of the fellow-
feeling with humanity, even at its lowliest, which contrasted
with his attitude of superiority and contempt for stupidity
and folly. This fellow-feeling and tenderness also differen-
tiates her from Hawthorne. He was, in comparison, purely
intellectual, and loved to elaborate such ideas as that of sin
as an agency in human education. In *The Scarlet Letter*, for
instance, their sin ultimately redeems the delinquents; whilst
the unrelenting pursuit of justice upon those who have wronged
him becomes in Roger Chillingworth the instrument of the
soul's perdition. That work is a more austere tragedy than
The Mill on the Floss, or indeed any of George Eliot's. In it,
Hawthorne abstained from humour, and even eliminated pathos,
putting in its place an awe and terror that benumb the heart.
But he was no realist; he dealt in symbolism, which turns
this, like others of his stories, into a parable. George Eliot
was conscious of some affinity with another novelist who was
by no means a realist, George Sand, who, she said, after putting
Jane Austen above "all the male novelists that ever lived,"
"had greater genius and incomparably deeper experience
than Miss Austen." She was attracted by George Sand's
handling of the theme of love and passion, which was as powerful

---

[1] "Vous choisissez un caractère, ou, comme vous dites, un tempérament; vous en
voulez 'démonter et remonter le méchanisme'; vous prétendez chercher 'ce que telle
passion, dans tel milieu et dans telles circonstances données, produira au point de vue
de l'individu et de la société?' Je le veux bien. Sans doute, puisque vous y tenez,
je vous fais remarquer en passant que, si l'homme n'est pas libre, il croit l'être; que les
sociétés de l'Occident sont fondées sur cette croyance—hypothèse, préjugé méta-
physique ou supersitition religieuse, comme il vous plaira de l'appeler;—et que, par
conséquent, vous éliminez de notre *roman expérimental* ce qu'il y a peut-être de plus
intéressant pour l'homme et plus vivant, au plein sens du mot, à savoir: la tragédie
d'une volonté qui pense" (*Le Roman naturaliste*—"Le Roman expérimental," 129).
"Human nature has the power at crucial moments of selecting among several
courses of action. Freedom, then, is possible. If freedom is characteristic of
human nature the self, then, is autonomous" (G. R. Swann: *Philosophical
Parallelisms* (1929), p. 92).

and unfettered as Rousseau's, another of her inspirers. The author of *Jacques, Valentine, Indiana, Jeanne* was a champion of the rights of the individual and a denouncer of all forms of tyranny and repression. But her passionate iteration of the value of the individual soul did not really correspond to George Eliot's gospel of personal development; it was entirely free from the tragical sense of a moral code and retributive justice. A closer bond was their belief in the inexhaustible strength of human charity. This was a mighty inspiration in George Sand. George Eliot has nothing to set beside that almost superhuman image of humble and unconscious magnanimity, the peasant Madeleine, in *François le Champi*, who shares her last crust with those still more destitute, and to succour her poorer neighbours inures herself to a sleepless life of sacrifice and self-devotion—it is superhuman, yet it rings true. In it George Sand transcended all her sentimentalism. This is really to say that in creative force and intensity of imagination George Sand was her superior; it is here George Eliot falls short of the greatest.

George Eliot's humour

There is a profundity in George Eliot's humour that tends to restore the balance. Her humour, however, was a variable faculty, and, like her genius in its totality, it grew, attained its highest development, and then deteriorated. At first, she seemed to condescend to be funny, as when Mr Gilfil asked little Corduroys whether they had milked the geese yet?

"Milked the geese! why, they don't milk the geese, you silly!"
"No! dear heart! why, how do the goslings live, then?"
The nutriment of goslings rather transcending Tommy's observations in natural history, he feigned to understand the question in an exclamatory rather than an interrogatory sense, and became absorbed in winding up his top.

Her child episodes in general, though full of truth and sympathy and not destitute of humour, tend to be far too serious and heavy-handed. There is often an uncertainty in her drawing of children; sometimes they are lifelike, more often they talk like elderly people and are preternaturally solemn and intelligent, like their begetter. As a child, George

Eliot herself left on many the impression of being precociously grown-up.[1] Tom, in *The Mill on the Floss*, reproving Maggie and assuring her, "I shall tell mother you know," seems to reflect the attitude of the Comtist Sunday School teacher. There is none of the lightness and gusto here of Meredith, or Lewis Carroll, or Kipling. In another of the clerical stories, "Janet's Repentance," the satirical irony in the portrait of Dempster tends towards caricature: the same was applied later on to Mr Casaubon.

"Presbyterians? what are they?" inquired Mr Tomlinson, who often said his father had given him "no eddication, and he didn't care who knowed it; he could buy up most o' th' eddicated men he'd ever come across."

"The Presbyterians," said Mr Dempster, in rather a louder tone than before, holding that every appeal for information must naturally be addressed to him, "are a sect founded in the reign of Charles I, by a man named John Presbyter, who hatched all the brood of Dissenting vermin that crawl about in dirty alleys, and circumvent the lord of the manor in order to get a few yards of ground for their pigeon-house conventicles."

"No, no, Dempster," said Mr Luke Byles, "you're wrong there. Presbyterianism is derived from the word presbyter, meaning an elder."

"Don't contradict *me*, sir!" stormed Dempster. "I say the word presbyterian is derived from John Presbyter, a miserable fanatic who wore a suit of leather, and went about from town to village, and from village to hamlet, inoculating the vulgar with the virus of Dissent."

"Come, Byles, that seems a deal more likely," said Mr Tomlinson, in a conciliatory tone, apparently of opinion that history was a process of ingenious guessing.

"It's not a question of likelihood; it's a known fact. I could fetch you my Encyclopædia, and show it you this moment."

"I don't care a straw, either for you or your Encyclopædia," said Mr Dempster; "a farrago of false information, of which

[1] It was partly the result of her loneliness and the old-fashioned policy of her instructors. "To these good ladies (the Misses Franklin at Coventry) the child was simply the less developed grown-up person who required no special treatment excepting that allowance had to be made for her limitations. And little Mary Anne played her part well and loved her funny grown-up books, and doubtless wrote her essays in the same grown-up language that now seems so odd and stilted" (Haldane, 23).

you picked up an imperfect copy in a cargo of wastepaper. Will you tell *me*, sir, that I don't know the origin of Presbyterianism? I, sir, a man known through the county, intrusted with the affairs of half a score parishes; while you, sir, are ignored by the very fleas that infest the miserable alley in which you were bred."

A loud and general laugh, with "You'd better let him alone, Byles"; "You'll not get the better of Dempster in a hurry," drowned the retort of the too well-informed Mr Byles, who, white with rage, rose and walked out of the bar.

"A meddlesome, upstart, Jacobinical fellow, gentlemen," continued Mr Dempster. "I was determined to get rid of him. What does he mean by thrusting himself into our company? A man with about as much principle as he has property, which, to my knowledge, is considerably less than none. An insolvent atheist, gentlemen. A deistical prater, fit to sit in the chimney-corner of a pot-house, and make blasphemous comments on the one greasy newspaper fingered by beer-swilling tinkers. I will not suffer in my company a man who speaks lightly of religion."

A much finer irony has already been appraised in the portrayal of the Tullivers. It grows rarer and fainter, in some of the vulgar gossip about Bulstrode, for instance, in *Middlemarch*, and how his wife Harriet bears their come-down in general esteem.

"Do you think any hint has reached her?" asks Mrs Hackbut. "I should hardly think so," said Mrs Tom Toller. "We hear that *he* is ill, and has never stirred out of the house since the meeting on Thursday; but she was with her girls at church yesterday, and they had new Tuscan bonnets. Her own had a feather in it. I have never seen that her religion made any difference in her dress."

"She wears very neat patterns always," said Mrs Plymdale, a little stung. "And that feather I know she's got dyed a pale lavender on purpose to be consistent. I must say it of Harriet that she wishes to do right."

Humour plays a diminishing part in the conversations in her later novels. Even the irony already noted in *Daniel Deronda* is held in check by her continual effort to convey the thought of persons consciously engaged in clarifying their ideas and developing a consistent view of life and conduct for their own behoof. Her three earliest novels contain the best of her humour, that humour which is the stamp of idiosyncrasy. Here most of the people betray themselves completely the moment they open their lips. It colours the dialogue, and is in other ways a source of admirable comedy. There is no need to cite further examples. But George Eliot's finest humour is that of her great aphorists. Very solemn and superior people would fain identify humour with folly and buffoonery, whereas on close examination it turns out to be near akin to if not the same thing as wisdom. The gnomic wisdom of Mrs Poyser is of course George Eliot's, put in the raciest and most vivacious form.

"Well, I like that woman even better than her cream-cheeses," said Mrs Irwine. "She has the spirit of three men, with that pale face of hers; and she says such sharp things too."

"Sharp! yes, her tongue is like a new-set razor. She's quite original in her talk, too; one of those untaught wits that help to stock a country with proverbs. I told you that capital thing I heard her say about Craig—that he was like a cock who thought the sun had risen to hear him crow. Now that's an Æsop's fable in a sentence."

George Eliot could have brought Æsop up to date, and her admirers did something of the sort by making a book out of her sayings.[1]

---

[1] *Wise, Witty, and Tender Sayings from the Works of George Eliot*, collected by Alexander Main (1872).

CHAPTER VII

GEORGE MEREDITH, POET AND NOVELIST

A poet,
like the
Brontës,
applying
poetry
to life

MEREDITH's earliest work of fiction, *The Shaving of Shagpat* (1856), was sympathetically reviewed by George Eliot, before she had begun writing fiction herself; but she could hardly foresee that one day he was to be her great successor as analyst of the mind and soul and as philosophic commentator on man in society. His first novel, *The Ordeal of Richard Feverel*, appeared the same year as hers, *Adam Bede* (1859), which happened to be the year of *The Origin of Species*, of FitzGerald's *Omar Khayyám*, and of Mill *On Liberty*. Ruskin was in the middle of *Modern Painters*, Carlyle of his *Frederick the Great*, and Herbert Spencer of his scientific and philosophical works. The Brontë sisters were all three dead, *The Professor* appearing posthumously in 1857. Meredith had published a little volume of *Poems* (1849), between *Shirley* and *Villette*. It was an almost negligible book, even as holding out some promise of better things [1]; and it was not till after his first two regular novels that he gave the world *Modern Love* (1862), almost a novel in verse, which proved that he was indeed a poet as well as a novelist, like Emily Brontë and Thomas Hardy, and not an obviously minor poet either, as so many novelists are, among them George Eliot. If Meredith, however, had never written a line of verse, his novels would have furnished the evidence required. For the breaking down, or repudiating, or simple ignoring of the time-worn barriers between poetry and fiction, begun by the Brontës, went on more drastically and more openly in Meredith's novels from the very beginning. He was to complete their work by finally re-establishing the original blood-relationship. George Eliot had been compared to

---

[1] Such as the first version of "Love in the Valley."

Shakespeare. But she was not a Shakespeare. Even had she
been his equal, her work would have fallen short of his, since
the novel as she had moulded it was still too imperfect a
medium for the prose and poetry which would have inter-
mingled. *Richard Feverel, Beauchamp's Career, Vittoria,* and
Rhoda Fleming may or may not be superior as tragic novels to
Adam Bede and *The Mill on the Floss;* but they move consistently at higher levels. *Shagpat* was a poetical fantasy, but
not intrinsically more poetical than *Richard Feverel,* his first
novel of contemporary life. He conceived life poetically. He
said later on, in *The Amazing Marriage,*

> Still we must have poetry to hallow this and other forms
> of energy: or say, if you like, the right view of them impels
> to poetry. Otherwise we are in the breeding yards, among
> the litters and the farrows. It is a question of looking down
> or looking up. If we are poor creatures—as we are if we do
> but feast and gamble and beget—we shall run for a time with
> the dogs and come to the finish of swine. Better say, life is
> holy!

Impressed by the doctrine of evolution, he gave it a spiritual
interpretation. Nature was to him spirit, the spirit of life
pervading all things; and her processes were spiritual processes,
with which man could labour in unison. His view was in
essence not very different from that of Butler, though he
would have allowed no evasion of the spiritual character of
nature's activity—something which is essentially soul or spirit
is virtually implied in any theory of semi-conscious volition or
semi-automatic evolution.

[margin note: View of evolution—a spiritual process]

Personal development was the phase of evolution in which
he was pre-eminently interested. In *Feverel,* "personality is
a progressive activity." [1] He blends the theme with the
Carlylean idea of biography. "Our world," he says, in *Diana
of the Crossways,* [2] "is all but a sensational world at present,
in maternal travail of a soberer, a braver, a brighter-eyed."
"Service is our destiny in life or in death. Then let it be my

---

[1] G. R. Swann, *Philosophical Parallelisms,* 94.

[2] *Diana of the Crossways,* in the pregnant discourse "Of Diaries and Diarists,"
forming the first chapter.

choice living to serve the living, and be fretted uncomplainingly.
If I can assure myself of doing service I have my home within."
The advance is towards a life illumined by philosophy; the
novelist should know this and minister thereto.

A thousand years! You may count full many a thousand
by this route before you are one with divine philosophy.
Whereas a single flight of brains will reach and embrace her;
give you the savour of Truth, the right use of the senses,
Reality's infinite sweetness; for these things are in philosophy;
and the fiction which is the summary of actual Life, the
within and without of us, is, prose or verse, plodding or soaring,
philosophy's elect handmaiden. To such an end let us bend
our aim to work, knowing that every form of labour, even this
flimsiest, should minister to growth.[1]

"Brainstuff is not lean stuff," he continues; "the brainstuff
of fiction is internal history." "The forecast may be hazarded,
that, if we do not speedily embrace philosophy in fiction, the
Art is doomed to extinction under the shining multitude of
its professors." That philosophy of his is a philosophy of
nature, and a philosophy of life, in the widest sense, in which
may be discerned a confluence of romanticism and modern
enlightenment, faith and reason, religion and science. His
poems crystallize the philosophy, the novels display it in action.
Nature is a living, developing, divine entity, in which man is
a living, developing, and divine part, finding his weal in the
joyous life of sensation and instinct, keeping true to Mother
Earth, whilst fulfilling himself in the exercise of mind and the
spiritual activities of art and zeal for the common welfare, in
the realization of beauty, love, and sacrifice for his fellows,

> Blood and brain and spirit, three
> Join for true felicity.[2]

Put in another way, man's earth-born nature grows, through
the stages of blood and brain, to spiritual completeness—from
instinct and the healthy exercise of the senses, to the intelligent

[1] *Diana of the Crossways.*
[2] "The Woods of Westermain."

control of the self and cheerful submission to the social order, and so, on to the loftiest ideals of love and devotion to the race. Throughout, man must keep firm hold on his kinship with Earth, his Mother.

'Tis Earth's, her gift, else have we nought.

He bans asceticism, mortification of the flesh. Redworth saw in love, in Diana,

a new start in our existence, a finer shoot of the tree stoutly planted in good gross earth; the senses running their live sap, and the minds companioned, and the spirits made one by the whole-natured conjunction. In sooth, a happy prospect for the sons and daughters of Earth, divinely indicating more than happiness: the speeding of us, compact of what we are, between the ascetic rocks and the sensual whirlpools, to the creation of certain nobler races, now very dimly imagined.

Even without the look so far ahead, this is a theme opening up poetic vistas, and Meredith from the outset swept the chords of all that poetry. His novels are no mere transcripts of experience, and no mere moralistic interpretation. What they give he calls "Poetic Comedy," in which characters who are relieved of much of the diurnal dust and mire which might clog their ardours contend and struggle towards their goal, on such a stage as shows them off more clearly than would the common arena of ordinary realistic fiction. It will speedily be seen what profound modifications of the structure and style of fiction were inevitably involved.

George Meredith (1828–1909) was son and grandson of naval *Mere-* outfitters at Portsmouth, where he was born. He died the *dith's* same year as Swinburne, who was nine years his junior. There *life* was Welsh blood in the family, much diluted, and his mother was a Macnamara, the name but little else Irish. The wife of his grandfather Melchizedec was the original of the Mrs Mel who makes such an admirable appearance in *Evan Harrington*. The question of his parentage, as the novelist treated it, was one of his poetic comedies. It must have irked him that he was the son of a tailor, though his feelings were not crude snobbishness. But as he was a poet, and posed as the critic of county society, and was personally, like his Evan Harrington, of a lordly presence and independent spirit, he felt acutely the ironical contrast with the tradesman who counts as the ninth part of a man. It was not exactly that he concealed the facts. Though strangely reticent about the spot where he first saw the light, yet, stranger still, he advertised this and his family history in one of his earliest novels, without however notifying that it all related to himself. It was as if to have put the harmless skeleton in a glass case and exhibited it on the mantelshelf, but without a label, at once satisfied his artistic relish for such a nice problem of character and gave him the same ease and relief as if he had made a clean breast of the secret. This novel, in spite of greater improbabilities than he usually allowed himself in fiction, tells more about his character and feelings at the threshold of manhood than any biographer could do. Some of Evan Harrington's circumstances, especially the incubus of the paternal debts, relate to Meredith's father, and Evan stands more or less for Meredith himself. It is the story of a young man brought up with tastes for gentility, at a time when social passports were rigorously demanded, who has been the plaything of a young lady and falls in love with her, but finds an almost insuperable obstacle to winning her in the fact that he came from a tailor's shop. Melchizedec Harrington was drawn from the famous outfitter, who looked like a marquess and left his son a load of debt through trying to live like one. The fellow-tradesmen who attended the great Mel's funeral have been recognized from the Portsmouth directory as householders in High Street, and Evan's sisters, Louisa, Harriet, Caroline, are Meredith's aunts, Louisa, Harriet, Catherine. The slight change in the last name is a measure of the thinness of the disguise, which indeed is no disguise. These ladies are good historical likenesses, even to the nature of their matrimonial alliances. Louisa and her husband did attain a distinguished position at the Court of Portugal. Harriet did marry a brewer, the original of Andrew Cogglesby. Catherine married a lieutenant of marines who has been identified in Major Strike, though the portrait is said to show

unfairness.[1] Meredith went to school first at Southsea, at
a more expensive place than was attended by most sons of
Portsmouth tradesmen, who thought him uppish. At thirteen,
when his father married a former housekeeper, he was sent to
Neuwied, on the Rhine, and entered a famous Moravian school,
where in his most impressionable years he imbibed, not merely
book-learning, but along with it that spirit of charity and
universal brotherhood which was inculcated by the gentle
Moravians. These two years left an indelible mark on
Meredith. They did not eradicate the pride and individualism
that even in old age kept him apart in a somewhat arrogant
aloofness. But they saved him from Victorian insularity, and
gave him broader horizons than hedged the vision of such
contemporaries as Dickens and Thackeray, Tennyson and
Browning, Kingsley, George Eliot, and even Matthew Arnold.
From the particular brand of virtues and foibles roughly
summed up in the term Victorianism he remained singularly
free: even less than Swinburne, and much less than Hardy,
who in later years was regarded as his rival in fiction and
poetry, could he be decried as an unilluminated Victorian.

The two years or so after Meredith's return to England are *Love and*
a blank. At the end of them he was articled to a solicitor, *poetry*
Charnock, starting on the usual short cut to literature by way
of the law. Charnock appears to have been a man of culture
with a deplorable digestive system, whose dyspeptic pangs
were, it is to be hoped, not so consuming as those of Uncle
Hippias, his supposed portrait in *Richard Feverel*. Through
him Meredith was introduced to a circle of literary and talkative
friends, among them the veteran poet and satirical novelist
Peacock. Peacock's son Edward was a chum of Meredith's,
and with the daughter, a dashing widow of thirty, the
susceptible young man fell in love. Meredith, who had cut
himself adrift from his father, now, when he was only just of

---

[1] It was Meredith's father who was left in the lurch at Melchizedec's demise.
But that Meredith sketched himself in Evan is confirmed by a curious slip in chap. iii.,
where Louisa, Countess de Saldar, is referred to inadvertently as Evan's aunt, instead
of his sister, though for dramatic purposes it was necessary to make her glorified
semblance Evan's sister (see also S. M. Ellis, *George Meredith, his Life and Friends,*
1920).

age, entered upon an ill-assorted marriage. The pair collaborated in writing poetry, and also in a cookery-book. For a while all went well. Sometimes they lived with Peacock, sometimes they visited, or travelled on the Continent, Meredith reading far and wide, as well as writing poetry, and tramping over the Surrey heaths, where throughout his life he felt most at home with nature. He dedicated the poems of 1851 to his father-in-law, whose learning and genial cynicism and leaning to extravaganza were by no means in disharmony with his own tendencies. Dr Middleton, in *The Egoist*, with his critical judgment of a great wine, his learning and his sesquipedalian humour, is a study of Peacock which recalls Peacock's Dr Opimian, in *Crotchet Castle*. Peacock must have read Meredith's first prose work, *The Shaving of Shagpat* (1856), and indirectly had a hand in it; for, not only is this so-called "Arabian Entertainment" a fantasy not of a totally different order from *Nightmare Abbey* and *Melincourt*, but the humour and extravagance, though dressed in Oriental colours, are recognizably akin to the *Mabinogion* and other romances of Celtic origin to which the author of *The Misfortunes of Elphin* may have introduced his son-in-law. But it contains more allegory, or at any rate symbolism. As Lafcadio Hearn pointed out, the sword of Aklis is the sword of intellect, of science, which cuts through the matted jungle of error and severs the root-hair of illusion—a truly Meredithian idea.[1] Mrs Meredith left her husband (1858) when their boy was five years old, and his situation was much the same as that of the baronet in *Richard Feverel* (1859), the story of a father and son, and of a mother who has run away with a trusted friend. In his greatest poem, *Modern Love* (1862), the pains and heart-searching of that unhappy time are recorded with a power that Shakespeare's sonnets alone have surpassed. But that poem is not more autobiographical than *Evan Harrington*. Meredith was not the man to recount actual events in a work of fiction, though he might represent the characters and the emotions. In the one case of his trying to combine what he believed to be historical incident with his own version of a

---

[1] Hearn, *On Art, Literature, and Philosophy* (Tokyo, 1932).

personality, the betrayal of the secret of State in *Diana of the Crossways*, he went grievously astray. The course of events darkly revealed in *Modern Love* is widely different from his domestic story. He had committed an error of judgment in his marriage, and he suffered the consequences, a further misfortune being his estrangement, long after, from his beloved son Arthur, who died twenty years before himself.

Modern Love is like a novel in having a plot; but, instead of a revelation, the end is an incident the exact nature of which it is left to the reader to divine. The story, indeed, is set forth in "tragic hints," not in explicit narrative; for here, as in his novels, Meredith flashes his lamp on the moments of highest tension, on the scenes in which emotion comes to a head, leaving mere events in twilight. He would have done the same had he elected to tell the tale in prose, though the feeling might not have had all the concentration, the same passionate intensity of utterance. The combat raging between mistrust and still unextinguished passion, set forth in this pregnant stanza, like the rest all but identical in form with a sonnet, has its analogues in Meredith's fiction. *"Modern Love," a novel in verse*

> This was the woman; what now of the man?
> But pass him. If he comes beneath a heel,
> He shall be crushed until he cannot feel,
> Or, being callous, haply till he can.
> But he is nothing—nothing? Only mark
> The rich light striking out from her on him!
> Ha! what a sense it is when her eyes swim
> Across the man she singles, leaving dark
> All else! Lord God, who mad'st the thing so fair,
> See that I am drawn to her even now!
> It cannot be such harm on her cool brow
> To put a kiss? Yet if I meet him there!
> But she is mine! Ah, no! I know too well
> I claim a star whose light is overcast:
> I claim a phantom-woman of the past.
> The hour has struck, though I heard not the bell!

The anguished husband examines his heart in soliloquy as a character might in a novel. He will not reproach Fate, or try to shuffle off his own peccability.

> I am not of those miserable males
> Who sniff at vice, and, daring not to snap,
> Do therefore hope for heaven.   I take the hap
> Of all my deeds.   The wind that fills my sails
> Propels, for I am helmsman.   Am I wrecked,
> I know the devil has sufficient weight
> To bear: I lay it not on him or fate,
> Besides, he's damned.
>
> If for those times I must ask charity,
> Have I not any charity to give?

He seeks distraction.   He philanders with a certain gold-haired lady.   But the game of sentiment has little solace: the ecstasy that might avail is fled.

> Where is the ancient wealth wherewith I clothed
> Our human nakedness, and could endow
> With spiritual splendour a pure brow
> That else had grinned at me the fact I loathed?
> A kiss is but a kiss now! and no wave
> Of a great flood that whirls me to the sea.
> But as you will! we'll sit contentedly
> And eat our pot of honey on the grave.

At last, he and his wife parley, for

> It is no vulgar nature I have wived.
> Secretive, sensitive, she takes a wound
> Deep to her soul, as if the sense had swooned,
> And not a thought of vengeance had survived.

The woman's agony is a dark enigma, only half-revealed in tragic hints.   Mutual suspicion has kept them apart.   She believes his love dead, and in a rush of magnanimity or "jealous devotion" resolves to free him.   She goes forth, he knows not whither:

> He found her by the ocean's roaring verge,
> Nor any wicked change in her discerned;
> And she believed his old love had returned,
> Which was her exultation and her scourge.
> She took his hand, and walked with him, and seemed
> The wife he sought, though shadow-like and dry.
> She had one terror, lest her heart should sigh,
> And tell her loudly she no longer dreamed.

She dared not say, "This is my breast, look in."
But there's a strength to help the desperate weak.
That night he learned how silence best can speak
The awful things when Pity pleads for Sin.
About the middle of the night her call
Was heard, and he came wondering to the bed.
"Now kiss me, dear! it may be now!" she said.
Lethe had passed those lips, and he knew all.

Three lines in a preceding stanza give the comment:

In tragic life, God wot,
No villain need be! Passions spin the plot:
We are betrayed by what is false within.

Searching imagination, beauty, rapture, despair, the occult
workings of the tortured heart, and the bitter irony of the
Comic Spirit—all the elements which appear in other combina-
tions in the novels—are to be found in this wonderful sequence,
which seemed to the *Spectator*, however, only a clever and
somewhat prurient treatment of a painful theme. That
organ of unredeemed Victorianism had previously accused *The
Ordeal of Richard Feverel* of "low ethical tone." Swinburne
was violently wroth, and in a protest to the captious journal
let himself go in his best style of denunciation.

In the same volume were included a charming group of *Char-*
"Poems of the English Roadside," simple eclogues of rustic *acters*
character, humorous and touching, and warm with a genuine *from the*
affection for the people that tends to be · overlooked in *roadside*
Meredith, through his insistence on the theory, diametrically
opposed to Fielding's, that high life, not low life, is the proper
sphere of comedy. The countryman, and what is nowadays
called the man in the street, make but an incidental appearance in his novels, though when they do figure they are drawn
with more realism than he thought appropriate for his drawing-
room scenes. For Meredith accurately describes himself, in a
letter of this period, as "an associate with owls and nightjars,
tramps and tinkers, who teach me nature and talk human
nature to me." [1] Juggling Jerry, in a lilting trochaic measure,

[1] To Miss Katherine Vulliamy, 28th October 1863 (*Letters*, i. 123).

speaks his sentiments on the life of man, a man like him, just
before the Great Juggler up above juggles him away:

> Pitch here the tent, while the old horse grazes;
> By the old hedge-side we'll halt a stage.
> It's nigh my last above the daisies:
> My next leaf'll be man's blank page.
> Yes, my old girl!' and it's no use crying:
> Juggler, constable, king, must bow.
> One that outjuggles us all's been spying
> Long to have me, and he has me now.

Equally affecting is the sketch of the "Old Chartist," drawn
with the sympathy of one who called himself a Radical, but
who, as *Beauchamp's Career* and his own letters were to show,
would now be a member of the Labour party, if he could bind
himself to any party at all. His wife was not of his way of
thinking; his daughter had married a respectable linendraper.
When he was transported, it was their disgrace. But the wife
had never failed in loyalty.

> She suffered for me:—women, you'll observe,
> Don't suffer for a cause, but for a man.
> When I was in the dock she show'd her nerve:
> I saw beneath her shawl my old tea-can.
> Trembling . . . she brought it
> To screw me for my work: she loath'd my plan,
> And therefore doubly kind I thought it.

> I've never lost the taste of that same tea:
> That liquor on my logic floats like oil,
> When I state facts, and fellows disagree.
> For human creatures all are in a coil;
> All may want pardon.
> I see a day when every pot will boil
> Harmonious in one great Tea-garden!

Later life

Meredith achieved what proved something like a perfect
union when he married Marie Vulliamy, who came of an old
Huguenot family settled in Surrey. She was his mate from
1864 to 1885, and her death evoked "A Faith on Trial," a
poem very different in spirit and thought from *Modern Love*.
But, in the main, the story of Meredith's later life is the story

of his works, and of the circumstances that helped to mould them.   The novelist who at eighty-one left *Celt and Saxon* unfinished was the same as at thirty-one published *The Ordeal of Richard Feverel*.   There is not much loss of power, or even of the spirit of youth, traceable in that fragment.   It is the same Meredith, with, however, one fatal difference, which is over all the work following *The Egoist*, whether in prose or verse—Meredith had become Meredithian.   After living with or near Peacock, at various rural spots in Surrey, and being half-domiciled with Rossetti and Swinburne for a time at 16 Cheyne Walk, he came at last to Flint Cottage, on the slopes of Box Hill, where, now that he was one of the most famous Englishmen of his day, he sat, like the earlier sage on the brow of Highgate Hill, "escaped from the inanity of life's battle, attracting toward him the thoughts of innumerable brave souls still engaged there."   He had enjoyed distinguished friendships, the objects of which have their best portraits in his novels. Those novels were the main occupation of his maturity, *The Amazing Marriage* (1895) being the last published in his lifetime, though he lived fourteen more years and left *Celt and Saxon* to his executors.   Betweenwhiles there appeared thin volumes of poetry, in which he formulated his philosophy of life.   For some eight years, whilst he was writing *Evan Harrington*, *Modern Love*, *Sandra Belloni*, and *Rhoda Fleming*, he was attached to the staff of a provincial newspaper, and wrote leaders and news columns from his home in Surrey.[1]   He went to Italy as a war correspondent (1866), gathering experiences which he afterwards utilized in *Vittoria* (1867), his novel of the Risorgimento.   For thirty-five years he was literary adviser to Chapman & Hall, and betrayed a lack of catholicity and an indiscreet contempt for the mercenary side of literature by rejecting *East Lynne* and other popular books, Butler's *Erewhon*, and the youthful novels of Bernard Shaw.

[1] Some admirers have been vexed by his supposed laxity in writing on politics for a Conservative organ.   But Meredith was never a party man.   His chief sympathies were Liberal, even Radical, and he would probably have voted for Labour at the present day.   On many questions, however, he was with the other side, and he seems to have been whole-heartedly with the South during the American Civil War.

Both Gissing and Hardy, on the other hand, bore witness to the wholesomeness of his advice when they were budding authors. He had no mercy for a remarkable young woman novelist, John Oliver Hobbes, though her mentality seems to have had some kinship with his.

Character and outlook

Meredith was always a person of abounding energy and vitality, who loved and was loved by troops of friends, but persistently went his own way, often in opposition to advice and entreaty, with contemptuous disregard for the inevitable results. He was an ardent votary of the open air, with a love of nature that was congenital, for his father, Augustus, who bowed the knee to tailordom, was a great walker. In the course of time it became philosophical; out of simple paganism he evolved a religion of nature. His friendships were based on intellectual affinities. Intellect as much as passion was the motive force in his finest poem, *Modern Love*, and more still in the rest of his poetry. Pride of intellect was perhaps his bane. If any of his intimates exercised any formative influence upon him, it was Peacock. But the influences that worked upon him through literature are a different matter. His wide and accurate scholarship was worthy of the best traditions of English letters. It was not his lot to go to a public school and proceed to a university; but if the fact could be deduced from his writings, it would not be from any deficiency of learning or critical appreciation. Whether at Neuwied or in his reading at home, he made himself conversant enough with classical literature to survey at ease the whole succession of Greek and Latin dramatists and comic writers, and disengage the characteristics of each and his relationship to the moderns. He produced some notable translations from the *Iliad*, and, more remarkably, from Mistral. His *Essay on Comedy* testifies to a sure and intimate command of French and English literature, and to far more than the usual smattering of Italian, Spanish, and German. Further testimony may be found in abundance in his novels and in his poems. If the *Essay on Comedy* yields a philosophy of literary history, a philosophy of history in the most profound sense is contained in the great odes to France. His German schooling taught him much that he could not have learned in England. Goethe, Richter, and Heine were live forces in his mind. The astringent German professor in *Harry Richmond* is one of his most penetrating critics of things English.

His indebtedness to the poets of his native land is less obvious, chiefly because it is so deeply and widely infused. *Debts to the great Romantics* Most of those early poems that showed touches of Rossetti and the Spasmodic poets disappeared in the later editions which are all that can be read now. Swinburne, with whose ideas Meredith's have a certain superficial analogy, and whom he painted winningly in the sprightly young Tracy Running-brook of *Sandra Belloni*, did not persuade Meredith to write in the Swinburnian way; sometimes it might be wished that he had. They had but lately met when *Modern Love* appeared. This is a poem in the great English tradition, with no trace of the idiosyncrasies marring his later poetry. But even in that later poetry, stamped as it is with the personality of George Meredith, the inspiration of the leading Romantics cannot escape notice. Different as he was from Wordsworth in his attitude to life, and still more different in his poetic style, Meredith shared the Wordsworthian vision. When he looked at Nature, he was not content to dwell on her visible beauties, he sought her inner being; he tried to discern her purposes, or at least the direction of her striving. For all his intellectualism, he was stanchly romantic in his implicit reliance on the inspired imagination as the interpreter of what the senses reveal. He did not assert, like Blake, that the imagination is an organ through which we perceive ultimate reality, and that mere intellect must be suspect; or, like Wordsworth and Coleridge, that imagination under the control of reason is an infallible seer. But he held that if mind is to penetrate to essence it can be only by surrendering itself to imaginative communion with the universal activities of Nature. To this mystical communion he gave the name of faith, distinguishing it from the lip-service that usurps the name, and is really unfaith,

> Unfaith clamouring to be coined
> To faith by proof.

Contact with science

In one of his best-remembered strictures, Matthew Arnold put his finger on "something premature" in the literature of the romantic era, splendid though it was. In spite of their energy and creative force, those poets, not excepting Wordsworth, were "wanting in completeness and variety," the reason being that they had insufficient materials to work with; in other words, they did not know enough. They lived and wrote before the acceptance of the historical method and the rise of modern science.[1] It was Meredith's good fortune to attain the height of his powers about the time when Arnold pronounced these animadversions. *Richard Feverel*, exactly contemporary with *The Origin of Species*, mirrors clearly the modern attitude to science, the interested, instructed, yet deeply critical attitude. Though Sir Austin Feverel's scheme for his son's education breaks down through its omission of certain human factors, the corrective satire is in the interests of science. Sir Austin held that "Man is a self-acting machine," and he left free will and various innate tendencies out of account; hence the utter miscarriage of the System and the tragedy of Richard's life.[2] In the later novels, Meredith can be seen studying the applications of scientific ideas to the conduct of life. But, again, it is the poems that summarize the thought in crystalline and perdurable phrases, and form both the entrance porch and the gate of remembrance to the novels. It is impossible to neglect them in any serious study of Meredith.

Contacts with other contemporaries

To what purpose he read his contemporaries is evident from numerous allusions in his books, though he does not cite them by name. Carlyle's ideas are seen in action in *Beauchamp's Career*, where, too, the spirit of Ruskin haunts the Venetian scenes. Many of those most eminent in thought and letters were among his nearest friends; Cotter Morison, Leslie

---

[1] *Essays in Criticism*, 1st series, "The Function of Criticism at the Present Time."

[2] The initial ethical structure of all Meredith's works is an erroneous conception of the nature and purpose of the self: *e.g.* Sir Austin Feverel, Evan Harrington, Diana. "The second step is disillusionment." "The third step is the discovery of the true conception of human nature and its field of action" (see G. R. Swann, *Philosophical Parallelisms*, 90–91). "It is the essential tragedy of Richard Feverel and Dr Alvan that they never realized wholeness" (*Ibid.*, 15).

Stephen, James Thomson, author of *The City of Dreadful Night*, Hyndman the socialist, John Morley, York Powell, G. W. Foote the rationalist, Edward Clodd, R. L. Stevenson. Stevenson and Leslie Stephen sat, and were aware that they sat, for two of his characters presented as types of modern man at his best. These were all people whom orthodoxy regarded as heretics, and so were other friends not of the same eminence. To a man they stood for no compromise. Tennyson and Browning had endeavoured to keep up with contemporary science; but its revelations, particularly the evidences of evolution, gave such a shock to their fixed convictions that they never entirely recovered their equilibrium. Tennyson was panic-stricken by the apparent consequences of the new interpretation of nature, "red in tooth and claw," and could not make up his mind whether the theory of evolution and the disclosure of the actual history of the globe was compatible with belief in his own personal immortality.[1] From *In Memoriam* to the end, he is seen oscillating between faith and doubt, and cleaving forlornly to the hope

> that somehow good
> Will be the final goal of ill.

Browning vaguely opined, after expressing himself antagonistically to Darwinism, that evolution levels upwards not downwards, the world being spiritual in essence; but argued that another existence must be postulated to rectify the injustices of the present.

Meredith and Swinburne, in different ways, tried to bring the new knowledge into their general scheme of things, and both aimed to find an altruistic religion reconciling scientific thought with human idealism. No religion can be valid that rejects knowledge. We may fail to arrive at truth; we must, at any rate, strive towards it unshrinkingly. Meredith accepted evolution as an hypothesis that cast floods of light on human history, and by enabling man to organize his life

The effort to reconcile science and human idealism

---

[1] Neither Meredith nor his father-in-law Peacock could stand the sentimentalism into which the "Sir Pandarus public . . . corrupted this fine singer. . . . Isn't there a scent of damned hypocrisy in all this lisping and vowelled purity of the *Idylls?* It is fashionable. It pleases the rose-pink ladies, it sells" (quoted from Meredith's *Letters* by Able, 47).

for attainable ends provided a basis for morality. For what may lie beyond, man must have faith in the wider incidence of all that is revealed. Swinburne's "Hertha," "The Hymn of Man," and "The Pilgrims" propound a different creed from that announced in "Earth and Man" and other statements of Meredith's beliefs; they start from different points, but they follow parallel lines. In Swinburne's symbolical interpretation of Kantian metaphysics the soul of all things attains its highest realization in man,

Man, pulse of my centre, and fruit of my body, and seed of my soul.

> One birth of my bosom:
> One beam of mine eye;
> One topmost blossom
> That scales the sky;
> Man, equal and one with me, man that is made of me, man that is I.

Meredith was no metaphysician. His cosmology is a bold speculation on the facts of existence, confirmed by what he felt to be his truly filial communion with Nature, his mother. It has its resemblances to that of Butler. Possibly, he had looked into *Erewhon* before he turned it down. Perhaps, at a later date, he read *Life and Habit* (1872), and Butler's later attempts to identify the motive agency of evolution. Unquestionably, in his poems and in his novels there are numerous examples of the working of instinct and obscure impulse and of an occult responsiveness to the influences of external nature, closely akin to the organic reactions described by Hering and Butler. But Meredith may have been thinking simply of the general process of evolution, without considering ultimate causes, when he invited us to behold Nature gazing on "her great venture, Man," and praying that her offspring may rise victorious above the lusts and terrors and distrusts that hold him down.

> But that the senses still
> Usurp the station of their issue mind,
> He would have burst the chrysalis of the blind:
> As yet he will;
>
> As yet he will, she prays,
> Yet will when his distempered devil of Self

shall have been subdued.

> Then shall the horrid pall
> Be lifted, and a spirit nigh divine,
> "Live in thy offspring as I live in mine,"
> Will hear her call.

But that consummation is yet afar; there is no terminus, indeed, to the forward and upward process. In an oft-quoted passage in *Diana of the Crossways* he speaks of "the speeding of us, compact of what we are, between the ascetic rocks and the sensual whirlpools, to the creation of certain nobler races, now very dimly imagined." For the goal of strife is in the illimitable distance; it is not an end, but a direction. Evolution, the survival of the fit to survive, progress through blood and tears, is the law of being; man will attain health and holiness only in its devout acceptance. By recognizing and accepting it in these latter days he makes it a law unto himself, and what had been an unconscious drift under conditions over which he exercised no control may become a conscious, purposive, and accelerated effort. But it is by listening to Nature's counsels, by the "Reading of Earth," that he learns the direction:

> She can lead us, only she,
> Unto God's footstool, whither she reaches;
> Loved, enjoyed, her gifts must be,
> Reverenced the truths she teaches,
> Ere a man may hope that he
> Ever can attain the glee
> Of things without a destiny.[1]

So man perceives the God in Earth and himself. By surveying the history of the Earth and tracing the path of evolution, he wins the rapture of the forward view.

The divinity in Nature

> She, judged of shrinking nerves, appears
> A Mother whom no cry can melt;
> But read her past desires and fears,
> The letters on her breast are spelt.

---

[1] "Ode to the Spirit of Earth in Autumn" (appendix to *The Poetry and Philosophy of George Meredith*, by G. M. Trevelyan).

A slayer, yea, as when she pressed
Her savage to the slaughter-heaps,
To sacrifice she prompts her best:
She reaps them as the sower reaps.

But read her thoughts to speed the race,
And stars rush forth of blackest night:
You chill not at a cold embrace
To come, nor dread a dubious might.

Her double visage, double voice,
In oneness rise to quench the doubt.
This breath, her gift, has only choice
Of service, breathe we in or out.

In the great "Hymn to Colour" he sings:

This way have men come out of brutishness
To spell the letters of the sky and read
A reflex upon earth else meaningless.
With thee, O fount of the Untimed! to lead;
Drink they of thee, thee eyeing, they unaged
Shall on through brave wars waged.

More gardens will they win than any lost;
The vile plucked out of them, the unlovely slain.
Not forfeiting the beast with which they are crossed,
To stature of the Gods will they attain.
They shall uplift their Earth to meet her Lord,
Themselves the attuning chord!

Yet he has even less expectation of Shelley's millennium,
the myth of perfectibility, than even Browning had, that other
tireless fighter.

It is a warfare but begun;
Unending, with no power to interpose;
No prayer, save for strength to keep his ground,
Heard of the Highest; never battle's close,
The victory complete and victor crowned:
Nor solace in defeat, save from that sense
Of strength well spent, which is the strength renewed.[1]

Matthew Arnold told the world of 1880 that, eventually,
"most of what now passes with us for religion and philosophy

[1] "The Test of Manhood."

will be replaced by poetry." Poetry had long been taking "*Spirit that exalted station, in the novel as well as in lyric and idyll, craves not pastoral and sonnet. Arnold was nominally an anti-Romantic; a goal"* yet, surely, this was the view of poetry held by the Romantics, and earlier than they. Before the age of Dryden and Pope, as well as afterwards, the poet who took himself seriously felt more or less certainly that he was a consecrated person performing a priestlike task. Equally with the scientist who sacrifices all to the quest of truth, the philosopher who seeks to penetrate the veil of the absolute, or the artist fashioning an image of supernal beauty, the poet is engaged on the loftiest service within the compass of his powers. To Blake, "Prayer was the study of art, praise the practice of art." Meredith, in his most significant poems, with sincerity if often with strain and effort, assumes the attitude of both prayer and praise. He preaches the religion of evolution. He bids us kneel with him to the God in Nature.

> She being Spirit in her clods
> Footway to the God of Gods,
> The Great Unseen, nowise the Dark Unknown.
>
> Do thou build
> Thy mind on her foundations in earth's bed;
> Behold man's mind the child of her keen rod,
> For teaching how the wits and passions wed
> To rear that temple of the credible God.[1]

He does not presume, in Rossetti's sarcastic phrase, to approve on God his "science of Theometry." Meredith is as far, on the one hand, from a formal pantheism, as, on the other, from the assured theosophy of Blake, who identified the prophetic mind, "called by mortals the Imagination," with the Logos, and accepted it as the infallible intermediary between man and the divine.[2] Meredith's faith was in the moral elements, the predominance of good, visible in nature's history. Sins are transgressions against natural laws, and bring their certain

[1] "The Sage enamoured and the Honest Lady."
[2] Meredith's references to Blake show that he knew Gilchrist's life and edition of the works. There are many contacts between his natural religion and that of the poet who said, "Everything that lives is holy" (*The Four Zoas*, ii. 358).

chastisement. Goodness is attained through obedience. To require definite certainties is unfaith, the scepticism of doubting Thomas.

> These are our sensual dreams;
> Of the yearning to touch, to feel
> The dark Impalpable sure,
> And have the Unveiled appear.[1]

Trust, rather, in the goodness that you know:

> Earth your haven, Earth your helm,
> You command a double realm:
> Labouring here to pay your debt,
> Till your little sun shall set;
> Leaving her the future task.[2]

"Spirit craves not a goal," he says in that pathetic declaration of his belief, "A Faith on Trial," wrung from him by the death of his wife. But he is sure that no dread secret has been kept from us for our destruction. The creatures in "Woodland Peace" know neither hope nor fear:

> what is dumb
> We question not, nor ask
> The silent to give sound,
> The hidden to unmask,
> The distant to draw near.

But to him spirit is very near:

> I neighbour the invisible
> So close that my consent
> Is only asked for spirits masked
> To leap from trees and flowers.

> And this because with them I dwell
> In thought, while calmly bent
> To read the lines dear Earth designs
> Shall speak her life on ours.[3]

But to attain that intimate vision, that harmony and deep content, we must put away fear, suspicion, the selfish impulses of the sensual man.

[1] "A Faith on Trial."   [2] "The Woods of Westermain."
[3] "Outer and Inner."

> Look with spirit past the sense,
> Spirit shines in permanence.
> That is She, the view of whom
> Is the dust within the tomb,
> Is the inner blush above,
> Look to loathe, or look to love;
> Think her Lump, or know her Flame;
> Dread her scourge, or read her aim;
> Shoot your hungers from their nerve;
> Or, in her example, serve.[1]

Not that he would inculcate asceticism; he has no belief in mortification of the flesh. The "ascetic rocks" are scarce less insidious than the "sensual whirlpools." Meredith would have man full-blooded as well as full-brained. It is a sin against nature to impute baseness to the desires of the body, which must however submit to the control of intelligence, and be directed to the loftiest purposes of the race.

> Count Nature devilish, and accept for doom
> The chasm between our passions and our wits.

Man finds his good in the joyous life of instinct and sensation, keeping true to Mother Earth, whilst using his mind to fathom her purposes, and with a large spiritual outlook co-operating with her in the general progress. But

> Only the rooted knowledge to high sense
> Of heavenly can mount, and feel the spur
> For fruitfullest advancement.[2]

So early as in *Richard Feverel*, Meredith out of his friendship *The same* with Nature had found comfort in her essential goodness and *phil-* in the signals she holds out of her beneficent aims. *osophy in poems and*

The wind that bowed the old elms, and shivered the dead *novels* leaves in the air, had a voice and a meaning for the baronet during that half-hour's lonely pacing up and down under the darkness awaiting his boy's return. The solemn gladness of his heart gave nature a tongue. Through the desolation flying overhead—the wailing of the Mother of Plenty across the bare-swept land—he caught intelligible signs of the beneficent

---

[1] "The Woods of Westermain."   [2] "The Sage enamoured."

order of the universe, from a heart newly confirmed in its grasp of the principle of human goodness, as manifested in the dear child who had just left him; confirmed in its belief in the ultimate victory of good within us, without which nature has neither music nor meaning, and is rock, stone, tree, and nothing more.

Meredith's confidence is rooted in his warm sense of reality, the solidarity of his fellowship with earth. Hence his faith is far more moving and appealing than the sublime but freezing philosophy of Swinburne's "Hertha," based on abstract ratiocination. It is a faith that questions not nor yet denies, but accepts the good that is granted, in the assurance that the best is designed. This is something very different from the stoical resignation to a blank destiny of Thomas Hardy, and still more different from the shrill defiance of such intellectuals as Henley, with his fierce braggadocio, "Out of the night that covers me," his vaunt, "I am the captain of my soul." Such violent insurgency was a natural reaction against Victorian cherishing of the dead bones instead of the live spirit of religion. But Meredith was not Victorian enough to be excited by these controversies. The mildness of soul and unaggressive free-thinking of the Moravians of Neuwied had taught him to be hostile to no one. He was also, perhaps, too proud to take sides. Thus he stood serenely aloof from the savage conflicts and mutual denunciations of churchman and infidel, theist and atheist. He was a romanticist, and the faith he held in the inscrutable is not to be distinguished from that held by Wordsworth and Coleridge, when they were still romantic poets, except that it is a faith illumined by the teachings of science. As Matthew Arnold might have said, Meredith was born later and had learned more.

A modern doctrine, moral, social, and political
A few decades before the Romantics, Dr Johnson's Imlac, in *Rasselas*, had easily pulverized the pseudo-philosopher mouthing his vague generalities and pompous phrases on life according to nature:

—in obedience to that universal and unalterable law with which every heart is originally impressed; which is not written on it by precept, but engraven by destiny; not instilled by

education, but infused at our nativity. He that lives according to nature will suffer nothing from the delusions of hope,
or importunities of desire; he will receive and reject with
equanimity of temper; and act or suffer as the reason of things
shall alternately prescribe. Other men may amuse themselves
with subtle definitions, or intricate ratiocination. Let them
learn to be wise by easier means: let them observe the hind
of the forest, and the linnet of the grove: let them consider
the life of animals, whose motions are regulated by instinct;
they obey their guide, and are happy. Let us, therefore, at
length, cease to dispute, learn to live: throw away the encum-
brance of precepts, which they who utter them with so much
pride and pomp do not understand, and carry with us this
simple and intelligible maxim, That deviation from nature is
deviation from happiness.

That was written exactly a hundred years before the publication of *Richard Feverel*, and attests how aboriginal is the issue
between the old school and the new. But the modern poet
and novelist sees a little deeper than Johnson's sage or Fielding's
philosopher Squarè into the life of both man and nature,
and his doctrines are not a sum of empty platitudes. From
nature's parental dealings with man and from the success
of those who "devoutly serve," Meredith deduces the laws of
man's life. His social doctrines are corollaries of his view of
nature; his ethics are complementary to his sociology. This
determines his basic values. His moral, social, and political
science is in consonance with the theory of nature and man
developing in unison. All is enunciated in the poems, sometimes
pellucidly, sometimes in the voice of oracles: the illustration
and touchstone is in his novels. The Spirit of Comedy that
hovers there over almost every scene is not only a muse inspiring
the artist, but the minister of reason, of the common sense of
untold generations schooled by Mother Earth, correcting and
guiding humanity. The Spirit of Comedy, in truth, is sister
of that other earth-born spirit, Love born of knowledge:

> Love born of knowledge, love that gains
> Vitality as Earth it mates,
> The meaning of the Pleasures, Pains,
> The Life, the Death, illuminates.

For love we Earth, then serve we all;
Her mystic secret then is ours:
We fall, or view our treasures fall,
Unclouded, as beholds her flowers

Earth, from a night of frosty wreck,
Enrobed in morning's mounted fire,
When lowly, with a broken neck,
The crocus lays her cheek to mire.[1]

Poetry in the novel   Obviously, when an eminent novelist writes poetry that is of importance in comparison with his novels, the fact must be taken into account from the outset in any assessment of his work in fiction. Not many poets of eminence have written novels, though most writers of fiction have written poetry, or at least verse. In Scott's case, the poet was merely the romancer writing first in the mediæval metrical way, who afterwards discovered that his vast experience of life and keen interest in the drama of human character were a better equipment for writing romantic novels. Fielding and Thackeray, Dickens and George Eliot, all wrote verse; but the fact is irrelevant—a busy novelist must have a recreation. But with such persons as Emily Brontë, George Meredith, and Thomas Hardy it is a different matter. The fiction and the poetry are felt to be somehow complementary to each other. In the former cases, novelist and poet were, not indeed two different minds at work, but different halves of the same brain. In the latter, the poems and the novels are two different but harmonious expressions of the same mind and the same imaginative view of the world, which could not be adequately expressed in either form alone. Both Hardy and Meredith adopted the gnomic form of verse for the most definite statement of their creeds, what they thought of the universe and man's place in it; and they gave the best illustration of their philosophy of life in a portrayal of life itself. Meredith's plan was similar to Hardy's; but in spirit and literary affinity he was nearer akin to the Brontës, in whom, as already contended, romanticism reawoke. Their poetry flowed over into their fiction. The Brontë novels

[1] "The Thrush in February."

were much more than portraiture of their own lives and
surroundings; they expressed the feelings and visions of two
earnest and imaginative souls, living in this imperfect world,
and striving to adjust its actualities to an exalted ideal of
human existence. The Meredithian novel likewise applies
imaginative thought to the relations between ideals and life,
but in a more systematic fashion and with ampler knowledge.
Fiction is to have a practical aim: it is to be an instrument of
the effort to raise humanity. "We must have poetry," says
Meredith, "to hallow this and other forms of energy. . . .
Better say life is holy."[1] Literature has a social function.
"We know that every form of energy, even this flimsiest, as
you esteem it, should minister to growth."

Both George Eliot and Meredith, it has been seen, had the *Phil-* approval of the oldest tradition of the English novel in making *osophy in* this a treatise on life. They had precedents enough. And, *the novel* convinced as they were that literature should minister to growth, they were doubly warranted in using fiction as the organ of their criticism of actualities and of their idealism. Now it is the insight of a mind that has already thought and generalized reviewing the facts in the representative instances which it sets before the eye, now the creative faculty bodying forth characters, thoughts, and actions, in which the secular process is seen going on: "The sensational world of the present in maternal travail of a soberer, a braver, a brighter-eyed." Meredith was without George Eliot's training in dialectical method, and less conversant with philosophical systems and philosophical literature. She might have regarded him as a mere amateur. His was an intuitive and poetic philosophy, rather than a system of doctrines worthy of the official stamp. So much the better, for it was a philosophy that appeared to evolve spontaneously from the problems and conjunctions surveyed in the novels. It was saner than George Eliot's, inasmuch as Meredith was never obsessed, as she had been, with the moral issues; which, on the contrary, he saw in their proper perspective, and when he dealt with them he made it clear that folly and error were delinquencies as serious in their

[1] *Diana.*

consequences as those which the moralist brands as sins. Meredith owed less to her than to the example of his father-in-law, Peacock, who, though he adopted a hostile and often cynical pose towards the thinkers and theorists of his day, was at any rate sincerely interested in the general questions mooted, and did apply thought worthy of a philosopher to their solution. The analogies between Meredith's social philosophy and Peacock's are too many and too close to be only accidental. It looks as if he were considerably in Peacock's debt for his outfit of ideas, and even that he may have imbibed from the sage who became his father-in-law that very habit of regarding life from a general and philosophic point of view which presently went on to embrace man's place and function in the cosmic scheme.

Probable indebtedness to Peacock   Peacock had his own view of the state of England, which, though stiffly reactionary, was no doubt as well founded on rational principles as those of the doctrinaires he quizzed. He was an intellectualist, like Meredith, who was later diagnosed by critics who did not like him as suffering from a dangerous hypertrophy of the intellect. He was even less inclined than his son-in-law to give way to any access of feeling. The intellectualism was no doubt the bond of affinity that brought and held them together; even after his matrimonial disaster, Meredith never let go of his elder's leading ideas, and he painted him with no lack of appreciation in Dr Middleton, in *The Egoist*. The author of *Nightmare Abbey*, *Melincourt*, and *Gryll Grange* was possessed by the Spirit of Comedy in the same full measure; he may have bequeathed the conception to his son-in-law. And a principal object of his detestation and ridicule was the very sentimentalism that Meredith was always exposing as the root of so many social evils. Sentiment. he called it: "sentiment, which is canting egoism in the mask of refined feeling."[1] It is burlesqued in the Scythrop of *Nightmare Abbey*, and shown chastened and cured in Mr Falconer, in *Gryll Grange*. To sentimentalism he opposes

[1] Quoted from *The Four Ages of Poetry* (1820), by A. H. Able, in *George Meredith and Thomas Love Peacock, a Study in Literary Influence*, which summarizes their coincidences not only of thought but also of literary methods and mannerisms.

the rule of Nature.   Conformity with Nature is the means by
which man attains a healthy, intelligent, and cheerful life, and
saves himself from error.   It is the great principle that Peacock
swears by; the objects of his satire are those who flout it.[1]
Meredith taught the same doctrine, which he blended with
the creed of evolution and developed into a general philosophy.
The theory of the Comic is a corollary.   Peacock's exponents
of the laughter which corrects aberrations, for instance, Friar
Tuck, in *Maid Marian,* who affirms, "Life is a farce, and he
that laughs most has most profit of the performance," and
Mr Hilary, in *Nightmare Abbey,* who says, "The highest
wisdom and the highest genius have been invariably
accompanied by cheerfulness," have their match in practically
every one of Meredith's fictions, from Shibli Bagarag, in
Shagpat, to Captain Baskelett, in *Beauchamp's Career,* and
Woodseer, in *The Amazing Marriage.*[2]   Meredith shared
Peacock's enthusiasm for Aristophanes, who receives his due
in the essay on Comedy, together with Molière, a nearer
example to himself of "the uses of comedy in teaching the
world to understand what ails it."   He was in full agreement
with Peacock on the rights of women to equal intellectual
development, to freedom, and a place of their own in the
social scheme.   Peacock's self-sufficient women, Anthelia, in
Melincourt, Stella, in *Nightmare Abbey,* and Morgana, in
Gryll Grange, have their still finer counterparts in Clara
Middleton, Vittoria, Cecilia Halkett, Diana, and Carinthia—
even if the last-named is the only one who has the strength
to stand alone and break opposition, with the self-resolution
of Peacock's heroines.[3]   Peacock and Meredith had the same
bent for fantasy, occasional farce, and sheer buffoonery, which
they both made contributory to the comedy of ideas.   The
machinery they employed is often identical—contrarieties and
clashes of manners, gatherings of incongruous individuals who
debate and dispute, rally and gibbet each other.   In two

---

[1] As Mr Hilary puts it, in *Nightmare Abbey,* "To reconcile man as he is to the
world as it is, to preserve and improve all that is good, to destroy all that is evil
in moral and physical nature" (quoted by Able, 52–53).
[2] Able, 37–45.
[3] *Ibid.,* 95.

interludes inserted in *One of our Conquerors*, Meredith gave a close reproduction of the characteristic Peacockian dialogue. But in the more urbane sphere of their fiction, where the social world is depicted, there are also close resemblances. Meredith did like Molière, who, he said, "seized his characters firmly for the central purpose of the play," and "stamped them in the idea"; Peacock stamped them all over with his ideas—a large proportion of his characters are little more than counters having dialectical values. They both made a practice of assembling their characters for polite talk and the exchange of ideas: Meredith's "society of cultivated men and women" is Peacock's favourite cast exactly, selected in like manner from the well-endowed in goods and station, to whom life is a fine art. How they both dwell on the æsthetics of dining and of savouring a great wine is a delight to every discerning reader. In George Eliot and Meredith the coalition of thought and fictive life works at a higher potential, especially in Meredith with his further coalition with poetry. It is his poetry, and his superior creative force, producing much more complex beings, though still profoundly rational beings, that lift him to other levels. Like Hardy, a little later, he sought to universalize fiction, according to dramatic formulas, taking a predominantly comic view of the world as the other took a tragic view. The optimism of his outlook, even when the logic of a story inevitably led to a tragic conclusion, was a contrast to the pessimism of both his elder and his younger contemporary.

The Meredithian novel

Several times in his letters Meredith protested that his real business in life was poetry, and that he wrote fiction only for a living, and to finance editions of the poems which a public, addicted to the ageing Tennyson's "fluting of creatures that have not a breath of vital humanity in them," refused to buy. The protest must be accepted with some reserve, especially as there are times when he confesses to a very different opinion of his novels, and shows himself not without confidence that, by "exposing and illustrating the natural history of man," he may have helped "to pave ways for the firmer footing of those who succeed us." In poetry and in fiction he tried to show what the theory of evolution means to the individual and the race. Hence there is nothing strange in the fact that the Meredithian novel is a product of evolution. He was a great and critical reader, and not likely to overlook anything worth learning from precursors or competitors. Enough has been said on the revival of romanticism in the Brontë novels, and of the way in which Charlotte's and Emily's poetry flowed over and saturated their fiction. The influence of Dickens, casual and less important, can be seen at a glance in Meredith's earlier novels, and may perhaps be attributed to his desire to show that he too could perform what the reader of that day thought the most brilliant of literary feats. The Peacock touch is continually evident; and in the romantic comedies of his maturity he is far from disguising that he is Molière's disciple. But before he reached that stage he had assimilated all he wanted of the art and craftsmanship of a good many more, novelists, playwrights, and others as well; and the result, the Meredithian novel all complete, was a thing entirely new, though constructed of elements that had been growing and ripening ever since the English novel emerged from the Elizabethan chaos. In that uproarious fantasy *The Shaving of Shagpat* the poet-novelist is trying his wings. In *The Ordeal of Richard Feverel*, and the novels that followed, he can be clearly seen working towards a new theory of fiction and learning how to apply it. Then, in a group comprising *Beauchamp's Career* and *The Egoist*, the theory and his mastery of it are complete. In the novels that come after, he can be seen showing off his dexterity, with some disdain for the conventional reader who might be entrapped into perusing him for mere amusement.[1]

It is not surprising that Meredith has been more heavily *Divers* criticized than any other novelist, the best or the worst, in *ingredients* English literature. He has been reproved through entire

---

[1] Swinburne and Watts-Dunton gave up Meredith at this latter stage. They were persons who took literary offences deeply to heart, and there was a real estrangement between Flint Cottage and the Pines, as I had from the best authorities, themselves; they lamented the coolness, however. Swinburne said he could not read *One of our Conquerors, Lord Ormont,* or *The Amazing Marriage.* There was some reconciliation in 1898 (see Ellis, 155–157).

misunderstanding of his intentions, and of the very nature of his fiction. The fact that he endeavoured to enlarge the boundaries of the art, to try certain new methods and drop certain old ones, is continually disregarded. Thus, the commonest objection is that he was weak at a story. But what if he did not want chiefly to tell a story, though, actually, he could dramatize a crucial incident with the best? After all, history, feigned or the reverse, is not all narrative. Narrative is of the very essence of fiction, but it need not be the predominant partner in the multiple alliance. Fiction is also portraiture, dramatic display, intellectual interpretation, a smile of tenderness, ironical laughter. Fiction absorbed the essay in Goldsmith and Sterne, it absorbed the drama in Fielding and Jane Austen, it absorbed satire, and it went on to absorb much of the finest poetry of the nineteenth century in the Brontës, in Meredith, in Thomas Hardy. The Meredithian novel might, with a little licence, be described as a synthesis of Richardson and Fielding, the intuitive process and the intellectual process of summarizing life and interpreting and judging character and conduct in the very moment of action; and, further, as a synthesis of Jane Austen and Peacock, with something of Lamb, the freakish and imaginative essayist, of Carlyle, the prophet and teacher, a dash of Congreve, and a stronger infusion of Molière. Sometimes it may almost be called a drama with annotations, the playwright standing in the wings and delivering the comment and fuller explanation which is the prerogative of the novelist. Meredith sets his action going, and expounds it at the same time; reveals the poetry and the plastic beauty in it, the philosophic vistas it opens up. He is story-teller and analyst of character, interpreter of motive, serious spectator, and smiling commentator, all at the same time.[1] And, though so many constituents had never before been poured into one mould, he is true to the English tradition. The novel that had descended from the old manuals of conduct, the character-books, and the didactic

[1] See Ramon Fernandez (*Messages*, 1ère série, 1926, "Le Message de Meredith") on Meredith's peculiar device, "dramatic analysis," by which "his knowledge of man and the dramatic expression of the individual unite in one and the same act of creation which is at once intuitive and rational."

sketches in the *Tatler* and *Spectator*, was not going out of the historical track in being a study of life and the universe as well as a portrayal of character and manners. Even with that prosy sermonizer Richardson, Meredith had a deep affinity. But on the artistic side he is nearer to Fielding, the ironic observer of the human comedy, who, moreover, expressly maintained that the novel had a social purpose, and was a treatise on life from which lessons of much practical value were to be gained. The tradition had remained unshaken down to Thackeray and George Eliot.

Whatever else they may be, Meredith's novels are essentially comedies. There is often tragedy in the histories recounted, as there must be in all high comedy: when life is viewed under the lash of the Comic Spirit many a stroke must needs touch our sympathies to the deepest. The sacrifice of Richard Feverel's young and unoffending wife, the wasteful end of Nevil Beauchamp, the immolation of the much-enduring Nataly in *One of our Conquerors*, tragic events in themselves, are integral parts of the comedy, for the comedy of a Molière or a Meredith does not keep the audience laughing all the time.[1] It is in the ironic attitude which he consistently maintains as the servant of the Comic Spirit that Meredith keeps close to Fielding, who adapted Molière to the English stage and was in fiction what Molière might have been had he written novels. Fielding had been under a cloud in Georgian and Victorian times. Carlyle, Tennyson, Browning, Fitz-Gerald, Charlotte Brontë, Ruskin could not abide him. Even Matthew Arnold had no good word for Fielding. Meredith was one of the first to restore the great comic novelist to his right eminence. The *Essay on Comedy* defines his spirit exactly, bracketing him with Aristophanes, Rabelais, Voltaire, Cervantes, and Molière, as one of those who test things by the common sense of an enlightened society and rouse to thoughtful laughter at follies and affectations. Such comedy was indeed "the fountain of good sense," a true counterpart of the poetic drama in which "Philosopher and Comic poet are of a cousin-

All his novels are comedies

---

[1] "To laugh at everything is to have no appreciation of the Comic of Comedy" (*Essay on Comedy*).

ship in the eye they cast on life"—and "equally unpopular with our wilful English of the hazy region and the ideal that is not to be disturbed." After the arch-ironist, Swift, Fielding was the first to sustain the ironic attitude throughout a long story. *Jonathan Wild* is the corrosive irony of Lucian, *Tom Jones* the bland, humane irony of high comedy. Meredith's novels, from first to last, are to be understood as "irony perusing history." Thus the lyrical outbursts in *Richard Feverel* and *Beauchamp's Career* are to be understood as Meredith intended only when the antithesis between the radiant dreams of youth and the harshness of reality is clearly perceived.

Meredith "idealized upon the real"

Fielding, however, was a realist; he drew life as he saw it. Meredith is not a realist like that. Since he undertakes to show "the sensational world of the present" in process of evolution towards "a soberer, a braver, a brighter-eyed," he is obliged to keep at "a pitch considerably above our common human." In short, to quote him again, he "idealized upon the real," like Menander and Molière, of whom he said, "the foundation of their types is real and in the quick, but they painted with spiritual strength, which is the solid in art." Hence it is beside the mark to complain that many of his characters are not true to common life, like Thackeray's or Arnold Bennett's. They were not meant to be. He idealized upon the real. Not, however, that any of his creations are pure idealisms, with no foothold on the solid earth. Those that go farthest beyond the average of probabilities—for instance, Roy Richmond, the Countess de Saldar, Sir Willoughby Patterne, the all-conquering financier Victor Radnor, or that "young man mysterious," the Earl of Fleetwood, in *The Amazing Marriage*—are in fundamentals manifestly true. Many of his most aspiring figures actually had their originals in Meredith's own circle of acquaintances; the original was but the starting-point for the "higher portraiture." He purposely increased their mental and moral stature; and, if they were to be protagonists of the comedy, he enlarged the frailties, manias, and perversities that were to subject them to the lash. Hazlitt said of Richardson that out of his own brain he evolved an artificial reality like nothing that ever existed. There never was an actual Lovelace or an actual Sir Charles Grandison. Meredith also creates an artificial reality; but types such as Sir Willoughby Patterne, the comic counterpart of Grandison, are not created out of nothing, not merely spun out of his inner consciousness. Richardson had little experience to work upon. Meredith starts from the groundwork of observation. Richardson passed off his artificial constructions as examples of reality. Meredith frankly announces that he idealizes upon the real, and his claim to take the midway path between plodding realism and idealistic creation is warranted by his design to show the way to the more splendid epoch that he sees ahead. Fielding's was the prose comedy of life, Meredith's the poetic comedy—a synthesis of the intellectual transcription of reality, illumined obliquely by the Comic Spirit, and his vision of a more perfect world now very dimly imagined. Fielding, to pursue the contrast, was first-rate at a story. Meredith did not envisage his subject as a succession of incidents, but as a group of characters brought into contact whose minds and feelings have to be searched and tested to show of what metal they are compounded. "A story should not always flow," says he, in *Sandra Belloni*, "or, at least, not to a given measure." "My method," he wrote to an American critic in 1887, "has been to prepare my readers for a crucial exhibition of the personæ, and then to give the scene in the fullest of the blood and brain under stress of a fiery situation."[1] This is what he did also in *Modern Love*; whereas in his other novel in verse, "The Sage enamoured and the Honest Lady," the fiery situation occurred long ago; this briefer piece is but the epilogue to a life that has been lived, a drama which still re-echoes in the woman's heart.

It is not strange that reviewers who appraised Meredith by the canons of ordinary fiction easily convicted him of incapacity. He could or would not tell a story; he could not draw a lifelike character; he would not write plain English, or let his people talk like plain Englishmen; and even the great scenes in which he triumphed, wonderful as they admittedly were, lacked the verisimilitude essential to any sort of realism, since it was so

Aberrations from the normal

[1] *Letters*, 22nd July 1870.

difficult to see how the situations had come about: the main facts, the very hinges of the structure, had to be taken for granted. The reader had to believe that Evan Harrington and his egregious sister, the Countess de Saldar, could hoax a crowd of intelligent persons about their family origin, when the gorgeous tailor, "that magnificent snob, that efflorescence of sublime imposture," had his noted shop not many miles away, and was the talk of the dinner-table. He must not decline to admit that rich old Tom Cogglesby, who was not a fool, would pay rattle-pated Jack Raikes a thousand a year to wear a tin plate sewn to the least dignified part of his anatomy; that the richest nobleman in England, a Nimrod of the sex, would pop the question to a strange girl at a dance, wed her in a huff, and desert her in the afternoon of this amazing marriage. The reader had to puzzle out for himself how Victor Radnor came to marry the lady old enough to be his mother, who makes such a dim figure but is the chief agent of fatality in *One of our Conquerors*. Obviously, those readers who were used to personally conducted tours would find a better Cook's agent in a Trollope, or a dozen efficient minor novelists, who would never leave them to fend for themselves in the intervals between events. Meredith seemed careless of everything that the orthodox novelist considers most important. He would accept the longest odds against probability, and hazard everything on one bold throw. All the time-worn devices for compelling poetic faith or realistic assurance are discarded, and he is less concerned with making us believe that we are looking at real life than with directing our eyes to the intricate drama going on inside the mind when self-love or affection is disturbed by the minutest shock.

"At present," he says,

I am aware, an audience impatient for blood and glory scorns the stress I am putting on incidents so minute, a picture so little imposing. An audience will come to whom it will be given to see the elementary machinery at work: who, as it were, from some slight hint of the straws, will feel the winds of March when they do not blow. To them will nothing be trivial, seeing that they will have in their eyes the invisible conflict going on around us, whose features a nod, a smile, a laugh of ours perpetually changes. And they will perceive, moreover, that in real life all hangs together: the train is laid in the lifting of an eyebrow, that bursts upon the field of thousands. They will see the links of things as they pass, and wonder not, as foolish people do now, that this great matter came out of that small one.[1]

Worst of all, to those who think that a Russian novel or a French or an American novel, with its artistic detachment and self-sufficiency of the action, is intrinsically superior to the easy-going English novel, which will not let the characters perform without talking at large about the performance, Meredith brings in an apparatus of pilgrim's scrips and Old Buccaneer's note-books, and a retinue of imps and other emissaries of the Comic Spirit, as elaborate as the chorus of interpreters in a Greek play. Why not let the drama explain itself? Why not embody his meaning in the action, as many playwrights, let alone novelists, have easily and satisfactorily done? How exquisitely Jane Austen's irony shines through, without a syllable of explanation! How competently Trollope's men and women do what is required of them, in spite of his ill-judged reminders that the whole thing is fiction! All this must be granted, except that the imps and other playful tropes and metaphors are much better than the abstractions which they enabled Meredith to avoid. But such considerations have to be set aside in his case. "Little writers should be realistic," he wrote to Jessop, and even the great writers must be realists in their groundwork. "But they have the broad arms of Idealism at command. They give us Earth; but it is earth with an atmosphere." Meredith gives both earth and atmosphere, both real and ideal, with the poetry that weds them and the irony that marks their difference. His reader must be prepared to read, no orthodox novelist, but a thinker, a critic, a teacher, a prophet—one who, like Aristophanes, blends poetry and the comedy of real life into such a harmony that they can no longer be held antagonistic. The seasoned novel-reader who embarks upon a course of

[1] *The Ordeal of Richard Feverel.*

Meredith must be prepared to discard some rooted tastes and prejudices, just as Meredith ignored many old-established regulations. Dr Johnson censured Fielding for disregarding the standards and conventions of that day. In the long run, it has not been Fielding that stands condemned.

The Mere-dithian style

Not improbably, before realizing that this is a new species of novel, such a reader will be disconcerted by the Meredithian style. That style, so plastic and multiform, in spite of its strong individuality, that it is almost necessary to call it styles, is the natural correlative of Meredith's fiction. The Mere-dithian novel is half poetry, and claims the privileges of poetry, continually transcending prose canons and rising into the upper region of poetic drama. The higher portraiture entailed the larger accents of characters idealized from the real, and the lyricism required to depict rare and uplifted states of mind. His outstanding characters are more complex beings, more cultivated and intellectual, wittier, more sensitive and impassioned, than common humanity; they are the dramatis personæ of poetic comedy. Life at such a pitch, on such a platform, requires a loftier idiom. Character, speech, and action are to produce an image of all life and all activity, even the thoughts and passions which are moulding possible existences. What was actually demanded was a highly flexible style. For ordinary routine, Meredith's prose and dialogue could be as plain, crisp, and businesslike as anyone's, though it is never commonplace. He cut out the dull, the inane, the otiose, of everyday conversation, even at some cost to verisimilitude: it exasperated him. For it must not be lost sight of that the Meredithian style was constitutional with him. He talked a sort of poetry; his ordinary speech was as far from ordinary prose as is his literary style at its most lawless. Discipline and convention had a tough subject in Meredith. His choice of a medium was assuredly not dictated by any craving to be unlike everyone else, but rather by a stubborn determination to be himself.[1] It came natural to him, and

[1] Let us repudiate the allegation: "Meredith sits in his chalet, biting his pen, and wondering how he can put it different from any other man living." And attacks on his English come chiefly from those who have never learned the language.

for the reasons stated it was exactly right for his semi-poetic purpose. It was as exactly right as were the heroic couplet and blank verse for poetic drama, and the hexameter for epic. It is by such standards as those that his choice of diction must be judged, rather than by the current rules of novel-writing.

But the Comic Spirit is ever hovering near. When Meredith is most lyrical, it is as sure as fate that some bitter reversal is imminent. The famous "Diversion played upon a Penny-whistle," in *Richard Feverel*, is commonly cited as a specimen of his affected word-painting, prose-poetry, and what-not, by critics who miss the arch smile of the spirit overhead, and seem totally unaware that there is irony about. It is a piece of lyrical prose contrasting the heaven of nature and innocence where the two lovers sit oblivious of harsh actualities, with the realism and the dehumanized logic of the father's System which is fated to blast them. Hence the high pitch of the induction:

His corrective—the comic repartee

Away with Systems! Away with a corrupt World! Let us breathe the air of the Enchanted Island. . . .
The Sun is coming down to earth, and the fields and the waters shout to him golden shouts. He comes, and his heralds run before him, and touch the leaves of oaks and planes and beeches lucid green, and the pine-stems redder gold; leaving brightest footprints upon thickly-weeded banks, where the foxglove's last upper-bells incline, and bramble-shoots wander amid moist rich herbage.

Musical, though less charged with imagery than a good deal of his prose, like the two paragraphs—strophes one is tempted to call them—where the ironic contrast is reiterated:

For this is the home of the enchantment. Here, secluded from vexed shores, the prince and princess of the island meet: here like darkling nightingales they sit, and into eyes and ears and hands pour endless ever-fresh treasures of their souls.
Roll on, grinding wheels of the world: cries of ships going down in a calm, groans of a System which will not know its rightful hour of exultation, complain to the universe. You are not heard here.

More lyrical still, for the irony is more remote, the disillusionment awaiting ecstatic young manhood lying below the
horizon, is another celebrated passage, the awakening of the
lovers, in *Beauchamp's Career*, in their boat on the Adriatic,
to see the Alps towering celestially at the head of the gulf.
Obviously, the scenery is part of the consciousness of the
actors, and has intense dramatic value. The vision is seen
through the eyes, first of Nevil, and then of Nevil and Renée,
both of them romantic, high-strung, tottering on the precipice
of love: hence the glories of physical nature become the
notes of a love-song. It is very different when, years later,
Beauchamp, joined in sober wedlock to Jenny Denham, sails
over the same waters with his wife: there is no lyric then.

Nevil Beauchamp dozed for an hour. He was awakened by
light on his eyelids, and starting up beheld the many pinnacles
of grey and red rocks and high white regions at the head of
the gulf waiting for the sun: and the sun struck them. One
by one they came out in crimson flame, till the vivid host
appeared to have stepped forward. The shadows on the snow-
fields deepened to purple below an irradiation of rose and pink
and dazzling silver. There of all the world you might imagine
Gods to sit. A crowd of mountains endless in range, erect, or
flowing, shattered and arid, or leaning in smooth lustre, hangs
above the gulf. The mountains are sovereign Alps, and the
sea is beneath them. The whole gigantic body keeps the sea,
as with a hand, to right and left.

Nevil's personal rapture craved for Renée with the second
long breath he drew; and now the curtain of her tent-cabin
parted, and greeting him with a half smile, she looked out.
The Adriatic was dark, the Alps had heaven to themselves.
Crescents and hollows, rosy mounds, white shelves, shining
ledges, domes and peaks, all the towering heights were in
illumination from Friuli into farthest Tyrol; beyond earth
to the stricken senses of the gazers. Colour was steadfast on
the massive front ranks: it wavered in the remoteness, and
was quick and dim as though it fell on beating wings; but
there too divine colour seized and shaped forth solid forms,
and thence away to others in uttermost distances where the
incredible flickering gleam of new heights arose, that soared,

or stretched their white uncertain curves in sky like wings traversing infinity.

It seemed unlike morning to the lovers, but as if night had broken with a revelation of the kingdom in the heart of night. While the broad smooth waters rolled unlighted beneath that transfigured upper sphere, it was possible to think the scene might vanish like a view caught out of darkness by lightning. Alp over burning Alp, and around them a hueless dawn! The two exulted: they threw off the load of wonderment, and in looking they had the delicious sensation of flight in their veins.

Hardy has passages fully equal to that, such, for instance, as the magnificent landscape-overture to *The Return of the Native*; but, though he uses scenery poetically, he is not lyrical. With Hardy, the visible scene symbolizes the vast, unfriendly universe which is the grim power behind the human drama. Meredith likewise is often symbolical, discerning, however, in the charms of Nature's face the signs of her inward bounty, "the tendency that makes for righteousness." His lyricism, and the dream-imagery through which he makes thoughts and recondite emotions concrete and legible, are the chief constituents of his semi-poetic prose. Poetry in a deeper sense, the poetry which, as he puts it, "makes romances pass-able, because it is the everlastingly and embracingly human," is the imaginative activity by which he prefigures in the world under scrutiny the greater world to which Nature is on the way. But it must be admitted that Meredith in both novels and poems in his later years misused the licences to which he had habituated himself. Much of his later prose is not good. It was as if he kept himself in a continual state of excitement. The metaphors tumble over one another, and he employed elec-trifying adjectives when the idea called for no such emphasis. It was the excess of his passion to be concrete. And his prose often failed to grapple with the congestion of ideas, when a strenuous gymnastic effort is demanded of the reader to construe him.

But other devices which he introduced or perfected were *His* invaluable additions to the technique of fiction, and among *dramatic* them the most useful for fiction such as his was his method *analysis* of dramatic analysis. Ordinarily, the novelist specializing in psychological portraiture begins with a description of the little world inhabited by his characters, and then of the characters themselves and their concerns and outlook, and goes on to a methodical account of their frames of mind and the motives prompting certain acts. Meredith skips all this, and lets character and the motives acting upon it come out in what takes place. Overt description is comparatively rare with him; the so-called word-painting is of another order and has different purposes. His leading figures are not mere unconscious symbols of his thought; they are mentally fully alive, and actively in quest of the mode of living that will realize their potentialities. There is no need in one of his pregnant scenes for any statement of the mental situation; the characters expound it in what they do and in the words they utter. Such a coincidence of intuition and action was a method not unknown to Fielding and Jane Austen, but they did not employ it with the same dramatic force and entire sufficiency. The Meredithian character expounds himself in the moment of acting; there is no call for further analysis. Again the inveterate dislike of abstractness triumphs over difficulties, and thought is conveyed in a way that puts no undue strain upon art.[1]

A good example is the scene immediately after Beauchamp and Renée's vision of the rosy peaks and pure white snow-fields, when Beauchamp presses her to fly with him, instead of returning to Venice and her father, and to the Marquis de Rouaillout, the elderly man to whom she has been pledged.

---

[1] Grâce à la parfaite harmonie qui règne chez Meredith entre l'intuition et l'analyse, entre l'intuition qui voit l'individu sentir et agir, et l'analyse qui explique et définit ses sentiments et ses actions, les personnages de ses romans mènent une double vie, une vie réelle et une vie possible, celle-ci étant suggérée par le jugement qui accompagne l'expression de celle-là. . . . Le jugement de fait se double d'un jugement de valeur, explicite ou non, qui suit (au lieu de précéder, comme dans le roman à thèse) l'intuition dramatique d'une personnalité. . . . L'idéal meridithien n'est pas introduit dans la vie comme un corps étranger; il se confondrait avec l'action elle-même si celle-ci devenait absolument transparente à l'intelligence de celui-ci qui agit (Ramon Fernandez, "Le Message de Meredith," in *Messages*, 1926). As M. Fernandez puts it later, "Son but est d'harmoniser l'acte de création et l'acte de jugement, et jusqu'à un certain point—nous allons le voir—de les *identifier*, en respectant leurs caractères propres: intentions complémentaires dont nous percevons les effets dans sa manière de poser les personnages et de les faire agir."

"She was mystically shaken and at his mercy; and had he said then, 'Over to the other land, away from Venice!' she would have bent her head." "She asked his permission to rouse her brother and madame, so that they should not miss the scene." Venice, however, is in sight.

"One night, and in a little time one hour! and next one minute! and there's the end," said Renée.

Her tone alarmed him. "Have you forgotten that you gave me your hand?"

"I gave my hand to my friend."

"You gave it to me for good."

"No; I dared not; it is not mine."

Renée pointed to the dots and severed lines and isolated columns of the rising city, black over bright sea.

"Mine there as well as here," said Beauchamp, and looked at her with the fiery zeal of eyes intent on minutest signs for a confirmation, to shake that sad negation of her face.

"Renée, you cannot break the pledge of the hand you gave me last night."

"You tell me how weak a creature I am."

"You are me, myself; more, better than me. And say, would you not rather coast here and keep the city under water?"

She could not refrain from confessing that she would be glad never to land there.

"So, when you land, go straight to your father," said Beauchamp, to whose conception it was a simple act resulting from the avowal.

"Oh! you torture me," she cried. Her eyelashes were heavy with tears. "I cannot do it. Think what you will of me! And, my friend, help me. Should you not help me? I have not once actually disobeyed my father, and he has indulged me, but he has been sure of me as a dutiful girl. That is my source of self-respect. My friend can always be my friend."

"Yes, while it's not too late," said Beauchamp.

She observed a sudden stringing of his features. He called to the chief boatman, made his command intelligible to that portly capitano, and went on to Roland, who was puffing his after-breakfast cigarette in conversation with the tolerant English lady.

"You condescend to notice us, signor Beauchamp?" said
Roland. "The vessel is up to some manœuvre?"

"We have decided not to land," replied Beauchamp. "And,
Roland," he checked the Frenchman's shout of laughter, "I
think of making for Trieste. Let me speak to you, to both.
Renée is in misery. She must not go back."

Roland sprang to his feet, stared, and walked over to Renée.

"Nevil," said Rosamund Culling, "do you know what you
are doing?"

"Perfectly," said he. "Come to her. She is a girl, and
I must think and act for her."

Roland met them.

"My dear Nevil, are you in a state of delusion? Renée
denies . . ."

"There's no delusion, Roland. I am determined to stop a
catastrophe. I see it as plainly as those Alps. There is only
one way, and that's the one I have chosen."

"Chosen! my friend. But allow me to remind you that
you have others to consult. And Renée herself . . ."

"She is a girl. She loves me, and I speak for her."

"She has said it?"

"She has more than said it."

"You strike me to the deck, Nevil. Either you are downright mad, which seems the likeliest, or we are all in a nightmare. Can you suppose I will let my sister be carried away
the deuce knows where, while her father is expecting her,
and to fulfil an engagement affecting his pledged word?"

Beauchamp simply replied,—

"Come to her."

The "singular council" in the chapter which ensues, at one
point in which Roland notices that Venice is no longer in sight,
Beauchamp having set a course in the other direction, is an
admirable comedy of four wills pulling weakly or fiercely in
different directions. Ultimately, they are met off Venice by
Renée's father and the marquis with a spare gondola. Renée
is told by her father to follow madame. He had jumped into
the spare boat and offered a seat to Beauchamp.

"No," cried Renée, arresting Beauchamp, "it is I who mean
to sit with papa."

Up sprang the marquis with an entreating "Mademoiselle!"

"M. Beauchamp will entertain you, M. le Marquis."

"I want him here," said the count; and Beauchamp showed that his wish was to enter the count's gondola; but Renée had recovered her aplomb, and decisively said "No," and Beauchamp had to yield.

That would have been an opportunity of speaking to her father without a formal asking of leave. She knew it as well as Nevil Beauchamp.

"Do nothing—nothing! until you hear from me."

The scene is complete. It has analysed itself.

CHAPTER VIII

MEREDITH—THE NOVELS OF HIS PRIME

"Shag-
pat"

The Ordeal of Richard Feverel, a history of a Father and Son (1859), was Meredith's first novel, but it was not his first story of that ordeal of life through which, as he said of Harry Richmond in a later one, man is changed from "the happy bubbling fool" to "the philosopher who has come to know himself and his relations towards the universe." That had been the gist of The Shaving of Shagpat, which deals fantastically —Meredith denied that it was an allegory—with the same moral problem as was to be handled more literally in the novels. The hero of the fable becomes a reformer of the world as well as of himself. Shagpat was written at Weybridge and Lower Halliford, when Meredith was in daily intercourse with Peacock; and it is not strange that the elder's influence on the book is clearly evident, and all the more evident when the Oriental disguise is seen through. For, though it is called "an Arabian entertainment," yet in the original preface Meredith avowed "that it springs from no Eastern source." The sources are, as already observed, Welsh, or at any rate Celtic, so far as he was not borrowing straight from Peacock and embroidering with his own fancy. Meredith loved to think of himself as a Celt, a mixture of Merediths and Macnamaras, Welsh and Irish; and he turned a charmed ear to what he took to be the authentic echoes of Welsh myth in his father-in-law's tales. Such was the true source of The Shaving of Shagpat, with its furious fancies, dazzling hyperbole, and gasconading rhetoric, and a dry realistic humour mingled throughout. The tone of the Mabinogion is heard from the outset. The barber, Shibli Bagarag, winged for his emprise by oracular prophecy, dauntlessly encounters

318

sorceresses and jinnees, baffles illusions and paralysing enchant-
ments, and at length succeeds in shaving the impostor Shagpat
and cleaving the Identical, so becoming Master of the Event.
There is no difficulty in tracing here the initial motive of the
great tale of Kilhwch,[1] who before he could wed Olwen was
called upon to perform a series of prodigious tasks, the most
desperate of which was to seize the comb and scissors that lay
between the ears of the frightful boar, son of Prince Tared:
these were the only implements that would serve to dress the
hair of his potential father-in-law, by reason of its rankness.
Meredith substitutes Arabian and Himalayan scenery for the
mountains of Wales, and adopts Oriental costumes and
Oriental imagery.   But the ordeals are Celtic in idea, and run
parallel to those surmounted by the Welsh hero.   Further, in
the inset story of Bhanavar and the serpents there are apparent
reminiscences of the mediæval tale of *Melusyne*,[2] the serpent-
woman; and the magic of the serpent-kiss which restores youth
and bloom to the withered and deformed lady must have been
suggested by the *fier baiser* in the other old tale of the *Bel
Inconnu*,[3] the kiss that releases the spellbound princess from
her dragon-shape.[4]   Several of Meredith's earliest and forgotten
poems are based on legends from the same group, and show
the direction of his interests at this period.

He might have called his first regular novel "The Ordeal of "*Richard*
Sir Austin Feverel," for it is Richard's overwise father that *Feverel*"
is really on trial, the man of science, the inditer of maxims,
who would in later days have been a psycho-analyst, with his
opinionated scheme based on the most advanced principles
of eugenics: he, not Richard, is to blame for the disasters.
But Meredith habitually sets an anti-hero over against his hero;
and, when they are fated to come to grief, it is the anti-hero
who is the active delinquent, the other falling a prey to the
comic scourge through weaknesses and blunders that experience
might have corrected.   As yet, he had not thought out his

---

[1] See Volume I. 90–94.
[2] *Ibid.*, 239–244.   [3] *Ibid.*, 135–138 and 145–147.
[4] Able (21–30) would trace the story of Bhanavar the Beautiful to Peacock's
poem *Rhododaphne*, and ultimately to traditions of Thessalian magic which Peacock
found in Apuleius and Petronius.

theory of poetic comedy, and this is a long way from the coherence and mastery of his riper work. But all the elements of his favourite problem are here. It is a study of real life, heightened by poetry, by the vision of what man may be. It is an intellectual study, ironically confronting good intentions with the terrible results of not keeping a strict profit-and-loss account with realities, especially the realities of one's own imperfect nature. But, though in the course of it Meredith reaches some of his highest summits, the book is not satisfactory as a whole. It may be viewed as a tragedy, or as a lyrical love-tale with a mournful ending, or as a satire on doctrinaire education. In sum, it is all these things; but in dry actuality it is a poetic comedy that has gone wrong through Meredith's besetting fault of not harmonizing all the constituents. The contrast between youthful lyricism and the harsh logic of facts is essential to the theme, and a tender and indulgent irony plays around it. But the change of key from the love-romance with its undertone of comedy is so harsh and abrupt that at a first perusal the reader is felled as by a bolt from the blue, and rebels at the seeming gratuitousness of the tragedy. Cold-blooded argument ought not to be the only means of justifying such pathos, especially in a satire of cold-blooded intellectualism. And is it Richard's story, or the story of the baronet, betrayed by his wife and friend, and "left to his loneliness with nothing to ease his heart upon save a little boy in a cradle"? All the while he was writing *Richard Feverel* Meredith had on his mind the question of his own motherless boy. Harassed by the identical problem, he was not unlikely to overweight the case against the father, and intensify the disastrous results of any mistake. It was not with complete artistic detachment that he studied the probable or possible consequences of the father's rigid System. He felt in his very bones that the other was the right way; that frankness, sympathy, tenderest confidence between father and son were the map and compass on which he must rely in his guardianship of Arthur Meredith. *Richard Feverel*, in short, is a kind of experimental novel, in which he worked out what would, he felt, be the wrong solution of his personal problem.

The raillery between the lines of that famous chapter *A pre-*
"Ferdinand and Miranda" is as significant of tragic irony on *conceived*
the watch as the "Diversion played upon a Penny-whistle," *catas-*
already quoted. *trophe*

He had landed on an isle of the still-vexed Bermoothes.
The world lay wrecked behind him: Raynham hung in mists,
remote, a phantom to the vivid reality of this white hand
which had drawn him thither away thousands of leagues in
an eye-twinkle. Hark, how Ariel sang overhead! What
splendour in the heavens! What marvels of beauty about his
enchanted head! And oh, you wonder! Fair Flame! by
whose light the glories of being are now first seen. . . . Radiant
Miranda! Prince Ferdinand is at your feet.

Properly understood, it foreshadows the dire reversal of all
those golden dreams. Richard's father had never taken into
his calculations such an event as his son's falling in love, without
due preparation and an exhaustive review of the possible
candidates for his hand. When Richard marries Lucy without
the baronet's consent, the acknowledged philosopher, author
of the Pilgrim's Scrip, decrees that the youth must do penance
and await his good pleasure before they can be reconciled. In
this state of uncertainty, Richard, separated from his wife and
waiting for his austere father's commands, falls into the toils
of a siren, bribed by a villainous rival to seduce him; and she,
charmed by his ingenuousness and boyish chivalry, succeeds.
This plot becomes the engine of fate. It fails to profit the
contriver in his designs upon Lucy. But Richard, crushed
with remorse, feels himself alienated from the wife he loves,
as he was already from his father. He burns unread all the
letters he receives. He wanders on the Continent, where the
news of his fatherhood, rendered more overpowering by a
strange experience in a German forest, at length sends him
home. But now the humiliating wrong done to him and
Lucy by the would-be seducer has to be wiped out. Before
he and his long-suffering wife can be reunited he must redeem
their honour. And so, scarce comprehending why or how,
the reader is faced with a catastrophe too pathetic to be borne.

Everyone, at the first reading, is staggered by what seems so utterly uncalled for. Meredith endues the hero of his first novel, like several later ones, with a nicety of conscience that looks like quixotism, which insists on punctiliously untying divers complicated knots that the ordinary man would have cut with the knife of common sense. The logic of events leading up to the duel is abstruse and somewhat fantastic, though any who go over it again will discover few weak links. But there are points in Richard's conduct that half confirm his father's doubts of him, and the article of the burnt letters is hard to credit. Things might easily have taken a dozen turns any one of which would have led to a different conclusion. But those who are inclined to accuse Richard of quixotism, because of his sensibility to the point of honour, and, later on, may nurse a like charge against Evan Harrington when he refuses the Beckley estates, or Beauchamp when he declines to give in to love or ambition, or, indeed, against almost any of Meredith's heroes or heroines who are worthy of the name, have to remember that these heroes and heroines are meant to be worthy of the name: they go through their crises in order that their natures may be disciplined for high destinies. Their moral standards must needs be finer than the standards of little people.[1] But why, as Stevenson and others have asked, should Lucy be sacrificed, who is of all concerned the most guiltless? That question would not be allowable if the story had been presented as a tragedy, for the very soul of tragedy is the suffering brought by the guilty on the innocent. Cordelia and Desdemona were not malefactors. Innocence and ignorance, as well as wilful violators of recognized commandments, are whelmed in a like doom. But the immolation of Lucy excites a protest and revolt which the death of Cordelia does not. There is something too accidental in the bias of events, confirming the sense of discord in a story running so light-heartedly at first and coming to such a dark conclusion. Tragedy demands a strictness and a transparent cogency in the articulation of cause and effect which Meredith does not

[1] "These half-comic little people have their place in the history of higher natures and darker destinies" (*Vittoria*, xl.).

observe. Subtlety and wilful intricacy always tend to suggest
sophistry, as in the case of Rhoda Fleming as well as that of
Richard Feverel. Meredith's preference for indirectness disables
him in those very points in which the tragic writer, whether
for the theatre or for the mental stage, is weak at his peril.

His strength is in his great scenes, in tense dramatic situations *The*
which are so enthralling that we forget to ask how they came *great*
about—in the dramatic analysis of souls in the stress of a *scenes*
moral conflict. Such is the pathetic scene of Richard's
parting from Lucy; such is another in which there is only one
actor, the chapter entitled "Nursing the Devil," where Sir
Austin, who has just promised his clear-sighted and clear-
judging Egeria, Lady Blandish, not to shut his heart to his
erring son, forthwith sets about "shutting it as tight as he
could." He had played providence to his boy; he had
experimented with a human creature, with one whom he loved
as his life,

and at once, when the experiment appeared to have failed,
all humanity's failings fell on the shoulders of his son. . . .
The young man had plotted this. From step to step Sir
Austin traced the plot. A Manichæan tendency, from which
the sententious eulogist of nature had been struggling for years
(and which was partly at the bottom of the System), now
began to cloud and usurp dominion of his mind. As he sat
alone in the forlorn dead-hush of his library, he saw the
devil. . . . There by the springs of Richard's future, his father
sat; and the devil said to him: "Only be quiet: do nothing:
resolutely do nothing: your object now is to keep a brave
face to the world, so that all may know you superior to this
human nature that has deceived you. For it is the shameless
deception, not the marriage, that has wounded you."
"Ay!" answered the baronet, "the shameless deception,
not the marriage; wicked and ruinous as it must be; a destroyer
of my tenderest hopes! my dearest schemes! Not the marriage
—the shameless deception!" and he crumpled up his son's
letter to him, and tossed it into the fire.

Eloquent of Meredith's creed of Mother Earth, and her
healing power over those whose primal instincts have not been

sophisticated away, is the chapter "Nature Speaks," in which the conscience-stricken Richard, wandering like an outcast through the German forest, after the news that he is a father, feels himself of a sudden mystically restored to harmony with the life that beats around him. Drenched by a tempest of lightning and rain, he picks up a half-drowned leveret and puts it in his breast. As he walks on in the dripping gloom he has a strange sensation, which presently runs through his blood, "wonderfully thrilling." "He grew aware that the little thing he carried in his breast was licking his hand there. The small rough tongue going over the palm of his hand produced the strange sensation he felt. . . . The gentle scraping continued without intermission as on he walked. What did it say to him? Human tongue could not have said so much just then."

A pale grey light on the skirts of the flying tempest displayed the dawn. Richard was walking hurriedly. The green drenched weeds lay all about in his path, bent thick, and the forest drooped glimmeringly. Impelled as a man who feels a revelation mounting obscurely to his brain, Richard was passing one of those little forest-chapels, hung with votive wreaths, where the peasant halts to kneel and pray. Cold, still, in the twilight it stood, rain-drops pattering round it. He looked within, and saw the Virgin holding her Child. He moved by. But not many steps had he gone ere his strength went out of him, and he shuddered. What was it? He asked not. He was in other hands. Vivid as lightning the Spirit of Life illumined him. He felt in his heart the cry of his child, his darling's touch. With shut eyes he saw them both. They drew him from the depths; they led him a blind and tottering man. And as they led him he had a sense of purification so sweet he shuddered again and again.

Flesh is very close to spirit. "I neighbour the Invisible" Meredith had sung. Here indeed is the spirit that "leaps from flowers and trees."

Character-drawing A number of the characters are almost conventional; others mere embodiments of an odd humour or idiosyncrasy fit to give colour and vivacity to the background. Meredith showed artistic economy in reserving depth of characterization for the personages, and not wasting it on mere accessories. But a tendency is perceptible to people the stage with various shadowy beings that might well be spared, a tendency which afterwards went to excess. Sir Austin, though so important as the mainspring of the action, is the least interesting of all Meredith's self-centred, sultanic persons, of whom Sir Willoughby Patterne is the most memorable because the most ruthlessly anatomized. That he is one of women's natural foes is detected by Lady Blandish, as the later egoist is brought to book by Clara Middleton. Meredith has already ranged himself on the side of women, and states their case more temperately and thus more persuasively than Charlotte Brontë had done. Like hers, his earlier heroes are not strongly individualized; often they are little more than points of view, or simply clay in the hands of the potter, circumstance and action. Outside the ring of those who are, or ought to have been, more intimately drawn, the crowd of by-characters play their allotted parts not amiss. The comic valetudinarian, Uncle Hippias, was drawn, as already noticed, from Meredith's friendly senior, Charnock. The "wise youth," Adrian, always ready with his drench of common sense, is said to be a portrait of Maurice FitzGerald, nephew of the translator of Omar, who used to revel with Meredith in the epicurean feasts cooked by their landlady at Seaford, Mrs Ockenden. That hospitable woman is sometimes put forward as Mrs Berry's original; she was certainly that of Mrs Crickledon, in the queer mixture of Dickensian farce and Meredithian comedy, "The House on the Beach." The motherly past-mistress of connubial lore, Mrs Berry, has also been taken for a variant of Mrs Gamp; but there is not much Dickens in her composition. She belongs to a traditional type as old as Juliet's nurse. A fair proportion of the material that went to the furnishing of this first novel may be set down to personal experience. But Meredith very reasonably objected when the sentiments which Sir Austin jotted down in the Pilgrim's Scrip were thrown in his teeth as if he held them himself. "It is hard on me," he said in his letters, "that the Scrip should be laid to my charge. These aphorisms came in the run of the pen, as dramatizings of the mind of the System-maker. I would not have owned to half a dozen of them. Sir Austin builds a system, quite unaware, on the unforgiveness of his wife. So, though it was a pretty system, it fell." [1] Sir Austin was the type of man he wanted none of us to be.

" *Evan Harrington* " The next novel is richer still in personal experience; in fact, of all his works it is the richest in both characters and circumstances that are historical. *Evan Harrington* (1861), as appeared from the summary of Meredith's life, is the romantic version of his own fight for freedom from the claims of the family shop. This time, the ordeal of young manhood is a comedy, pure and simple, except when it degenerates into farce. Truly, much of the story is wildly improbable. The whole structure, at some crazy moments, seems to pivot on a cluster of pretences, threatening to collapse at a breath of sober criticism. But the Saldar, if largely a figment of the comic imagination, is a masterpiece that entrances; they would be the losers who insisted too shrewishly on the laws of verisimilitude and refused to bow to her seductions. The cream of the comedy is that this indomitable lady, with her talent for over-reaching herself as well as other people, placidly believing that she is Evan's best ally, should prove herself the most dangerous enemy of his interests. When Meredith, as in this instance, portrayed a character from flesh-and-blood reality, he was not less creative than when he produced one that was brand-new. The countess and Richmond Roy are among the boldest and most original products of his imagination; yet both were idealized portraits. The countess was drawn from his aunt, Louisa; Roy, that shady Don Quixote, had his origin in a certain magnificent pretender of whose bombastic claims to royal blood Meredith told hilarious anecdotes. Behind the well-known features it was his way to insert a personality that would fit. He constructed a lifelike effigy, and put his own machinery inside. Thus the characters that were identified by his friends and acquaintances are as markedly Meredithian as any. Nevil Beauchamp and Diana are cases in point. No doubt, also, he

[1] *Letters*, 75.

often drew upon his own past experiences, especially in those heroes of his who are depicted as going through their ordeal and attaining wisdom through error and suffering. Richard Feverel, Evan Harrington, and Harry Richmond, all look like impersonations of his own young manhood. Something of the sort was inevitable, with a theme so compulsive, and was probably involuntary and unconscious. Arthur Rhodes, the young writer in *Diana of the Crossways* who is the heroine's devoted esquire, was, on the other hand, a more deliberate, and hence a more detached and laboured, study of what he conceived himself to have been at the same age.

It is as if the analytical novelist were continually collaborat- *Dramatic* ing with the playwright. Meredith frequently stops to explain *analysis* the peculiar working of the Countess de Saldar's mind. The "mapping out of consequences followed the countess's deeds, and did not inspire them. Her passions sharpened her instincts, which produced her actions. The reflections ensued: as in nature the consequences were all seen subsequently! Observe the difference between your male and female Generals." An excellent illustration of how the great lady's strategic instinct seized upon the thing to do, and darted instantaneously from perception to action, is her exploit in capturing Mr Harry Jocelyn, the son of the house, and the most to be feared of the young bloods who were scandalized by the appearance of Evan among them, and wondered "what the deuce little Rosey was doing with the tailor-fellow." The countess did not waste a moment.

She put on her bonnet hastily, tried the effect of a peculiar smile in the mirror, and lightly ran downstairs.

The three youths were standing in the portico when the Countess appeared among them. She singled out him who was specially obnoxious to her, and sweetly inquired the direction to the village post. With the renowned gallantry of his nation, he offered to accompany her, but presently, with a different exhibition of the same, proposed that they should spare themselves the trouble by dropping the letter she held prominently, in the bag.

"Thanks," murmured the Countess, "I will go." Upon

which his eager air subsided, and he fell into an awkward silent march at her side, looking so like the victim he was to be, that the Countess could have emulated his power of laughter.

"And you are Mr Harry Jocelyn, the very famous cricketer?"

He answered, glancing back at his friends, that he was, but did not know about the "famous."

"Oh! but I saw you—I saw you hit the ball most beautifully, and dearly wished my brother had an equal ability. Brought up in the Court of Portugal, he is barely English. *There* they have no manly sports. You saw him pass you?"

"Him! Whom?" asked Harry.

"My brother, on the lawn, this moment. Your sweet sister's friend. Your Uncle Melville's secretary."

"What's his name?" said Harry, in blunt perplexity.

The Countess repeated his name, which in her pronunciation was "Hawington," adding, "That was my brother. I am his sister. Have you heard of the Countess de Saldar?"

"Countess!" muttered Harry. "Dash it! here's a mistake."

She continued, with elegant fan-like motion of her gloved fingers: "They say there is a likeness between us. The dear Queen of Portugal often remarked it, and in her it was a compliment to me, for she thought my brother a model! You I should have known from your extreme resemblance to your lovely young sister."

Coarse food, but then Harry was a youthful Englishman; and the Countess dieted the vanity according to the nationality. With good wine to wash it down, one can swallow anything. The Countess lent him her eyes for that purpose; eyes that had a liquid glow under the dove-like drooping lids. It was a principle of hers, pampering our poor sex with swinish solids or the lightest ambrosia, never to let the accompanying cordial be other than of the finest quality. She knew that clowns, even more than aristocrats, are flattered by the inebriation of delicate celestial liquors.

The clownish young squire falls at once into her toils, and is henceforth her servile ally. By way of contrast, set beside this delectable creature the boisterous humours of Jack Raikes, and note the hand of Dickens.

Mr Raikes laughed mildly. "When I was in Town, sir, on my late fortunate expedition, I happened to be driving round

St Paul's. Rather a crush. Some particular service going on. In my desire to study humanity in all its aspects, I preferred to acquiesce in the block of carriages and avoid manslaughter. My optics were attracted by several effulgent men that stood and made a blaze at the lofty doors of the cathedral. Nor mine alone. A dame with an umbrella—she likewise did regard the pageant show. 'Sir,' says she to me. I leaned over to her, affably as usual. 'Sir, can you be so good as to tell me the names of they noblemen there?" Atrocious grammar is common among the people, but a gentleman passes it by: it being his duty to understand what is *meant* by the poor creatures. You laugh, sir! You agree with me. Consequently I looked about me for the representatives of the country's pride. 'What great lords are they?' she repeats. I followed the level of her umbrella, and felt—astonishment was uppermost. Should I rebuke her? Should I enlighten her? Never, I said to myself: but one, a wretch, a brute, had not those scruples. 'Them 'ere chaps, ma'am?' says he. 'Lords, ma'am? why, Lor' bless you, they're the Lord Mayor's footmen!' The illusion of her life was scattered."

Jack's speech goes off into flourishes that are anything but Dickens; but who it was that Meredith was vying with, in this character and in Tom Cogglesby, and again in Dandy the postilion, cannot easily be mistaken. None the less, there is no lack of originality in Tom, that "upside-down old despot," whom his brother Andrew describes as "a deuced deal prouder than fifty peers." Besides unlimited hospitality, which helps Evan to gain a footing at Beckley Court, he provides some excellent farce, and his inverted snobbishness, which stubbornly attributes Lady Jocelyn's former rejection of his suit "to the fact of his descent from a cobbler, or, as he put it, to her infernal worship of rank," gives another fillip of irony to Meredith's comic treatment of class prejudice, an integral item in the main theme. These droll creatures are diverting enough to atone for their being somewhat second-hand.

Rose Jocelyn, another image of fresh young girlhood, is a *The pair* change from Lucy Desborough, for she has more of the mind *of lovers* that thinks and the will that can make decisions and abide by them. She was drawn, as everybody, not excepting the original, knew, from Meredith's dearest female friend, Janet Duff-Gordon, afterwards Mrs Ross. That lady was a child when he first knew her at Weybridge. He wrote to her, in every key of playfulness and of intimate self-confession, down to the last years of his life. Her mother, Lady Duff-Gordon, supplied the lineaments of Lady Jocelyn, one of Meredith's fine portraits of mature womanhood; she was also to supply those of a still more exquisite being, Diana's friend, Lady Dunstane. Her father, Sir Alexander Duff-Gordon, has been recognized in Sir Franks. Thus, with the daughters of the Great Mel, and the solid bulk of Mrs Mel, all in the picture, Meredith was well supplied with household material for his characters. And there may be other portraits which have escaped identification. The aristocratic cubs who bait the tradesman's son, so much better a gentleman than themselves, seem to be depicted by one with a personal grudge to wipe out. Evan himself is a nice, good-humoured young man, one of the sort likely to make a stronger impression on the nice young lady of the novel than on the reader. Heroes are peculiarly difficult to make interesting; and, after all, these early heroes of Meredith's have their character to shape; their lives are written to show how they shape it.

Most youths are like Pope's women, they have no character at all. And indeed a character that does not wait for circumstances to shape it, is of small worth in the race that must be run. To be set too early, is to take the work out of the hands of the Sculptor who fashions men.

The view that he made Evan in his own image is confirmed by the dash of quixotry in that youth's constitution, a general trait of this group of otherwise plastic young fellows. When Evan takes upon himself the stigma of the anonymous letter written by his sister, and when he renounces the bequest of the Beckley estates, he sincerely thinks he is giving up Rose Jocelyn and all that he has lived for. It was actually the master-stroke in the proving of his soundness and for the winning of his love. But for this, Rose might have gone on doubting "whether it really was in Nature's power, unaided by family-portraits, coats-of-arms, ball-room practice, and at least one small phial of Essence of Society, to make a Gentleman." Here and elsewhere, Meredith's mockery plays round the convention that gentility is a matter of birth. It plays more subtly over the various degrees and disguises of the opposite foible, vulgarity, convicting even that ultra-refined lady, the Countess de Saldar herself, who hated her brother the brewer, "for vulgarity in others evoked vulgarity in her, which was the reason why she hated vulgarity as the chief of the deadly sins."

Meredith at this period was busy with three pieces of work: "*Sandra* a novel, *Emilia in England*, afterwards entitled *Sandra Belloni*; *Belloni*" his short story, "The House on the Beach"; and a comedy, *The Sentimentalists*, which was played as a curiosity after his death, only to show conclusively that he had not missed his vocation by not turning playwright. The short story is chiefly interesting as a mixture of incongruities: Meredith was still under the impression that if he was to attract readers he must give them Dickens. He did his best to ruin the novel also by overloading it with a heavy and clumsy caricature, the Dickensian Mrs Chump, a singular monstrosity in such a study as the author of *Sense and Sensibility* might appropriately have undertaken. This time, it is the ordeal of a whole group of characters, especially the Pole family, and more especially the only son, Wilfrid Pole, who reappears as pseudo-hero in the sequel. Meredith explains, "This is the game of Fine Shades and Nice Feelings, under whose empire you see this family, and from which they are to emerge considerably shorn, but purified—examples of one present passage of our civilization." These types of affectation are carefully graduated. First come the ladies of Brookfield, the three Miss Poles, daughters of a prosperous City merchant, all intent on "scaling society by the help of the arts." In their privacy together, they nickname each other, Pole, Polar, and North Pole, designating "the three shades of distance which they could convey in a bow," names which were transformed by their envious rivals, the Tinleys, to Pole, Polony, and Maypole. Wilfrid, the petted son, is the typical sentimental youth, a fellow with plenty of physical courage, who morally is such a weakling that he cannot even fall in love until other men in hot pursuit of the lady kindle his ardour and show him what a chance he is missing. It is love that will test him: love in all Meredith's novels is the touchstone by which we know of what we are made.

Is it any waste of time to write of love? The trials of life are in it, but in a narrow ring and a fiercer. You may learn to know yourself through love, as you do after years of life, whether you are fit to lift them that are about you, or whether you are but a cheat, and a load on the backs of your fellows. The impure perishes, the inefficient languishes, the moderate comes to its autumn of decay—these are of the kinds which aim at satisfaction to die of it soon or late. The love that survives has strangled craving; it lives because it lives to nourish and succour like the heavens.

Wilfrid's steady declension is traced to its last phase, in this and the sequel, *Vittoria*, in which the principal characters are transferred to a very different stage.

The anatomy of sentimentalism

Sandra Belloni is his principal treatise on sentimentalism, "fiddling harmonics on the strings of sensualism"; but he often applied his microscope to the same malady in other sickrooms. For the present, the novelist is in partnership with a "garrulous, super-subtle, so-called Philosopher," who will retire when the action shifts to Italy, "where life fights for plain issues," and the novelist can only "sum results."

Let us, he entreats, be true to time and space. In our fat England, the gardener Time is playing all sorts of delicate freaks with the hues and traceries of the flower of life, and shall we not note them? If we are to understand our species, and mark the progress of civilisation at all, we must. Thus the Philosopher.[1]

---

[1] He wrote of this novel to Mrs Ross: "It is called 'Emilia in England' antiposed to 'Emilia in Italy,' which is to follow—both in 3 vols. The first is a contrast between a girl of simplicity and passion and our English sentimental, socially-aspiring damsels. The second (in Italy) is vivid narrative, or should be" (*Letters*, i. 130). He told Jessopp: "The novel has good points, and some of my worst ones. It has no plot albeit a current series of events: but being based on character and continuous development, it is not unlikely to miss a striking success" (*Ibid.*, 377). He was right.

There are still other vagaries of sentimentalism to be noted. The least credible is the case of that refined soul Sir Purcell Barrett, who escapes from a world that is too gross by quietly putting a pistol to his head. Two other persons, almost as shadowy, though Meredith gives one of them later a more heroic rôle, are Merthyr Powys and his sister Georgiana—the sister in love with her brother and a hater of all other men. She is a hater, too, of most women, so jealous is she of her superfine brother. It is in regard to this pair of idealists that he observes, not without a glance at his own cherished genealogy, "There is human nature and Welsh nature." But, as must also be said of another Welshman, the oracular Gower Woodseer, in *The Amazing Marriage*, these characters are well conceived, but not so well substantiated.

In contradistinction to these artificialities, Meredith brings *The* forward a set of common or uncommon persons who are *converse* unaffected specimens of human nature. Sandra, who gives her name to the book, was evidently meant to be a very complete exponent of his philosophy. She, the future *prima donna*, comes on the stage singing, in a memorable scene in the second chapter. In this first volume of her history she appears as "a little unformed girl, who had no care to conceal that she was an animal, nor any notion of the necessity for doing so." In the epical sequel she reappears grown up, and her powers of heart and genius perfected; at least, the author avers that it is the identical woman, else some might find her a little difficult to recognize. Emilia-Sandra-Vittoria, to cite her successive names, does in her final avatar fulfil the prophecy of Diana of the Crossways: "If you prove to be of some spiritual stature, you may reach to an ideal of the heroical feminine type for the worship of mankind, an image as yet in poetical outline only on our upper skies." She it is with whom Wilfrid plays at love-making, in the manner of the ingrained sentimentalist. The scene "By Wilming Weir" recalls the purer ecstasies beside another weir-pool, in *Richard Feverel*; but this time the irony is not far to seek. Sandra is the lover, the artist, the poet: she it is who in the noise of the water sees hundreds of pictures.

"I thought—what could stir music in me more than this? and, am I not just as rich if I stay here with my lover, instead of flying to strange countries, that I shall not care for now? So, you shall take me as I am. I do not feel poor any longer."

With that she gave him both her hands.

"Yes," said Wilfrid.

As if struck by the ridicule of so feeble a note, falling upon her passionate speech, he followed it up with the "yes!" of a man; adding: "Whatever you are, you are my dear girl; my own love; mine!"

Having said it, he was screwed up to feel it as nearly as possible, such virtue is there in uttered words.

Sometimes, for irony—but it is comparatively rare with him —Meredith offers humour, that which arises from the collision of disparate temperaments, as when the half-Italian girl appeals to the sedate and startled City man, Mr Pole senior:

"You are not cruel. I knew it. I should have died, if you had come between us. Oh, Wilfrid's father, I love you! . . . You are Wilfrid's father, whom I can kneel to. My lover's father! my own father! my friend next to heaven. . . . The thought of losing him goes like perishing cold through my bones;—my heart jerks, as if it had to pull up my body from the grave every time it beats."

"God in heaven!" cried the horrified merchant, on whose susceptible nerves these images wrought with such a force that he absolutely had dread of her. He gasped, and felt at his heart, and then at his pulse; rubbed the moisture from his forehead, and throwing a fixedly wild look on her eyes, he jumped up and left her kneeling.

Humour was not Meredith's strong point. His comedy was purely intellectual, and did not easily combine both, as Shakespeare and Jane Austen did without effort. More characteristic of his maturing technique is the dialogue in which Wilfrid tries and fails to extricate himself from his entanglement with Lady Charlotte Chillingworth: here emotions and incipient motives are caught on the wing with a skill seldom rivalled.

While she was speaking, Wilfrid's thoughts ran: "My time has come to strike for liberty."

This too she perceived, and was prepared for him.

He said: "Lady Charlotte. I feel that I must tell you . . . I fear that I have been calculating rather more hopefully. . . ." Here the pitfall of sentiment yawned before him on a sudden. "I mean" (he struggled to avoid it, but was at the brink in the next sentence)—"I mean, dear lady, that I had hopes . . . Besworth pleased you . . . to offer this . . ."

"With yourself?" she relieved him. A different manner in protesting male would have charmed her better. She excused him, knowing what stood in his way.

"*That* I scarcely dared to hope," said Wilfrid, bewildered to see the loose chain he had striven to cast off gather tightly round him.

"You do hope it?"

"I have."

"You have hoped that I . . ." (she was not insolent by nature, and corrected the form)—"to marry me?"

"Yes, Lady Charlotte, I—I had that hope . . . if I could have offered this place—Besworth. I find that my father will never buy it; I have misunderstood him."

He fixed his eyes on her, expecting a cool, or an ironical, rejoinder to end the colloquy; after which, fair freedom! She answered, "We may do very well without it."

Wilfrid was not equal to a start and the trick of rapturous astonishment. He heard the words like the shooting of dungeon-bolts, thinking, "Oh, heaven! if at the first I had only told the woman I do not love her!" But that sentimental lead had ruined him. And, on second thoughts, how could he have spoken thus to the point, when they had never previously dealt in anything save sentimental implications? The folly was in his speaking at all. The game was now in Lady Charlotte's hands.

Sandra was drawn from a half-Italian whom the Merediths *Portraits* knew at Weybridge, and whose unlikeness to the conventional English miss captivated the novelist.[1] No original has been ascertained for the Greek musical connoisseur, Antonio Pericles, brilliant combination of the artistic soul and the hard practical brain of the man of business, with his passionate

---

[1] This Emilia Macirone was the daughter of a lady, formerly Miss Williams, with whom they lived at Weybridge.

reverence for the divine gift of song and his savage contempt for all that is second-rate. Never since George Sand wrote *Consuelo* has any succeeded better than Meredith in conveying by mere words the effect of great music. And he achieves this, partly by the Homeric device of showing how the listeners are held spellbound, partly by the poetry of the scene—the moonlit woods and the nightingales outsung, the hushed theatre and the glorious voice issuing into space.

This is what the great voice does for us. It rarely astonishes our ears. It illumines our souls, as you see the lightning make the unintelligible craving darkness leap into long mountain ridges, and twisted vales, and spires of cities, and inner recesses of light within light, rose-like, toward a central core of violet heat.

Last but not least of the authenticated likenesses is that of the youthful Swinburne, in the red-haired, impetuous boy, Tracy Runningbrook: his effervescent talk and the explosive rhetoric of his controversial prose are caught to the life. It is a pity that the sentimental Miss Poles and their bugbear Mrs Chump are creations often too fantastic for belief. They could be tolerated in serious comedy only if Meredith's dictum in *The Egoist* were accepted: "The Comic Spirit has not a thought of persuading you to believe in him."

"Rhoda Fleming" His hands were very full at the time he was meditating *Vittoria*, the story of Sandra or Emilia in Italy. He was writing for two newspapers, working by fits and starts on *Rhoda Fleming*, and had plans in his head for *Harry Richmond*, not to be carried out for several years. *Vittoria* had to be put aside, and the hiatus may account for some difficulty in our making the threads of the character-drawing tally between the English and the Italian portions of the story. Several of those in Sandra's retinue of friends seem to have undergone more than a sea-change when they are met again in a foreign land. Stern tragedy is the keynote of *Rhoda Fleming* (1865), a novel which seems to bid for comparison with George Eliot.[1]

---

[1] The circumstance that most of the leading characters are farm-hands or at any rate country folk has misled some into comparing this with the typical Hardy novel. "Rhoda Fleming, in that curious novel which always suggests a Meredith masquerading as a Hardy" (J. B. Priestley, *Meredith*, 183). Hardy had not yet begun writing fiction.

It is the highly Meredithian form of such a story as *Adam Bede*, of a girl of the yeoman class seduced and deserted by the squire's son, and of the love-affairs of two others implicated in her sad fortunes. The strong-minded Rhoda, the weak and betrayed Dahlia, the sturdy Robert Eccles, and the culpable Edward Blancove, correspond symmetrically with Dinah Morris, poor little Hetty, Adam Bede, and Arthur Donnithorne. The correspondences are really contrasts; a world of difference stretched between the two novelists. And yet George Eliot might also have written of misguided young men, "What father teaches them that a human act once set in motion flows on for ever to the great account? Our deathlessness is in what we do, not in what we are." Blancove, like Arthur Donnithorne, is another of the sentimentalists, "they who seek to enjoy without incurring the Immense Debtorship for a thing done." There is no festive conclusion in this case: nowhere has Meredith played more movingly on the strings of suspense. When the last stage of Dahlia's mortal pilgrimage is reached, it is as if patience and renunciation of earthly good were all that befits the spirit refined and redeemed by suffering. George Eliot's characters were simpler. Dinah Morris and Mrs Poyser are what Meredith would call "exceptional"; but the others are ordinary types of humanity portrayed to the depths. Meredith's four, whilst actuated by those feelings and motives which are universal and without which tragedy would make no impression on the soul, are of marked individuality. Rhoda, the strong, resolute, enduring, is cast in the same mould as the tragic heroines, Vittoria, Chloe, Nataly, Carinthia; though, like them, having a mind of her own and being responsible for her own actions, she is a distinct personality. And Dahlia is no Hetty Sorrel. Like all Meredith's central characters, she grows in spirit under the buffetings of life; and in her last phase this martyr to the immense endurance and inexhaustible charity of love shines out even among Meredith's embodiments of feminine beauty. Still less is Rhoda, that indomitable pagan, a representative of the conventional attitude towards the "fallen woman." Determined as she is to right her sister's good name by compelling her, with the strength of a superior will, into an unwelcome marriage, she does not fail in tenderest fellow-feeling towards the victim of another's fault. She does not dream of forgiving her, or urging her to ask forgiveness of her sins. Her error is too implacable a sense of justice. As no penance or contrition can move Carinthia, in *The Amazing Marriage*, to pardon the husband who has changed his heart, so no awakening of Edward Blancove to the worth of the treasure he has lost, no moral revolution, can avail with Rhoda to let him cast himself at the feet of Dahlia, who would have forgiven everything. Meredith repeatedly reminds the studious reader of Richardson, that older investigator of the clockwork of the mind and heart. The end of *Rhoda Fleming* is like the end of *Clarissa*: the man who has outraged womanhood is indignantly rejected when he comes back on hands and knees to offer reparation. But the part of Clarissa is divided between the two sisters: Dahlia, the betrayed virgin, remains passive; it is Rhoda who supplies the inflexible will and vindicates the dignity of woman. As in *Clarissa* also, there is a greatness and sublimity here which the story of Hetty entirely lacks, though George Eliot's workmanship is more thorough. Meredith again provokes doubts of the inevitability of the events that bring down the catastrophe. Granted that it was thoroughly in character for Rhoda, out of her pride in her sister and devotion to the heart-broken father, to turn a deaf ear to the reluctant Dahlia's protests and urge on the union with the unknown man, that the family's self-respect might be restored by her bringing back her sister a married woman, it verges on the incredible that so many chances should have been missed of identifying the unknown with the infamous Sedgett. But the prime weakness in the causal chain is the supposition that Edward Blancove would have let the fool Algernon have a chief finger in the business. This inconsequent buffoon thus becomes the arbiter of destiny. At the very moment when Sedgett would have been unmasked, the wedding takes place; the stricken lover and the distracted Robert, hurrying to the rescue, arrive just too late. It is forcing the hand of the Comic Spirit with a vengeance. There is too much here of what Meredith brands as "a delusion . . .

a poet's brain, a bottle of gin, and a theatrical wardrobe," of melodrama, to wit; and so again, in the affair of Major Waring and the captivating Mrs Lovel. As to the fantastic doings of old Anthony Hackbut, ridden by the money-demon, which so strangely provide the funds later on to buy off Sedgett, it is bad Dickens again, Dickens psychologized, but a hybrid and a monstrosity.

The rustics are drawn with a firm hand, but with a sort *A rustic* of contemptuous tolerance, very unlike George Eliot's kindly *novel* attitude or Thomas Hardy's, who makes his country people mouthpieces of his sardonic humour and of his cosmic philosophy, to which they give a homelier enunciation. They are still more stolid, more racy of the soil, and manifestly taken from the life. The inmates of Queen Anne's Farm, the original of which was not in Kent, but has been identified with Byfleet Manor House, do not number a Mrs Poyser amongst them. On the other hand, primitive, nay, prehistoric, wisdom flows from the lips of that old Saurian, Mas' Gammon, imperturbable consumer of dumplings, who will not be hurried, when everybody is on tenterhooks for him to speak, until he feels his buttons.

"Yes, I calculate I save threepence a day in beer alone," said Anthony.

"Three times seven's twenty-one, ain't it?"

Mr Fleming said this, and let out his elbow in a small perplexity, as Anthony took him up:—"And fifty-two times twenty-one?"

"Well, that's, that's—how much is that, Mas' Gammon?" the farmer asked in a bellow.

Master Gammon was laboriously and steadily engaged in tightening himself with dumpling. He relaxed his exertions sufficiently to take his new burden on his brain, and immediately cast it off.

"Ah never thinks when I feeds—Ah was al'ays a bad hand at 'counts. Gi'es it up."

"Why, you're like a horse that never was rode! Try again, old man," said the farmer.

"If I drags a cart," Master Gammon replied, "that ain't no reason why I should leap a gate."

Master Gammon had chosen his pace, and was not of a mind to change it for anybody or anything. It was his boast that he had never ridden by railway: "nor ever means to, if I can help it," he would say. He was very much in harmony with universal nature, if to be that is the secret of human life.

Let Robert Eccles himself paint the picture of Rhoda, in this bit of talk with his old regimental friend, Major Waring:

"She saw you, did she? Did she colour when she heard your name?"

"Very much," said Major Waring.

"Was dressed in—?"

"Black, with a crimson ribbon round the collar."

Robert waved the image from his eyes. . . .

"She wore a red ribbon? If it had been Spring, you'd have seen roses. Oh! what a stanch heart that girl has. Where she sets it, mind! Her life where that creature sets her heart! But, for *me*, not a penny of comfort! Now for a whole week of her, day and night, in that black dress with the coloured ribbon. On she goes: walking to church; sitting at table; looking out of the window!—

"Will you believe I thought those thick eyebrows of hers ugly once—a tremendous long time ago. Yes; but what eyes she has under them! And if she looks tender, one corner of her mouth goes quivering; and the eyes are steady, so that it looks like some wonderful bit of mercy.

"I think of that true-hearted creature praying and longing for her sister, and fearing there's shame—that's why she hates me. I wouldn't say I was certain her sister had not fallen into a pit. I couldn't. I was an idiot. I thought I wouldn't be a hypocrite. I might have said I believed as she did. There she stood ready to be taken—ready to have given herself to me, if I had only spoken a word! It was a moment of heaven, and God the Father could not give it to me twice! The chance has gone."

"*Vittoria*"

Rhoda Fleming was a digression from the path Meredith had marked out for himself. It is in his comedies that he found the aptest method of expounding that "closer knowledge of our fellows, discernment of the laws of existence," which "leads to great civilization"; for it is comedy that teaches man to act with sanity by laughing at his aberrations. And comedy goes hand in hand with poetry. Comedy is only a corrector, poetry points the way. Poetry discerns the perfection towards which Nature is everlastingly tending. His finer creations—Sandra and Rhoda are of the number, and will soon be joined by others—are at once of the present and the future, citizens of a more beautiful epoch in man's history than any yet realized. Poetic comedy in *Richard Feverel* had fought a losing battle with tragedy. *Evan Harrington* and *Sandra Belloni*, though imperfect, were better examples of the kind of fiction at which he was aiming. They are in a sense plays reduced to narrative, in which the characters are kept at a distance, as on a stage, but at critical moments are brought close to the spectator, and their inmost selves illumined, not only the drama of human relations, but also the drama in the individual mind and the reactions upon that mind of all which is going on around it, being set before the eye. Though the four novels from *Vittoria* (1866) to *The Egoist* (1879) are not all pure comedy, yet in every one, even in the epical *Vittoria* and the romantic story of the idealist Beauchamp, with its bitter ending, the irony of the Comic Spirit is never far away. *The Egoist* is his most elaborate exemplification of the theory set forth in the *Essay on Comedy*. *Vittoria*, in which Sandra and her friends are transported to Italy and plunged amid the plots and counterplots, the insurrections and battles of an abortive rising against the Austrians, and mixed with a vast crowd of patriots and intriguers and Austrian campaigners and their women-folk, is Meredith's one novel of action. It deals with an historical event, the outbreak of 1848, when the Austrians, driven from Milan, advanced again under Radetzki, and after several engagements took possession of the city. The king was not in full sympathy with the Milanese, who for the most part wanted a republic. There were dissensions, and no fully concerted action. After the defeats of Custozza and Novara, Sardinia made peace, and Carlo Alberto abdicated. These crucial events, however, so important in the history of the Risorgimento, are not given any prominence by Meredith. The advance and retreat, with

all the confused incidents of a popular rising, looking all the
more intricate from being viewed from both sides alternately,
form the background, against which the personal drama is
silhouetted. He abstains from any but an impressionistic view
of the fighting. Even such a scene of fiery action as the duel
in the Stelvio Pass is memorable chiefly for the thrilling
glimpses into the souls of the two combatants. Like Scott,
Meredith rarely brings famous personages to the front of the
stage. There is a brief glance at Custozza, a rumour of Novara.
Carlo Alberto remains in the distance; Mazzini is shown for
a moment, but not even named. It is left to the reader to
identify the old marshal with Radetzki. The real drama is
enacted by a great body of characters created for the purpose,
at once individuals of well-marked traits and epitomes of the
various types of humanity engaged in the vast, many-sided
strife.

*The
leading
personages* The opening scene on the mountain-top overlooking
Maggiore and the Lombard plain is magnificent, and deftly
introduces most of the foremost actors. Here the ringleaders
of the insurgent Milanese have a rendezvous with the chief,
who is of course Mazzini, and with the great singer Vittoria.
She is our old acquaintance Sandra. Pericles has provided for
her training, and she is to appear shortly at La Scala in a new
opera, which is a covert attack on the Austrian regime. She
has further been entrusted with the glorious duty of singing
an insurrectionary song, which is to be the signal of revolt.
But even at this critical moment there is no unanimity of
outlook or plan; dangerous disputes can already be foreseen.
Before the party has quite dispersed a band of tourists appear
ascending the peak: they are Vittoria's English friends.
Wilfrid Pole is not among them; but she hears that he has
become an Austrian officer, and is quartered not far off in
Verona. Thus the previous novel is linked up with the new,
and the presence on the scene of these ancient friends, free
of both camps, and, still more, the fact that her old flame
Wilfrid is with the enemy, foreshadow complications bristling
with tragic possibilities. The drama has begun. Very in-
discreetly, though Meredith never puts it in that light, Vittoria

conveys a hint to the newcomers that Milan may soon be too hot to hold them. The news finds its way inevitably to the other side; Wilfrid's sister was sure to warn her brother. The fact leaks out among the revolutionaries. That terrible plotter, Barto Rizzo, "The Miner," "The Great Cat," knows that the secret has been blabbed, and takes measures to cancel the intended outbreak. Count Carlo Ammiani, one of the youngest and most chivalrous of the republican army, hotly in love with the *prima donna*, strives in the dark and all in vain to exonerate her from the suspicion of treachery. He and Vittoria, amid the clash of pure and sinister motives and the cross-currents of intrigue, hardly know where they stand: the reader must follow the swift and tortuous narrative with the utmost alertness not to be bewildered. With the young enthusiast Ammiani, whose fine sense of honour, bordering on quixotry, brings him at last to his grave, are abruptly contrasted such men of affairs as Colonel Corte, a stern, bluff soldier, the sane and clear-sighted Agostino Balderini, gently satirical of the eccentricities of his allies and of the enemy, and Count Medole, vain of his position as leader of the revolt, but a reed to the blast of circumstance. Nearer to his heart and sharers of his generous idealism are his venerable mother, the Countess Ammiani, who has buried her dearest, and now resigns herself heroically to see the last of the name go to the sacrifice, without a word to shake his fortitude; and the fierce young widow, Laura Piaveni, nursing the memory of her slain husband and the thirst for revenge. Equal justice is dealt to the other side: in truth, Meredith's impartial attitude is sometimes an obstacle to our seizing the drift of the complicated action going on. Even the parasitic old courtier and diplomatic time-server, Count Serabiglione, is drawn with no unkindness; and the political courtesan, the bewitching Countess Violetta, whose double-dealing helps to lure Carlo to his death, is treated with the same courtesy as she meets with from that doomed young knight-errant himself. The Lenkensteins, soldierly Count Karl, gay and coquettish Countess Lena, and the savage and sullen Countess Anna, together with their neutral friend, the Duchess Amalia, loving Laura as the widow of the slaughtered man she herself had loved, are drawn with the same graciousness as the Italians, and are equally lifelike and representative. Still more prominent is the invincible swordsman, Weisspriess, picturesque embodiment of the devil-may-care gallantry and unquestioning submission of the Austrian officer. Lastly, in a grim under-plot closely intertwined, the brothers Guidascarpi, hunted down like wolves for a fearful deed of vengeance, bring a lurid crimson into the many-coloured skein. Characteristically, Meredith reserves the complete story of this relentless vendetta till the latter pages of the book. But perhaps the mystery veiling their past deepens the terror they inspire. Often in reading *Vittoria* it is as if we were watching some great Elizabethan drama of blood, insensate passion, and superhuman heroism, and nowhere so much as in the tragic adventures of the Guidascarpi.

An heroic story Vittoria makes her début and sings her incendiary song, rousing a tempest of enthusiasm. But the Austrians have taken precautions that there shall be no outbreak. The theatre is packed with soldiers. At Camilla's death-scene the house was hushed as if it were reality and not a play. "It was more like a cathedral service than an operatic pageant." The theme of the final stanzas is that of Swinburne's "Pilgrims," in *Songs before Sunrise*, which was to appear four years later: the cheerful self-immolation of those who die before "their thrones are won," but will live and triumph in the liberation of their children—

> Enough of life is this for one life's span,
> That all men born are mortal, but not man;
> And we men bring death lives by night to sow,
> That man may eat and reap and live by day.

Such is the burden of Camilla's dying speech:

> Our life is but a little holding, lent
> To do a mighty labour: we are one
> With heaven and the stars when it is spent
> To serve God's aim: else die we with the sun.

The curtain is rung down; but a dozen youths hold it up,

whilst Vittoria sings the proscribed song. It drops after the last stanza:

> I enter the black boat
> Upon the wide grey sea,
> Where all her set suns float;
> Thence hear my voice remote:
> Italia, Italia shall be free!

Her arrest is instantly ordered. But the lights have been extinguished, the theatre is a howling cavern of plaudits and battle-cries. Before the military can get her out of the building she is hurried away by other hands, and when she wakes from the stupor following excitement and utter exhaustion she finds herself in a carriage rolling swiftly up an Alpine valley towards Tyrol. Late next day a horseman overtakes the carriage. It is an Austrian officer, no less a person indeed than the redoubtable Captain Weisspriess, who, hearing that Vittoria's friends were sending her out of harm's way, had got leave to follow, partly out of professional zeal and partly on the chance of an amour. All this she finds out bit by bit through her courier, who, however, is not the faithful Beppo, but a stranger who slipt into the seat behind the carriage and so got past the sentinels at Milan gates. It is in fact Angelo Guidascarpi, like his brother Rinaldo a fugitive, with Austrian bloodhounds hot on his trail. And Weisspriess, hottest of all the bloodhounds, sits up in front beside the driver. Either Vittoria or Angelo would be a prize: to capture both, and bring them in triumph to Meran, would make his fortune, and win him the hand of the Countess Anna, most implacable of the Guidascarpis' foes.

The situation is romantic in the extreme, and Meredith *The* has managed so far with skill and an eye for effect. Angelo *flight and* and Vittoria are in the lion's mouth; but, before the lion finds *the duel* out that Angelo as well as Vittoria is in his clutches, the fugitives are away. They take to the mountains, with two hours' start; and Vittoria, still in Camilla's pink and gold, with silken slippers on her feet, follows Angelo through the fringes of forest and high rocky pastures below the glaciers, nearer and nearer to the frontiers of Switzerland. But an episode that might have outdone Stevenson's breathless story of the flight through the heather, in *Kidnapped* twenty years later, does not come up to that level. The wayside incidents, the colloquies with chance-met peasants and treacherous innkeepers, who are sketched with a flying pen, are excellent; but the run of the narrative in between is vague and confusing. Meredith extricates his runaways from their peril somehow, but we hardly know how he does it; and subsequently he gets Angelo, lying wounded and disabled in Meran itself, out of the enemy's stronghold, much to the reader's astonishment. In this after-affair, Wilfrid Pierson, *alias* Pole, plumbs the uttermost depths of ignominy, when he breaks his military oath and helps the condemned man to elude those on watch, all for an approving smile from his lost love. The folly and abasement of the sentimentalist, all through the book, are tacitly contrasted with the selfless heroism of the young patriots. But, again, the scenes in which the drama culminates are magnificent. That of the duel in the pass is of unique interest, as an example of the mental historian dealing with passions at the death-grapple; once more the real drama is internal. As the two fugitives near Meran, Angelo leaves Vittoria to finish the journey alone, and the vigilant Weisspriess intercepts her. But Angelo had never let her out of his sight. He drops from the forest above the road. Weisspriess has his sword; Angelo's only weapon is his Italian stiletto. The Austrian's military gorge rises at the idea of fighting a man so unarmed; but he cannot refuse the challenge.

"Killing you, Angelo Guidascarpi, is the killing of a dog. But there are such things as mad dogs. This is not a duel. It is a righteous execution, since you force me to it: I shall deserve your thanks for saving you from the hangman. I think you have heard that I can use my weapon. There's death on this point for you. Make your peace with your Maker."

Weisspriess spoke sternly. He delayed the lifting of his sword that the bloody soul might pray.

But Angelo has chosen the ground. It is a patch of meadow where he can dart from side to side, and avoid the deadly point.

The combatants are not so unequally matched after all. Blood is drawn on both sides, Weisspriess bewildered and scandalized by his opponent's unconventional tactics. It is the guerrilla against the trained soldier. At length, bleeding from many cuts, Angelo springs on the sword, taking it in his side, and throwing it square out drives in the stiletto. "It was at a moment when Weisspriess was courteously bantering him with the question whether he was ready, meaning that the affirmative should open the gates of death to him." He tottered and fell: "amazement was on his features." "'Finish me,' he moaned. 'Good-evening to the old army.'"

A vision of leaping tumbrils, and long marching columns about to deploy, passed before his eyelids: he thought he had fallen on the battle-field, and heard a drum beat furiously in the back of his head; and on streamed the cavalry, wonderfully caught away to such a distance that the figures were all diminutive, and the regimental colours swam in smoke, and the enemy danced a plume here and there out of the sea, while his mother and a forgotten Viennese girl gazed at him with exactly the same unfamiliar countenance, and refused to hear that they were unintelligible in the roaring of guns and floods and hurrahs, and the thumping of the tremendous big drum behind his head—"somewhere in the middle of the earth": he tried to explain the locality of that terrible drumming noise to them, and Vittoria conceived him to be delirious; but he knew that he was sensible: he knew her and Angelo and the mountain-pass, and that he had a cigar-case in his pocket worked in embroidery of crimson, blue, and gold, by the hands of Countess Anna. He said distinctly that he desired the cigar-case to be delivered to Countess Anna at the Castle of Sonnenberg, and rejoiced on being assured that his wish was comprehended and should be fulfilled; but the marvel was, that his mother should still refuse to give him wine, and suppose him to be a boy: and when he was so thirsty and dry-lipped that though Mina was bending over him, just fresh from Mariazell, he had not the heart to kiss her or lift an arm to her!—He was going down with a company of infantry in the Gulf of Venice: cards were in his hand, visible, though he could not feel them, and as the vessel settled for the black plunge, the cards flushed all honours, and his mother shook her head at him: he sank, and heard Mina singing all the length of the water to the bottom, which grated and gave him two horrid shocks of pain: and he cried for a doctor, and admitted that his horse had managed to throw him; but wine was the cure, brandy was the cure, or water, water!

Considering that diagnosis of a mind in delirium, or that deep plunge, in *Richard Feverel*, into the unconscious region where man feels his mystic kinship with Mother Earth, or the strange hallucinations of Richmond Roy or Victor Radnor in later novels, one is bound to wonder whether, after all, the extravagant fancies of Anthony Hackbut, in *Rhoda Fleming*, were not the phenomena of monomania observed by an accurate psychologist. Alienists have written books on Shakespeare's knowledge of mental derangements. Meredith deprecated any such compliment, no doubt pluming himself on the normality of his characters. But

Great wits are sure to madness near allied,

and the novelist who delineated genius could hardly have been unable to give its counterpart and opposite.

"A doctor of the insane wrote to my publishers from Australia that the opening chapter [of *One of our Conquerors*] showed all the symptoms of incipient lesion of the brain, and he wondered whether I had studied the disease. Had I done so I should not have written of it." [1]

A sublime ending When the revolt collapsed, and the city was reoccupied, rebellion still smouldered underground, though there were divisions in the camp, some of the patriots fleeing to Rome to join Mazzini, other still fomenting insurrection in Lombardy. And there were spies in their counsels. Carlo Ammiani did not see eye to eye with Vittoria, now his wife, though he was beginning to understand that she was of "the nobler order of women" who have "a craving for idealistic truths, which men are apt, under the heat and hurry of their energies, to put aside as stars that are meant merely for shining." His chivalry and sense of honour have carried him to a position from which

[1] *Letters*, ii. 586.

there is no receding. He sets out to lead his forlorn enterprise, aware that it must fail, that the enemy have been warned by the venal Countess Violetta. Merthyr Powys reasons with him, though "in his wise mind he knew Carlo to have surveyed things justly, and that the Fates are within us. . . . In the imminent hour Carlo had recognized his position as Merthyr with the wisdom of years looked on it." Meredith keeps his instrument strung up to epic pitch in the infinitely moving scene where Carlo bids farewell to the women who have loved him. But the ironic comedy which is only the other face of tragedy steadies the tone of lofty enthusiasm. As the novelist says in his last book, "Humour in its intense strain has a seat somewhere about the mouth of tragedy, giving it the enigmatical faint wry pull at a corner visible at times upon the dreadful mask."

Carlo smiled. . . . "The Brescians are up: that's an hour that has struck, and there's no calling it to move a step in the rear. Brescia under the big Eastern hill which throws a cloak on it at sunrise! Brescia is always the eagle that looks over Lombardy! And Bergamo! you know the terraces of Bergamo. Aren't they like a morning sky? Dying there is not death; it's flying into the dawn. You Romans envy us. Come confess it, you envy us. You have no Alps, no crimson hills, nothing but old walls to look on while you fight. Farewell, Merthyr Powys. I hear my servant's foot outside. My horse is awaiting me saddled, a mile from the city. Perhaps I shall see my wife again at the door below, or in heaven. Addio! Kiss Luciano for me. Tell him that I knew myself as well as he did, before the end came. Enrico, Emilio, and the others—tell them that I love them. . . ."

They embraced. Merthyr said no more than that he would place messengers on the road to Brescia to carry news of the king's army. His voice was thick, and when Carlo laughed at him, his sensations strangely reversed their situations.

There were two cloaked figures at different points in the descent of the stairs. These rose severally at Carlo's approach, took him to their bosoms, and kissed him in silence. They were his mother and Laura. A third crouched by the door of the courtyard, which was his wife.

Meredith never did anything more Meredithian than *The Adventures of Harry Richmond* (1871), a novel which calls for an effort, not always forthcoming, on the reader's intelligence, by having a dual subject, the nominal hero not being the real one. Put more accurately, the titular hero is in this case entirely subordinate to the anti-hero, who is magnified by several dimensions. Superficially, it is two things at once: the autobiography of the usual young man who goes through a series of varicoloured trials and vicissitudes before he proves his manhood, and the history of the magnificent, self-deluded impostor, Roy Richmond, who is drawn on such a scale and dominates the story to the final page so overbearingly that Harry becomes a sheer cipher. The cynosure of understanding eyes is Roy, who by this device is detached and projected on the mental screen, and· stands out substantial, alive, and coherent, to the last fibre. Harry is secondary, hardly a character at all, a point of view for the real interest, the epic of the illustrious adventurer, recounted by the boyish and confiding, the idolizing, then the disillusioned, and lastly the ruthful son. There is usually irony in the titles of Meredith's books when these are not simply names. It turned out that Richard Feverel's ordeal was really his father's. It will be seen that the irony of "Beauchamp's Career" was that Beauchamp did not have a career, in spite of his aspirations and furious energy, and of "Lord Ormont and his Aminta," that Aminta speedily ceased to be his.[1] Whether the double theme was perfectly harmonized is another matter: at all events, it makes the same demand on the reader's sympathetic perceptiveness as the division of interest in *Richard Feverel*.

It is one of Meredith's poetic romances, and a bare summary of the situations as they arise would suggest that he had ridden

---

[1] That the anti-hero is here the great figure is continually missed.' It is beside the mark to say that "The detachment demanded by intellectual Comedy is clearly impossible when one of the chief actors is himself the narrator and we are to see everything through his eyes" (*George Meredith*, by J. B. Priestley, 155). That was exactly how Meredith secured detachment: Harry is not really a "chief actor." "We see him [Roy] through the eyes of his admiring young son, and though we may dislike the kind of thing for which he stands, we find it impossible to dislike him." Of course, any more than by a parity of reasoning we should dislike Don Quixote!

the fantastic Pegasus so hard that his steed had bolted into the *Romance* inane. But it is the glamour that does this: there is no gross *turning to* violation of probability. The air of a fairy-story is natural *comedy* to Harry's boyish chronicle. To him at that age all was strange and unexpected; and in later life, when he penned his reminiscences, the swift succession of vivid and ever-changing incidents, from the opening chapter telling of the midnight rape of Harry by his amazing father to the incandescent final scene when Roy perishes in the burning of Riversley, are inevitably telescoped, and seem all the stranger. All is seen through a golden haze—the haze that hangs over our earliest experiences—until the change from high-flying romance to the social comedy of discordant characters in conflict—a change which is itself as much in Harry's more mature vision as in the new interests to which he is now alive. Meredith always scored heavily over his rivals in recapturing the spirit of boyhood: did he ever grow old himself? He can recall the tiny lad's sense of the vast, mysterious world beyond the circle of familiar faces, the comedy and romance of his schooldays, and the mystery and wonder of the quest for his father in London, with a zest and truth to the boy's point of view which are infallible. Harry and his chum at Mr Rippinger's academy are as good as young Feverel, or as the lad Crossjay, in *The Egoist*. A full-blown Meredithian heroine appears also, in Irish-eyed Julia Rippinger, daughter of the head; and the rivalry of Harry and young Heriot and the spiteful usher for the damsel's favour is neither farce nor the mawkish sentiment usual in schoolboy love-tales. Harry makes a god of his father, that wonderful magician, half-charlatan, half-genius, whose fascination none can resist but hard-headed haters of poetry and romantic feeling, like Squire Beltham. It takes years of disenchantment in later life to wean Harry from his devotion. For there is a greatness about Roy, as there was about his prototypes, the Great Mel and the Countess de Saldar; and his character is fairly summed in Colonel Heddon's dictum: "Now Roy was an adventurer, but he had a soul of true chivalry, by gad, he had." But the comet-like Roy disappears. Harry runs away with the gipsies, and then he and Temple

are carried aboard the barque *Priscilla*, and sail under the God-
fearing Captain Welsh from the Thames to the other side.
This is one of the most piquant chapters in all Meredith. The
captain, whose mission in life it is to save the souls of his crew,
and of any other unregenerate persons who come within reach
of his discipline, finding two youths in suspicious company
with the marks of dissipation on their faces, draws his own
conclusions. When they demand to be set ashore he refers
them to the tale of the Prodigal Son. The Lord has thrown
them into his hands, not without a purpose. They shall do
hard labour for their souls' health. They shall read the Bible.
"And when I hand you back to your parents, why, they'll
thank me if you won't. But it's not thanks I look for: it's my
bounden Christian duty I look to. I reckon a couple o' stray
lambs equal to one lost sheep." This militant but most
gentle of Christians plays a further part in the story, when the
Priscilla founders, and drowns two sinful persons whose removal
is singularly opportune.

*Romantic
comedy
and
comic
tragedy*
But the boys find themselves touching port in a German
city, and escape. By accident they get on the track of the
elusive one, and the most astounding chapters of the wondrous
Odyssey ensue. Their chance encounter with the young
Princess Ottilia, who has already heard of his son from the
inimitable Roy, the famous recognition scene when Roy,
posing as the statue, steps down from the horse of bronze at
hearing Harry's English shout, and the adventurer's plot to
marry the heir of Squire Beltham's enormous fortune to the
princess, are incidents draped in fantasy but not too romantic
as prelude to the comedy which follows, at the Court of
Eppenwelzen-Sarkeld and then in England. Harry's mind
and conscience become the theatre for the strife of motive,
passion tugging one way and chivalry the other; the father
outraging chivalry by his crafty manœuvres for capturing the
princess, Squire Beltham summoning back Harry's filial loyalty
with his merciless jibes and blind hatred of the pretender.
Externally, it is a duel between Roy and the squire for the
soul of Harry, who remains passive between them, except
that his awakening conscience rebels against his father's

chicanery. Roy's crowning exploit is to decoy the prince and his daughter to England by an urgent letter to Ottilia intimating that Harry is ill and in danger. Then comes Roy's discomfiture, in one of the strongest chapters Meredith ever penned: "Strange Revelations, and my Grandfather has his last out-burst." Roy has counted on Harry's pliability and his love for the princess, on Ottilia's passion for Harry, and her father's solicitude for her good name. He thought there was no way out of the dilemma he had contrived. But Harry's sense of honour rebels, and Perseus arrives in the nick of time to save the lady from the wily old dragon, in the person of her loyal German suitor, Prince Hermann, ready to marry Ottilia on the spot. Simultaneously with this rebuff, Roy staggers under a still more crushing blow from Squire Beltham, who has been looking into his grandson's banking-account and making strange discoveries. Harry's fortune has been squandered away on wild schemes to promote the marriage, and a huge deficit has been recently made up by the squire's daughter Dorothy, the tender-hearted sister of Roy's dead wife. The two combatants face each other at last, and fight it out—to the death, for the squire "lived eight months after a scene that had afforded him high gratification at the heaviest cost a plain man can pay for his pleasures: it killed him"; and Roy dropped into the mere futility of monomania. His towering self-confidence had wilted under the squire's thundering invective. It sounds like the voice of Squire Western, but Mr Beltham's Meredithian eloquence is finer than that:

"I'll thank my God for anything short of your foul blood in the family. You married the boy's mother to craze and kill her, and guttle her property. You waited for the boy to come of age to swallow what was settled on him. You wait for me to lie in my coffin to pounce on the strong-box you think me the fool to toss to a young donkey ready to ruin all his belongings for you! For nine-and-twenty years you've sucked the veins of my family, and struck through my house like a rotting-disease. Nine-and-twenty years ago you gave a singing-lesson in my house: the pest has been in it ever since! You breed vermin in the brain, to think of you! Your wife, your son, your dupes, every soul that touches you, mildews from a blight! You were born of ropery, and you go at it straight, like a webfoot to water. What's your boast? —your mother's disgrace! You shame your mother. Your whole life's a ballad o' bastardy. You cry up the woman's infamy to hook at a father. You swell and strut on her pickings. You're a cock forced from the smoke of the dunghill! You shame your mother, damned adventurer! You train your boy for a swindler after your own pattern; you twirl him in your curst harlequinade to a damnation as sure as your own."

Even in his overthrow Roy cannot forgo the histrionic display of his broken heart.

He put out a swimming hand that trembled when it rested, like that of an aged man grasping a staff. I feared for a moment he was acting, he spoke so like himself, miserable though he appeared: but it was his well-known native old style in a state of decrepitude.
"I am broken," he repeated, "I am like the ancient figure of mortality entering the mouth of the tomb on a sepulchral monument, somewhere, by a celebrated sculptor: I have seen it: I forget the city. I shall presently forget names of men. It is not your abuse, Mr Beltham. I should have bowed my head to it till the storm passed. Your facts . . . Oh! Miss Beltham."

Some of the women characters

The many women in the book are drawn with the same truth and distinction as the men. As in the majority of his stories, Meredith accords a kind of symbolic value to one contrasted pair, Harry's lodestar and goddess, the Princess Ottilia, who was to him the call of high romance, and Janet Ilchester, whom he married. The difference between them is that of the two poles of Harry's career. Ottilia was "not a romantic little lady of semi-celestial rank," or at least not that alone, "but a touchstone, a relentless mirror, a piercing eye, a mind severe as the Goddess of the God's head: a princess indeed, but essentially a princess above women: a remorseless intellect, an actual soul visible in the flesh." Harry's soul, saved and ennobled, was almost her handiwork: it was this vision that inspired him at the crisis of his destiny. But plain and trusty English Janet, who stands for plain and honest matter of fact, was after all the best mate for him. A similar contrast, though embodied in three finely differenced heroines, is the key to the story that followed, *Beauchamp's Career*. Among the other female characters, all of course presented in Harry's vision of them, the most fascinating is the gipsy girl Kiomi, pursued by his schoolmate Heriot, because she was so like a panther. Meredith must have met some such a one on his Surrey heaths. She is better than Watts-Dunton's Sinfi, for if Sinfi is good literature Kiomi is the real thing. She is as good as a dozen Carmens. Here is Harry's vision of her:

She had grown a superb savage, proof against weather and compliments. Her face was like an Egyptian sky fronting night. The strong old Eastern blood put ruddy flame for the red colour; tawny olive edged from the red; rare vivid yellow, all but amber. The light that first looks down upon the fallen sun was her complexion above the brows, and round the cheeks, the neck's nape, the throat, and the firm bosom prompt to lift and sink with her vigour of speech, as her eyes were to flash and darken. Meeting her you swore she was the personification of wandering Asia. There was no question of beauty and grace, for these have laws. The curve of her brows broke like a beaten wave; the lips and nostrils were wide, tragic in repose. But when she laughed she illuminated you; where she stepped she made the earth hers. She was as fresh of her East as the morning when her ancient people struck tents in the track of their shadows. I write of her in the style consonant to my ideas of her at the time. I would have carried her off on the impulse and lived her life, merely to have had such a picture moving in my sight, and call it mine.

CHAPTER IX

BEAUCHAMP'S CAREER, THE EGOIST,
AND LATER NOVELS

THE *Essay on Comedy* first appeared midway between *Beauchamp's Career* (1875) and *The Egoist* (1879), the two finest illustrations of its doctrines. Both are comedies, in different keys; and in both Meredith showed himself as absolute a master as he ever was to be of the subtle and complicated instrument that he had made out of the novel. *The Egoist* is the more drastic in its remodelling of method and structure: it is his epitome and show-piece. His new idea of the scope and potentialities of fiction was accepted as a challenge. Henceforth, everyone born into the world of those who read and think was destined to be a Meredithian or of the other party.

"*Beauch-
amp's
Career*" If into *Evan Harrington* he introduced a larger number of his relatives and close acquaintances, he did not make so much out of one intimate as he did in *Beauchamp's Career*. A well-loved friend, Frederick Augustus Maxse, was notoriously the original of Beauchamp. Meredith took an active part in Maxse's canvass before the Southampton election of 1868, the tale of which he retells here in the account of the election for Bevisham. And, though Meredith attends strictly to his duty as a novelist and does not advertise his own political convictions, he was doubtless whole-heartedly with Maxse in his criticism of the state of England and his forecast of a regenerated social system. But Maxse was in too much of a hurry. Meredith had written to him, ten years before the novel appeared, "I think you altogether too impetuous: 500 years too fast for the human race." Yet Meredith was not ultimately the one left behind, for Maxse, who first became a Radical through his experiences of Government mismanage-

ment and the sufferings of the under-dog during the Crimean war, at a riper age turned Unionist.[1] Meredith believed in evolution, and showed in his novels how man could take an active part in it. Maxse held and Beauchamp holds the same opinions as he on the next stage in human advancement; but they thought it could be brought about at once if they only pointed out its benefits and the injustice of the existing state of things. Beauchamp is very emphatic on the right and duty of the community to exploit the natural resources of the land. He deplores that the State failed to retain possession of the railways; and assures Cecilia Halkett that the national debt might have been paid off and taxation remitted had those profits been secured for the community, along with the valuable land adjoining stations. "What think you," he says to the less than lukewarm young lady, "of a Government of landowners decreeing the enclosure of millions of acres of common land amongst themselves; taking the property of the people to add to their own! Say, is not that plunder?" He believes in universal suffrage, in the limitation of private wealth, in a host of things which are now the chief heads of the Labour programme. Such views are the corollaries ·of Meredith's gospel of service and of brotherhood, set forth in "The Test of Manhood" and other poems. Beauchamp's creed is summed up in "The Empty Purse," composed nearly a score of years later: its main articles are justice to all men now, and enlightened provision for those who will come after—

> Keep the young generations in hail,
> And bequeath them no tumbled house!

The doctrine of primogeniture, contends this scion of aristocracy, is a survival of barbarism—

> Men's right of bequeathing their all to their own
> (With little regard for the creatures they squeezed).

---

[1] Meredith's or Beauchamp's or Maxse's reflections on the war-fever are strikingly unlike those of the fire-eating hero of *Maud*. But he was by no means a pacifist; on the contrary, the satire is largely directed at our besetting lack of preparation, and our accompanying absurd habit of blustering at the pretences of foreign governments to take their own line of action without consulting us. Meredith's patriotism was as enlightened as his humanity, which was cosmopolitan.

"The Empty Purse," that sermon to a prodigal son, puts into aphoristic terms Beauchamp's fierce denunciations of the wastefulness of the great houses, the pampering of the young by rich parents, the evasion of public duty, and their recalcitrance when even "a sliding scale of taxation" is proposed to remedy old-established iniquities of fortune and rectify the debit-and-credit account of the rich to the community.

The comedy of love and politics

It is to the hopeless enterprise of rousing a wealthy commercial nation, whose policy is dictated by a mercantile class and a nobility both equally dependent on our commercial ascendancy, to a consciousness of their human responsibilities, that Beauchamp applies his energies and idealism. He is nephew and heir-presumptive to Everard Romfrey, "a noticeable gentleman, in mind a mediæval baron, in politics a crotchety and unintelligible Whig," who stands in much the same relation to him as Squire Beltham to Harry Richmond, even to the extent of having a suitable bride duly marked out for his heir, in the fair Cecilia, daughter of an opulent neighbour, Colonel Halkett, a stanch, unintelligent Tory. To his uncle's chagrin Nevil Beauchamp, after winning laurels in the Crimea, throws himself headlong into politics, declares himself a Radical, and nearly runs off with a Frenchwoman encountered at Venice, sister of a brother officer whose life he had saved at the risk of his own. This feud with his uncle, complicated with his relations to the French Renée and the English Cecilia, is the backbone of the novel, which is thus a story of love and politics, the two so closely bound up together that they form one theme. Love is in conflict with a lofty political mission. The self-interest which an ordinary man would entertain in regard to Nevil's uncle, whose heritage he stands to lose, vanishes in the stress of finer motives. Hence, it is nothing to Nevil, but, by a fine stroke of irony, much to his uncle, when towards the end of the story that old patrician, to avenge himself on his disappointing nephew, marries Rosamund Culling and begets an heir, who dies almost as soon as born. With his usual indifference to mere story-interest, Meredith tells the reader early in the book that Beauchamp is doomed to fail. Beauchamp is the hero of a poetic comedy, and the appointed target for irony. His passionate idealism and pure self-devotion have in the end no discernible results on a stolid, idea-less electorate, beyond a few ripples in the restless sea of politics. And the futility of such a career is bitterly emphasized by its end, when he flings his life away to save a mudlark from drowning. A strange end for a comedy, though entirely in character; quite the appropriate fate, in truth, for a mediæval knight born out of due time. Beauchamp is an English Carlo Ammiani, with the heroism and the quixotic excess of his predecessor.

Beauchampism may be said to stand for nearly everything which is the obverse of Byronism, and rarely woos your sympathy, shuns the statuesque pathetic, or any kind of posturing. For Beauchamp will not even look at happiness to mourn its absence; melodious lamentation, demoniacal scorn, are quite alien to him. His faith is in working and fighting. With every inducement to offer himself for a romantic figure, he despises the pomades and curling-irons of modern romance, its shears and its labels.

The allusion is to Carlyle's sarcasms at the expense of Byron's complaint that he was not happy. Carlyle's name is not mentioned, though we are told that Beauchamp was deeply influenced by a writer on Heroes, with "a wind-in-the-orchard style," "a style resembling either early architecture or utter dilapidation"; and later he comes under the closer tutelage of the philosopher Dr Shrapnel, a curious figure, almost a grotesque combination of Carlyle and Emerson, preaching the gospel of work and service to our fellow-men.

Meredith holds the scales even; the irony falls on both *Irony* sides, in proportion to their deviations from intelligence. *equally* There is irony upon irony in the chapter headed "The Epistle *distri-* of Dr Shrapnel to Commander Beauchamp," when Captain *buted* Baskelett reads out a long exhortation on the same text as "The Empty Purse" to a crowd of Beauchamp's Conservative friends. "I've had enough!" Colonel Halkett ejaculated. In their comments and protests, Beauchamp's adversaries depict their own prejudices and imperviousness to ideas. But they are drawn, every one, with admirable fairness, except Captain Baskelett, the unscrupulous and predatory man of pleasure, ready to snap up an heiress or betray his cousin Nevil for the reversion of his inheritance. They are estimable people in their several ways. That generous old fighting baron, Nevil's uncle, who becomes Earl of Romfrey, is one of Meredith's most taking creations. Even Colonel Halkett is a good-natured, well-meaning gentleman, with the mental limitations of one who took his station and his political opinions as they were given him.

"I would rather have a good Administration than all your talk of principles: one's a fact, but principles? principles?" He languished for a phrase to describe the hazy things. "I have mine, and you have yours. It's like a dispute between religions. There's no settling it except by main force. That's what principles lead you to."

The serene, stable, fair-minded Seymour Austin is one of the strong, reliable, intelligent types, like the Vernon Whitfords and Tom Redworths who were about to supplant his more impetuous heroes and win his later heroines. Only in the case of Blackburn Tuckham, the solid young Tory lawyer who becomes the solid, philistine husband of Cecilia Halkett, is there a dash of satirical raillery. And this portrait he drew from one of his most intimate and cherished friends, William Hardman, who became editor of the *Morning Post* (1872). "Tuck," as Meredith commonly addressed him, was an old comrade of Meredith's walks in Surrey and the recipient of many of his most fraternal letters. That he could view himself in so frank and unflattering a mirror without offence was a tribute to the essential good nature of both men. Tuck's stocky personal appearance is sketched with more freedom than kindness, before he is heard holding forth to the superfine Miss Halkett:

"Let me set you right, sir," he said sometimes to Colonel Halkett, and that was his modesty. "You are altogether wrong," Miss Halkett heard herself informed, which was his courtesy. . . . On the question of politics, "I venture to state," he remarked, in anything but the tone of a venture, "that no educated man of ordinary sense who has visited our colonies will come back a Liberal." As for a man of sense and education being a Radical, he scouted the notion with a pooh sufficient to awaken a vessel in the doldrums. . . . Either the Radical candidate for Bevisham stood self-deceived, or—the other supposition. Mr Tuckham would venture to state that no English gentleman, exempt from an examination by order of the Commissioners of Lunacy, could be sincerely a Radical.

This is hard on Tuck, who must have had a heart of gold to put up with Meredith's eagle-eyed scrutiny of his foibles.

This gentleman betrayed his accomplishments one by one. He sketched, and was no artist; he planted, and was no gardener; he touched the piano neatly, and was no musician; he sang, and he had no voice.

Cecilia Halkett is the fine flower, the exquisite artificial *Love and* product, of the social system against which Beauchamp is *political* contending. Conservatism, privilege, prejudice are imperson- *idealism* ated in their more attractive aspects in this beautiful creature. And his failure to win her over, in love with him as she is, gives the finishing-touch to Beauchamp's general futility. He "had not the faculty of reading inside men"; hence he lays himself open to the counterstroke of his uncle Everard, who, tired of his persistence in demanding an apology to Dr Shrapnel for the assault committed through a pure misunderstanding, turns the tables by insisting on an apology from Nevil to the unoffended Rosamund Culling. Nor could he read inside women, else he would have won Cecilia in the way she should have been won, instead of calling out her resistance by his dogged efforts to convert her; just as, years before, he might have carried off Renée, if he had seized the moment when she was as wax in his hands. His love-affairs are the vital factor in the problem of his career. He outlived his passion for Renée, but Renée's claim on his old-standing allegiance still cripples his devotion to the social crusade. Dr Shrapnel had written: "Rebellion against society and advocacy of humanity

run counter." When Renée claimed his word, on the eve of
the election, he obeyed, and took his holiday at Tourdestelle,
losing whatever chances he had through the slanderous reports
which were spread among his constituents. But he had
learned his duty when Renée, like Clementina in Richardson's
last novel, a character with whom she has something in common,
fled in despair of happiness to the one man she had ever loved.
Renée had urged him to marry Cecilia, and he knew that
Cecilia might be his if he asked her fairly. But Meredith's
young men are not as other young men, if the strife of impulse
and inhibition that determines their actions be contemplated
with exclusively intellectual interest. Their control of passion
is almost incredible. The reader is more in love with
Meredith's heroines than his lovers are.

The three women

Cecilia is lost to Nevil before he knows clearly what has
happened. The irony of the situation falls on her.

The room she had looked to as a refuge from Nevil was
now her stronghold against the man whom she had incredibly
accepted. . . . Feeling entrapped, she considered that she
must have been encircled and betrayed. She looked back on
herself as a giddy figure falling into a pit: and in the pit she lay.

There is no plot in *Beauchamp's Career*; but there is something better, the mental and moral situation, and that is stated
clearly in such a piece of analysis as this of Cecilia's mind, and
then of Beauchamp's:

Cecilia's intuition told her that by leading to a discussion
of politics, and adopting Beauchamp's views, she could kindle
him. Why did she refrain? It was that the conquered young
lady was a captive, not an ally. To touch the subject in cold
blood, voluntarily to launch on those vexed waters, as if his
cause were her heart's, as much as her heart was the man's,
she felt to be impossible. He at the same time felt that the
heiress, endowing him with money to speed the good cause,
should be his match in ardour for it, otherwise he was but a
common adventurer, winning and despoiling an heiress.

Our Paris stands long hesitating before he can make up his
mind to which of his three divinities he shall give the apple;

but he comes to the right decision at last. From the day when he listened to her "chattering snatches of Venetian caught from the gondoliers," when "she was like a delicate cup of crystal brimming with the beauty of the place, and making one drink in all his impressions through her," Renée was the call of romance to Beauchamp. But he chose his path; and then, this beautiful thing, clouded by the tragic destiny that had blotted out her trust in life, became merely the disturbing influence, the foreigner, the wife of another man, to snatch at whom would have been treason to his work for mankind. Cecilia might well have been his helpmate; but his career would have lost much of its ardour and disinterestedness had he married a woman of the philistines. Both drew him by the charm of sex; but if Beauchamp ever was in love it was with Renée.

Decidedly, Cecilia was a more beautiful woman than Renée: but on which does the eye linger longest—which draws the heart? a radiant landscape, where the tall ripe wheat flashes between shadow and shine in the stately march of summer, or the peep into dewy woodland on to dark water?

In Jenny Denham he found something more substantial than romance or beauty: when, chastened and taught by harsh experience, he weds the devoted niece of the old Radical doctor, it is his spiritual home-coming.

There are as many commanding, striking, or at any rate "The typical and well-differentiated figures in *Beauchamp's Career Egoist*" as in *Vittoria*, and a much larger number than in *The Egoist*, where, though the stage always seems full, the important characters are few, the rest being supernumeraries who play minor parts and give the sense of an animated background. Here the real personages are two, or at most three: the Egoist himself and his affianced, Clara Middleton, through whose minds alternately we observe the drama when we are not invited to contemplate it as a whole from an external point of view, and Lætitia Dale, whose mental changes as the tale unfolds are explored with similar minuteness. On a secondary plane are grouped such figures as Vernon Whitford, Clara's

father, Dr Middleton, and the lad Crossjay, clearly characterized but not deeply anatomized; whilst further back are
ranged the minor performers in the comedy, Mrs Mountstuart
Jenkinson, Colonel De Craye, Mr Dale, Sir Willoughby's
aunts, Lady Busshe and Lady Culmer, and others holding
small parts. Meredith describes *The Egoist* as "a Comedy in
Narrative," and accepts such dramatic restrictions as the
unities of time and place, whilst taking the utmost freedom to
put the spectator where he can see the character from without
or within, as may be needful. The subtlety and complexity of
the interplay of motive exceed anything hitherto attempted
in fiction. Even with the aid of Meredith's running commentary, it is hard to extract the utmost flavour out of such
an opulent dish, without returning to it again and again.[1]
Yet the story is extremely simple. Sir Willoughby Patterne
is the man who has rounded Seraglio Point but has not yet
doubled Cape Turk. He philanders with Lætitia, who adores
him, and, having secured the exquisite Clara Middleton, flatters
himself that she is "essentially feminine, in other words, a
parasite and a chalice." But Clara turns out to be a modern
woman, intent on living a life of her own; and, through
his purblindness, the admired Sir Willoughby, the idol of his
county, is dragged step by step through the lacerating torments
of jealousy and public derision, and has to go on his knees at
last to the woman he has slighted and humiliated. From the
day when in his fatuous conceit he says to Clara, "Beware of
marrying an Egoist, my dear!" to his last despairing clutch at
the woman he has despised, Sir Willoughby passes through
the nine circles of irony: his comic history is an epitome of
Meredithian fiction.

Richard-   Meredith's affinities to his great predecessor in the subtle
son again lore of the psychological analyst have been alluded to already.
Richardson, however, constructing his facsimile of reality out
of a mind thinly stocked with the living material drawn from
experience, when he most excites admiration often fails to
establish conviction. Compared with the observant realist, he

---

[1] Stevenson said, "I have just re-read for the third or fourth time *The Egoist*.
When I shall have read it the sixth or seventh, I begin to see I shall know all about it."

was a mere introvert. Sir Willoughby inevitably calls up Sir Charles Grandison: he is a Grandison contemplated from every side, cut open to the marrow, and put under the microscope in the glare of the most relentless irony. Yet not relentless, for Meredith asks you to "consider him indulgently": his is a tragic state, and therefore pathetic.[1] The Egoist is the old Adam in all of us. "There," Meredith, all through the book, seems to be saying, "but for the grace of common sense, go you, go I, go all of us!"

The Egoist is our fountain-head, primeval man: the primitive is born again, the elementary reconstituted. Born again, into new conditions, the primitive may be highly polished of men, and forfeit nothing save the roughness of his original nature. He is not only his own father, he is ours; and he is also our son. We have produced him, he us. Such were we, to such we are returning.

That is, if we relax our labours and cease to go forward.

There are fifty chapters, each a definite scene forwarding *Progress* the action or illuminating the state of mind of one of the *of the* three protagonists. Some missfire; certain by-characters, the *drama* impossible Colonel De Craye, for instance, fail to make good Meredith's designs; and many of the conversations, meant to impress with their brilliance, are so stilted as to overtax the most willing efforts at illusion. But, on the whole, the drama moves swiftly and surely through the labyrinth of confidences and deceptions, attractions and repulsions, manœuvres, equivocations, and dramatic exposures, to a close that satisfies the sense of justice and verisimilitude. An instance of the general soundness of construction is the entertaining chapter, "An Aged and Great Wine," which seems at first to have little to do with Clara's anxious predicament, but proves no digression; for Willoughby understands how to play upon Dr Middleton's epicurean tastes, and induce him to resist more

---

[1] "The Egoist surely inspires pity. He who would desire to clothe himself at everybody's expense, and is of that desire condemned to strip himself stark naked, he, if pathos ever had a form, might be taken for the actual person. Only he is not allowed to rush at you, roll you over, and squeeze your body for the briny drops. There is the innovation."

stubbornly than ever Clara's flighty eagerness to leave the house of such a rare amphitryon. Clara was stupefied at the result.

He had won her father for an ally. Strangely, she knew not how, he had succeeded in swaying her father, who had previously not more than tolerated him. "Son Willoughby" on her father's lips meant something that scenes and scenes would have to struggle with, to the outwearying of her father and herself. She revolved the "Son Willoughby" through moods of stupefaction, contempt, revolt, subjection. It meant that her father's esteem for her was forfeited. She saw him a gigantic image of discomposure.

Willoughby's offence was that "he slew imagination."

Woman can bear revelations—they are exciting: but the monotonousness. . . . There is no direr disaster in love than the death of imagination. He dragged her through the labyrinths of his penetralia, in his hungry coveting to be loved more and still more, more still, until imagination gave up the ghost, and he talked to her plain hearing like a monster. It must have been that; for the spell of the primitive upon woman is masterful up to the point of contact.

The girl's disillusionment commences the moment he has brought her and her father to Patterne Hall, after capturing her by storm, in his fever to retrieve the blow to his self-esteem and the stain upon his reputation of a recent jilting, which he tries to explain away. It proceeds rapidly, with his indefatigable lectures on the æsthetics of love, his efforts to subdue her whole personality, to make her his for this life and after. It struggles with her perception of the universal and, "as she was compelled to see, honest admiration" of his superlative merits. "She tried to cheat herself with the thought that they were right and that she was the foolish and wicked inconstant." But, "if she partly succeeded in stupefying her antagonism, five minutes of him undid the work." Her insight, sharpened by distress and fear, frightens Lætitia Dale, still constant to the idol of her girlhood: "Miss Middleton, you have a dreadful power," she exclaims. In the

talks of the two women, in which Lætitia gradually learns to
see the predaceous monster as he really is, the thoughts seem
to become visible, flashing out like sparks from the heart to
the brain.

But the dialogue for the most part fails in this spontaneous-
ness. There are scenes in the two preceding novels more
lifelike than any in *The Egoist*, where Meredith is at his best
in the analysis of a brooding or rebellious heart. Hundreds of
passages might be quoted; but this, tracing Clara's reflections
on the boy Crossjay's behaviour to Willoughby, who treats the
lad as he treats women, is as good as any: *Dialogue versus cold analysis*

> The boy raised a shout and scampered away to Sir Willoughby,
> at the appearance of whom Clara felt herself nipped and
> curling inward. Crossjay ran up to him with every sign of
> pleasure. Yet he had not mentioned him during the walk;
> and Clara took it for a sign that the boy understood the entire
> satisfaction Willoughby had in mere shows of affection, and
> acted up to it. Hardly blaming Crossjay, she was a critic
> of the scene, for the reason that youthful creatures who have
> ceased to love a person, hunger for evidence against him to
> confirm their hard animus, which will seem to them sometimes,
> when he is not immediately irritating them, brutish, because
> they cannot analyse it and reduce it to the multitude of just
> antagonisms whereof it came. It has passed by large accumula-
> tion into a sombre and speechless load upon the senses, and
> fresh evidence, the smallest item, is a champion to speak for it.
> Being about to do wrong, she grasped at this eagerly, and
> brooded on the little of vital and truthful that there was in
> the man, and how he corrupted the boy. Nevertheless she
> instinctively imitated Crossjay in an almost sparkling salute
> to him.

But in the dialogue of two such clever fencers as Sir
Willoughby and Mrs Mountstuart Jenkinson, when that astute
lady guesses the real state of affairs which he strives desperately
to conceal, with due allowance for the fact that the most important things are those left unsaid, there is no shortage of wit
or of the humour of character. Not even Sterne in *Tristram
Shandy* and *The Sentimental Journey* was more skilful in the

visualizing of gesture, without which conversation would be like prose without its stops and verse without its beats.

Mrs Mountstuart pricked the turf with the point of her parasol. She looked down and she looked up.

"Well?" said he to her eyes.

"Well, and where is Lætitia Dale?"

He turned about to show his face elsewhere. When he fronted her again she looked very fixedly, and set her head shaking.

"It will not do, my dear Sir Willoughby!"

"What?"

"It."

"I never could solve enigmas."

"Playing ta-ta-ta-ta ad infinitum, then. Things have gone far. All parties would be happier for an excursion. Send her home."

"Lætitia? I can't part with her."

Mrs Mountstuart put a tooth on her under-lip as her head renewed its brushing negative.

"In what way can it be hurtful that she should be here, ma'am?" he ventured to persist.

"Think."

"She is proof."

"Twice!"

The word was big artillery. He tried the affectation of a staring stupidity. She might have seen his heart thump, and he quitted the mask for an agreeable grimace.

"She is inaccessible. She is my friend. I guarantee her, on my honour. Have no fear for her. I beg you to have confidence in me. I would perish rather. No soul on earth to be compared with her."

Mrs Mountstuart repeated, "Twice!"

The low monosyllable, musically spoken in the same tone of warning of a gentle ghost, rolled a thunder that maddened him, but he dared not take it up to fight against it on plain terms.

"Is it for my sake?" he said.

"It will not do, Sir Willoughby!"

She spurred him to a frenzy.

The long-drawn agony of the Egoist has begun. His pangs and contortions, his feints and stratagems, his efforts to hoodwink observers and dissemble his wounds, alternate with frantic *The* attempts even now to entrap the escaping bird. "It would *comic* be glorious to swing round on Lady Busshe and the world, *catas-* with Clara nestling under an arm, and protest astonishment *trophe* at the erroneous and utterly unfounded anticipations of any other development." His final discomfiture comes from the hand of Lætitia. Some have objected to the concluding turn of the story. Why should Sir Willoughby have gone back to the faded woman he had trifled with, when, surely, there was no lack of young ladies only too ready to marry fifty thousand a year? But this is to forget that he had brought himself into a dilemma from which there was no other exit, by his stealthy manœuvring to retain Lætitia as his second string. And, apart from the likelihood that a jilted lover would fly instinctively to the nearest woman, to the woman, that is, with whom he has been on a sentimental footing, there is the peculiar situation of the Egoist. He was an inveterate *poseur*. He has to save his face somehow, to maintain the fiction that he is still following his own inclinations, that he is no one's victim. And only one way remains open. When Constantia Durham left him, he pretended to be drawn by Lætitia. When Clara leaves him, he can only repeat his former shift, and this time it has to be in earnest. The bitterness for Sir Willoughby is that Lætitia knows him now exactly for what he is, and he must sue to be taken on her own terms. As soon as the report leaks out of the midnight conference of Willoughby and Lætitia in the drawing-room, with young Crossjay not asleep on the sofa, Clara is irrecoverably lost. And Lætitia clearly sees the motive of everything he has done, or said, or pretended. His last disguise is rent. There is no alternative but to marry Lætitia or face the laughter of the world. Through a whole night he pleaded with her.

He stooped so far as to kneel, and not gracefully. Nay, it is in the chronicle of the invisible host around him, that in a fit of supplication, upon a cry of "Lætitia!" twice repeated, he whimpered, "Lætitia's heart is dead. If she consents, it will be without one."

"I was once a foolish romantic girl," she tells his bewildered
aunts, "now I am a sickly woman, all illusions vanished. . . .
My girl's view of him has entirely changed, and I am almost
indifferent to the change. I can endeavour to respect him,
I cannot venerate."

"An
artificial
reality"

Deliberately framed as a complete example of his theory
of comedy, *The Egoist* has a homogeneousness and a unity
conspicuously lacking in several of Meredith's novels. It
contains nothing extraneous, even so well-adapted to his
purposes as the chunks of personal experience in *Beauchamp's
Career*, Maxse's political doings, the eccentricities of William
Hardman, his own unfortunate experiments with vegetarianism,
utilized in Beauchamp and Cecilia's discussions of the topic
and Beauchamp's dangerous illness brought on by his foolhardy
abstention from meat. No such crude shreds of actuality
are traceable here, and the characters are as much his own
invention as the comedy itself. Only Dr Middleton and
Vernon Whitford have been pointed out as exceptions. Dr
Middleton is something like Peacock, and still more like a
character out of Peacock's stories. Whitford was a sketch of
Leslie Stephen: the acute intellect, the strong self-reliance,
the scholarship and the competent pen, the passion for the
mountains. But the likeness is not one that jumps to the eye,
any more than that of Woodseer to R. L. Stevenson, in *The
Amazing Marriage*. "Vernon had no irony," it is stated.
That, at any rate, does not reproduce the author of *Hours in
a Library* and the biographer of Swift. Meredith in *The
Egoist* worked in the Richardsonian manner, and evolved an
artificial simulacrum of life to tally with and illustrate his
social philosophy. But, being better grounded in concrete
experience, he drew characters that are nearly all exquisitely
alive. The Egoist himself is one of his exceptional characters,
"actual yet uncommon," like Richmond Roy, the Countess
de Saldar, Alvan, or Victor Radnor, that transcend the common
orbit. But the uncommon is not the abnormal. The
exceptional characters of literature, the Falstaffs, Hamlets,
Don Quixotes, Parson Adamses, and Uncle Tobys, have more,
not less, of human nature in their composition than our next-

door neighbours. Idealizing upon the real produces these large-scale beings, and sets them going in a field of action which gives scope to their superabundance of mental energy. Their performances in that field are to be scrutinized by the bright eyes of Comedy, which means that the presence of critical and intelligent women is essential. Women, Meredith reiterates, are both physically and mentally nearer than man to Mother Earth. Women are man's test: they are not so much the prize of superiority as man's judges. True comedy, he maintained, can exist only in a high state of civilization, and in a community where women are held in high esteem. Hence the importance of Clara and Lætitia in the dramatic scheme: deputies of the Comic Spirit, by them man is tested and judged, chastised, or rewarded. Beside them stand a whole crowd of critical spectators, nearly all women. Sir Willoughby shivers in his shoes at the bare idea of being found out by Mrs Mountstuart or Lady Busshe or Lady Culmer, who actually know him much better than he knows himself. But these are only the witnesses. Clara and Lætitia are prosecuting counsel and jury. They fulfil more formally and conspicuously the same function as Ottilia and Janet in *Harry Richmond*, the trio of fair women in *Beauchamp's Career*, Vittoria in the histories of Wilfrid Pole and Carlo Ammiani, and Rose Jocelyn and Lucy in the two previous novels. They rank high among Meredith's creations because they have to officiate in his most important leading case, and he made them worthy of its importance. Both are at once women of unmistakable individuality and types of their sex of contrasted kinds—the eager, intelligent girl just entering on life, and the woman who has suffered grievous disappointment and readjusted the demands of her heart to insistent realities. Both achieve their victory over this most formidable enemy of the sex, Clara winning the freedom which had seemed lost beyond hope, Lætitia the security of fortune and the opportunity for social labour for which she had longed. But their appointed task, that for which the novelist gave them being, was the stripping and castigation of the Egoist. Even Clara and Lætitia are only subordinates; he is the central figure, the anti-hero, this time without any prominent opposite: the unity of the book is complete.

Some short stories

Meredith wrote three short stories. "The House on the Beach," which was in hand sixteen years before he published it, has been roughly characterized already. More like him is the other little comedy, "The Case of General Ople and Lady Camper," which he made up out of a diverting affair, ending in a legal suit, that occurred between some neighbours when he was living at Kingston. It is very light and rather broad comedy—*The Egoist* in miniature and in coarser terms. General Ople, a simple retired gentleman, "Wilsonople" as the exasperated and exasperating Lady Camper dubs him, is of the common herd of egoists, a dense, unimaginative person, with no sense of humour, whose obtuseness and submissiveness under provocation make him even attractive. Whilst his daughter is being made love to under his nose, he remains calmly unobservant, engrossed in his gentlemanlike residence and his garden; and he mistakes the great lady's tactful feelers, when she sees it is high time to discuss the subject, for an overture to himself. The hail of caricatures with which she brings him to his senses is one of those devices that seem far-fetched in a novel, but are among the facts borrowed from unadorned history. That brief tragedy "The Tale of Chloe" stands on a loftier plane; it is one of Meredith's rare gems of fine workmanship. Chloe herself deserves a place beside his noblest heroines, Rhoda Fleming, or Nataly, or Carinthia. It is a piece in which he refrains from talking round the story as well as telling it. And he is content with a small scale, almost that of a miniature. Yet all the essentials are there, and all, as so seldom with him, are kept in strict order and proportion. It is a little episode of life in Bath or Tunbridge Wells during the eighteenth century: the sprightly Beau Beamish might well stand for a Beau Nash without the bullying manners. Chloe, whose heart still yearns for the specious rake who villainously deserted her, sees with anguish the giddy young duchess who has been put under her protection about to fall a prey to the same raptorial beast. She sacrifices her life to save her friend. In the last quiet speech before the fatal night are heard again the heroic accents that sounded in *Vittoria.*

"Friend, my dear, true friend," Chloe said in her deeper voice of melody, "set your mind at ease about to-morrow and her. Her safety is assured. I stake my life on it. She shall not be a victim. At the worst she will but have learnt a lesson. So, then, adieu! The West hangs like a garland of unwatered flowers, neglected by the mistress they adorned. Remember the scene, and that here we parted, and that Chloe wished you the happiness it was out of her power to bestow, because she was of another world, with her history written out to the last red streak before ever you knew her. Adieu; this time adieu for good!"

In the curious work entitled *The Tragic Comedians: a study in a Well-Known Story* (1880), which is not a novel, for Meredith, so he assured the reader, put in nothing of his own invention, he related in his own way the actual history of Ferdinand Lassalle and Hélène von Dönniges. Alvan, under whose name is vividly presented the volcanic temper and dominating will of the great socialist, is a variety of the genus egoist. He and Clothilde, who as accurately represents the lady, fall tempestuously in love; and Alvan might, for the lifting of a finger, have carried her off. But in his superb conceit he refuses the gift of the gods, unless it be also the gift of the lady's parents. He will have no runaway bride. He wills that those who hate and revile him as an upstart Jew, a profligate, a republican, shall quietly accept him as their son-in-law; that the pariah shall become a respected member of society and of the ruling order. So, when she has fled to him he restores her to her mother's arms, confiding in his own ability to win her parents over. From that moment, the critical moment of the story, Clotilde foresees the end. She tells herself: "You that offered yourself in flight to him who once proposed it, he had the choice of you and he abjured you. He has cast you off!" He can never retrieve that error. Clotilde was no heroine, but an enamoured girl who had nerved herself to one act of courage. He had failed her then; she is powerless to help him now. He never sees her again. Her parents shut her up, and defy Alvan. Driven to desperation, he challenges the lady's father, and meets the rival her parents have destined for her hand. Alvan, the superhuman, the dead-shot, so invincible that he can denounce duelling without the risk of being thought a craven, falls at the hands of a boy who had hardly fired a pistol before. Alvan's failing was that he did not understand women. He had been too successful.

Women for him were objects to be chased, the politician's relaxation, taken like the sportsman's business, with keen relish both for the pursuit and the prey, and a view of the termination of his pastime. Their feelings he could appreciate during the time when they flew and fell, perhaps a little longer; but the change in his own feelings withdrew him from the communion of sentiment.

He and Clotilde are self-deceivers, tragic comedians. There was no true confidence between them, and without that their mutual desires were foredoomed.

"Diana of the Cross-ways" Meredith's first real novel after *The Egoist,* actually six years after, was *Diana of the Crossways* (1885), in which he made a bid for popularity by taking and adapting the romantic story of the celebrated Mrs Caroline Norton, Sheridan's grand-daughter, who had separated from her husband after his unsuccessful divorce suit, and won a certain vogue by her novels and poems. He handles both the character and the story with praiseworthy freedom. Diana's friendship with the Premier, Lord Dannisburgh, which gives rise to so much scandal, her husband's attempts to reassert his rights, and the famous legend of the Cabinet secret sold to *The Times,* are borrowed however from the traditional story. Meredith unfortunately accepted the last-named item as historical, and forced it into the frame-work of the novel. Whether historical or not, and it has been proved unfounded, it was one of those bizarre odds and ends to which fiction should give a wide berth. More than once in *Diana,* but this is the crucial instance, he makes fiction subservient to fact. That one of the facts turned out to be unhistorical is irrelevant. Fiction cannot afford to follow

fact, which as often as not is notable because exceptional, because it is one of the real occurrences which are too strange for fiction. Diana is endowed with much of the enthusiasm, the impetuousness, and the rashness of Meredith's earliest quixotic heroes. But not one of those headstrong young fellows would commit an act of treachery; and Meredith has not revealed anything in Diana's nature to make it credible in her.

Though he held out the lure of romance and a brilliant *Manner-* heroine associated with a *cause célèbre*, Meredith prefixed an *isms and* introductory chapter that was crabbed and cryptic enough *redeem-* to repel those who did not warily evade it; and he thought *ing virtues* to authenticate his heroine's brilliance by putting in her mouth such showers of coruscating epigrams that he almost failed to authenticate her at all. The trouble with Meredith's style begins with *Diana of the Crossways*. It reaches its maximum in the next novel, *One of our Conquerors*, and in his poems from this date onwards. It is not to be supposed that he was obscure on purpose, or that he deliberately cherished and emphasized his mannerisms or wanted to show off his cleverness: to suppose it would be puerile. He simply declined to study the weaknesses of the common reader: he probably did not know of them, and did not trouble to know. Meredith—reports of his metaphorical conversation, his eloquent thinking aloud, confirm it—was an intellectual expressing himself poetically, whether in verse or prose: hence his poetry is over-intellectual and his prose over-poetical. *Diana* is not one of his best novels, but it contains many of his best things. With such a heroine in the forefront, there was no need for a hero. But several lovers present themselves, who are shrewdly anatomized; and, instead of the hero of romance such as might have been anticipated, the staid and sensible, anti-romantic Redworth, who provides a refuge, peace and safety for Diana after her chequered career of independence, is perhaps the most interesting among his later knights. The friendship of Diana and Lady Dunstane is a beautiful thing, more beautiful than most love-stories; and Lady Dunstane, another study of Meredith's old friend Lady

Duff-Gordon, is memorable among his vignettes of exquisite womanhood. Her husband, Sir Lukin, is as true and touching a picture of "the sinner honourably remorseful" as was ever painted, a surprising and creditable feat by one who was supposed to have little mercy for the brainless, even when their hearts were in the right place. And the book contains some biting sketches of the pharisaic tribe of scandal-mongers and officious peacemakers, such as Lady Watkin, "one of the order of women who can do anything in a worthy cause," who dares so many rebuffs in her efforts to reclaim a lady whom she would fain see ostracized.

One of our Conquerors (1891) appeared after *Ballads and Poems of Tragic Life* (1887). In style it is the most uncompromising of all his novels. It is also one in which Meredith's disregard for clarity or logical connectedness in the story, that winds its subterranean course somewhere behind the scenes, is a serious defect; for the story had the makings of impressive drama. This is unfortunate in other respects. Readers not baffled by the contorted diction and the elusiveness of the central motive, which does not transpire for many chapters full of irrelevant brilliance, would make the acquaintance of two of Meredith's finest heroines: the tragic Nataly, and that gallant young champion of the unfortunate of her sex, Nataly's daughter, Nesta. There is a largeness, also, if not a greatness, in Victor Radnor, Nesta's father, a mighty optimist compared with whom Mr Micawber is a prattling babe. The reactions of this "histrionic self-deceiver," and deceiver of many others who come within range of his magnetism, make a profoundly interesting study of the influence of temperament. The psychological insight shown in it as a case of incipient insanity has been already noted. Victor and Nataly are not married. A raw youth, with his way to make in the world, he had accepted the hand of a rich widow, many years his senior, who still lives. He and the lovely Nataly, whom she had imprudently thrown together, were irresistibly attracted by each other, entered into a union, and have been waiting ever since for a divorce or the death that never comes. Mrs Burman Radnor refuses to release her husband, and, always ailing, will not die. At every effort

"One of our Conquerors"

of Victor, now heaping million upon million, to make a show
in society, she threatens them with exposure. Between this
avenging fate in the background and Victor's unquenchable
ambition, Nataly's life is a ceaseless torment. And her cup
is brimmed with tragic irony when her daughter, the beloved
Nesta, who has been kept in ignorance of her father's and
mother's plight, in pure tenderness of heart and girlish
innocence, takes up the cause of a woman of doubtful character
whom she conceives to be grossly wronged, and gets herself
talked about. Little could she know of the fragility of the
glass house that sheltered her—Nesta, the one person in the
world who could least afford a murmur of scandal! Retribution
falls on Victor and Nataly, breaking the woman, and wrecking
the father's mind. Nesta is left, her nobility proved by
endurance and self-sacrifice, for a happier lot.

A broken union is the theme of all the four novels from *"Lord
Diana* to *The Amazing Marriage.* There is an illusory *Ormont
and his*
resemblance to the current problem-novel in the last three. *Aminta"*
But Meredith proffers no consistent solution of the cases
submitted, handling them strictly and impartially as studies
of the particular characters and circumstances involved. Hence
the sociologist who seeks a definite verdict from him on the
marriage question is nonplussed. His attitude towards Nataly
seems to be the converse of his attitude towards the rebellious
wife in *Lord Ormont and his Aminta* (1894), and the solution
of the question at issue in that novel appears to be contradicted
by the unrelenting close of *The Amazing Marriage.* Evidently it
is not wise to assume that Meredith was engaging in sociological
polemics when he wrote these interesting novels. He was
simply a novelist, treating the discords of character and conduct
with that exclusive regard for the general and theoretic which
was incumbent upon him in his artistic capacity. *Lord Ormont
and his Aminta* is written in an easy, vivacious style, and tries
the reader's patience with no obscurities of character or con-
tingency. The curious matrimonial imbroglio seems to have
been suggested by the history of that masterful soldier, the
third Earl of Peterborough, and the unfortunate Anastasia
Robinson, who claimed that he had married her. But the

novel is in no sense historical, and the Peninsular war once or twice referred to was a later and more famous war. Aminta, a schoolgirl worshipper of the military hero, meets him by accident, and he marries her in haste to neglect her at leisure. The marriage took place abroad, and at home he declines to acknowledge her as his countess. He is a lordly and capricious person, who would have done her justice in his own good time. But Aminta, burning with her wrongs, takes the law into her own hands. "Laws," she tells herself, "are necessary instruments of the majority: but when they grind the sane human being to dust for their maintenance, their enthronement is the rule of the savage's old deity, sniffing blood-sacrifice. There cannot be a based society upon such conditions." In this case, too, Perseus is ready. The chivalrous young schoolmaster Weyburn rescues the lady, and the pair settle in Switzerland, where they carry out together Weyburn's great scheme for co-education. Lady Charlotte Eglet, in this novel, is another inspiring example of femininity and true humanity.

"The Amazing Marriage" Meredith's defiance of the ordinary laws of probability in *The Amazing Marriage* (1895), which followed in a year, has been touched upon already. This has a fairly simple plot. Carinthia, whose strange upbringing in a foreign environment under the care of that veritable Melampus, the Old Buccaneer, has left her a child of Nature, innocent, trustful, true, is another of those women who judge men's failures as sternly and unforgivingly as Nature herself. She fascinates the Byronic Lord Fleetwood, who proposes to her on an impulse of which he speedily repents. Called to account by her penurious uncle, Lord Levellier, he formally fulfils his pledge, but quits her after the ceremony. In her childlike ignorance of the world, Carinthia does not understand that this attitude is simply contemptuous, and tries submissively to do her duty as his wife. But his outrageous slights open her eyes. For the sake of their child, whose advent is perfunctorily accounted for by obscure hints dropped long after, she insists on a proper maintenance, but will have nothing more to do with him. Fleetwood's eyes are opened also in the course of time to her supreme worth, but too late: treachery in love is inexpiable.

The histories of Dahlia and Edward Blancove, of Vittoria and Wilfrid Pole, have shown that already. Carinthia rejects Fleetwood as Clarissa rejected Lovelace. Mere repentance is futile.

Was he not another man? By the leap of his heart to the woman standing down there, he was a better man. But recent spiritual exercises brought him to see superstitiously how by that sign she was lost to him; for everlastingly in this life the better pays for the worse; thus is the better a proved thing.

This is no mere problem-novel, but a penetrating inquest into the roots of character, as exposed in the antagonism of two singular personalities and unbending wills.

Such was the inexorable and characteristic finale of the last "*Celt* novel Meredith completed. The one that he left unfinished *and* at his death fourteen years later, *Celt and Saxon* (1910), was *Saxon"* presumably the work of his latter days, but there is no information as to when he wrote it. The three hundred pages or so that there are of it seem rather like a conversation-novel by Peacock. There are a group of Welsh characters, the Adiantes, an Irish group in the O'Donnells, and the great Mr Bull is typified in the self-made Mattock family, especially the two splendid representatives of to-day, John and Jane. Perhaps *Celt and Saxon* would have been a Meredithian rival to *John Bull's Other Island*. But the stage is set for a promising drama, and then the reader is left, with hardly a clue to the course of events intended.

Every one of Meredith's novels has an individuality of its *Meredith* own; but from first to last he kept consistently to the pro- *and* gramme which he had in his mind's eye when he wrote *Richard George* *Feverel*. They make up a body of work at least as distinct *Eliot* from that of other novelists as is the work of Henry James or Conrad or Hardy. Hardy's genius for poetic tragedy is paralleled by Meredith's for poetic comedy. This poetic strain in his fiction is even more significant than the comic treatment of his themes in the interests of his philosophy of human life. It is here that he contrasts with George Eliot, with whose works his otherwise challenge comparison. She was ten years his senior, but his junior as a writer of fiction. A student of philosophy before she became a novelist, she so continued. Her seriousness seems to be opposed to his lightness, her solemn conscientiousness and sense of responsibility to his spirit of comedy. She had humour, more humour than Meredith, if his differentiation of humour from other forms of the comic be accepted. But George Eliot's prevailing gravity does not prove that she took life more seriously than Meredith did. His comic mask often covers the face of tragedy: he never pretends that life is not a strenuous and momentous affair. Their chief unlikeness was in their artistic attitudes, and perhaps it comes out nowhere more emphatically than in the aphoristic sayings both were so fond of. Meredith's are cast into poetic symbols, George Eliot's into the terminology of the scientist. Here are some of hers:

"Iteration, like friction, is likely to generate heat instead of progress."
"The responsibility of tolerance lies with those who have the wider vision."
"All yielding is attended with a less vivid consciousness than resistance; it is the partial sleep of thought; it is the submergence of our own personality by another."

Meredith's are utterly different in expression:

"The light of every soul burns upward. Let us allow for atmospheric disturbance."
"Expediency is man's wisdom. Doing right is God's."
"Planting the past in the present like a perceptible ghost."
"Woman's reason is in the milk of her breasts."

The view that Meredith dates

George Eliot has lost the unexampled hold she once had on the intelligent reader; and Meredith, superior people affirm, is already out of date. His windmills, they say, have all been overthrown: there are no sentimentalists now, women have asserted their freedom, their equality, and so on through the catalogue of his watchwords and war-cries. But Meredith was never in date. His portrayal of life, whatever its demerits, is peculiarly untrammelled by considerations of time. Those critics who complain that he dates, that he was a mere Victorian depicting an age that has disappeared, and those who, on the other hand, imagine that, because he stood aloof, he knew nothing and had nothing to say of the age in which he lived, not merely cancel each other out, but also illustrate the truth, that he saw what were the permanent characteristics of his countrymen, their virtues and their failings, and judged them by the standard of what they might be. He reviewed the present in the light of the future, as befitted the apostle of spiritual evolution. Nor was his vision of an evolving society, an evolving race, restricted to such narrow objects as women, for instance, have recently attained. He would not admit, even to-day, that women have won their emancipation, or have reached that level in a fully civilized society in which Comedy can flourish and their wits keep mankind in the right road. The anti-grundyism and flouting of convention that rejoice many hearts at the present time are possibly not a sign of "noble strength on fire" or of true freedom, which according to Meredith must be based on a whole-hearted belief in the orderliness as well as the goodness of Nature. He believed in taking counsel not of the sensations but of the intelligence: "I let the former have free play but deny them the right to bring me to a decision." Sentimentalism is now a byword, thanks to Meredith, who gave it a name. Everybody now is as afraid of being thought a sentimentalist as of being found wanting in a sense of humour. Whether the thing itself is dead is a very different matter. Congenital vices of human nature do not disappear at the touch of a conjurer's wand. It would be more than rash to say that Meredith has been fully assimilated and done with: the very opposite might be as plausibly maintained. For what we have received we are indebted to the ideas in his novels and in his poems, and those ideas have plenty of work to do still. And why not add Meredith's *Letters*? It was in a review of those letters, given to the world in 1912 by Meredith's son, that a lamented critic, Dixon Scott, wrote these significant words on Meredith's vogue, at that time and in the time to come:

We are approaching him now; the day will come when we will be his contemporaries. Meanwhile his past is our future, and these letters may help us like maps into the unknown. They will pass immediately into the stuff of living thought, making blood and tissue instantly; for they show us the fluttering ideals and dim desires of our day clearly formulated and alive. To read them is to find a groping track suddenly stiffening and straightening into highroad. Down that, towards that figure, we now press.[1]

[1] Dixon Scott, *Men of Letters* (1916), "George Meredith's Letters," 244, originally an article in the *Manchester Guardian* (1912). Dixon Scott was one of the English critics who understood Meredith: they are not too numerous. It seems odd, but it is the countrymen of Molière who have produced the most intelligent appreciations of Molière's English disciple, as the names of Photiadès, Galland, Chevalley, Ramon Fernandez remind us. When Molière died, he had long been ostracized and persecuted by the established orders, including the scholars and the men of letters; he was given a pauper's funeral, and it was not till a century and a half later that his bones—or someone else's—were exhumed from the common fosse and given a sepulture more worthy of a national hero. The reputation of the other great emissary of the Spirit of Comedy seems to be going through similar vicissitudes. It cannot be that these grudging critics are lacking in what Meredith was always pleading for, intelligence; in fact, they themselves candidly acknowledge that they are well furnished with that. But they are guardians of the flock, and must protect the general reader from violent assaults upon his peace and composure. This seems the only reasonable explanation.

SELECT READING AND REFERENCE LIST

GENERAL

BROWN, STEPHEN J. *Ireland in Fiction: a guide to Irish novels, tales, romances, and folklore.* 1916.

BROWNELL, W. C. *Victorian Prose Masters.* 1902.

CAZAMIAN, LOUIS. *Le Roman social en Angleterre* (1830–1850). 1903.

CAZAMIAN, MADELEINE L. *Le Roman et les idées en Angleterre.* I, *L'Influence de la science* (1860–1890) (1923); II. *L'Anti-intellectualisme et l'esthéticisme* (1935).

CECIL, LORD DAVID. *Early Victorian Novelists.* 1935.
Dickens, Thackeray, Brontës, Trollope, Gaskell, George Eliot.

CHANDLER, FRANK WADLEIGH. *The Literature of Roguery.* 2 vols. 1907.

CHEVALLEY, ABEL. *Le Roman anglais de notre temps.* 1921.

CROSS, WILBUR L. *The Development of the English Novel.* 1899.

DRINKWATER, JOHN. *The Eighteen-Sixties: essays by Fellows of the Royal Society of Literature.* 1932.

EDGAR, PELHAM. *The Art of the Novel, from 1700 to the present time.* 1923.

ELTON, OLIVER. *A Survey of English Literature, 1830–1880.* 2 vols. 1920.

GRANVILLE-BARKER, HARLEY. *The Eighteen-Seventies: essays by Fellows of the Royal Society of Literature.* 1929.

HARRISON, FREDERIC. *Studies in Early Victorian Literature.* 1895.
Disraeli, Dickens, Thackeray, George Eliot, Charlotte Brontë, Kingsley, Trollope.

HENLEY, W. E. *Views and Reviews: Essays in Appreciation—Literature.* 1890.
Dickens, Thackeray, Disraeli, Dumas, Meredith, Hugo, Rabelais, George Eliot, Borrow, Balzac, Lever, Richardson, Tolstoi, Fielding, etc.

JAMES, HENRY. *The Art of the Novel: critical prefaces.* 1935

KRANS, HORATIO SHEAFE. *Irish Life in Irish Fiction.* 1903.

LANG, ANDREW. *Essays in Little.* 1891.
Dumas, Stevenson, Thackeray, Dickens, Kingsley, Lever, Kipling, etc.

MANSFIELD, KATHERINE. *Novels and Novelists.* 1930.

MASEFIELD, MURIEL. *Women Novelists from Fanny Burney to George Eliot.* 1934.

MASSINGHAM, H.J. and HUGH (ed.). *The Great Victorians.* 1932.

OLIPHANT, JAMES. *Victorian Novelists.* 1899.

OMOND, T. S. *The Romantic Triumph (Periods of European Literature).* 1909.

SHEPPARD, ARTHUR TRESIDDER. *The Art and Practice of Historical Fiction.* 1930.

SHEPPERSON, A. B. *The Novel in Motley: a history of the burlesque novel in English.* 1936.

STRACHEY, LYTTON. *Characters and Commentaries.* 1933.

VERSCHOYLE, DEREK (ed.). *The English Novelists.* 1936.

WHITMORE, CLARA H. *Woman's Work in English Fiction.* 1910.

CHAPTERS I–II.—THE BRONTË SISTERS

BENSON, E. F. *The Life of Charlotte Brontë.* 1932.

BONNELL, H. H. *Charlotte Brontë, George Eliot, Jane Austen: Studies in their Works.* 1902.

BRADBY, G. F. *The Brontës, and other Essays.* 1932.

BRONTË, CHARLOTTE and PATRICK. *Poems.* 1934.
The Poems of Emily Jane Brontë and Anne Brontë. Edited by F. J. Wise and J. A. Symington. 2 vols. Blackwell, 1934.

BRONTË, EMILY JANE. *Complete Poems.* Edited by C. K. Shorter. 1923.

BRONTËS: *their lives, friendships, and correspondence.* Edited by F. J. Wise and J. Alexander Symington. 1932.

CHADWICK, MRS E. H. *In the Footsteps of the Brontës.* 1914.

DELAFIELD, E. M. (ed.). *The Brontës: their lives recorded by their contemporaries.* 1935.

DIMNET, ERNEST. *Les Sœurs Brontë.* 1910.

HARRISON, G. ELSIE. *Methodist Good Companions.* 1935.

LANGBRIDGE, ROSAMOND. *Charlotte Brontë: a psychological study.* 1929.

MACKAY, ANGUS M. *The Brontës: fact and fiction.* 1897.

REID, SIR T. WEMYSS. *Charlotte Brontë: a monograph.* 1877.

ROBINSON, AGNES MARY FRANCES, afterwards MME DUCLAUX. *Emily Brontë (Eminent Women).* 1883.

ROMIEU, E. and G. *The Brontë Sisters.* 1931.

SHORTER, C. K. *The Brontës and their Circle.* 1896. *The Brontës: life and letters.* 2 vols. 1908.

SINCLAIR, MAY. *The Three Brontës.* 1914.

SMITH, J. C. *Emily Brontë (Essays and Studies of the English Association,* 1914).

SUGDEN, KAYE ASPINALL RAMSDEN. *A Short History of the Brontës.* 1928.

SWINBURNE, ALGERNON CHARLES. *A Note on Charlotte Brontë.* 1877.

WILLIS, IRENE COOPER. *The Authorship of Wuthering Heights.* 1936.

WROOT, HERBERT E. (ed.). *Sources of Charlotte Brontë's Novels: Persons and Places (Publications of the Brontë Society,* VIII., pt. 4). 1935.

CHAPTERS III–V

COLERIDGE, CHRISTABEL. *Charlotte Mary Yonge.* 1903.

ELLIS, S. M. *Wilkie Collins, Le Fanu, and Others.* 1931.

ELWIN, MALCOLM. *Charles Reade: a biography.* 1931.

PHILLIPS, WALTER C. *Dickens, Reade, and Collins: sensation novelists.* 1919.

ROMANES, ETHEL M. *Charlotte Mary Yonge: an appreciation.* 1908.

SADLEIR, MICHAEL. *Trollope: a commentary.* 1927. *Trollope: a bibliography.* 1928.

WALPOLE, HUGH. *Anthony Trollope (English Men of Letters).* 1928.

CHAPTER VI.—GEORGE ELIOT

BLIND, MATHILDE. *George Eliot (Eminent Women).* 1883.

BOURL'HONNE, P. *George Eliot: essai de biographie intellectuelle et morale, 1819–1854 — Influences anglaises et étrangères.* 1933.

BRUNETIÈRE, FERDINAND. *Le Roman naturaliste.* 1896.

GARDNER, CHARLES. *The Inner Life of George Eliot.* 1912.

HALDANE, ELIZABETH. *George Eliot and her Times.* 1927.

PATERSON, ARTHUR. *George Eliot: life and letters.* 1928.

SPEARE, MORRIS EDMUND. *The Political Novel: its development in England and in America.* 1924.

WILLIAMS, BLANCHE COTTON. *George Eliot: a biography.* 1936.

CHAPTER VII.—GEORGE MEREDITH

ABLE, A. H. *George Meredith and T. L. Peacock: a study of literary influences.* 1933.

CURLE, R. H. P. *Aspects of George Meredith.* 1908.

ELLIS, S. M. *George Meredith: his life and friends in relation to his work.* 1920.

FERNANDEZ, RAMON. *Messages.* 1926.
"Le Message de Meredith."

GALLAND, RENÉ. *George Meredith: les cinquante premières années (1828–1878).* 1923.

JERROLD, WALTER. *George Meredith: an essay towards appreciation.* 1902.

LE GALLIENNE, RICHARD. *George Meredith: some characteristics.* 1905.

MEREDITH, GEORGE. *The Letters of George Meredith to Alice Meynell, 1896–1907.* 1923.

PHOTIADÈS, CONSTANTIN. *George Meredith: his life, genius, and teaching; rendered into English by A. Price.* 1913.

PRIESTLEY, J. B. *George Meredith (English Men of Letters).* 1926.

SENCOURT, R. E. *The Life of George Meredith.* 1929.

SWANN, GEORGE ROGERS. *Philosophical Parallelisms in Six English Novelists.* 1929.

TREVELYAN, G. M. *The Poetry and Philosophy of George Meredith.* 1906.

INDEX

INDEX

A

Abercrombie, Lascelles, on romanticism, 20–21, note
Allen, Grant, learned from Wilkie Collins, 219
Arnold, Matthew, 166
— criticism of the "Muscular" school, 183
— narrower outlook than Meredith's, 279
— on religion and poetry in Meredith's time, 292
— on the Romantic literature, 288, 296
Austen, Jane, 49, note, 223, 304
— admired by Trollope, 119
— attitude to romanticism, 11–13
— Charlotte Brontë on, 26
— compared with Mrs Gaskell, 81–82, 99, 100
— compared with Trollope, 118, 159
— comparison with George Eliot, 234
— comparison with Meredith, 309, 314, 331, 334
— George Eliot on, 269
— read by Charlotte Yonge, 102

B

Babbitt, Irving, on romanticism, 15, note
Baculard d'Arnaud, 24
Bailey, Philip James, *Festus*, 17
Banim, John and Michael, 25, 115
Barnes, William, 18
Barton, Bernard, 17
Beckford, William, his romanticism, 15
Beddoes, Thomas Lovell, 17–18
Bel Inconnu, Le, 319

391

G

H

W